HERAKLES

There is more material available on Herakles than any other Greek god or hero. His story has many more episodes than those of other heroes, concerning his life and death as well as his battles with myriad monsters and other opponents. In literature, he appears in our earliest Greek epic and lyric poetry, is reinvented for the tragic and comic stage, and later finds his way into such unlikely areas as philosophical writing and love poetry. In art, his exploits are amongst the earliest identifiable mythological scenes, and his easily recognisable figure with lionskin and club was a familiar sight throughout antiquity in sculpture, vase-painting and other media. He was held up as an ancestor and role-model for both Greek and Roman rulers, and widely worshipped as a god, his unusual status as a hero-god being reinforced by the story of his apotheosis. Often referred to by his Roman name Hercules, he has continued to fascinate writers and artists right up to the present day.

In *Herakles*, Emma Stafford has successfully tackled the 'Herculean task' of surveying both the ancient sources and the extensive modern scholarship in order to present a hugely accessible account of this important mythical figure. Covering both Greek and Roman material, the book highlights areas of consensus and dissent, indicating avenues for further study on both details and broader issues. Easy to read, *Herakles* is perfectly suited to students of classics and related disciplines, and of interest to anyone looking for an insight into ancient Greece's most popular hero.

Emma Stafford is Senior Lecturer in Classics at the University of Leeds. Her research and teaching interests lie in Greek cultural history, especially religion, myth and art. She is author of *Worshipping Virtues: Personification and the Divine in Ancient Greece* (2000), and *Life, Myth and Art in Ancient Greece* (2004), and co-editor of *Personification in the Greek World* (2005). She has also written numerous articles on Greek religion and iconography.

Gods and Heroes of the Ancient World

Series editor Susan Deacy
Roehampton University

Routledge is pleased to present an exciting new series, Gods and Heroes of the Ancient World. These figures from antiquity are embedded in our culture, many functioning as the source of creative inspiration for poets, novelists, artists, composers and filmmakers. Concerned with their multifaceted aspects within the world of ancient paganism and how and why these figures continue to fascinate, the books provide a route into understanding Greek and Roman polytheism in the 21st century.

These concise and comprehensive guides provide a thorough understanding of each figure, offering the latest in critical research from the leading scholars in the field in an accessible and approachable form, making them ideal for undergraduates in Classics and related disciplines.

Each volume includes illustrations, time charts, family trees and maps where appropriate.

Also available:

Aphrodite
Monica S. Cyrino

Apollo
Fritz Graf

Perseus
Daniel Ogden

Athena
Susan Deacy

Zeus
Ken Dowden

Prometheus
Carol Dougherty

Medea
Emma Griffiths

Dionysos
Richard Seaford

Oedipus
Lowell Edmunds

Forthcoming:

Diana
Fay Glinister

Susan Deacy is Lecturer in Greek History and Literature at Roehampton University. Her main research interests are Greek religion, and gender and sexuality. Publications include the co-edited volumes *Rape in Antiquity* (1997), and *Athena in the Classical World* (2001), and the monograph *A Traitor to Her Sex? Athena the Trickster* (forthcoming).

HERAKLES

Emma Stafford

Routledge
Taylor & Francis Group

LONDON AND NEW YORK

First published 2012
by Routledge
2 Park Square, Milton Park, Abingdon, Oxon OX14 4RN

Simultaneously published in the USA and Canada
by Routledge
711 Third Avenue, New York, NY 10017

Routledge is an imprint of the Taylor & Francis Group, an informa business

British Library Cataloguing in Publication Data
A catalogue record for this book is available from the British Library

Library of Congress Cataloging in Publication Data
Stafford, Emma.
Herakles / Emma Stafford.
    p. cm.—(Gods and heroes of the ancient world)
Includes bibliographical references (p.) and index.
    1. Heracles (Greek mythology) I. Title.
BL820.H5S83 2011
398.20938—dc23
2011023977

ISBN: 978–0–415–30067–4 (hbk)
ISBN: 978–0–415–30068–1 (pbk)
ISBN: 978–0–203–15245–4 (ebk)

Typeset in Utopia
by Swales & Willis Ltd, Exeter, Devon

For Gabriella

CONTENTS

SERIES FOREWORD

It is proper for a person who is beginning any serious discourse and task to begin first with the gods.

(Demosthenes, *Epistula* 1.1)

WHY GODS AND HEROES?

The gods and heroes of classical antiquity are part of our culture. Many function as sources of creative inspiration for poets, novelists, artists, composers, film makers and designers. Greek tragedy's enduring appeal has ensured an ongoing familiarity with its protagonists' experiences and sufferings, while the choice of Minerva as the logo of one of the newest British universities, the University of Lincoln, demonstrates the ancient gods' continued emblematic potential. Even the world of management has used them as representatives of different styles: Zeus and the "club" culture for example, and Apollo and the "role" culture (see C. Handy, *The Gods of Management: Who they are, how they work and why they fail*, London, 1978).

This series is concerned with how and why these figures continue to fascinate and intrigue. But it has another aim too, namely to explore their strangeness. The familiarity of the gods and heroes risks obscuring a vital difference between modern meanings and ancient functions and purpose. With certain exceptions, people today do not worship them, yet to the Greeks and Romans they were real beings in a system comprising literally hundreds of divine powers. These range from the major gods, each of whom was worshipped in many guises via their epithets or "surnames," to the heroes – deceased individuals associated with local communities – to other figures such as daemons and nymphs. The landscape was dotted with sanctuaries, while natural features such as mountains, trees and rivers were thought to be inhabited by religious beings. Studying ancient paganism involves finding strategies to comprehend a world where everything was, in the often quoted words of Thales, "full of gods."

In order to get to grips with this world, it is necessary to set aside our preconceptions of the divine, shaped as they are in large part by Christianised notions of a transcendent, omnipotent God who is morally good. The Greeks and Romans worshipped numerous beings, both male and female, who looked, behaved and suffered like humans, but who, as immortals, were not bound by the human condition. Far from being omnipotent, each had limited powers: even the sovereign, Zeus/Jupiter, shared control of the universe with his brothers Poseidon/Neptune (the sea) and Hades/Pluto (the underworld). Lacking a creed or anything like an organised church, ancient paganism was open to continual reinterpretation, with the result that we should not expect to find figures with a uniform essence. It is common to begin accounts of the pantheon with a list of the major gods and their function(s) (Hephaistos/Vulcan: craft, Aphrodite/Venus: love, and Artemis/Diana: the hunt and so on), but few are this straightforward. Aphrodite, for example, is much more than the goddess of love, vital though that function is. Her epithets include *hetaira* ("courtesan") and *porne* ("prostitute"), but also attest roles as varied as patron of the citizen body (*pandemos*: "of all the people") and protectress of seafaring (*Euploia, Pontia, Limenia*).

Recognising this diversity, the series consists not of biographies of each god or hero (though such have been attempted in the past), but of investigations into their multifaceted aspects within the complex world of ancient paganism. Its approach has been shaped partly in response to two distinctive patterns in previous research. Until the middle of the twentieth century, scholarship largely took the form of studies of individual gods and heroes. Many works presented a detailed appraisal of such issues as each figure's origins, myth and cult; these include L.R. Farnell's examination of major deities in his *Cults of the Greek States* (five volumes, Oxford, 1896–1909) and A.B. Cook's huge three-volume *Zeus* (Cambridge, 1914–1940). Others applied theoretical developments to the study of gods and heroes, notably (and in the closest existing works to a uniform series), K. Kerényi in his investigations of gods as Jungian archetypes, including *Prometheus: Archetypal image of human existence* (English trans. London 1963) and *Dionysos: Archetypal image of indestructible life* (English trans. London 1976).

In contrast, under the influence of French structuralism, the later part of the century saw a deliberate shift away from research into particular gods and heroes towards an investigation of the system of which they were part. Fuelled by a conviction that the study of isolated gods could not do justice to the dynamics of ancient religion, the pantheon came to be represented as a logical and coherent network in which the various powers were systematically opposed to one another. In a classic study by J.-P. Vernant for example, the Greek concept of space was shown to be consecrated through the opposition between Hestia (goddess of the hearth – fixed space) and Hermes (messenger and traveller god – moveable space: Vernant, *Myth and Thought among the Greeks* London, 1983, 127–75). The gods as individual entities were far from neglected however, as may be exemplified by the works by Vernant, and his colleague M. Detienne, on particular deities, including Artemis, Dionysos and Apollo: see, most recently, Detienne's *Apollon, le couteau en main: une approche expérimentale du polythéisme grec* (Paris, 1998).

In a sense, this series is seeking a middle ground. While approaching its subjects as unique (if diverse) individuals, it pays attention to their significance as powers within the collectivity of religious beings. *Gods and Heroes of the Ancient World* sheds new light on many of the most important religious beings of classical antiquity; it also provides a route into understanding Greek and Roman polytheism in the twenty-first century.

The series is intended to interest the general reader as well as being geared to the needs of students in a wide range of fields from Greek and Roman religion and mythology, classical literature and anthropology, to Renaissance literature and cultural studies. Each book presents an authoritative, accessible and refreshing account of its subject via three main sections. The introduction brings out what it is about the god or hero that merits particular attention. This is followed by a central section which introduces key themes and ideas, including (to varying degrees) origins, myth, cult, and representations in literature and art. Recognising that the heritage of myth is a crucial factor in its continued appeal, the reception of each figure since antiquity forms the subject of the third part of the book. The books include illustrations of each god/hero and, where appropriate, time charts, family trees and maps. An annotated bibliography synthesises past research and indicates useful follow-up reading.

For convenience, the masculine terms "gods" and "heroes" have been selected for the series title, although (and with an apology for the male-dominated language), the choice partly reflects ancient usage in that the Greek *theos* ("god") is used of goddesses too. For convenience and consistency, Greek spellings are used for ancient names, except for famous Latinised exceptions, and BC/AD has been selected rather than BCE/CE.

I am indebted to Catherine Bousfield, the editorial assistant until 2004, who (literally) dreamt up the series and whose thoroughness and motivation brought it close to its launch. The hard work and efficiency of her successor, Matthew Gibbons, has overseen its progress to publication, and the former classics publisher of Routledge, Richard Stoneman, has provided support and expertise throughout. The anonymous readers for each proposal gave frank and helpful advice, while the authors' commitments to advancing scholarship while producing accessible accounts of their designated subjects has made it a pleasure to work with them.

Susan Deacy, Roehampton University, June 2005

ACKNOWLEDGEMENTS

I should thank the University of Leeds for funding two periods of study leave in 2003 and 2010, at the beginning and end of the book's protracted gestation. More significant, however, is my debt to my immediate colleagues in Leeds' Department of Classics, who have been remarkably patient with me, and especially supportive in the difficult period leading up to the book's completion. Most particularly, Malcolm Heath and Steve Green have been endlessly generous in their provision of practical, as well as moral, support; Malcolm also read drafts of the entire manuscript, while Steve made me clarify my thoughts on the modern Herakles by inviting me to co-teach a Classics on Screen module in 2011. In earlier years I have been able to try out ideas on undergraduate classes taking my Greek Myth Through Art module, and a number of postgraduate students have contributed to my thinking on aspects of Herakles' iconography and cult, especially Katie Bell and Sam Gartland. Also at Leeds, Roger Brock commented on the politics and cult chapters, Fabio Sarranito helped me with some Renaissance Spanish, and Valerie Mainz supplied extensive bibliography on Hercules in the French Revolution. Eleanor OKell has introduced me to the whole area of modern performances of Heraklean tragedies, in addition to being a mine of information on the hero's many incarnations in twenty-first century popular culture.

Beyond Leeds, I should thank Susan Deacy for inviting me to write this book in the first place, after we had both been involved in the conference organized by Louis Rawlings at Cardiff in 1997. My initial proposal was approved by Timothy Gantz, whose 1993 work on Greek myth is an invaluable tool for any endeavour of this kind; I am sorry that he is no longer with us, as I should have liked to have his comments on the finished product. Both Susan and more than one editor at Routledge offered formative feedback on early drafts of individual chapters, while Nick Fisher offered useful comments on the final version of the cult chapter. Others have kindly answered questions and offered suggestions on Herakles' appearances in their own fields of scholarship: Douglas Cairns on Bakchylides, Bob Fowler on early Greek Mythography Keith Rutter on South Italian coins, Dominic Berry on Cicero, Lucy Grig on early Christian art, Fiona Hobden on banqueting, Daniele Miano on Etruscan art. Scripts of the two 2010 plays discussed in the final chapter were generously supplied by their authors, George Rodosthenous and Helen Eastman, and I thank Russell Richardson, the original Erymanthian Bore, for bringing the latter play to my attention. I am indebted to Andreas and Haris Michalopoulos for information on various modern Greek instantiations of our hero, especially Iraklis F.C. Administrators at the National Maritime Museum, Greenwich, and the city of Hercules, California, were courteous in their answer to queries.

The laborious task of acquiring illustrations and permissions was greatly facilitated by some efficient individuals at the various museums involved. I am grateful also to Hans Goette for advice and assistance in obtaining Figure 1.1, and to Elizabeth Moignard for introducing me to Figure 4.1. I must thank John Prag for drawing Marianne Maguire's work to my attention, and the artist herself for her generosity in allowing me to reproduce Figure 7.5 free of charge.

Sheila Bewley not only executed Figure 5.2, but acted as guinea-pig reader for most of the manuscript. Other members of my family and friends have all contributed to the effort one way or another over the years, and the book would not have made it to the light of publication without their support. Thank you.

Whilst every effort has been made to trace copyright holders and obtain permission, this may not have been possible in all cases. Any omissions brought to our attention will be remedied in future editions.

Emma Stafford, University of Leeds, September 2011

LIST OF FIGURES

ABBREVIATIONS AND CONVENTIONS

The following conventional abbreviations are used to cite inscriptions, some visual material, and ancient literary works which only survive in fragmentary form. Ancient authors and works referred to in the text are given in full. Works by modern scholars are referred to by author-surname and date; full bibliographical details of these can be found in the Works Cited section. Where works of art are referred to I have included conventional details, such as material and shape (of vases) and museum location, so that readers may identify the sculpture or vase concerned in other scholarship (e.g. if pursuing the suggested Further Reading).

BMC   *A Catalogue of Greek Coins in the British Museum*, London 1888–94

Caizzi   Caizzi, F.D. (1966) *Antisthenis Fragmenta*, Milan/Varese

CPG   Leutsch, E.L. and Schneidewin, F.G. (1839) *Corpus Paroemiographorum Graecorum*, Göttingen

F   Fowler, R.L. (2000) *Early Greek Mythography*, vol. 1, Oxford

FGrH   Jacoby, F. (1923–58) *Die Fragmente der Griechischen Historiker*, Leiden. This collection of fragments of Greek historical writing has recently been made a great deal more accessible to students via the online project *Brill's New Jacoby* (ed. I. Worthington, Leiden 2006–), available via university libraries which have an institutional site licence. Each fragment is provided with an English translation as well as the Greek text, a commentary and bibliography

IG   *Inscriptiones Graecae*

LGPN   Fraser, P.M. and Matthews, E. (eds) *A Lexicon of Greek Personal Names*, Oxford. vol. I, *The Aegean Islands, Cyprus, Cyrenaica* (1987); vol. II, *Attica* (1994); vol. IIIa, *The Peloponnese, western Greece, Sicily and Magna Graecia* (1997); vol. IIIb, *Central Greece, from the Megarid to Thessaly* (2000); vol. IV, Macedonia, *Thrace,*

	Northern regions of the Black Sea (2005)
LIMC	*Lexicon Iconographicum Mythologiae Classicae*, Zurich and Munich 1981–99
LP	Lobel, E. and Page, D. (1955) *Poetarum Lesbiorum Fragmenta*, Oxford
LSCG	Sokolowski, F. (1969) *Lois sacrées des cités grecques*, Paris
LSS	Sokolowski, F. (1962) *Lois sacrées des cités grecques: supplement*, Paris
ML	Meiggs, R. and Lewis, D.M. (1988) *Greek Historical Inscriptions to the End of the Fifth Century BC*, rev. ed. Oxford
MW	Merkelback, R. and West, M.L. (1967) *Fragmenta Hesiodea*, Oxford
PCG	Kassel, R. and Austin, C. (1983–2001) *Poetae Comici Graeci*, Berlin
PEG	Bernabé, A. (1996) *Poetarum Epicorum Graecorum*, 2nd ed. Leipzig
Pfeiffer	Pfeiffer, R. (1945–53), *Callimachus*, Oxford
PMG	Page, D.L. (1962) *Poetae Melici Graeci*, Oxford
PMG²	Davies, M. (1991) *Poetarum Melicorum Graecorum Fragmenta* I, Oxford
SEG	*Supplementum Epigraphicum Graecum*, Leiden 1923–
SM	Snell, B. and Maehler, H. (1987–9) *Pindari carmina cum fragmentis*, Leipzig
ThesCRA	*Thesaurus cultus et rituum antiquorum*, Los Angeles 2004–6
TrGF	Snell, B., Radt, S. and Kannicht, R. (1971–2004) *Tragicorum Graecorum Fragmenta* I-V, Göttingen
W	West, M.L. (2003) *Greek Epic Fragments*, Cambridge, MA and London
West	West, M.L. (1989–92) *Iambi et Elegi Graeci*, 2nd ed. Oxford

Spelling of names

It is impossible to be entirely consistent in the spelling of Greek names without making some familiar ones look very strange. I have therefore adopted the common compromise position of using spellings which follow the Greek as closely as possible where the result is intelligible to a modern reader (e.g. 'Herakles' rather than 'Heracles'), but keeping the traditional Latinized forms of such names as 'Thucydides' (rather than the unwieldy 'Thoukudides'). When discussing Roman material I have used the Latin versions of characters' names – as a general rule, the Greek 'k' changes to a Latin 'c', Greek 'ai' to Latin 'ae', Greek '-os' to Latin '-us', but in a few cases the Latin name is quite different from the Greek. Principal characters include:

Greek name	Latin name
Alkmene	Alcmena
Amphitryon	Amphitryo
Antaios	Antaeus
Deianeira	Deianira
Hera	Juno
Herakles	Hercules
Hermes	Mercury
Iolaos	Iolaus
Kerberos	Cerberus
Zeus	Jupiter

All translations are the author's own unless otherwise specified.

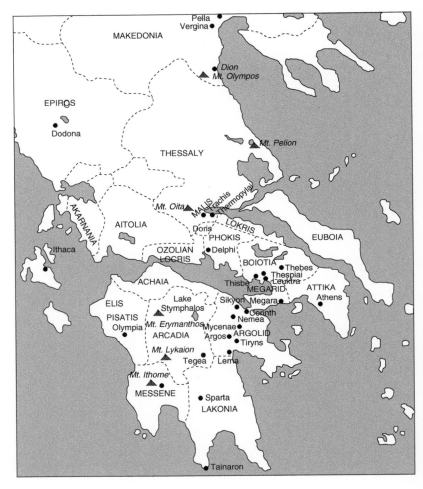

Map. 1 The regions of mainland Greece.

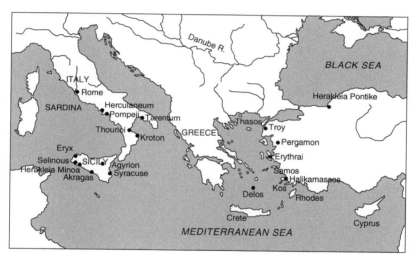

Map. 2 Italy, Greece and Asia Minor.

HERAKLES' FAMILY TREE

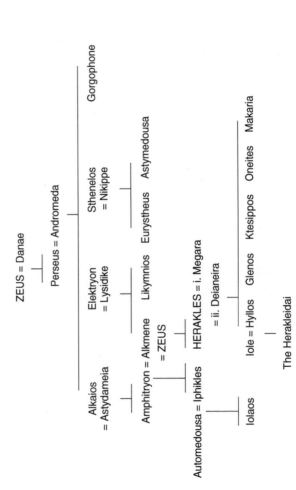

ZEUS = Danae

Perseus = Andromeda

Alkaios = Astydameia

Elektryon = Lysidike

Sthenelos = Nikippe

Gorgophone

Amphitryon = Alkmene = ZEUS

Likymnios

Eurystheus

Astymedousa

Automedousa = Iphikles

HERAKLES = i. Megara = ii. Deianeira

Iolaos

Iole = Hyllos   Glenos   Ktesippos   Oneites   Makaria

The Herakleidai

FOREWORD: WHY HERAKLES?

The figure of the hero who is always strong, never defeated, and exceptionally potent sexually seems, like many fairy-tale motifs, to be drawn from a wish-fulfilment fantasy. Yet not only does this hero meet a terrible or, at any rate an ambivalent end, but he also contains his own antithesis. The glorious hero is also a slave, a woman, and a madman.

(Burkert 1985, 210)

Herakles is the quintessential Greek hero. In antiquity he featured in more stories and was represented more frequently in art than other hero or god – some ancient writers speculated that there must have been two, three, six, eight or even as many as forty-three heroes of the same name. His exploits took him all over Greece, to the furthest extents of the known world to east and west, and beyond this world to Hades and eventually to the home of the gods on Olympos. He entered Roman mythology early on, his worship supposedly started by the legendary king Evander before the city of Rome was even founded. Both the Greek Herakles and the Latin Hercules were part of everyday life because they were invoked in the exclamation 'By Herakles!' (*Herakleis, mehercule*), which expresses surprise or indignation, or is used for emphasis. Greeks and Romans alike worshipped him as invincible warder-off of evils, their belief in his power demonstrated by state-financed sacrifices and festivals as well as the private offerings of individuals and families. With the rise of Christianity in the first few centuries AD Herakles' cult inevitably died, but the hero himself continued to fascinate writers and artists, who romanticized him as a medieval knight, allegorized him as the incarnation of Renaissance virtue, and even proclaimed him as a prototype of Christ.

The figure of Herakles continues to appeal today, at the beginning of the twenty-first century. In the English-speaking world everyone has heard of him by his Roman name Hercules, centuries of tradition making this more familiar than the Greek 'Herakles'. His adventures have provided comic-book writers and film-makers with subject matter, his physical prowess making him the preeminent strong man of the 'sword-and-sandals' genre of the late 1950s and early 60s. The movie-star hero has enjoyed a revival of popularity since the mid-1990s with Disney's animation *Hercules* and the TV series *Hercules: the Legendary Journeys*, which continues to be screened around the world today. In addition to his appearance in such stories, Herakles also continues to exist as a concept. The name Hercules is synonymous with physical strength, and a 'Herculean task' is something beyond the abilities of any ordinary mortal. It is presumably this association with extraordinary strength that lies behind the appropriation of his name for such diverse things as the Hercules C130J transporter plane, a Californian dynamite manufacturer, a major Greek cement company, and a number of football teams. In the academic world, Herakles has received particular attention since the publication of Galinksy's *The Herakles Theme* in 1972, a masterful survey of Herakles' literary incarnations from Homer to the twentieth century. Numerous monographs and articles have followed, on every aspect of Herakles' myth, cult and representations in literature and art, while since the late 1980s at least one exhibition and six entire conferences have been devoted to the subject.[1]

There are various accessible works available on Herakles' myth, but no book-length study provides what I attempt to give here: an overview of Herakles' myth in ancient literature and art, and of his worship across the Greek and Roman worlds, with a postscript on what has happened to him since antiquity.[2] The survey begins with Herakles the slayer of monsters (Chapters 1 and 2), since this is the most persistent aspect of his myth and the one by which he is best known. There are other sides to Herakles' character, however, which are the subject of Chapters 3 and 4: he can be portrayed as both the tragic and the comic hero *par excellence*, he has an active love life, and some even credit him with intellectual virtues. Herakles' adaptability is further demonstrated by the many instances of his exploitation by political leaders to legitimize claims to power (Chapter 5). Beyond all the stories and variations of his image, though, the most alien aspect for the modern reader to come to terms with is Herakles' status as a god, worshipped with full ritual and all due seriousness throughout antiquity (Chapter 6). A final chapter looks at those elements of Herakles' complex nature which survived the end of antiquity, bringing the survey up to the present day.

Before embarking on more detailed study, however, first we need to familiarize ourselves with Herakles' story, so the Introduction provides a synopsis of the myth and deals with some general questions on how to approach it.

WHY HERAKLES?

INTRODUCING HERAKLES

It is a Herculean task to cover the whole story of Hercules.
(Lilio Gregorio Giraldi, preface to *Life of Hercules*, 1539)

TELLING THE STORY

Relating the myth of Herakles is not as simple as it sounds, because he has a more complicated life-story, and a more extensive portfolio of exploits, than any other Greek hero. Anyone who attempts to reduce all the stories, in all their variations, to a single account must sympathize with the Renaissance writer Giraldi's remark which heads this chapter. Nonetheless, such systematizations of the stories of Herakles were already undertaken in antiquity, first by the writers of epic poetry. No complete Herakles epic survives, but we know of a *Herakleia*, 'Deeds of Herakles', written around 600 BC by Peisandros of Rhodes. Peisandros was reputedly the first poet to give Herakles a club and lionskin (fr. 1 W), and the few fragments preserved by later authors suggest that this told the story in considerable detail, in two books, covering at least five of the twelve labours, as well as a number of minor exploits. Another *Herakleia* known to us only from fragments is that of the mid-fifth-century poet Panyassis of Halikarnassos, a relative of Herodotus. This ran to a substantial fourteen books, with a total of 9,000 lines, spending longer on Herakles' more obscure exploits than on the labours.[1] In the fourth century, such epics attracted criticism from Aristotle, for whom the disparate episodes of the story presented a dissatisfying lack of unity (*Poetics* 1451a16–22, tr. Heath):

> A plot is not (as some think) unified because it is concerned with a single person . . . It is clear that a mistake has been made by all those poets who have composed a *Heracleid* or a *Theseid*, or poems of that kind, on the assumption that, just because Heracles was one person, the plot too is bound to be unified.

Aristotle's concern is with poetry, so he makes no mention of the other important genre in which Herakles' story was being recounted by his time:

the prose work of the mythographers ('writers of myth') who began to appear c.500 BC. We have fragments from a substantial work by the Athenian Pherekydes, c.450 BC, covering episodes from Herakles' childhood, several of the labours and later exploits, and some of the events leading up to his death. The Herakles work by Herodoros of Herakleia, c.400 BC, must have included even greater detail, since it ran to at least seventeen books. The only mythographical work to survive in relatively complete form is the *Library* of Apollodoros; the authorship of this work has been much disputed, but it was most likely written in the first or second century AD. A whole section (2.5–7) is devoted to Herakles, beginning with his parents' marriage and his own birth, ending with his death and apotheosis, and a list of his many sons by various women; at least half of the narrative is taken up with a detailed account of the twelve labours performed at the command of Eurystheus. Herakles also features largely in Diodoros of Sicily's *Historical Library*, written in the latter half of the first century BC, a 'universal history' of Greece from mythological times to 60 BC. The section on Herakles begins with a cautionary discussion of the difficulties faced by the teller of ancient tales in general, and myths about Herakles in particular (4.8.1):

> For it is generally agreed that this man has come down to us as having surpassed, in the greatness of the deeds he accomplished, all those handed down in memory from antiquity; so it is difficult to report each of his exploits in a worthy manner and to make the account equal to such deeds, the greatness of which won him the prize of immortality.

Diodoros nevertheless attempts to do Herakles justice by recounting his life and deeds at great length, including much more detail than Apollodoros, especially on Herakles' travels in the western Mediterranean (4.9–39).[2]

SYNOPSIS OF THE MYTH

The following synopsis, which more or less follows Apollodoros' account, will provide a framework for more detailed discussion of individual episodes in later chapters. The story falls into four sections: birth and early years, the twelve labours, minor exploits, events leading up to Herakles' death and apotheosis. See the genealogical table and maps (pp. xxii–iv).

Birth and early years

Herakles' great-grandfather Perseus inherited the throne of Argos, but exchanged it with Megapenthes for rule over Tiryns, from where he founded Mycenae; here his three sons Alkaios, Elektryon and Sthenelos were born. Alkaios inherited Tiryns while Mycenae went to Elektryon, so that when

Alkaios' son Amphitryon married Elektryon's daughter Alkmene, he became heir to both cities. However, Amphitryon accidentally killed Elektryon and had to go into exile in Thebes, upon which Perseus' third son Sthenelos seized power over Mycenae and Tiryns. In Thebes, meanwhile, Amphitryon set out on an expedition against the Teleboans, inhabitants of an island in the Corinthian Gulf who had murdered Alkmene's brothers in the course of a dispute over land and cattle. While he was away, Zeus, motivated either by a particular desire to beget a mighty child or simply by his customary predilection for beautiful women, took on Amphitryon's likeness and slipped into Alkmene's bed, prolonging the night to three times its usual length. When Amphitryon himself returned shortly after the god's departure, he too enjoyed his wife's embraces, and so Alkmene conceived twins, Herakles by Zeus and the fully mortal Iphikles by Amphitryon. Jealous of Zeus' infidelity, Hera displayed her disapproval from the outset by delaying Herakles' birth, allowing Sthenelos' son Eurystheus to be born first back in Mycenae/Tiryns. Because of an incautious declaration by Zeus, that the child born that day would become lord of those around him, Eurystheus was put in a position of potential power over Herakles.

Hera's animosity next manifested itself in the sending of snakes to kill Herakles and Iphikles in their cradle, but the infant hero easily strangled them. Later in his childhood he betrayed the first signs of his legendary temper by killing his music-teacher Linos in a fit of rage. As a young man, Herakles killed the lion of Kithairon, in return for which the king of Thespiai arranged for him to sleep with each of his fifty daughters, in the hope of getting noble grandchildren. Later, Herakles helped his father to defend Thebes against Erginos and the Minyans, a battle in which Amphitryon was killed, but the victorious Herakles was rewarded by Kreon, king of Thebes, with his daughter Megara's hand in marriage. The couple had three sons, but Hera's enmity once again intervened, striking Herakles with a fit of madness in which he killed all the children, and Megara too according to some. Seeking purification from this blood-guilt, Herakles was told by the oracle at Delphi that he must serve Eurystheus as a slave and accomplish whatever tasks he might set.

The twelve labours

These tasks were the twelve labours for which Herakles would become best known, each involving the killing of a monster or the fetching of an impossible prize. First was the Nemean lion, whose hide was invulnerable to any weapon, so Herakles had to kill it with his bare hands; he flayed it with its own claws and wore the lionskin in all his subsequent adventures. Next was the Lernaian hydra, a monstrous serpent living in the swamps not far from Argos. Every time one of its multiple heads was cut off two grew in its place, so Herakles enlisted the help of his nephew Iolaos in cauterizing the stumps before the heads could regenerate, and buried the one immortal head under a rock, before collecting some of the hydra's poisoned blood for future use; to make the task more difficult, Hera sent a giant crab to help the hydra. The object of Herakles' third labour, the Keryneian (sometimes Kerynitian) hind, was entirely harmless but under the protection of Artemis, so it had to be taken to Eurystheus alive and later returned; it had horns, despite being female, of gold. Also brought back alive, but rather more dangerous, was the Erymanthian boar, a monster which had been terrorizing the region of Psophis; Herakles succeeded in trapping it with nets, and presented it to Eurystheus who was so terrified that he hid in a storage jar. Labour number five, the Augeian stables, involved more cunning than brute force: Herakles undertook to clean out the cattle-sheds of Augeias, king of Elis, in a single day, and achieved this by diverting two local rivers so that they swept through the stables. The Stymphalian birds, which had been infesting the Arkadian Lake Stymphalos, likewise required a strategic approach: Herakles frightened them into flight using bronze castanets supplied by Athena, before shooting them down with his arrows.

The first labour to take Herakles beyond the Peloponnese is number seven, the capture of the Cretan bull, which he brought back to Eurystheus alive; it was then set free, to be captured once again by Theseus at Marathon in Attika. Next came the mares of Diomedes, man-eating horses kept by the king of a wild Thracian tribe; Herakles tamed the mares by feeding them Diomedes himself, or his stable-boy, before fetching them back to Mycenae. Herakles had to travel further away still, to the northern limits of the world, to reach the land of the Amazons and fetch the belt of Hippolyte, after killing the queen herself in battle. Labours ten and eleven took Herakles to the far west, in search first of the cattle of Geryon, a three-headed monster who lived beyond Okeanos, his cattle guarded by a herdsman Eurytion and a two-headed dog Orthos; Herakles killed all three and drove the cattle back to Mycenae, where Eurystheus sacrificed them to Hera. In order to fetch the apples of the Hesperides Herakles had to return to the distant west, where the three daughters of Hesperos had their garden, its tree of golden apples guarded by the serpent Ladon. In some versions Herakles did not go himself, but held up the sky in Atlas' place while the latter went on his behalf. The final and most difficult of the labours was the fetching of Kerberos, the three-headed hound of Hades, from the Underworld; Hades allowed Herakles to take Kerberos on condition that he used no weapons, which he succeeded in doing, and he returned the hound to its rightful place once Eurystheus had seen him.

Minor exploits

Numerous other exploits are attributed to Herakles, some of which are fitted in around the labours, others not securely placed. On the way to fetch the Erymanthian boar Herakles encountered Pholos and the centaurs of Mount Pholoe, and after delivering the boar to Eurystheus he took a break from the labours to participate in the voyage of the Argo. On the way back from the land of the Amazons he rescued Laomedon's daughter Hesione from a sea-monster at Troy. In order to reach Geryon's home in Erytheia he travelled through Europe and Libya, setting up the Pillars at the boundary between the two, and crossed the sea in a golden cup borrowed from the Sun. To find the way to the garden of the Hesperides he had to wrestle with the shape-shifting sea-god Nereus, and when passing through the Caucasus mountains he set Prometheus free. Also often associated with the journey to or from these last two labours are Herakles' combats with the giant Antaios, the Egyptian king Bousiris, Emathion, Eryx, Alkyoneus and the Roman Cacus, as well the foundation of various cities in Italy and Sicily. During Herakles' visit to the Underworld he rescued Theseus and Peirithous, chained up there for having attempted to abduct Persephone, and heard of his future wife Deianeira from the shade of her brother Meleager.

Herakles' first wife Megara was either killed along with her children or was later given to his nephew Iolaos. Seeking a new wife, Herakles took part in an archery competition set up by Eurytos, king of Oichalia (usually located in Euboia), for his daughter Iole's hand in marriage; Herakles won, but for some reason was denied his prize. Later he murdered Eurytos' son Iphitos, either in madness or in a dispute over some cattle, for which he sought purification at Delphi. The Pythia initially refused to see him, so he tried to carry off her tripod and fought with Apollo until Zeus intervened. The oracle then promised him purification in return for spending three years in slavery to Omphale, queen of Lydia. During this enslavement Herakles encounterd the vineyard-owner Syleus, the cheeky Kerkopes and the Itonoi.

After the rescue of Hesione, Laomedon had promised Herakles horses but reneged, so Herakles returned and sacked the city of Troy, assisted by Telamon. On his way home, Hera sent storms to blow him off course to Kos. Later, Athena enlisted Herakles' help on the gods' side in their battle against the giants. Back in the Peloponnese, Herakles encountered the Molione twins, sacked Elis and founded the Olympic Games, then went on to sack Pylos, where he killed the sons of Neleus. While passing through Arkadia, Herakles raped Auge, daughter of Aleos, king of Tegea, who bore him a son, Telephos.

Events leading up to Herakles' death and apotheosis

In Kalydonia, Herakles married Deianeira, daughter of Oineus, after wrestling with a rival suitor, the river-god Acheloos, whose horn was broken off in the fight. The couple went to Trachis in central Greece, where they had to cross the river Euenos. The centaur Nessos offered to carry Deianeira across, but attempted to rape her on the way, so Herakles shot him down, using arrows poisoned with the hydra's blood. As he lay dying, Nessos tricked Deianeira into taking some of the blood from his wound, pretending that it would act as a love-potion on her husband should she ever need one. Later, after a visit to king Keyx in Trachis and the defeat of Kyknos, Herakles mounted an expedition against Eurytos, in revenge for his earlier refusal to hand over his daughter, sacked Oichalia and brought Iole home as a concubine. Deianeira decided to use the 'love-potion' to regain Herakles' affections, discovering too late that it was in fact poison. Dying in agony, Herakles asked for a funeral pyre to be built on Mount Oita, which he threw himself onto. Just before his death he instructed Hyllos, his oldest son by Deianeira, to marry Iole, and handed over his bow and arrows to Philoktetes (or his father Poias) as a reward for lighting the pyre. He was taken up from the pyre to Olympos, where he was reconciled with Hera and spent a happy eternity married to Hebe ('Youth' personified). After Herakles' death, his old enemy Eurystheus continued to harrass his children, but was eventually killed by Hyllos or by Iolaos, sometimes with help of the Athenians.

EXPLAINING HERAKLES

Having established the basic outline of Herakles' story, we should pause for a moment to consider ways in which we might go about a closer study. Myth was already a subject for reflection in antiquity, and modern scholars have been proposing and elaborating universal theories of myth since at least the eighteenth century. What follows is a brief survey of how some of the most influential of these approaches have been applied specifically to Herakles.

What's in a name?

One line of enquiry which was popular in antiquity was etymology, the attempt to discover the truth about a thing by analyzing its name. Most ancient writers interpreted Herakles' name as meaning 'glory (*kleos*) of Hera', some attempting to explain the apparent paradox this involves, given Herakles' notoriously bad relationship with the goddess. According to Pindar (fr. 291 SM), the hero was originally called Alkeides, 'descendant of Alkaios', but was renamed Herakles by Hera herself in grudging recognition that his *kleos* had been won as result of her harassment; Apollodoros attributes this name change to the Delphic oracle. According to Diodoros (4.10.1) and others the original name was simply Alkaios ('Strong'), which would reflect what we know of historical naming practices, since this is the name of his paternal grandfather. The change to Herakles was made by the people of Argos, impressed by the infant hero's feat in strangling the snakes sent by Hera, or else it came about much later, when Herakles had assisted Hera by overcoming the giant Porphyrion.

Such explanations have not entirely satisfied modern scholars. The name appears to be formed on a principle common to many others familiar from ancient Greece, i.e. by adding a suffix to the name of a deity – Herodotus and Apollodoros are 'gifts' of Hera and Apollo respectively, while Herakles is exactly paralleled by Diokles and Themistokles, 'glory of' Zeus ('Dios' is the genitive case) and Themis, goddess of Order. This kind of name might well reflect the parents' relationship with a particular deity, expressing thanks for answered prayers or dedicating the child to the god's future protection. As goddess of marriage, as well as principle deity of the city of Argos, Hera would be an entirely appropriate choice for real Argolid parents to honour in the naming of their son. Farnell (1921, 99–101) indeed took the very normal formulation of Herakles' name as support for the supposition that he began his career as a mortal (whether fictional or real) and was only later deified. Pötscher (1971) dispensed with the apparent inappropriateness of 'glory of Hera' by supposing an original version of the story in which Herakles' deeds were performed on Hera's orders, to which the motifs of Hera's hostility and jealousy of Alkmene were only added subsequently. More recently, West (1997, 471) has revived the theory that the first part of Herakles' name is related to the word *hêrôs*, 'hero', as well as to Hera, both of which may be derived from the Indo-European root **yêr-* meaning 'year'.[3]

Rationalizing accounts

Another ancient approach is allegorical interpretation, according to which myth is a kind of philosophy or theology in disguise, hiding its real moral message beneath the surface of the story. This has its roots in the work of the ancient mythographers, and Herodoros (fr. 14 F) provides a good example in his account of Herakles' visit to the garden of the Hesperides: the three apples represent three virtues (abstinence from anger, avarice and hedonism), all guarded by the serpent of desire, which Herakles, dressed in the lionskin of wise reason, kills with the club of strong spirit. In a similar vein, the first-century AD writer Herakleitos gives a succinct interpretation of Herakles' labours in terms of the Stoic philosopher's struggle against earthly passions (*Homeric Problems* 33.3–10):

> The boar he captured is intemperance, habitual amongst men, and the lion, the instinctive urge which drives us to evil; in the same way, because he shackled the irrational emotions, he was considered to have chained the unruly bull, and he chased cowardice, the Keryneian hind, from life. And something incorrectly called a labour was achieved when he purged the heaped up dung, the disgusting state which overruns mankind. The birds he dispersed are the fleeting hopes which devour our life, and the many-headed insolence, which begins to sprout again whenever you cut a head off, he decapitated like a hydra by the fire of his exhortation. And that three-headed Kerberos which he brought into the light of day would in all likelihood signify the three parts of philosophy, which we call logic, physics and ethics; these grow, as it were, from a single neck but divide into three separate heads.

A different kind of rationalizing approach, again with ancient roots, holds that myth is merely distorted history. Some exponents, notably Euhemeros of Messene, used this to argue the gods out of existence, but others confined themselves to the myths of heroes and aimed rather to encourage belief by removing the more improbable elements of their stories. An early example is Hekataios of Miletos, writing in the 490s BC, who explained Herakles' fetching of Kerberos by supposing that the hero had in fact captured a huge snake named the 'Hound of Hades' near Cape Tainaron in southern Lakonia, where a cave was widely believed to be an entrance to Hades (fr. 27a F). In the late fourth century BC, several of Herakles' exploits receive this kind of treatment in Palaiphatos' treatise *On Unbelievable Tales* (44):

> It is said about Omphale that Herakles was enslaved to her – a silly story, for he could have been lord over her and her belongings. It happened like this. Omphale was daughter of Iardanos, king of Lydia. This woman, hearing of Herakles' strength, pretended to be in love with him. Once in her company, Herakles was seized by love for her, and fathered a son from her; because he was delighted by her, he did whatever Omphale asked. The simple-minded, however, supposed he was enslaved to her.

In a similar vein, both ancient and modern scholars have interpreted such exploits as the killing of the hydra, the cleaning of Augeias stables or the Stymphalian birds as reflecting major water management projects of the Mycenaean period.[4]

Historicism in modern scholarship has especially informed discussion of the 'Return of the Herakleidai' (pp. 137–9) and of Herakles' origins. The idea that a myth can be explained if we know where it comes from is an attractive one, but centuries of debate have produced no firm consensus in Herakles' case. The problem is that our earliest Greek sources, the epic poems of Homer and Hesiod, allude to stories about Herakles only in passing, assuming the audience's familiarity with the myth. They also introduce his name with a stock epic formula *biê Heraklêeiê*, literally 'Herakleian might' though usually translated 'mighty Herakles', the sort of formulaic expression which was used in the oral tradition of epic long before Homer. This indicates that stories were being told about Herakles in the so-called Dark Age of Greece, which preceded Homer (c.1100–750 BC), but we cannot be sure exactly what these stories involved, or how far back they went.

Scholars have speculated that Herakles was imported by, and was somehow the embodiment of, the Dorians, a shadowy people supposed to have invaded Greece from the north around the eleventh century BC and taken control over the Peloponnese and Crete. This idea was popular in the nineteenth century, but it was convincingly refuted by Farnell (1921) on the grounds that there is no consistent correlation between Herakles' cult and Dorian areas, and today many dispute that there was an invasion at all. Other early twentieth-century scholars argued that Herakles originated within Greece itself, either in the Mycenaean period or in the Dark Age, more specifically in eighth-century Argos. It is certainly true that Herakles has a strong mythological attachment to the Argolid, as we have seen in the story of his ancestry. Six of his labours are set in various parts of the Peloponnese, and their traditional sequence follows a geographical expansion which adherents of the historicist approach would see as representing the historical spread of Argive power: Nemea (the lion) and Lerna (the hydra) are in the Argolid itself; Mount Erymanthos (the boar), Keryneia (the hind) and Lake Stymphalos (the birds) in Arkadia; and the stables of Augeias at Olympia.[5]

Comparative approaches

A variation on the ancient allegorical approach surfaced in the mid-nineteenth century with F. Max Müller's theory of natural allegory, whereby all myths are expressions of the religious awe aroused in primitive man by natural phenomena. Müller's 'comparative mythology', as he called it, was based on philology, prompted by his study of the Sanskrit *Rig Veda*, in which he saw all kinds of parallels with the Greek myth: for him Herakles, like the Hindu god Indra, was essentially a solar deity, and his death on the pyre reflected the fiery rays of the setting sun. The germ of the 'solar deity' idea in fact goes back to the early fifth-century AD Macrobius, who declared that 'Hercules is that power of the sun which provides to the human race virtue like that of the gods' (*Saturnalia* 1.20.6), and had been taken up in the Renaissance by writers such as George Sandys (commentary on Ovid's *Metamorphoses* 440):

For what signifies Hercules but the Glory of the Aire? And what is the Glory of the aire, but the Suns illumination, which expelleth the Spirit of Darknesse?

A more empirical approach to comparative mythology was inspired by the publication, in 1890, of J.G. Frazer's *Golden Bough*, a vast collection of data on 'primitive' beliefs and rituals from around the world. Frazer's main interest was in rituals concerned, in his view, with fertility, and this strongly influenced the interpretations of the 'Cambridge ritualists', a group of scholars who used this material to shed light on Greek religious thought and practice. Jane Harrison broadened the enquiry to take in social rituals too, but her assessment of Herakles is dominated by the fertility paradigm. According to her (1912, 364–81), Herakles is a 'year-daimon', a spirit of the natural cycle of decay, death and renewal; his twelve labours reflect the solar year, and he can borrow the cup of the Sun because he is Helios' humanized double; his club was originally the magical bough which brings fertility; the horn of Acheloos, broken off by Herakles, becomes the cornucopia, symbol of plenty and regeneration. Harrison's concept of the year-daimon has generally been discarded, but her broader contention that myths were originally the spoken accompaniments to ritual, or at least expressed parallel concerns, forms the basis for a debate which continues to this day on the relationship between myth and ritual. As we shall see in Chapter 6, some of the rituals performed in Herakles' honour were explained in antiquity as commemorating particular mythological events, while others have been interpreted by modern scholars in the light of episodes of Herakles' story – as in the case of rituals on Kos, which may reflect his marriage to Hebe. Conversely, even where no specific ritual is known, some elements of the myth can be understood as reflecting *types* of ritual – the Geryon story, for example, is one of several Greek cattle-raiding myths thought to mirror young men's maturation rites.

Harrison's work was a strong influence on Georges Dumézil, who from the 1930s developed a more restrained version of Müller's comparative mythology. According to this, all the institutions of Indo-European societies could be divided into three ideological classes, or 'functions', reflected in their mythology: the priest/king, the warrior and the farmer/craftsman. While much of Greek mythology seems not to fit the pattern, a reasonable case has been made for Herakles as the epitome of the warrior function, and numerous parallels drawn with warrior-figures in other Indo-European mythologies. Herakles' story has elements in common with heroes such as the Germanic Starkaðr and the Indian Śiśupāla: his conception is accompanied by reproductive excess; he has great physical strength, but is subject to one god who favours him, one who persecutes him; he violates various fundamental social principles in the course of his career, for which he is punished; on his death he is returned to his divine source, having passed his warrior attributes to another. The myths of Herakles and his like all reflect the warrior's ambiguous relationship to society, for which he is at once an essential guardian and a potential threat.[6] Drawing on this comparative approach, Burkert (1979) argues that the figure of Herakles belongs to a prehistoric, proto-Indo-European hunter culture, his animal encounters reflecting the everyday struggle with the wild, while his journeys to the land beyond the sun and the underworld belong to shamanistic hunting magic.

Most recently scholars have concentrated on Near Eastern mythology, where there are some very striking parallels especially for Herakles' monster-fighting. Mesopotamian seals as early as 2500 BC feature a hero strangling a huge snake in either hand, an exploit attributed to the infant Herakles, or fighting a huge bird, or against a seven-headed serpent strongly reminiscent of the hydra. Ninurta or Ningirsu, hero of the *Epic of Anzu* and *The Return of Ninurta to Nippur*, appears with lionskin, club and bow, and is son of Enlil the storm-god, ruler of the pantheon, just as Herakles is son of 'storm-gathering' Zeus. He fights against eleven or twelve fabulous monsters and brings them back to his city as trophies; monsters which include the seven-headed serpent, a wild bull, a stag, the Anzu-bird, and a lion. The idea of a cycle of twelve labours may also be seen in the case of the god Marduk, who has to vanquish the sea-god Tiamat and eleven monsters in the Babylonian *Epic of Creation*. Herakles has been compared with the eponymous hero of the *Epic of Gilgamesh*, too, who wears an animal (lion or dog) skin while on his quest for immortality, and finds jewelled fruit growing in a fantastic garden at the ends of the earth.

Similarities have also been noted between Herakles and the Biblical Samson, who kills a lion with his bare hands, breaks out of his bonds, pulls down a house and, though previously invincible, is eventually undone by a woman (Judges 16:3–30). The lion in particular makes much more sense as an opponent of Ninurta, Gilgamesh or Samson than of Herakles, since lions were relatively common in Syria, Palestine and North Africa, but almost unknown in Greece. Egyptian myth provides another possible model for the number twelve in the form of the Sun-god Ra's journey through the twelve hours of the night, encountering gods and monsters in each hour-sector, while an odd detail of Egyptian tradition is that various Pharoahs were supposedly begotten by Amun impersonating their mortal father. The chronological priority of Near Eastern mythology once again raises the possibility of finding Herakles' origins, but Burkert (1987, 17) warns against any simplistic derivation of the Greek Herakles from one oriental prototype: 'there is no single "Herakles myth" that could have been passed, like sealed parcel, to new possessors at a certain time and place'.[7]

Psychoanalysis, structuralism and after

The idea that certain characters and story-lines recur in different cultures was taken over from comparative studies by a number of approaches developed in the twentieth century. Psychoanalytic studies, in particular, depend on the Jungian idea of 'archetypes', images that appear in dreams and folktales the world over because they are somehow inherent in the human mind. An extensive application of such an approach to Herakles can be found in Slater (1968, 337–94), who finds parallels in modern psychoanalytical case studies for many aspects of his character, and explains his many exploits as a 'compulsive assertion of strength' in response to persecution by Hera, the 'hostile, depriving mother'. Herakles' various serpentine opponents, in particular, represent aspects of 'the oral-narcissistic conflict' caused by the traumatic process of individuation, as the child gains a separate identity from his mother. Against this kind of threat, Herakles adopts such basic human defence strategies as 'identification with the aggressor', e.g. by dipping his arrows in the poisoned blood of the Lernaean hydra he assimilates the monster's power. A more recent exponent of the psychoanalytical approach (Caldwell 1989, 161) interprets the Hesperides episode in terms of the trauma of individuation: like the Garden of Eden, the Hesperides' home can be understood as an unconscious memory of the infant's earliest symbiotic relationship with the mother, a place of primal gratification, while the golden apples symbolize maternal breasts; Herakles' visit to this 'symbiotic paradise' represents 'the wish to be reunited with the nurturant mother'.

Other interpretative trends of the twentieth century look rather to the internal structures of myth in their search for significance. In the 1920s Vladimir Propp developed a theory, based on an analysis of Russian folktales, that stories can be reduced to a recurrent structural type, made up of thirty-one units of action, or 'functions', which remain constant whatever the changes of character and detail. Though only of limited application to Greek myth, some elements of the analysis do adapt quite well to a group of 'quest' stories, which include Herakles' labours and the adventures of Bellerophon, Perseus and Jason: in each case the hero is sent off on an apparently impossible mission, receives supernatural help, defeats a villain and/or obtains the object of the quest, and eventually returns home. Such analysis of linear structure usefully highlights narrative patterns, facilitating comparison between stories, but its focus on action excludes such important elements as character, human relationships, motivation and location.

A more influential kind of structuralist analysis was that developed by

Claude Lévi-Strauss in the 1950s and 60s. This is concerned not with narrative sequence but rather with identifying deeper underlying patterns, based on binary oppositions which are understood to be fundamental to human thought (raw/cooked, nature/culture, hunter/hunted); for the structuralists, myth is a means of mediating between the two polarities and resolving, or at least alleviating, the inherent conflict. The structuralist approach has been applied to Greek myth especially by Jean-Pierre Vernant and Marcel Detienne, who emphasize the importance of social and historical context in 'decoding' the stories, which reflect and reinforce the dominant values of the particular culture which produced them. Herakles' complex character offers a great deal of scope for such analysis, as suggested towards the end of Kirk's summary (1974, 176–212) of the hero's career: Herakles' many civilized actions are juxtaposed to bestial lack of restraint and fits of rage, an opposition nicely mirrored by his apparent affinity with centaurs, the ultimate mythological embodiment of the nature/culture polarity.

Similar concerns can be seen in the post-structuralist 'ideological' approach, most recently demonstrated in relation to Herakles by Csapo (2005, 301–15). Put very briefly, the myth articulates Greek ideas about labour and freedom, as associated with three social classes: aristocrats, who voluntarily engage in the 'work' of athletic competition and war in order to win glory; merchants, who voluntarily engage in trade in order to satisfy their greed for money; and peasants, who are compelled to work on the land in order to gain food. All of these categories are represented amongst Herakles' exploits – he defeats a number of opponents by the aristocratic means of wrestling (the Nemean lion, the giant Antaios) and ultimately achieves great glory, but he is also known to work for the promise of financial reward (some versions of the Augeian stables, the rescue of Hesione), and he submits to the most extreme form of compulsion in his enslavement to Eurystheus and Omphale. This complexity in the modes and motives of Herakles' exploits goes some way towards explaining the hero's universal appeal, but the supreme value of voluntary, aristocratic labour is constantly reinforced by the problematization of the other forms of labour, all of which are dependent on others, who invariably prove to be unreliable.

CONTEXTS AND SOURCES

While some of these approaches have insights to offer, most suffer to a greater or lesser degree from a tendency to divorce Greek myth from the contexts in which the stories were told, and they often work on the basis of a synthetic account of the myth drawn indiscriminately from sources of widely differing type and date. Modern handbooks of Greek myth likewise follow the precedent of the ancient mythographers in trying to create a systematic account, which is liable to obscure the glorious wealth of material available. A strong trend in current scholarship, however, is rather to break myths down, looking at the literary and visual sources available for individual elements, in order to trace the historical development of the story in different geographical areas. Although this approach is limited by the material which has happened to survive, it gets us as close as possible to how the stories were communicated in antiquity. We can never fully reconstruct informal tellings around the family hearth or the soldiers' campfire, but glimpses appear in popular visual media, and for the more formal types of performance we sometimes have preserved texts. My own approach in the following chapters will be very much concerned with what can actually be seen in the ancient sources for Herakles' myth, and what this may tell us about the societies which produced them. The brief overview here puts these sources into chronological order, taking literature first, then art.[8]

Literature provides the most obvious medium for storytelling, and Herakles appears in a great variety of literary genres. We have already discussed works of epic and mythography which set out to cover the whole of Herakles' career, but much more commonly we find just an individual episode of the story, or a reference made to Herakles as an aside to the main subject. The predominant literary genre of the archaic period is epic poetry, beginning with Homer. Although the date and method of Homeric composition remains the subject of scholarly debate, reasonable working dates are 750–700 BC for the *Iliad*, with the *Odyssey* just a little later; also composed c.700 BC was Hesiod's *Theogony*, where the bare 'x begat y' format of the genealogy is enlivened throughout by allusions to the stories surrounding each character. The earliest epic known to have focused on a particular episode of Herakles' story is the seventh- or sixth-century *Capture of Oichalia* by Kreophylos of Samos, which presumably told the story of Herakles' quarrel with Eurytos. Two more episodes from the later part of Herakles' story are treated individually by epics attributed in antiquity to Hesiod, though likely to date from the later seventh or early sixth century. The *Wedding of Keyx* told of a feast at Trachis apparently gate-crashed by Herakles at some point after the incident with Nessos, while the *Aigimios* had him assisting Aigimios, king of the city of Doris in Phokis, in a boundary dispute against the Lapiths. Again traditionally attributed to Hesiod, but probably written c.580–520 BC, is the *Catalogue of Women*, sometimes referred to by its Greek title the *Ehoiai* ('Or like she who . . .'). Only a small proportion of the *Catalogue*'s original five or six books is preserved in fragments, but these include some important contributions to our knowledge of the early development of Herakles' story. Also attributed to Hesiod, but written towards the end of the sixth century, is the *Shield of Herakles*, which recounts the hero's battle against Kyknos.

Individual exploits also provide subject-matter for lyric poetry, the archaic period's other significant genre, which might be performed at the symposium by a solo singer accompanying himself on the lyre, or in the more public context of a religious festival by a soloist or chorus. Especially important for Herakles is Stesichoros of Himera, working in Sicily in the first half of the sixth century, who according to Athenaios (12.512e–13a) was the first poet to represent Herakles as a lone bandit, with the club, lionskin and bow; we have surviving fragments of his *Geryoneis*, a *Kerberos* and a *Kyknos*.

The classical period saw further works in these genres – the lyric odes of Bakchylides and Pindar, and Panyassis' lost epic – but is more significant for the development of drama and various kinds of prose writing. Surviving tragedies include two which take Herakles as their central character, Sophokles' *Women of Trachis* and Euripides' *Herakles*, substantial reworkings of the story of his death and of his madness. He was also a familiar sight on the comic stage, in comedy proper and in satyr drama, although for the most part we only have fragments of the plays concerned. In prose, Herakles features surprisingly often in historiography, his origins and divine/ heroic nature being a subject of discussion for Herodotus, for example, and he even finds his way into the major fourth-century genres of oratory and philosophy. In the third century Herakles is one of Jason's companions in Apollonios of Rhodes' epic, the *Argonautika*, but he also appears in more characteristically hellenistic poetic genres, such as the pastoral idylls of Theokritos. Roman writers took Herakles up as part of the whole package of Greek culture that influenced their work, so that he appears, for example, in Virgil's *Aeneid*, Ovid's *Metamorphoses*, and the literary tragedies of the younger Seneca.

Storytelling is not confined to literature, however; the visual arts provide a wealth of information on the development of mythological narrative, especially in its early stages. Of particular importance is architectural sculpture, which begins to be used around 600 BC to decorate temples and other buildings with mythological scenes, among which a wide variety of Herakles' exploits features. Such scenes are not nearly as plentiful as those in smaller-scale media, but they are by definition both for public viewing and geographically fixed, which provides us with sound information on how widely known the episodes depicted were, and how Herakles stories might have special significance in particular locations. Important buildings include the temple of Hera at Foce del Sele in Campania (c.560 BC), temples on the mid-sixth-century Athenian Akropolis, the temple of Athena at Assos in the Troad (c.540–520 BC), the late sixth-century Throne of Bathykles at Amyklai near Sparta, and the Siphnian and Athenian Treasuries at Delphi (c.525 and 490 BC respectively).

Small-scale media expand the picture both chronologically and geographically. The earliest securely identifiable Herakles scenes date from the early seventh century, decorating a variety of bronze and other artefacts as well as pottery. Notable are the mythological scenes which decorate bronze fibulae from Boiotia, dating from the late eighth and early seventh centuries, and the shield-bands from the sanctuary of Zeus at Olympia, dating from the late seventh to the early sixth centuries. Herakles also features prominently on pottery from the Peloponnese, with Corinthian ware providing us with some of our earliest visual representations of a good many episodes of the myth between about 670 and 570 BC. We have far fewer painted pots from Lakonia, the region around Sparta, but Herakles appears on more than 20 per cent of them, dating between c.570 and 540 BC, reflecting the special place Herakles occupied in Spartan mythology. By far the most abundant source of representations of Herakles, however, is Attic vase-painting. Attic black-figure proper develops from the early sixth century, causing a veritable explosion of material available for the study of mythological narrative. Herakles stories account for almost half of all mythological scenes in surviving Attic black-figure, and he is still very much in evidence in the earliest red-figure, c.530–500 BC. Herakles continues to appear in vase-painting of fifth-century Athens and fourth-century southern Italy, though not with anything like the frequency of his archaic image. Figure-painting on vases more or less stops around 300 BC, but in the hellenistic period Herakles becomes a favourite subject in both large- and small-scale free-standing sculpture.[9]

Many Greek vases were exported to Etruria in the late archaic period, and the Etruscans began depicting Herakles in their own art from the early sixth century BC. He is recognizable by his lionskin and club when he appears alone, especially in small-scale sculpture and on gems, while the narrative scenes of vase-painting, on mirror-cases and in relief sculpture present him in contexts usually familiar from Greek art; inscriptions giving him the Etruscan name 'Hercle' appear alongside the images from c.480 BC. Both Greek and Etruscan art influenced the image of the Roman Hercules. Versions of Greek sculptural types were much reproduced as both full-scale statues and statuettes, while various Heraklean exploits appear in Roman wall-painting and mosaic, and the labours feature especially in the relief decoration of sarcophagi. The figure of Herakles, alone or with a single opponent, is also a regular subject for such small-scale Roman items as gems, coins and jewellery; for example, earrings in the shape of Herakles' club (San Francisco 3921-b).[10]

OVERVIEW

Herakles was a hugely popular character in antiquity, with a great number of exploits to his name. We have the systematic accounts of Diodoros and Apollodoros as guides, but there is no one 'correct' version of Herakles' story, nor even of its individual episodes; we should rather think of many different tellings of the story at different times and in different places, which are partially reflected in surviving literature and art. Numerous theoretical approaches have been applied to Herakles, the most promising of which point to parallels in Near Eastern mythology. The name Herakles, however, is distinctively Greek and specifically Greek locations for his life and the majority of his exploits are elaborated by our sources. It is most likely that the individual figure of Herakles was a hero of Peloponnesian tradition, to whom more and more stories gradually attached, at first from local sources and later from further afield, as the people who told his story gradually came into contact with new cultures. Such a piecemeal development goes some way to explaining the many contradictions in Herakles' character.

A neat summary of the story is provided as early as the sixth century BC by the *Homeric Hymn* (15) to 'Herakles the lion-hearted':

> I shall sing of Herakles, son of Zeus, by far the best of men on the earth,
> whom Alkmene bore in fair-dancing Thebes,
> after she had lain with the dark-clouded son of Kronos.
> Once he used to wander over the unmeasured land
> and the sea, sent by lord Eurystheus, and on his own account
> he both performed and endured many violent deeds.
> But now he lives happily in the fine seat of snowy Olympos,
> and has fair-ankled Hebe as his wife.
> Hail, lord, son of Zeus: Grant me excellence (*aretê*) and wealth!

KEY THEMES

I

MONSTERS AND THE HERO I: THE TWELVE LABOURS

The father of men and gods contrived a plan in his mind,
that he would beget for gods and bread-eating men a protector from slaughter.
(*Catalogue of Women*, Hesiod fr. 195.27–9 MW)

THE STRONG MAN FIGURE AND MONSTER-FIGHTING

The most abiding image of Herakles is that of the strong man fighting a monster. This is how he appears in his earliest visual representations in archaic Greece, and how he is portrayed in film right up to the beginning of the twenty-first century. Monster-slaying is indeed a common occupation for Greek heroes – Theseus kills the Minotaur, Perseus beheads the Gorgon Medusa and rescues Andromeda from a sea-monster, Bellerophon frees the land of Lykia from the ravages of the Chimaira, Jason kills the dragon which guards the golden fleece, Kadmos has to kill a dragon before he can found Thebes – and the hero-monster opposition is common in the popular stories of many other cultures, from St George and the dragon all the way through to Buffy the Vampire-Slayer. The particular nature of the monster and details of the hero's character vary from case to case, but the essential story-line is always the same: the monster, which is threatening a maiden or a whole community or barring the way to a treasure, has proved invincible against all previous comers, but, after a hard battle, is brought down by the hero's superior abilities. The hero may have some kind of supernatural aid, and often has to apply a degree of cunning when sheer brawn is not enough, but his most clearly characteristic feature is physical strength.

Why is the monster-fighting hero motif so perennially popular? One might point to allegorical meanings and underlying psychology, the timeless battle of good against evil, the restoration of civilization threatened by chaos, the universal desire for a champion. But just as important is the powerful attraction of the basic plot-line involved: with its combination of action, straightforward morality, and temporary fear quickly resolved by the hero's reassuring victory, killing monsters makes an excellent story.[1]

DEVELOPMENT OF THE CANON OF LABOURS

As we saw in the introduction, there are early oriental parallels for the idea of a 'cycle' of heroic deeds, and even the specific number twelve, but Herakles' canonical twelve labours do not seem to be established in Greek myth before the classical period. The Greek word traditionally translated as 'labour' is *athlon*, meaning a contest for a prize and especially associated with the panhellenic games, which underlines Herakles' aristocratic aspect as the 'athlete' par excellence; the group of twelve is sometimes referred to by the Greek term *dôdekathlos*, though this was not used in antiquity.

The first clear instance of such a collection of twelve labours is on the temple of Zeus at Olympia, built c.460 BC, decorating the metopes within the porches over the front and back entrances. There were six metopes at each end, and the episodes depicted correspond to those which later sources agree were the canonical twelve labours (Figure 1.1). The sculptural programme of the whole temple is carefully planned with its location in mind: the west pediment depicts a lively battle of the Lapiths against the centaurs, a myth used all over the Greek world to symbolize the triumph of Greek civilization over barbarian chaos; but the east pediment represents a myth of more local significance, the chariot race between Pelops and Oinomaos, the result of which will be the establishment of Pelops' reign at Elis (the state which had control over Olympia). It is no accident, then, that the metopes depict the civilizing influence and athleticism of Herakles, who is particularly connected with Olympia as mythological founder of the Games. It has been suggested that the Olympia metopes created the canon of labours, the number dictated by the spaces available for decoration.[2]

While the number twelve is not seen before this, however, there are several examples in archaic literature which make it clear that Herakles was already known as performing a series of tasks at the command of Eurystheus. The earliest references come in the *Iliad*, though only one of the labours is actually specified. Details of the hero's birth are given in a speech by Agamemnon, who is trying to excuse his own former folly in quarrelling with Achilles by demonstrating that even Zeus could be deceived (19.95–125): when Alkmene was due to give birth, Zeus declared that the man born that day would be lord over all those around him, whereupon Hera delayed Herakles' birth at Thebes, but brought on premature labour in Sthenelos' wife at Argos, so that Herakles' relative (first cousin once removed) Eurystheus could be born first. Zeus punished the goddess

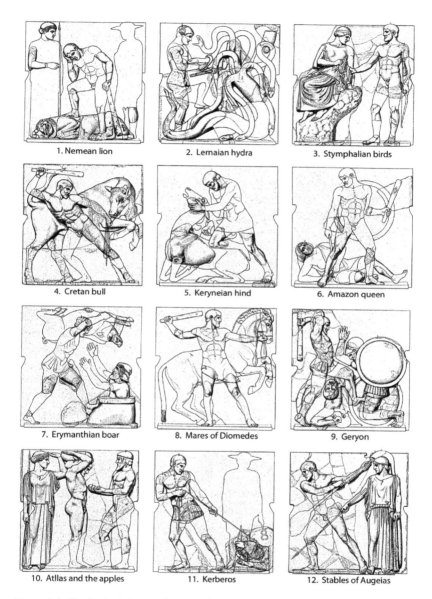

1. Nemean lion   2. Lernaian hydra   3. Stymphalian birds

4. Cretan bull   5. Keryneian hind   6. Amazon queen

7. Erymanthian boar   8. Mares of Diomedes   9. Geryon

10. Atllas and the apples   11. Kerberos   12. Stables of Augeias

Figure 1.1 The Twelve Labours: drawing of metopes from the temple of Zeus at Olympia. According to Pausanias, 1–6 were in the west porch, 7–12 in the east porch. Drawing: after E. Curtius and F. Adler, *Olympia. Die Ergebnisse der von dem Deutschen Reich veranstalteten Grabung* III. *Die Bildwerke in Stein und Thon* (Berlin 1894), pl. XLV.

Delusion for this deception, and continues to groan over her 'whenever he sees his dear son doing some shameful deed of the labours set him by Eurystheus' (19.132–3). These labours are alluded to again in the description of Kopreus, 'who often used to go as messenger from lord Eurystheus to mighty Herakles' (15.639–40), and explicit mention is made of the fetching of Kerberos: Athena complains that Zeus has forgotten 'how often I saved his son when he was worn down by the tasks of Eurystheus', including the occasion when 'he was sent down to the House of Hades, Warden of the Gates, to bring the hound of hateful Hades from Erebos' (8.362–3 and 367–8).

Some of the same details recur in *Odyssey* Book 11, where Odysseus visits the Underworld. He encounters Alkmene, 'Amphitryon's wife, who bore the daring lion-hearted Herakles having lain in the arms of mighty Zeus' (ll.266–8), and Megara, daughter of Kreon, wife of 'the indomitable son of Amphitryon' (ll.269–70). Later on (ll.601–26), Odysseus meets Herakles himself, who is described as a fearsome figure, with bow, arrows and an elaborately decorated gold breastplate, but no lionskin or club. Herakles complains of the servitude he suffered during his life to 'a lesser man', who inflicted 'difficult labours' on him, specifying the one most suited to the situation (ll.623–6):

> And once he sent me here to fetch the hound – for he thought that no other labour would be harder than this. I, however, brought him up and led him out of Hades. And Hermes escorted me, and grey-eyed Athena.

In Hesiod's *Theogony* as many as five of the labours appear. Geryon is described as three-headed, offspring of Medusa's son Chrysaor and the Okeanid Kallirhoë, and Herakles' fetching of the cattle is summarized in a few lines which already contain all the essential details (ll.289–94): Geryon's home is in 'sea-girt Erytheia' beyond Okeanos, i.e. the edge of the earth, and he is killed alongside his cowherd Eurytion and the dog Orthos before Herakles drives his oxen back to Tiryns. Orthos is linked genealogically with three of Herakles' other monstrous opponents – Kerberos, the Lernaian hydra and the Nemean lion – all four being offspring of the snakey monsters Echidna and Typhaon (ll.306–32). There is no mention of Herakles in relation to the fifty-headed, raw-flesh-eating Kerberos who guards Hades, but the hydra and the lion, both raised by Hera, are explicitly overcome by 'mighty Herakles', the former with the help of his nephew Iolaos and Athena. Finally, the Hesperides are described as guarding their golden apples 'beyond glorious Okeanos' (ll.215–16), and Herakles' exploit is obliquely alluded to in the genealogy of Atlas and Prometheus, sons of Iapetos and Klymene (ll.517–31): Atlas is described as standing 'at the borders of the earth, before the clear-voiced Hesperides', and a few lines later it is noted that the eagle which Zeus set to peck out Prometheus' liver daily was eventually killed by Herakles; this would accord with Apollodoros' account (2.5.11), which places the rescue on Herakles' return from the Hesperides' garden (pp. 66–8).[3]

The few surviving fragments of Peisandros' *Herakleia* (frs 1–11 *PEG*) specify that Herakles wrestled with the Nemean lion and subsequently wore its skin, characterize the Lernaian hydra as 'many headed', and refer to Herakles travelling across Okeanos in the cup of Helios, which implies the journey to fetch either Geryon's cattle or the Hesperides' apples; they also add two more labours, with references to the Keryneian hind, female and golden-horned, and the Stymphalian birds, and mention Antaios.

Groups of Heraklean exploits also appear in archaic art. The earliest example is the late seventh- or early sixth-century Chest of Kypselos, which is no longer extant but is described in detail by Pausanias (5.17.5–19.10), who saw it when he visited Olympia in the late second century AD. It seems to have been an intricately carved cedar-wood chest, decorated with inlaid ivory and gold, depicting a whole compendium of mythological scenes. These include several relating to Herakles: a man offering Alkmene a cup and a necklace, which Pausanias explains as referring to the myth that Zeus lay with Alkmene in the form of Amphitryon; Herakles battling with Geryon or centaurs; Atlas supporting the sky and still holding the apples of the Hesperides as Herakles approaches with a sword. In connection with a scene showing the killing of the hydra, Pausanias makes the interesting comment that Herakles' name is not inscribed, but the hero is recognizable 'because of both his labours and the way he is represented' (5.17.11); presumably Pausanias means he has the lionskin, club and bow which had become such standard attributes by his own time.

Another archaic work which only survives in Pausanias' description (3.18.9–19.5) is the Throne of Bathykles at Amyklai near Sparta, an elaborate architectural surround for the ancient statue of Apollo, by the late sixth-century sculptor Bathykles of Magnesia. Herakles featured prominently in the sculptural decoration, in no fewer than thirteen scenes, mirroring his popularity in Lakonian vase-painting. Once again there is no distinction between the labours and other exploits, nor does Pausanias make it clear how the scenes were represented (e.g. on metopes or a continuous frieze), but simply lists the characters concerned, sometimes with an indication of the action involved: 'Atlas, Herakles' single combat with Kyknos, and the battle of the centaurs at Pholos' home'; 'Herakles' battle against the giant Thourios, Athena leading Herakles to Olympos'; 'Herakles taking revenge upon Diomedes the Thracian and upon Nessos by the river Euenos'; 'the slaying of the hydra, the fetching of Kerberos and the cattle of Geryon';

'Herakles killing the sons of Aktor (the Moliones)'; 'Herakles' combat with a centaur called Oreios and his wrestling-match with the river Acheloos'. On the akropolis of Sparta itself, again according to Pausanias (3.17.3), the sixth-century temple of Athena of the Bronze House was decorated with bronze panels which featured 'many of Herakles' labours and many of the things he accomplished of his own free will' amongst other mythological scenes.[4]

In extant architectural sculpture, the earliest and most remarkable representations of Herakles are on the first temple of Hera at Foce del Sele in Campania, built c.560 BC by Greek colonists from Troizen who had settled at nearby Paestum. At least half of the forty-odd metopes from its Doric frieze feature Herakles, which might seem an odd choice for a temple dedicated to his arch enemy. It is perhaps to be explained by the Peloponnesian origins of its builders, who, according to Pliny (*Natural History* 3.5.7), dedicated the temple specifically to 'Argive Hera'. Two of the labours are depicted: Herakles wrestling with the Nemean lion, and presenting the Erymanthian boar to Eurystheus. These are in no way distinguished, however, from the exploits depicted on the other metopes: Herakles trying to make off with Apollo's tripod, carrying the Kerkopes, wrestling with Antaios, killing a giant, and fighting yet another centaur. A whole set of six metopes, possibly placed along the east side of the temple over the entrance, shows the encounter with the centaurs of Mount Pholoe: Pholos himself stands behind the archer Herakles, while four other centaurs canter in to attack. Another pair of metopes show Deianeira behind Herakles, who crouches to shoot the oncoming centaur Nessos, while a group of three metopes present what may be Herakles protecting Hera from the attack of four Silenoi, an episode not attested at all in literature, but found again in early fifth-century vase-painting at Athens. The same promiscuity of labours and other exploits can be seen in the metopes of the Athenian Treasury at Delphi (pp. 168–9), and in carvings on the door of the temple of Herakles-Melqart at Cadiz (pp. 191–2).[5]

There are, then, plenty of precedents for grouping together a number of Herakles' exploits. The significance of the Olympia metopes is that they distinguish the particular twelve, but it is debatable at what point these became canonical. Only nine labours appear, for example, on the temple of Hephaistos in the Athenian Agora (p. 169), built a decade or so after Zeus' temple at Olympia. Similarly, Pausanias (9.11.6) comments that 'the birds at Stymphalos and how Herakles cleaned the territory of Elis' are missing from the labours depicted on the fourth-century temple of Herakles at Thebes, their place apparently taken by the wrestling match with Antaios; the rather unheroic nature of the birds and the stables episodes might account for their omission. Later in the fourth century, a sanctuary of

Herakles at Alyzia, on the west coast of central Greece, was adorned with a statue group by the sculptor Lysippos apparently entitled *The Labours of Herakles*, but we have no indication of their number or content; according to Strabo (10.2.21) this was looted by a Roman commander, probably in the late second century BC. The same lack of consistency can be seen in literature, too. Not much earlier than the Olympia metopes, there is a possible reference to a 'twelfth' labour in a fragment of Pindar (fr. 169a.43 SM), though only part of the relevant word (*dôd)ekatos* survives. Indications that the twelve were not yet settled in the fifth century can be seen in Sophokles' *Women of Trachis* (ll.1098–1100), where Herakles himself lists just five, while the chorus of Euripides' *Herakles* (ll. 359–42) include other exploits in a rambling account of seven of the labours.

The number twelve seems to be more firmly established by the third century BC, when several explicit references can be found. In Theokritos' *Idyll* 24, for example, the seer Teiresias predicts 'it is fated that, having completed twelve labours, he shall live with Zeus' (ll.82–3). Similarly in Apollonious' *Argonautika* (1.1317–18) the sea-god Nereus predicts that 'in Argos it is his fate to accomplish with toil a whole twelve labours for the wicked Eurystheus', while in a fragment of Kallimachos' *Aetia* (fr. 23.19–20 Pfeiffer) someone addresses Herakles as having performed 'twice six commands'. In hellenistic art, a clay relief bowl from the Boiotian town of Anthedon, of the mid-second century BC (Berlin 3161g), depicts only six of the labours but has an inscription saying 'of Herakles' twelve labours', which suggests that the remaining six featured on a companion piece. All twelve may also have appeared on a frieze from the theatre at Delphi of the second or first century BC, although only seven can be made out, alongside two or three other exploits, in the extant remains (Delphi Museum).

It is, however, only with the systematic account of Diodoros in the late first century BC that the twelve are actually listed, and even after this instances of the whole cycle related in literature or depicted in art are not all that common. A complete list is found on the *Tabula Albana*, a striking Roman relief panel variously dated between the first century BC and the second AD, which depicts Herakles reclining with satyrs and maenads on an enormous lionskin in an upper frieze, while below, Victory assists a man and a woman (Herakles and Alkmene?) in making a libation. The images have been subject to a variety of interpretations, but more relevant here are the accompanying inscriptions: on pilasters to either side of the libation scene is a lengthy prose synopsis of Herakles' minor deeds, while beneath is a metrical account of the twelve labours 'which he was compelled to complete by Eurystheus', followed by some of his other exploits (*IG* XIV 1293 = *FGrH* 40F1). The labours are enumerated here in just the same way that they are in an anonymous epigram from the *Greek Anthology* (16.92): 'First, in Nemea he slew the mighty lion; second, in Lerna he destroyed the many-necked hydra; third after these he killed the Erymanthian boar . . . .'

Eight or more labours are found on a number of Roman sarcophagi, for example one of AD 150–200 (Rome, Museo Torlonia 420) from Asia Minor, which presents all twelve in a series of inter-columnated arches. Half a dozen Roman mosaics also depict a collection of labours, such as the dining room of the early fourth-century AD villa at Piazza Armerina in Sicily, where the central part of the floor depicts Herakles' vanquished opponents in glorious confusion, while one apse is taken up by Herakles himself being crowned, another by defeated giants. More tidily, a splendid third-century AD floor from Liria near Valencia (Madrid 2/1943) places the canonical twelve in a series of panels around a large central image of Herakles and Omphale. The twelve also feature on one or two series of coins, such as a set minted at Alexandria under Antoninus Pius, each coin in the set depicting one of the labours. Finally, a papyrus from Greco-Roman Oxyrhynchos in Egypt preserves what looks like a comic-book version of the twelve labours, with cartoon-like drawings illustrating a verse dialogue between Herakles and a narrator who constantly undercuts his achievements.[6]

INDIVIDUAL LABOURS

Representations of groups of labours are relatively rare when compared to the huge popularity of individual episodes, especially in media like vase-painting, where a single scene is usually all that can be shown in the space available. There are literally hundreds of representations (both artistic and literary) of some of the labours, but in what follows we shall focus on the most important points – first appearances, popularity in particular places/periods, significant variations in the story or its iconography – and some of the more striking examples and interesting interpretations which have been suggested. I am following the order given by Apollodoros; Diodoros' account reverses numbers three and four, so that the boar comes before the hind, five and six, so that the birds come before the stables, and eleven and twelve, so that the Hesperides come last. The images referred to can be found in works detailed in the Further Reading section.

The Nemean lion

In addition to its early appearance in epic, the killing of the Nemean lion is the most popular of all Herakles' exploits for representation in the visual arts of the archaic period. This is hardly surprising, since this first labour not only provides the lionskin subsequently worn by Herakles throughout his career, but it displays him at his aristocratic-athletic best. Also to be considered is the likelihood, as we have seen (p. 13), that the lion-killing motif is adapted from oriental prototypes which draw on the lion's status as noble adversary – the lion is, for example, the object of the Assyrian Royal Hunt.

A man killing a lion appears on a sixteenth-century BC gold seal from Mycenae (Athens NM 33), but the earliest possible sightings of the episode in Greek art proper are from the late eighth century, on a clay tripod from Athens (Kerameikos 407) and a bronze fibula from Boiotia (London 3204), more or less contemporary with the earliest literary allusion in Hesiod. It is impossible to be sure, however, that the man in these cases is indeed Herakles, since he has no distinguishing attributes, and he is killing the lion with a sword or a spear rather than wrestling it into submission. The idea that the lion's skin was invulnerable may not in fact have become standard until the sixth century, since both sword and wrestling versions are found in the late seventh and early sixth centuries on shield-band reliefs from Olympia. Alternatively, the images might reflect versions of the story in which Herakles attempted to use his sword or arrows at first, resorting to his bare hands only when these proved unsuccessful. The earliest certain attestation of the invulnerability motif in literature comes in a victory ode by Bakchylides (13.46–54) for one Pytheas of Aigina, winner of the *pankration* at Nemea in the 480s BC, a context where the emphasis on Herakles' athletic expertise is highly appropriate:

> . . . with all kinds of skill Perseus' descendant lays neck-breaking hand on the flesh-eating lion, for glittering, man-taming bronze refuses to pierce its unapproachable body, and his sword was bent back.

The property of invulnerability was imagined as continuing after the lion's death, so that the skin is effectively worn by Herakles as armour. It is often depicted with the paws carefully arranged around the hero's neck in a reef or square knot (see e.g. Figure 2.1), a ligature which came to be known in antiquity as the 'knot of Herakles', and which was believed to have magic properties of healing and averting harm.[7]

In the sixth century, the lion episode appears on Lakonian, Caeretan and Chalkidian vases, but its greatest popularity is in Attic vase-painting: more than seven hundred black-figure and nearly one hundred early red-figure examples survive. The composition of these scenes varies, the artist being free to choose any moment of the fight, and whether to include subsidiary figures such as Herakles' regular helpers Iolaos and Athena; Herakles may be upright grappling with a lion reared on its hind legs, or the pair may be down on the ground, the lion often scratching at his adversary with a hind paw; occasionally Herakles is depicted as a beardless youth, a device meant to indicate that this is his first labour. In Exekias' version of the scene (Figure 1.2), confidently signed 'Exekias my painter was my potter too', Herakles has a stranglehold on the lion, which is gasping for breath; the central pair are flanked by an encouraging Athena and by Iolaos, who holds his uncle's club and bow.

The Nemean lion is not quite so frequently seen in classical and later art, although it remains the most popular of his labours for depiction. Some later Attic red-figure and South Italian vases reprise the archaic 'action shot' of the wrestling, but a completely different schema appears in the Olympia metope (Figure 1.1). Here we see the aftermath of the fight: flanked by Athena and Hermes, a tired young Herakles leans his head on his hand, his elbow supported by a knee, his foot resting on the body of the dead lion, its tongue rather pathetically lolling out of its defeated mouth. A nice detail is that Herakles here sports the cauliflower ear of a boxer or pankratiast, making quietly explicit the link between the hero of the metopes and the real-life athletes competing in the sanctuary below. In the third century, a colourful literary account of the story appears in Theokritos,

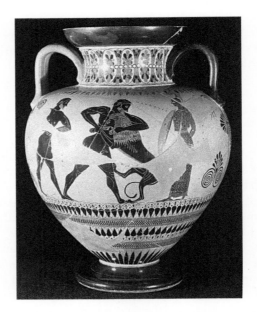

Figure 1.2 Herakles and the Nemean lion. Attic red-figure amphora signed by Exekias, c.540 BC (Berlin F1720). Photo: © bpk, Antikensammlung, Staatliche Museen zu Berlin, Gerhard Murza.

Idyll 25 (ll.153–281), where Herakles himself describes the lion returning to its den – 'fed full of meat and blood, defiled with gore around his squalid mane, his bright-eyed face and chest, licking all around his cheeks with his tongue' (ll.224–6) – and recounts the struggle, in which he at first attempted to shoot the lion with arrows, then stunned it with a blow from his club before finishing it off in a strangle-hold. The lion was supposed by ancient astronomers to have been immortalized by becoming the constellation Leo (Pseudo-Eratosthenes, *Katasterismoi* 1.12).

The Lernaian hydra

The encounter with the Lernaian hydra is not only attested in epic, as we have seen, but is the subject of some of the earliest securely identifiable Herakles scenes in Greek art, probably again adapted from oriental proto-types. On two Boiotian fibulae of c.750–700 BC (London 3205; Philadelphia 75–35–1) a six-headed snake is attacked by a hero, at whose feet is a crab, while a second figure assists with a sickle-shaped sword or *harpe*: these details are remarkably consistent with later representations of the scene, which seems to be especially popular in Corinthian vase-painting from c.630 BC. The hydra is in any case easy to recognize, but the other figures are sometimes identified by inscriptions, as in Figure 1.3, where the names HERAKLES and ATHANA are clearly in view. Athena holds a small jug,

Figure 1.3 Herakles and the Lernaian hydra. Corinthian aryballos, c.600 BC, height 11.2 cm (Malibu 92.AE.4). Photo: The J. Paul Getty Museum, Villa Collection, Malibu, California.

presumably to catch the hydra's poisonous blood, which both Apollodoros (2.5.2) and Diodoros (4.11.5–6) specify was subsequently used by Herakles to poison his arrows. Snapping at Herakles' ankle is the crab, which appears in at least half the Corinthian examples, while (just out of view here) Iolaos, also inscribed, lops off heads with a *harpe*.

Attic versions of the scene are not especially remarkable, but there is a lively Caeretan example on a hydria of c.530 BC by the Eagle Painter (Malibu 83.AE.346). Here Herakles and his nephew attack a nine-headed hydra from either side, with club and *harpe* respectively, but at Iolaos' feet is a fire, consistent with the tradition that Iolaos prevented the hydra's severed heads from re-growing by cauterizing the stumps. The first literary attestation of this motif only comes a century later, in two plays by Euripides: in the *Herakles* (ll.419–21) Herakles has 'destroyed by fire the many-headed, murderous hound, the hydra of Lerna'; in the *Ion* (ll.190–200; 413 BC), a chorus of Athenian girls visiting the sanctuary of Apollo at Delphi exclaim over a sculptural group of Herakles killing the hydra with a golden sickle, assisted by someone 'raising a flaming torch – is this the man whose story accompanies my weaving, the shield-bearer Iolaos, who suffered with the son of Zeus, taking a share in his labours?' The text does not make it clear whether this is a free-standing group or architectural sculpture such as a metope, though the latter is more likely; the fact that the girls relate the image to a story heard at home is a nice reminder of the informal contexts in which myths were regularly communicated in ancient Greece.

The number of the hydra's heads never really becomes fixed. Both Corinthian and Attic painters give it between six and ten, the latter often depicting the necks sprouting from a fat body, which is sometimes coiled round a tree. This scheme is adopted also on a late fourth-century BC coin type from Phaistos in Crete, which manages still to include the crab despite its small scale. Even writers, unconstrained by the technical difficulty of depicting a multiplicity of heads, reach no clear consensus: around 600 BC Alkaios (fr. 443 LP) is the earliest poet to specify the number as nine, but a century later Simonides of Keos (fr. 569 *PMG*) ups the stakes to fifty; Apollodoros goes for nine, Diodoros a hundred. On visiting Lerna, Pausanias (2.37.4) is uncharacteristically critical, commenting that the monster only really had one head but that 'Peisandros of Kamiros gave the hydra many heads so that the beast might seem more frightening and his own poetry might be more noteworthy'. Apollodoros is the only author to attest the detail that one of the heads was immortal, and he adds that Eurystheus discounted this labour because Herakles had been unable to achieve it without help. According to Pseudo-Eratosthenes (*Katasterismoi* 1.11), Hera rewarded the crab by making it the constellation Cancer; there is also a constellation 'Hydra', but no extant writer explicitly makes the connection with Herakles.[8]

The Keryneian hind

The Keryneian hind episode is less obviously dramatic than the first two labours, since the animal in question is hardly monstrous and no killing is involved (usually); this probably accounts for the paucity of representations in the visual arts, even in the archaic period. It may, however, appear as early as c.750–700 BC, on the reverse of one of the Boiotian fibulae featuring the hydra (London 3205), where a man grasps by the horn a deer which is nursing a fawn – the pairing of the scenes makes it plausible to identity this as Herakles' labour. After this there are just a few examples of the episode in Attic black-figure vase-painting, and one or two in Attic and South Italian red-figure. In some of these Apollo is trying to intervene, presumably in order to regain possession of the deer for his sister Artemis (sometimes also present herself), suggesting a version of the story only hinted at in Apollodoros (2.5.3), where the altercation is resolved by Herakles 'pleading necessity and saying that Eurystheus was the culprit', which allays Artemis' anger. On one of the metopes of the Athenian Treasury at Delphi (pp. 168–9) the lone Herakles subdues the hind with a knee on her rear-quarters while grasping her horns, a schema taken up in the hellenistic period for free-standing sculptural groups.

Our earliest literary account of the story, apart from the short fragment of Peisandros, is in Pindar's *Olympian* 3, written for Theron of Akragas, winner of the chariot race of 476 BC. Here (ll.26–30) the golden-horned hind seems to have been dedicated to Artemis by Taygete, a daughter of Atlas who, according to an ancient commentator on Pindar, was once herself turned into a deer by the goddess in order to escape Zeus' amorous advances. Euripides (*Herakles* 375–9) is the one source to make the hind a menace, 'a robber of the fields', and to have her killed by Herakles; both Diodoros (4.13.1) and Apollodoros (2.5.3) make the encounter rather an endurance test for Herakles, who has to use some ingenuity to get the hind alive to Eurystheus. The most intriguing aspect of the story is the animal's odd anatomy, given that female deer do not have horns – this is commented on as an error by ancient writers from Aristotle (*Poetics* 1460b31–2) onwards. The anomaly has been variously explained as an element retained from a northern European tale about hunting a female reindeer (which would quite properly have antlers), or by assuming that the story is somehow 'really' about the river Kerynites, the horns representing its various branches. Most recently, Burkert (1998, 14–15) has suggested that the myth is aetiological, explaining *why* the female deer has no horns. However, sexual ambiguity in animals is not unheard of elsewhere in Greek art – an archaic pediment from the Athenian Akropolis features a suckling lioness with a mane, Io transformed into a cow is sometimes represented as a bull – and it might be easier to assume that an early story-teller either made a mistake, or simply wanted to add to the animal's mystique.

The Erymanthian boar

The Erymanthian boar is only mentioned once in archaic literature, in a fragment of the historian Hekataios, writing c.500 BC: 'There was a boar on the mountain and it was doing much harm to the people of Psophis' (*FGrH* 1F6). Later sources, however, give details of how it was presented to Eurystheus, which make the episode more obviously visually appealing than the hind's capture. As Diodoros (4.12.2) tells it: 'when the king saw Herakles carrying it on his shoulders, he was afraid, and hid himself in a bronze *pithos*' (large storage jar). Apollodoros (2.5.1) does not mention the jar in connection with this labour, but he does report that when Herakles returned with the Nemean lion, 'he was afraid and had prepared for himself a bronze *pithos* to hide in under the ground'.

The motif is not found in earlier literary accounts, but its antiquity is demonstrated by a number of scenes in archaic art where Herakles presents the boar to Eurystheus who is indeed cowering in his *pithos*. On the mid-sixth-century Foce del Sele metope mentioned above all that can be seen of the king is his head and an arm, as he peers out from beneath the *pithos*' lid at the beast on Herakles' shoulders looming above him. The scene appears around the same time on a shield-band from Olympia and a Lakonian cup (formerly in Kavala Museum), and it is especially popular in Attic pottery in the latter part of the sixth century. There are a few alternative versions of the episode in Attic black-figure which do not feature Eurystheus – Herakles either carries the boar or pushes it wheelbarrow-fashion, sometimes watched by Athena and Iolaos – but the *pithos* schema is taken up again on the metopes at Olympia (Figure 1.1) and on the temple of Hephaistos in Athens. It is interesting that it so often this rather humorous scene which is represented, rather than a more obvious celebration of Herakles' prowess in overpowering the beast, especially since boars, like lions, are such prestigious prey for the aristocratic hunter. The idea would seem to be to foreground Herakles' heroic qualities by contrast with his weak and cowardly opposite, underlining the irony of his servitude to a lesser man.[9]

The stables of Augeias

The one labour that does not appear in the archaic period is the cleaning of Augeias' stables. The earliest allusion in literature is in Pindar's *Olympian* 10 (ll.26–30), written in 476 BC in celebration of the victory of Hagesidamos of Western Lokroi in the boys' boxing. Here it is said that Herakles' killing of the Molione twins (p. 65) was meant to compel Augeias to pay for the service he had performed, though no mention is made of what that service entailed. Just two decades later, the labour's first appearance in art is on the Olympia metope (Figure 1.1), conspicuously placed at the end of the sequence in the east porch. Here Herakles is in vigorous action, under Athena's direction, but unfortunately it is not entirely clear from the fragmentary sculpture what he is doing: he could be wielding a shovel or pitchfork, although the position of his hands suggest that the missing implement is rather a long crowbar, with which he is poised to breach the stable walls in order to let in the water. In the third century, Theokritos' *Idyll* 25 concerns a visit by Herakles to Augeias' farm and includes a lengthy description of the vast herd of cattle (ll.1–152), but there is no explicit reference to any cleaning of the stables.[10]

The full story of this labour is not told in surviving literature until Diodoros (4.13.3), who indicates that the task was demeaning, but that Herakles diverted a local river in order to complete the job while avoiding the ignominy of actually shovelling dung. Apollodoros (2.5.5) recounts a more detailed version, in which Herakles conceals the fact that he is acting under Eurystheus' orders and makes a proposal, to which Augeias agrees, to remove the dung in a single day in return for a tenth of the cattle. When he achieves this apparently impossible task, however, Augeias refuses to pay, having discovered the deception, and despite arbitration Herakles ends up leaving empty-handed; nonetheless, Eurystheus would not accept this labour because it had been done for a fee. This version of the story makes sense of Pindar's allusion, which confirms that the motif of payment withheld goes back to at least the early fifth century, although the double-motivation involved is slightly awkward.

Because it is so different, it has been suggested that this episode was not originally one of the labours, as perhaps hinted by Apollodoros, but only became one because of its association with Olympia, and the influence of the metopes on the subsequent development of the canon. Ancient authors disagree on exactly which local rivers Herakles diverted to achieve his task – one or two of the Peneios, Meneios and Alpheios – but viewers entering the east porch of Zeus' temple would perhaps have recalled the two river-gods they had just seen reclining in the corners of the pediment above, identified by Pausanias (5.10.7) as Alpheios and Kladeos.

The Stymphalian birds

The Stymphalian birds are rarely depicted in art, probably because they do not offer such an obviously satisfying compositional scheme as a single opponent, but there are two possible early sightings from the late eighth century. One scene is on the bronze fibula already mentioned in connection with the Nemean lion (London 3204), which also features two men holding birds by their necks; the other is on the shoulder of a Geometric oinochoe (Copenhagen, private collection), where a man holds one bird by the neck while several others run or fly away. There is no guarantee in either case that the man is Herakles, but the scheme of Herakles and Iolaos strangling the birds recurs on a rather crudely painted Attic black-figure lekythos of the mid-sixth century (Munich 1842). More sophisticated is the scene on an amphora attributed to the 'Group E' painters, c.530 BC (London B163), where Herakles uses a catapult to shoot at the birds which flock around him, their plumage decoratively picked out in added white and red paint. On the Olympia metope the heat of action has been rejected, as it was in the case of the lion, in favour of a quieter moment later in the proceedings, with Herakles standing before a seated Athena, calmly handing over the dead birds – the birds themselves can no longer be seen, but were probably added in paint.

The people of the historical town of Stymphalos in Arkadia seem to have been proud of their link with Herakles, because they alluded to the labour on coins of the late fifth/early fourth century, which have the head of a young Herakles on one side and the head of a water-bird on the other. Mid-fourth-century coins depict the head of Artemis on one side, and on the other Herakles vigorously wielding his club with the inscription 'Saviour of the Stymphalians', possibly a reference to the town's recent liberation from Spartan control. Sculptures of birds and bird-maidens were also a feature of the ancient temple of Stymphalian Artemis, according to Pausanias (8.22.7).

The images all present Herakles killing the birds, but the earliest literary source, Peisandros (followed by Apollonios, *Argonautika* 2.1052–7 and Diodoros 4.13.2), has Herakles just frightening them off with the noise of a rattle. Some later writers, like Apollodoros (2.5.6), compromise by supposing that Herakles shot the birds down with his arrows after first frightening them, with the rattle or with bronze castanets made by the craftsman-god Hephaistos. Exactly what threat the birds presented is unclear: Apollodoros merely cites their large numbers, Diodoros has them despoiling the surrounding countryside of fruit. Only Pausanias (8.22.4) claims that they were man-eating, a detail which has given rise to the unlikely idea that the story could reflect problems in the area caused by malaria-bearing dampness, or even mosquitoes. Other historicizing interpretations focus on the rattle, seeing this as representing the noise of water falling down limestone sinkholes, or the tools of workmen on a Mycenaean water control project connected with Lake Stymphalos.[11]

The Cretan bull

The Cretan bull, like the hind and the boar, has to be captured and shown to Eurystheus rather than destroyed. It is variously identified by ancient authors as being the bull (more usually thought to be Zeus himself in disguise) that carried Europa to Crete, or the bull sent from the sea by Poseidon to an ungrateful king Minos, which subsequently fathered the Minotaur on Minos' infatuated wife Pasiphae. This slightly contrived link with Cretan mythology is matched by the equally awkward tradition that the same bull, having been set free by Herakles in the Argolid, made its way to Attika, where it harassed the people of Marathon and was eventually killed by Theseus. It has been suggested that the bull represents an earthquake originating in Crete, or that its capture reflects an ancestral memory of the Mycenaean conquest of Crete, but perhaps more plausible is the theory that the specific links with Crete and Theseus were added to the story as a by-product of the development of a Theseus cycle in late sixth-century Athens (pp. 167–8). The journey to Crete certainly makes this the first labour to take Herakles outside the Peloponnese, preparing the way for the more extensive travels involved in the later tasks.

In extant literature the episode is not attested before the hellenistic period, but Apollodoros cites as one of his sources Akousilaos of Argos (*FGrH* 2F29), who was writing around 500 BC, and the scene can be found in art from the mid-sixth century onwards. Some of its earliest probable appearances are on four Lakonian cups of c.550–540 BC by the Rider Painter (e.g. New York 59.15), all of which feature a man struggling with a bull; Herakles has no identifying attributes here, but he is the most likely candidate for such a scene in non-Athenian works of this period. More or less contemporary is a metope from temple Y at Selinous in Sicily (Palermo 3914), which is too damaged to make out any detail, but that the city had a particular affinity with the story is suggested by its appearance on Selinuntine coins of c.450 BC.

The episode appears in Attic vase-painting from c.560 BC, but becomes noticeably popular towards the end of the century, with over two hundred black-figure and early red-figure examples surviving, the majority dating from around 510–500 BC. Herakles sometimes tackles the bull head on, wrestling it with his arms around its neck, and sometimes approaches from behind, seizing its hind quarters or casting a rope around its horns. As with the Nemean lion, the labour's basic motif of the bare-handed subduing of a physically powerful animal provides the artist with the perfect excuse for dwelling on Herakles' strength, as seen in the Olympia metope (Figure 1.1), where the hero's muscular torso is displayed to particularly good advantage.[12]

The mares of Diomedes

The fetching of the mares of the Thracian king Diomedes appears only rarely in archaic art, on the Throne of Bathykles (above) and on two or three late sixth-century Attic black-figure vases. Most striking is the tondo of a cup by Psiax, c.520 BC (St Petersburg 9270), where Herakles has his arm around the neck of a horse out of whose mouth a human arm and head are protruding. The earliest literary account of the story comes in the very fragmentary poem by Pindar (fr. 169a SM) referred to above, which includes the detail of Herakles throwing someone to the horses before harnessing them – this is perhaps a reference to the 'be done by as you did' motif, spelt out in Diodoros (4.15.3), of the mares' own master being fed to them.

Later in the fifth century the horses' nature is colourfully described in Euripides' *Alkestis* (438 BC), in which Herakles is passing through the Thessalian city of Pherai on his way to carry out the task. The Chorus of elderly citizens questions how Herakles will manage to capture the horses (ll.492–96):

> CHORUS: You won't easily insert a bit between their jaws.
> HERAKLES: As long as they don't breathe fire from their nostrils!
> CHORUS: No, but they rip men apart with their swift jaws.
> HERAKLES: You're talking about the feeding of mountain beasts, not horses!
> CHORUS: You'll see their mangers wet with blood.

Herakles goes on (ll.497–506) to establish that Diomedes is a son of the war-god Ares, and comments on the fact that he has already faced two other sons of Ares, Lykaon and Kyknos, but none can frighten him. Diodoros (4.15.4) has the mares duly delivered to Eurystheus and subsequently dedicated to Hera, adding that 'their breed continued going strong until the reign of Alexander of Makedon'. Such a legacy is denied by the tradition Apollodoros reports (2.5.8), however, which has the horses released by Eurystheus and killed by wild beasts on Mount Olympos. Apollodoros' version is also different in providing Herakles with a company of volunteers, one of whom, Abderos, is a son of Hermes and Herakles' lover; when the boy is killed by the horses, Herakles founds the city of Abdera by his grave.

This last element of the story is a typical city-foundation myth, presumably developed some time after Abdera's refoundation by Greek colonists from Teos in the mid-sixth century BC. The main narrative, too, is susceptible of historicizing interpretations. Palaiphatos (*On Unbelievable Tales* 7) rationalizes the 'man-eating' element simply as the great expense of keeping horses. Schoo (1969, 77–80) elaborates improbably on the detail reported by Diodoros that the mangers were made of bronze, supposing them to represent Thracian metal-mines in which many enslaved foreigners died working, and the entire exploit as an expedition which seized control over the mines, forcing their former owners to work in them. More broadly, the episode is an extreme example of the idea that horses are potentially dangerous, a theme raised elsewhere in Greek myth by the horrific death of the Thracian king Lykourgos, torn limb from limb by wild horses as a punishment for denying the power of Dionysos.

The Amazons

Herakles' battle with the Amazons takes him even further afield than Thrace, their capital Themiskyra supposedly being situated at the mouth of the river Thermodon on the Black Sea. The story invites comparison with other heroes' encounters – Achilles' killing of Penthesileia, Theseus' carrying off of Antiope or Hippolyta – and it is not always easy to distinguish between the stories in visual representations, although the Herakles story is the most common in the archaic period. The earliest securely identifiable example of Herakles' Amazonomachy is on a Corinthian alabastron of c.600 BC from Samothrace (now lost), where inscriptions guarantee some of the figures as Herakles, Iolaos and the Amazon Andromeda. The episode is also probably shown on a Lakonian cup by the Arkesilas Painter, c.560 BC (Rome, private collection), although the hero pursuing the two female warriors has none of Herakles' usual distinguishing features.

It is in Attic black-figure, however, that the scene really develops, with almost four hundred examples making this second only to the Nemean lion in popularity. Herakles' particular opponent, where named, is usually Andromache rather than Hippolyta, and there is no sign that Herakles is especially after her belt, or any other item of clothing. One of the earliest Attic examples is a Tyrrhenian amphora by the Timiades Painter, c.570 BC (Boston 98.916), where Herakles grasps the arm of Andromache, her name inscribed, as she turns to run away. There are also some archaic red-figure versions of the battle, notably on an amphora by the Andokides Painter, c.520 BC (Orvieto, Faina 64), which uses the compositional scheme of Herakles' combat with the triple-bodied Geryon, with a pair of Amazons attacking from the right and one fallen at Herakles' feet. The same scheme appears on a krater by Euphronios, c.500 BC (Arezzo 1465), where one of the Amazons is in Persian dress.

In the classical period and later, Amazonomachies are popular themes for architectural sculpture, being quite transparent metaphors for the superiority of Greek civilization over eastern barbarity. More or less contemporary with the temple of Zeus at Olympia, a metope from Temple E at Selinous portrays a youthful Herakles in single combat with an Amazon, the toes of his left foot curling over her right foot, echoing the grip his left hand has on her Phrygian hat. A more extensive battle is the subject of half of the frieze of the temple of Apollo at Bassai (430–390 BC); in the thick of battle, Herakles is identifiable by the lion-skin swirling dramatically behind his otherwise nude body, as he starts back from the Amazon he is fighting.[13]

Ibykos (fr. 299 *PMG*), writing in the second half of the sixth century, is the only archaic writer to specify that Herakles went in search of the Amazon's belt, although he names the Amazon in question as Oiolyke, daughter of Briareus, rather than the more familiar Amazon queen Hippolyta. After Ibykos, the first sign of the girdle is in the title of a comedy by the early fifth-century Sicilian playwright Epicharmos, *Herakles After the Girdle*, and in a passing reference to plural girdles in Pindar (fr. 172 SM). The chorus' account of the labour in Euripides' *Herakles* (ll.408–18) makes definite reference to 'the girdle of the gold-decked cloak of Ares' daughter', a barbarian spoil now preserved in Mycenae; a similar dedication of Amazons' clothing is referred to in Euripides' *Ion* (1143–58) as having been made by Herakles himself at Delphi, but these are the elaborately woven tunics (*peploi*) of a multiplicity of Amazons, with no specific mention of belts. In art, the belt is first definitely seen around 400 BC on early South Italian vases. It may have featured before this in the scene on the Olympia metope (Figure 1.1), which Pausanias (5.10.9) describes as 'Herakles taking the belt', but this interpretation could easily have been influenced by the writer's knowledge of the later development of the story, and not enough of the actual sculpture survives to decide the issue.

Geryon

Herakles' next labour takes him to the opposite edge of the world in the far west. As we have seen, the Geryon encounter is first attested in Hesiod's *Theogony*, and it was probably related at more length in Peisandros' *Herakleia*, but the most extensive archaic literary account seems to have been the sixth-century *Geryoneis* of Stesichoros. One fragment has a number in the margin signifying 'line 1,300', making this a poem of almost epic proportions, although only around seventy lines actually survive, many not known before 1950 when they were discovered on a papyrus in Egypt. These give us a flavour of the whole poem as well as adding some details to the story as we know it from Hesiod and Peisandros: Geryon's home Erytheia is located across the Tartessos River (i.e. the Guadelquivir) in Spain; Herakles travels to the island in the cup of Helios, which he later returns to the Sun; Geryon himself has six hands and feet, and wings; the gods take sides in the encounter, Poseidon supporting his grandson Geryon and Athena helping Herakles. Unusually, Stesichoros seems to have visualized the encounter at least partly from Geryon's point of view, with such humanizing touches as conversations in which family and friends try to dissuade Geryon from fighting, and Geryon's death itself is described with a rather touching simile comparing him to a poppy shedding its petals. Two other episodes of Herakles' story are referred to in the course of the narrative, the slaying of the hydra and his visit to the centaur Pholos. Later versions of the story elaborate on Herakles' journey, especially his encounter with Helios, which sometimes involves negotiation or the threat of violence on Herakles' part, and some have him seeking help from the sea-god Nereus, though others attach this motif to the Hesperides labour.

We will consider the encounter with Nereus in the next chapter (pp. 72–3), but the borrowing of Helios' cup as a vessel in which to cross Okeanos caught the imagination of one or two artists. A particularly fine rendering can be seen in the interior of an Attic red-figure cup by Douris c.480 BC (Vatican 16563), where the circular frame of the tondo is half filled by the cauldron-shaped cup, with fish-filled waves lapping at its sides; just the top half of Herakles can be seen above the rim of his vessel, wearing the lion-skin and clutching his club and bow rather determinedly, as though uneasy with this unusual mode of transport. Boardman (2002, 174–5) suggests that the idea of bringing Geryon's cattle back in a cup might have been inspired by the bull friezes often used to decorate the interior of Syrian *phialai* (shallow dishes). According to Servius' commentary on Virgil (on *Aeneid* 8.278), a huge wooden cup, preserved in pitch and supposed to be that of the Sun, was used in ritual for Hercules at the Ara Maxima in the Forum Boarium (pp. 195–6).

The actual fight with Geryon is always easy to recognize in art because of the monster himself, represented with three heads and various numbers of limbs. It appears amongst our earliest Herakles scenes, not long after Hesiod's account in the *Theogony*, on a Protocorinthian pyxis of c.670 BC (London A487): although the painting is quite crude, Geryon clearly has three heads and bodies, defended by three shields against Herakles' bow, while the cattle occupy the reverse of the pot. Another Geryon scene includes our earliest sighting of Herakles wearing the lionskin, on a beautiful bronze pectoral from Samos dating from c.600 BC (Figure 1.4). Here Geryon's three heads seem to be attached to a single body, any difficulty about the join being covered by the shields; also included in the scene are the two-headed dog Orthos, the already dead herdsman Eurytion, and the disputed cattle.

Figure 1.4 Herakles fights Geryon and the dog Orthos. Bronze pectoral from Samos, c.600 BC (Samos B2518). Photo: Archaeological Museum of Samos.

Stesichoros' poem may have been the influence behind the popularity of the episode in vase-painting from c.560–510 BC. Painting Geryon was obviously something of a challenge, and from the Euboian colony of Rhegion in southern Italy we have two versions by the same artist, the Inscription Painter. On both of these so-called Chalkidian amphoras, of c.530 BC, Geryon has three heads and bodies, one pair of legs, and wings; these last may be a west Greek speciality, since they also appear in Stesichoros' description of the monster. On one (London B155), Geryon's three bodies seem to rotate around his shield, with one head still upright and active, one swung back looking dead, and one swung forward in a strikingly frontal position, looking straight out at the viewer. On the other amphora (Paris, Cabinet des Médailles 202), the three heads of Geryon are still very much alive, but the herdsman Eurytion and his dog are already dead at his feet, while the reverse of the pot is taken up by the cattle in question.

Three sets of limbs, as well as the three heads and torsos, are to be seen on a shield-band from Olympia c.550 BC, and this is the standard scheme adopted in Attic vase-painting. Among more than seventy Attic black-figure examples is a notable Group E amphora, signed by Exekias as a potter, c.550 BC (Paris F53), where one of Geryon's three bodies turns backwards while two remain intent on the battle; between the opponents, Eurytion lies collapsed onto his elbow, wearing a delightfully un-heroic sun-hat. A particularly fine archaic red-figure version of the scene is Euphronios' cup (Munich 2620), where the central figures fight over the dead body of the two-headed Orthos; this would appear to be especially faithful to Stesichoros' version of the story because behind Geryon stands a woman making gestures of distress, who must be his mother Kallirhoe.[14]

The episode has attracted a wide range of interpretations. In antiquity, Palaiphatos (*On Unbelievable Tales* 24) offered the explanation that Geryon's three-headedness is simply a misunderstanding of the geographical epithet Trikarenios ('three-headed'), from a town called Trikarenia. Schoo (1969, 85–92) again provides an elaborate modern version of such rationalizing, taking Geryon to represent the volcano of Tenerife, linking the 'red' (*phoinikes*) cattle mentioned by Apollodoros (2.5.10), as well as the name Erytheia (*erythros* is another kind of 'red') with a red/purple dye much prized by Phoenician traders, made from a special kind of lichen (*roccella tinctoria*) which grows in the Canaries; an alternative link would be with the islands' 'dragon tree' (*dracaena draco*), which produces red resin. More promising approaches invoke the universal appeal of the cattle-raiding motif, suggesting that the story has its origins in the remote past when the ancestors of the Greeks were nomadic and loss of livestock a serious threat; a Hercules who protects cattle-herds on the move is the recipient of dedications found in passes of the Apennine mountains, probably made by herders engaged in transhumance. Others point out that the Geryon episode quite nicely fits Propp's scheme of the heroic quest (p. 14), the details of the encounter with Nereus and Helios' cup being good examples of the classic folktale motifs of the reluctant helper and the borrowing of a magical object.

Comparisons can also be drawn with the remaining two labours which both again involve the fetching of supposedly unattainable objects, the apples of the Hesperides and Kerberos, all three episodes being interpreted by some scholars as representing successful return-journeys to the land of the dead and therefore Herakles' triumph over death. This characterization of the Geryon story depends on a number of details about Erytheia which seem to parallel the Underworld: it is located in the far west, beyond the edge of this world and the sunset, and reaching it requires the crossing of water; Orthos is brother of Kerberos; either Eurytion or Geryon himself might be identified with the herdsman of the dead. More prosaically, the journeys involved in the Geryon and Hesperides episodes have often been linked with Greek colonization in the western Mediterranean, the stories providing a context for more localized tales of individual cities' foundation by Herakles, as we shall see in Chapter 5.[15]

The apples of the Hesperides

Also situated in the far west is the garden of the Hesperides, daughters of the Evening Star. As noted above, the labour is alluded to in the *Theogony*, but Hesiod does not provide a narrative as such, and we have no other archaic literary source. In the mid-fifth century the story seems to have been told in some detail by Pherekydes (frs 16–17 F), although we only have a para-phrase, preserved by an ancient commentator on Apollonios, in which the narrative is sometimes confused. One point which is clear, however, is that Pherekydes' account had Herakles sending Atlas to fetch the apples on his behalf while he (Herakles) held up the heavens. Apollodoros (2.5.11) fol-lows this tradition, but Diodoros (4.26.2) keeps to a more straightforward version in which Herakles slays the serpent guardian of the apples and fetches them himself. This version is clearly referred to in Panyassis' epic (fr. 11 *PEG*), in Sophokles' *Trachiniae* (ll.1099–1100), where Herakles him-self speaks of killing the dragon, and in Euripides' *Herakles* (ll.394–400), where the chorus sing of the exploit:

> CHORUS: He came to the maiden singers, to their home in the west, in order to pluck with his own hand the golden fruit from the apple-bearing leaves, killing the red-backed serpent which guarded them, coiling its tail around formidably.

In the hellenistic period, the story is given a more negative spin in Apollonios' *Argonautika* (4.1432–49) in the mouth of Aigle, one of the Hesperides themselves, who tells it as having happened the day before the arrival of the Argonauts. She does not name Herakles, but refers to him as 'that most shameless man . . . most murderous in his violence', describing him as brutish in both appearance and behaviour, and speaking of the 'bit-ter grief' he has left behind.

The two stories, then, are equally well attested in literature, and art does little to help us distinguish which might have been the original, since scenes relating to both can be found already in the archaic period. The ver-sion involving Atlas is what seems to have been portrayed on the Chest of Kypselos, and it is clearly depicted on a shield-band from Olympia, c.550–540 BC (Basel Lu 217), on which Atlas has just resumed holding up the sky as Herakles strides away, holding his club and an apple, towards Athena. The same scene appears on a more or less contemporary Attic black-figure cup signed by the potter Nearchos (Bern, private collection), on which Herakles' epic character is emphasized by the epithet *melapheres*, 'apple-bearer', inscribed between palmettes. A slightly earlier moment in the story appears on a black-figure lekythos by the Athena Painter, c.500 BC (Athens 1132), where Herakles is still holding up the heavens and Atlas is returning with the apples. This is also the moment chosen by the sculptor of the Hesperides metope on the temple of Zeus at Olympia (Figure 1.1): Herakles is shown with a cushion on his shoulders holding up the heavens, with a little help from Athena, facing Atlas, who has just returned with the golden apples.

The alternative version, in which Herakles goes himself, is already seen on a rather crudely painted lekythos of c.520 BC (Mainz, private collection), where Herakles brandishes his club at a serpent coiled around a tree. In the classical period both versions can still be found, sometimes slightly romanticized, as in the scene on the Meidias Painter's well-known hydria (London E224). Here a youthful Herakles, attended by Iolaos, sits on his lionskin apparently in conversation with three Hesperides who are picking the apples for him, unhindered by the presence of a fairly harmless-looking snake coiled around the tree.

The exact location of the Hesperides' home has been variously identified, by commentators ancient and modern, as western Libya, the land of the Hyperboreans, the Canary Islands, the Azores, and even America – the important point seems to be that they are situated at the very edge of the known world, towards the sunset. As we saw in the previous chapter (p. 14), their garden has sometimes been seen as a kind of paradise, an idea which the Meidias Painter's scene alludes to by including a figure labelled as Hygieia, 'Health' personified, alongside the Hesperides. Nowhere in ancient literature is it specified that the apples convey immortality or youth on their possessor, although they certainly have divine associations – Apollodoros follows Pherekydes in explaining that the apples had been given by Earth as a wedding present to Hera and Zeus – and the episode has often been interpreted as foreshadowing Herakles' apotheosis. Just one piece of evidence provides a direct link between the Hesperides' apples and Herakles' immortality: on an Attic red-figure stamnos of c.470 BC (St Petersburg B640) Herakles is depicted arriving on Olympos, accompanied by Athena, holding out an apple towards Zeus, while behind Athena is a snake coiled in a tree.[16]

Diodoros (4.26.3) has come across a more mundane interpretation of the apples, that they are in fact sheep, called 'golden' because of their beauty; the usual Greek word for apple, *mêlon*, can indeed also mean 'sheep', but the absence of sheep from visual representations of the labour confirms that this is just an intellectual hypothesis rather than a genuine mythological tradition. Once again this episode is associated by ancient astronomers with the stars: Pseudo-Eratosthenes (*Katasterismoi* 3–4) explains the constellation Draco as the snake which had guarded the Hesperides' apples, while 'The Kneeler' (known today as 'Hercules') is Herakles in the process of killing the serpent.

Kerberos

As we have seen, the fetching of Kerberos from the Underworld is the one labour to be specifically mentioned in the *Iliad* and the *Odyssey*, while Kerberos is one of many monsters to feature in Hesiod's *Theogony*. The story was presumably told in considerable detail in Stesichoros' poem *Kerberos*, but unfortunately no more than the title of this survives. At the very end of the archaic period the episode is referred to briefly in Bakchylides' ode for Hieron, tyrant of Syracuse, celebrating his victory in the horse-race at Olympia in 476 BC (5.56–62):

> Once, they say, the gate-smashing, unconquerable son of thunder-flashing Zeus went down to the halls of slender-ankled Persephone to fetch the jagged-toothed dog, son of terrible Echidna, up to the light out of Hades.

In the fifth century, the episode must have been the subject of Sophokles' *Kerberos* and his satyr play *Herakles at Tainaron* (Tainaron being a traditional entrance to the Underworld), but we have little more than the titles to go on. The story is alluded to in Euripides' *Herakles* (pp. 89–92), since the hero's absence during the first part of play is due to its performance, and it was the focus of the action of the same writer's satyr play *Eurystheus* and of the lost tragedy *Peirithous* (pp. 95–6). Seneca's adaptation (pp. 99–101) of Euripides' *Herakles* makes much more of the hound than the original, apparently even bringing Cerberus on stage when Hercules first returns to Thebes (*Hercules Furens* 592ff.). Theseus, who in this version seems to have been an eye-witness, gives a dramatic account of the fight and a description of the aftermath which nicely presents the now-subdued Cerberus as a normal dog (ll.807–12):

> THESEUS: Then, stroking the monster's heavy necks with his hand, Hercules binds him with a web of adamant; forgetful of himself, the dog who is watchful guardian of the shady realm lowers his ears, timid and willing to be led, having acknowledged his master, and follows after with lowered muzzle, beating both his flanks with snaky tail.

Kerberos' monstrous appearance has great visual potential, and unsurprisingly the episode is represented in vase-painting from all over the Greek world. The earliest example is on a Corinthian skyphos of c.580 BC (now lost), where Kerberos has just one dog's head but a body covered in snakes, and the scene is paired with the hydra episode. Not much later is the very striking Lakonian cup by the Hunt Painter, c.560–50 BC (London, Erskine collection), which depicts a magnificent three-headed Kerberos, again covered in snakes. The hound takes up most of the circular space available, one head snapping at the winged heels of Hermes who is almost out of shot to the left, another looking back towards Herakles; all that is visible of the hero is a leg and two hands holding fast the hound's chain, but he is identifiable by the club he wields. Three heads and snakes are seen again on the often-reproduced Caeretan hydria by the Eagle Painter (Louvre E701), which borrows the motif of Eurystheus cowering in a *pithos* usually associated with the delivery of the Erymanthian boar; it certainly seems appropriate here in the face of the terrifying Kerberos, whose heads are made very clear by being painted in different colours (black, white and red), barely restrained by Herakles' leash.

The scene appears on nearly a hundred Attic black-figure vases as well as a few early red-figure ones. A notable point about the archaic Attic Kerberos, for which no compelling explanation has been offered, is that he only has two heads, rather than the three we see elsewhere and which will become standard even at Athens in the fifth century. In the fourth century the labour features on a number of South Italian vases, Kerberos straining on Herakles' leash amongst other Underworld characters. The labour's setting in the world of the dead also accounts for its appearance on Roman sarcophagi, where Kerberos sometimes sports a variety of different animal heads, or is dragged out through a doorway, perhaps conveying an optimistic message about the fate of the deceased.

It is not difficult to see why Herakles' journey to the Underworld might be read as such an allegory of the overcoming of death. As we have already seen, both the Geryon and Hesperides episodes have sometimes been understood as variations on this same theme, but the message is much more overt in the case of the hero's triumphant return to the upper world with Kerberos. As we shall discover (pp. 165–6), from the late sixth century onwards the Athenians explained Herakles' success as a result of his initiation into the Eleusinian Mysteries, which promised a happy afterlife to all initiates, and had him rescue their hero Theseus from the Underworld while he was there; Herakles' adventure also served as a starting-point for both comic and philosophical explorations of the afterlife in the classical period. It has also been suggested that the scene's iconography may draw on ancient Near Eastern and Egyptian traditions of the presentation to the king of tributes from distant lands, the more exotic the creature the more potent a symbol of the king's far-reaching power; as a denizen of the land of the dead, Kerberos would be a particularly valuable form of tribute.[17]

OVERVIEW

Herakles' character as a monster-slayer is established in the earliest literature and art to survive from ancient Greece. The idea of his performing a

succession of labours in servitude to the inferior Eursytheus is also apparent already in the *Iliad*, although it is not clear that the number twelve was
established before the fifth century. Nonetheless, all but one of the exploits
which would become the canonical twelve can be found in art and/or literature of the archaic period, and several of the labours were depicted so
frequently that we still have literally hundreds of examples surviving. In
the sixth century, most popular in Attic vase-painting are Herakles' battles with the Nemean lion and against the Amazons, but appearances of
the Lernaian hydra in Corinthian vase-painting and of Geryon in western colonies are also worthy of note for their local significance. There is
a dramatic reduction in visual representations of Herakles' labours in the
classical period, although they are certainly still to be found in both vase-
painting and sculpture. Likewise, surviving literature of the fifth century
and later continues to make occasional mention of the labours, although
it tends to emphasize other aspects of Herakles' character, as we shall see
in Chapters 3–4. Interpretations of individual labours range from the possible to the elaborate and frankly implausible, but the one unifying feature
of the twelve is the image of Herakles as the eternally reliable strong man,
always victorious in the apparently hopeless battle and able to attain the
unattainable.

2

MONSTERS AND THE HERO II:
OTHER BATTLES

Do you not know that it was not by staying in Tiryns or Argos, nor in the Peloponnese or Thebes, that our ancestor Herakles reached such great glory that he became, or seemed to become, a god from a man?

(Arrian, *Anabasis* 5.26.5)

A WEALTH OF OPPONENTS

As if the twelve labours had not presented Herakles with enough monstrous opponents, the format is extended to a large number of his other exploits. The story of the infant Herakles strangling the snakes prefigures both the labours proper and the motif of Hera's enmity, while other tales from his youth further establish his physical prowess, though pointing to a tendency to excess which we will be exploring in Chapters 3–4. Apart from the encounter with Nessos, which is clearly embedded in the complex of stories surrounding Herakles' death, the battles of Herakles' adulthood are only really distinguished from the labours by their accidental nature – instead of being tasks set by Eurystheus, they are encounters with opponents who simply got in the way, and are sometimes referred to by the Greek term *parerga*, 'secondary works'. Many of the opponents in question are transgressive in some way, so that Herakles' ultimate victory quite clearly represents the triumph of civilized values; some are disturbing by their very nature, being the hybrid centaurs or shape-shifting deities.

As in Chapter 1, in what follows we will focus on the most important points – first appearances, popularity in particular places/periods, significant variations in the story or its iconography – and some of the more striking examples and interesting interpretations that have been suggested. Many of the episodes here are not securely placed within Herakles' career, but I have divided them into a number of general categories, and within each category I follow the order adopted in the synopsis provided in the introduction (pp. 4–8). As before, the images referred to can be found in works on the Further Reading list.

EARLY EXPLOITS

Baby Herakles and the snakes

As we have seen, the idea that Hera hated Herakles even before he was born was already established in the *Iliad*, with her delaying of his birth. The story of Hera sending snakes to kill the infant Herakles and his brother in their cradle seems to be a later creation, not attested before the fifth century, and it may well owe its inspiration to a general artistic interest in children which seems to begin at the outset of the classical period. Our earliest source is Pindar's *Nemean* 1, written to celebrate the victory of Chromios of Aitna, a distinguished Sicilian Greek who claimed descent from Herakles, in the chariot race of 476 or 472 BC. After praise of both Chromios and Sicily, the second half of the poem (ll.33–72) relates how the baby Herakles strangled the two snakes, sent by an angry Hera, before his parents could come to the rescue; amazed, Amphitryon sent for the seer Teiresias, who prophesied 'what fortunes Herakles would encounter, how many lawless beasts he would kill on dry land, how many on the sea' (ll.61–3) before his eventual promotion to Olympos and marriage to Hebe. Pindar's fragmentary *Paean* 20 also seems to have included at least the basic snake-strangling story.

An alternative version is offered by Pherekydes (fr. 69 F), cited by Apollodoros (2.4.8), who has the snakes supplied, not by a jealous Hera, but by Amphitryon in a bid to find out which child is his and which the son of Zeus. It is, however, Pindar's account which is followed in Theokritos' colourful rendition of the story in *Idyll* 24, a poem we have already mentioned (p. 29). Entitled 'The Little Herakles', this tells the snake-strangling story with a great deal more domestic detail than Pindar (ll.1–63), painting a delightful picture of the sleeping household being awoken in the middle of the night, and making much of the contrast between the bold Herakles and his terrified brother Iphikles, attacked as they sleep in a bronze shield (ll.23–9):

> When he became aware of the evil beasts above the hollow shield and saw their shameless teeth, Iphikles immediately cried out, and kicked away the woollen blanket with his feet in his hurry to get away; but Herakles, facing them, shot out his hands and bound them both in a forceful grip, having seized them by the throat, there where the baneful venom of deadly snakes is found, which even gods detest.

Here it is Alkmene, rather than Amphitryon, who summons Teiresias for an interpretation of the event (ll.64–102), and his prophecy is followed by a further account of Herakles' upbringing (ll.103–40) before the manuscript breaks off in the middle of a description of the boy's daily life.

In art the story first appears around 480 BC, only slightly earlier than Pindar's poem, on an Attic red-figure stamnos by the Berlin Painter (Louvre G192). The two children are depicted on a couch, Iphikles dark-haired and leaping into Alkmene's arms while the lighter-haired Herakles holds the two snakes by the neck; to the left, Athena watches her protégé, as in so many depictions of his adult labours, and the scene is flanked by the helpless Amphitryon and a female servant. This scene is repeated, with minor variations, on a few other fifth-century Attic and fourth-century Etruscan vases, and in a painting by Zeuxis c.400 BC which Pliny (*Natural History* 35.61) describes as 'magnificent', though all he tells us of its appearance is that it features Amphitryon and 'Alkmene his mother trembling with fear'. In the late fifth and fourth centuries most intriguing is the political use made of the story on coins, as we shall see in Chapter 6 (p. 183), but its greatest popularity is in the hellenistic and Roman periods, when it provides both sculptors and painters with an opportunity to experiment with the depiction of children. In sculpture the main type is the single figure of the infant Herakles either seated or kneeling, much as evoked by Theokritos (*Idyll* 24.55) happily 'holding the two beasts fast in his soft hands'. One or two Roman versions reproduce the figure of Herakles with a portrait-head as a monument to a dead child, reference to the story suggesting the hope of an afterlife where death is overcome.[1]

Other youthful exploits

The one other battle of Herakles' childhood presents him in a less glorious light. This is the slaying of his music teacher Linos in a fit of temper, in retaliation against a blow from Linos' kithara. Diodoros (3.67.2) has Linos' action prompted by Herakles' inability to learn 'because of his slowness of spirit', and according to Apollodoros (2.4.9) Herakles successfully countered the consequent charge of murder by claiming it was self-defence. We have no extant earlier accounts to confirm the motivations involved or the outcome, but the story was probably the subject of a satyr play entitled *Linos* by the fifth-century Achaios (fr. 26 *TrGF*) and of a comedy of the same name by the fourth-century Alexis (fr. 140 *PCG*). It also appears on a number of fifth-century Attic vases, such as the red-figure cup by Douris, c.480 BC (Munich 2646), on which the young Herakles wields a broken stool against Linos, who tries to defend himself with a lyre but is clearly losing the fight, while four other youths flee the scene; the lyre, incidentally, is a lighter instrument than the kithara of our literary sources.

Just as the snake-strangling episode foreshadows later achievements, this story translates to childhood a tendency to angry violence which recurs in Herakles' adult life, notably in the murders of his first family and of Eurytos' son Iphitos, although our surviving sources make no suggestion in this case that divine-inflicted madness might be an extentuating circumstance – Apollodoros' mention of a trial sounds like an attempt to tidy up a slightly uncomfortable tale. Herakles is not alone amongst Greek heroes in displaying excessive violence – think of Achilles' rampage against the Trojans in *Iliad* Book 21 after the death of Patroklos – and excess characterizes other areas of his behaviour too, as we shall see in Chapters 3–4.

Two further battles belong to Herakles' young manhood. The first is attested only by Apollodoros (2.4.9–10), who merely records that Herakles 'destroyed the lion of Kithairon; for from its base in Kithairon this was laying waste the cattle of Amphitryon and of Thespios' and later dressed in its skin. This is clearly a duplicate of the better-known Nemean lion story, transferred from the Peloponnese to Thebes, Kithairon being the mountain range between Boiotia and Attika. It is possible that this is a vestige of an alternative Theban tradition, but there is no trace of such a geographical transposition of the other Peloponnesian labours, and the skin worn by Herakles is identified as that of the Nemean lion as early as Peisandros (fr. 1 *PEG*). While this other lion is elusive, however, the episode is related by Apollodoros to the much better known story of Herakles' prodigious feat in sleeping with king Thespios' fifty daughters, to which we will return (pp. 183–4).

The second battle has Herakles leading a Theban army rather than acting alone, restoring his city's freedom when it has been forced to pay tribute to Erginos, king of the Minyans in the neighbouring city of Orchomenos. The story is alluded to in Euripides' *Herakles* (ll.48–50, 220–1), and it may have been the subject of a satyr play by Aeschylus (p. 110), but the most colourful details come from Apollodoros (2.4.11), who records that Herakles intercepted the heralds who were on their way to collect the tribute, cut off their ears, noses and hands, and sent them back with these tied around their necks to Erginos, who henceforth had to pay Thebes double the original tribute of a hundred cattle. The gory detail concerning the heralds is reduced by Diodoros (4.10.3) to the convenient single verb *akrôtêriazein*, to 'cut off the extremities', and he chooses rather to expand on Herakles' gathering together of an army of Theban youths 'of his own age', equipped with old weapons taken from the city's temples where they had been left as dedications to the gods, putting the emphasis on the triumph of youthful refusal to bow to oppression rather than Herakles' individual fighting prowess.

STRONG MEN AND TRANSGRESSORS

Enemies of the Argonauts

According to Apollonios' *Argonautika*, the most authoritative account of the expedition, Herakles had just delivered the Erymanthian boar to Eurystheus when he heard the call for heroes to join the voyage of the Argo (1.122–32). Other sources leave this episode's placing in Herakles' career vague, including Apollodoros (1.9.19), who cites authorities for different opinions as to where Herakles left the expedition, and for the idea that Herakles missed the expedition entirely because it coincided with his servitude to Omphale. Herakles' involvement, however, is attested as early as the *Wedding of Keyx* (fr. 263 MW) and most agree on his inclusion amongst the crew, as listed for example by Pindar (*Pythian* 4.171–2).

In Apollonios' account (*Argonautika* 1.989–1011), Herakles plays a notable part in one of the Argonauts' earlier battles, when their visit to king Kyzikos and the Doliones in the Propontis is interrupted by an attack from the Gegeneis, 'the Earthborn ones', six-armed monsters (described at ll.942–6) who live nearby:

> But Herakles had been left behind there with the younger men, and, immediately stretching the back-bent bow, he brought them to earth one after another; and they in turn lifted and threw jagged rocks. For these grim monsters too, I suppose, the goddess Hera, wife of Zeus, had reared to be a trial for Herakles.

A few lines later (ll.1040–1) Herakles is involved in a fight which accidentally breaks out between the Argonauts and their hosts, killing the Doliones Telekles and Megabrontes. Not long afterwards the expedition moves on to Kios where Hylas disappears, a story to which we shall return (pp. 134–6), and Herakles departs, returning to his labours. Diodoros (4.43.3–44.6) keeps Herakles on board rather longer, involving him in the Argonauts' encounter with the Thracian king Phineus. Rather than the better-known story of Phineus' blinding by the gods and his torment by the Harpies, Diodoros' version has Phineus killed by Herakles in a battle which follows the Argonauts' rescue of his mistreated sons, presenting Herakles as the defender of civilized values as much as the monster-slayer.

Antaios

A more popular story is Herakles' fight against Antaios, which Apollodoros (2.5.11) sets on his way to the garden of the Hesperides, Diodoros (4.17.4) en route for Geryon's Erytheia. Most sources agree that Antaios lived in Libya, was a son of Poseidon, and that he specialized in forcing strangers to wrestle with him; one or two specify that his mother was Earth, or imply that he was a giant, and Pindar (*Isthmian* 4.52–5) mentions the grisly detail that he used his opponents' skulls to roof Poseidon's temple. The episode is alluded to in Peisandros and in art it may appear first on a metope of the Heraion at Foce del Sele, although the subject's identity is not entirely certain. Then there are about thirty-five examples of Herakles wrestling with Antaios in extant Attic vase-painting, all from around 530–480 BC, including a fine red-figure krater signed by Euphronios, c.510 BC (Louvre G103). On this, the two opponents are locked in a complicated scrum on the ground, and Antaios is represented as an over-sized man, his barbaric nature indicated by his unkempt hair and beard, which is contrasted with Herakles' neat coiffure.

There is no indication in any of these archaic images of the motif of Antaios gaining strength from contact with the earth. Its earliest appearances are in the hellenistic period, when a silver coin from third-century Taras (*BMC* Italy 208) features Herakles with Antaios in a realistic wrestling pose, raised up to shoulder-height in a firm hold around the waist; the same pose can also be seen in a type of statue group which originated in the third or second century BC. In literature the first writer to make the motif explicit is Ovid, his Hercules speaking of having taken away from Antaeus his 'parent's nourishment' (*Metamorphoses* 9.183–4). Much is made of the motif in the vivid account of the first-century AD Lucan's *Pharsalia* (4.593–655). The story is put in the mouth of an African peasant, who is telling the visiting Romans why some hills are known as Antaeus' home. He explains Antaeus' parentage and his reputation as an invincible killer before introducing Hercules (ll.612–19):

> Hercules threw off the skin of the lion of Cleonae [*i.e. Nemea*], Antaeus that of a Libyan lion; the visitor (Hercules) drenched his limbs with oil in the traditional manner of the Olympian wrestling-ground; the other (Antaeus), not trusting that he should touch his mother with his feet alone, poured hot sand over his limbs as an aid. They locked hands and arms in many a grip; for a long time they tested each other's neck with weighty arms in vain; they kept their heads immobile with brows fixed, and each was amazed to have met his match.

Hercules, of course, eventually realizes how Antaeus is able to regain his strength and wins by holding him up, away from contact with the earth.

Bousiris

Immediately after his victory over Antaios, in both Apollodoros' and Diodoros' accounts, Herakles comes to Egypt where he encounters the king

Bousiris, another inhospitable son of Poseidon. Our earliest literary source is a fragment of Pherekydes (fr. 17 F), which has Herakles kill Bousiris and various companions at 'the altar of Zeus, where he used to slay strangers', but not until Apollodoros (2.5.11) do we get full details of the episode: Bousiris took to sacrificing foreigners in accordance with an oracle which prescribed the sacrifice of one man a year in honour of Zeus to stave off barrenness; the first victim had been the seer Phrasios who delivered the oracle in the first place.

Since Zeus is the god particularly concerned with the proper observance of guest-friendship (*xenia*) and protection of strangers, the locating of such a sacrifice at his altar seems particularly impious, and it is paradoxical that Zeus himself should have ordained it. One possible explanation is that Bousiris had misunderstood, or even been misled by the seer, but in fact there are parallels for such apparently inconsistent behaviour by Greek gods. The sacrifice of Iphigeneia, for example, is required by Artemis, a goddess usually regarded as protector of the young; many versions of the story restore the goddess' more kindly reputation by having her replace the girl at the last minute by an animal victim, but in some Iphigeneia does die. In a more historical context, Herodotus (1.57–9) recounts how Apollo deliberately instructed the people of Kyme to commit the impiety of surrendering a suppliant in order that they might be punished – the thought here may be that Apollo is predisposed to punish them for some unspecified offence, or that the Kymeans have displayed impiety by even contemplating the act and approaching the oracle in the first place.

In the end, however, the fact that Bousiris is punished confirms that his human sacrifices were an offence against the gods. The story was the subject of a satyr play by Euripides entitled *Bousiris*, and comedies of the same name by Epicharmos and Kratinos in the fifth century; in the fourth century further *Bousiris* comedies are attributed to Kratinos the younger, Antiphanes, Ephippos and Mnesimachos. In the 380s or 370s BC an unusual work by Isokrates purports to be a private communication to his contemporary Polykrates criticizing the latter's *Defence of Bousiris*, but in fact offers an alternative encomium of the Egyptian king. In a display of rhetorical virtuosity, Isokrates picks up every point which could possibly be adduced in Bousiris' favour, the most devastating argument he can propose being that Bousiris lived some three hundred years or more before Herakles and therefore cannot possibly have been killed by him, so all the stories must be false (*Bousiris* 36). Altogether the speech rather emphasizes the enormity of Bousiris' crimes, which only the deftest of barristers could possibly hope to defend.

In art the story appears on around thirty vases, ranging from the mid-sixth century to the fourth century BC. The encounter is depicted in particularly lively fashion on a Caeretan hydria of c.530 BC, name vase of the Bousiris Painter (Vienna 3576). Herakles deals with the king's servants here by throwing them down and trampling them, just as a Pharaoh tramples his enemies on Egyptian reliefs, while the king himself is the only figure apart from Herakles to have a beard, and is wearing a cobra headdress, which again suggests an awareness of Egyptian iconographical conventions; some attempt is also made to distinguish between racial types, with half of the servants depicted as Nubians, being bald/close-shaven, with snub noses, earrings and long tunics. Such an interest in racial types, rare in Greek art before the hellenistic period, is characteristic of the Attic representations too, and emphasizes the centrality of the Greek-barbarian opposition to the story. On a red-figure pelike by the Pan Painter of c.460 BC (Figure 2.1), for example, the three Egyptians of negroid appearance are carefully posed with their tunics tucked out of the way in order to display circumcized genitalia. The incidental details of the images, however, such

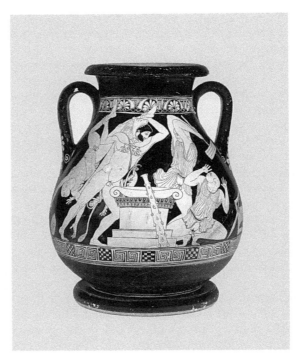

Figure 2.1 Herakles and Bousiris. Attic red-figure stamnos by the Pan Painter, c.460 BC (Athens 9683). Photo: National Archaeological Museum, Athens © Hellenic Ministry of Culture and Tourism / Archaeological Receipts Fund.

as altars and sacrificial utensils, are entirely Greek, and indeed provide useful information about regular Greek sacrificial practices.

Herodotus (2.45) criticizes this as a 'silly story' indicative of the Greeks' ignorance of Egyptian character and customs, because the Egyptians do not even sacrifice many animals, let alone human beings, but the majority of Greeks would probably not have found the idea of foreigners behaving badly so difficult to believe. The episode's obvious message is that both human sacrifice and the flouting of the laws of hospitality are barbaric, but in addition it highlights the issue that sacrifice/meat-eating entails killing, a problem also articulated in one or two Greek rituals (see p. 187).[2]

Roman Cacus

One episode which really has to be located on the return journey from Erytheia is Herakles' encounter with the robber Cacus, who attempts to steal the cattle of Geryon. This is very much a Roman story, set at the site of the future Rome and providing the foundation myth for the cult of Hercules at the Ara Maxima in Rome's Forum Boarium (pp. 195–6). It is first attested in the late first century BC, in Dionysios of Halikarnassos' *Roman Antiquities* (1.39), which tells how Hercules was driving Geryon's cattle back through Italy when he decided to rest at a place with good pasture beside the river Tiber; while he was sleeping, Cacus removed a few choice beasts, dragging them backwards by the tail into his cave so that their footprints would not give away their location; Hercules was at first fooled by this ruse, but then the cattle inside the cave heard their fellows lowing and betrayed their whereabouts by their answering calls; Hercules summarily despatched Cacus with a blow from his club. The same story is noted in Livy's history of Rome (1.7.4–8), and recounted by the Augustan poets Propertius (4.9) and Ovid (*Fasti* 1.543–82).

The most extensive and memorable version of the story, however, is that related by Virgil in the *Aeneid* (8.184–305), where it is put in the mouth of Evander, king of the area which would one day become Rome, explaining to Aeneas and his companions the origins of the sacrifice in which they have just participated. Evander points out the cave which was once Cacus's squalid home and describes how Cacus, afraid for the first time in his life when confronted by Hercules, attempts to shut himself in there. The denouement is dramatic, with Hercules wrenching a great rock away to uncover Cacus trapped in his den (ll.251–61):[3]

But he, for now there was no escape from the danger above, belched out thick smoke from his throat (astonishing to report) and wrapped his home in blind darkness, robbing the eyes of sight, and gathered smoke-bearing night in his cave, with fire and shadows mixed together. Alcides [*i.e. Hercules*] could not endure this in his spirit, and with a headlong jump he threw himself through the fire, where the densest smoke came in a wave and the huge cave heaved with black cloud. Hercules seized Cacus, who was spewing ineffectual fire in the darkness, clasping him in a knot, and throttled him, clinging until his eyes were squeezed out and his throat was dry of blood.

Syleus and the Kerkopes

Later, Herakles is supposed to have dealt with a number of local menaces during his period of servitude to Omphale. The Itonoi are attested only in Diodoros (4.31.7), who merely says they had been plundering Omphale's territory, so Herakles razed their city to the ground and enslaved its inhabitants. More substantial a character is Syleus, who forced passers-by to dig his vineyard until Herakles killed him with his own hoe. Fragments of a satyr play by Euripides entitled *Syleus* (frs 686a–94 *TrGF*) include Herakles being sold to Syleus to work in his vineyard, uprooting vines and using the wood to roast an ox, which he feasted on washed down with his master's wine. A daughter, Xenodoke or Xenodike, was also involved, and her part in the story is amplified by Apollodoros (2.6.3), who has her killed by Herakles before he burns the vineyard to the ground. The daughter also features in a more romantic version in a *Herakleia* by the first century BC/AD Knidian historian Konon (*FGrH* 26F1.17), in which Herakles falls in love with the daughter, but she dies of longing when he goes away.

Earlier than Euripides, the story is first attested c.480 BC on an Attic red-figure stamnos which is name-vase of the Syleus Painter (Copenhagen 3293), on which Herakles, accompanied by Athena, stands holding a mattock while Syleus talks to him. Other Attic representations all date between about 490 and 460 BC, and are identifiable by the agricultural tool held by Herakles, either a mattock or a double axe. On one, a red-figure skyphos of c.460 BC (Zurich ETH B19), while Herakles works with the mattock, a girl runs off to the right with his club and lionskin; this might be Syleus' daughter, given her later role in the story, but her actions here strongly echo the appropriation of Herakles' clothes by Omphale herself. The 'be done by as you did' motif, which we have already seen in connection with the mares of Diomedes story (pp. 40–1), is reminiscent of Theseus' youthful deeds, which were a popular subject in Attic vase-painting especially in the early fifth century, and may have influenced the Syleus scenes.

Best known of this group of Lydian 'baddies', however, are the Kerkopes. The development of their story is even more than usually difficult to trace, since our stalwarts Apollodoros and Diodoros only mention them very briefly, and fail to recount the more colourful elements of the episode. More complete accounts are found in one edition of the second-century AD Zenobios' collection of proverbs (the 'Athoan recension' 2.85) and in a sixth-century AD Christian work, the *Commentary on Gregory of Nazianzus' Sermons* (4.39). These relate how the Kerkopes' mother had told the brothers to beware of the *melampygos*, the 'black-buttocked' one, but one day they found Herakles asleep under a tree and were about to make off with his weapons when he woke up and carried them away, hung upside-down from a pole; from here they had a good view of Herakles' black bottom and remembered their mother's warning, but proceeded to talk to each other and laugh at their captor; he immediately untied them and let them go.[4]

Very little of this detail can be traced in earlier literature. The episode was the subject of a number of lost comedies entitled *Kerkopes*, in the fifth century by Hermippos and Plato, and in the fourth by Euboulos and Menippos; there is also at least mention of the Kerkopes in a few other comedies, such as Kratinos' *Archilochoi* – but not enough survives to indicate the course of the story. The one classical source to contain a hint of the later story is Herodotus (7.216), in the unlikely context of his account of the battle of Thermopylai: the mountain track which enabled the Persians to get behind the Greek army came out to the east 'near the stone called Black-Buttocked and the seats of the Kerkopes, where the narrowest part of the pass is'. Not until c.AD 100 do we find the suggestion that Herakles enjoyed his captives' jokes, in a frustratingly brief allusion in Plutarch (*Moralia* 60c): 'even Herakles was amused by certain Kerkopes, and Dionysos by Silenoi'. A less cheerful tradition is hinted at by a fragment of Pherekydes (fr. 77 F), which has the Kerkopes turned to stone, and by Diodoros (4.31.7), who talks of multiple Kerkopes 'robbing and doing many evil deeds', of whom Herakles kills some and hands others over to Omphale; Apollodoros (2.6.3) merely states that Herakles 'captured and bound the Kerkopes', locating their home at Ephesos.

In contrast to the literary evidence, the visual record provides unusually consistent attestation of one element of the story: from as early as c.600 BC, the Kerkopes are always depicted slung upside-down from a pole over Herakles' shoulders, usually symmetrically posed looking in towards their captor. The earliest examples appear in the Peloponnese, on Corinthian vases c.600–575 BC, and then c.560 BC on a shield-band relief from Olympia and on a fragmentary Lakonian cup (Tocra 934). Around the same time the scene is depicted on a metope of the Heraion at Foce del Sele, and on a metope from Temple C, possibly of Apollo, at Selinous (Palermo 3920C). The Selinous metope varies the composition slightly by presenting both Herakles and his captives frontally, staring out at the viewer as though just caught in mid-action; the sculptor has also attempted to represent the effect of gravity on the Kerkopes' hair, which hangs down beside their heads in rather comical fashion. In Attic black-figure vase-painting there are around ten examples of the scene, sometimes including Athena or other subsidiary figures, but the central group of Herakles and the Kerkopes reprises the usual scheme.

Many scholars have read the archaic images as comical, but it is possible that a modern view of the scenes is distorted by our knowledge of the later story, which might only have acquired its humorous elements via comedy in the classical period. Marconi (2007, 150–9 and 205–7) takes this line, noting that the scene is similar to representations of the hunter with his prey, the upside-down position of the Kerkopes emphasizing Herakles' domination. He concludes that the Selinous metope is part of a broader sculptural trend asserting the city's cultural identity, with Herakles representing the civilized Greek colonists, the Kerkopes their brigand non-Greek neighbours.

Undoubtedly humorous, however, is the remarkable image on a Sicilian krater of c.380–370 BC (Catania MB 4232), which presents two figures in comic costume. The actor to the left carries a club, Herakles' standard attribute, and has two basket-cages slung on a yoke over his shoulders containing small figures who must be the Kerkopes; to the right sits another actor holding a staff, who might be Omphale, although the character's sex is unclear. This suggests that the Kerkopes story was the subject of dramatic performances in fourth-century Sicily, either in comedies like those mentioned above, or in the native South Italian genre of the phlyax play (pp. 112–14).

One other South Italian image, from a little earlier in the century, is worth mentioning for its representation of the Kerkopes, who have previously been entirely anthropomorphic. This is a Lucanian pelike of c.380 BC (Malibu 81.AE.189), on which Herakles is depicted as a young man, contrasting strongly with the two Kerkopes suspended from his yoke, who have pot bellies, over-sized genitalia and monkey-like faces with large pointy ears. This links in with yet another strand to the story possibly suggested by the Kerkopes' name, which may be derived from *kerkos*, 'tail', implying their animal status. A more specific connection is supplied by the geographer Xenagoras, in a work *On the Islands* (*FGH* 240F28; fourth to first century BC), which explains that the island of Pithekoussai (modern Ischia, in the Bay of Naples) was called after the Kerkopes who had been turned into monkeys (*pithêkoi*). This idea is enlarged upon by Ovid in his *Metamorphoses* (14.89–100), who provides characteristically vivid detail of the physical transformation involved:

> Once upon a time the father of the gods, detesting the deceit and perjuries of the Cercopes and the crimes of that treacherous people, changed the men into a misshapen

animal, so that they appeared both like and unlike humans: he contracted their limbs, beat their noses so they were turned up on their faces, and furrowed their brows with an old woman's wrinkles, and, having covered their whole bodies in yellow hair, sent them to this home – not before he had taken away their use of words and of the tongues born for terrible perjuries; he left them the ability to complain only in a raucous shriek.

Giants

Herakles has a number of encounters with individual opponents described as giants, such as Antaios and Alkyoneus (p. 118), but by far the most significant of his *parerga* is his involvement in the Gigantomachy, the battle of the gods against the giants who threatened the establishment of Zeus' power on Olympos. Apollodoros (2.7.1) puts this between Herakles' sack of Troy and his campaigns in the Peloponnese, Diodoros (4.15.1) just before his rescue of Prometheus, between the Cretan bull labour and the mares of Diomedes. Most sources, however, are less precise in relating the battle to Herakles' career – this is, after all, as much the gods' story as Herakles', being significant especially for Zeus and Athena.[5]

The Gigantomachy is not narrated in surviving literature until Pindar (*Nemean* 1.67–72), where it is included in Teiresias' prophecy concerning the infant Herakles' future, and it is juxtaposed to mention of his eventual apotheosis. A particular connection between the Gigantomachy and Herakles' deification may earlier have been implied by Hesiod (*Theogony* 954), where the description of Herakles' happy life on Olympos is said to follow the accomplishment of 'a great deed amongst the gods' – but other interpretations of this line are possible, and the poem does not explicitly mention the Gigantomachy at all. A line from the *Catalogue of Women* (fr.43a.65 MW) is more helpful, specifying that Herakles 'slew the overbearing Giants at Phlegrai', but we have to wait until Apollodoros (1.6.1) to hear a rationale for his participation: an oracle had pronounced that only the presence of a mortal fighting on their side would guarantee the gods' victory. The site of the battle is variously supposed to be in Italy, on the Phlegraian Plain in Campania, or in northern Greece, on the westernmost peninsular of Chalkidiki, which is sometimes called Pallene, sometimes (confusingly) Phlegra.

Visual evidence confirms that Herakles had an important part to play in the battle at least as early as the mid-sixth century. The earliest relevant scenes appear on four black-figure Attic vases of c.560 BC found on the Athenian Akropolis, where they must have been dedications to Athena. These include a fragmentary dinos by Lydos (Akropolis 607), on which Herakles fights alongside Zeus, aiming his bow from a chariot in the midst of the action. The scene remains popular in Attic black-figure, and is typified by an amphora of c.520 BC by the Lysippides Painter (London B208), on which Zeus mounts his chariot brandishing a thunderbolt, while ahead of him Herakles is stepping forward onto the chariot's shaft in his eagerness to join Athena as she strides forward into the fray. The Gigantomachy had particular resonance at Athens because of the significant part which Athena was supposed to have played in it: her victories were reputedly woven into the robe presented to the goddess at the Panathenaia festival every year, and she is prominent in the battle's representation on the pediment of Athena's temple of c.520 BC on the Akropolis.

Nonetheless, the story can be understood as having a more general significance, representing the triumph of order over chaos, or civilization over barbarity, like so many of Herakles' individual combats. This must be at least part of the reason for its popularity outside of Athens, too, in the late sixth century, when it appears for example on the pediments of the temple of Apollo at Delphi and the Megarian Treasury at Olympia, although these, like the Athena temple, are too poorly preserved for us to be sure of Herakles' involvement. A reasonable case has been made, however, for reconstructing Herakles in the Gigantomachy which occupies the north frieze of the Siphnian Treasury at Delphi, c.525 BC: the critical section at the centre of the frieze is damaged, but comparison of the composition as a whole with vase-painting suggests that Herakles may have been depicted fighting from Zeus' chariot.

The battle is less common in later art, and does not always include our hero, but there are one or two examples which feature Herakles in Attic red-figure, and half a dozen on south Italian vases. He can also be found in two notable post-archaic sculptural Gigantomachies: in one of the Parthenon's east metopes Herakles has been identified as the dominant figure on the grounds of his pose, wielding both club and bow; on the hellenistic Altar of Zeus at Pergamon (pp. 149–50), although the relevant portion of the east frieze is incomplete, his position near to Zeus and Athena is quite certainly established by an inscription. A notable element of all these representations is the appearance of the giants: in the archaic and classical periods the giants are entirely anthropomorphic, sometimes dressed as hoplite soldiers, sometimes wearing animal skins to emphasize their barbarity. On the Pergamon Altar, however, although a few maintain hoplite form, many have wings, bushy hair and legs which end in snakes' heads, much as we find them described by Apollodoros (1.6.1):

> . . . unsurpassable in physical size, unconquerable in strength, who appeared fearful to the eyes, with thick hair hanging down from their head and cheeks, and they had dragon-scale feet.

These hellenistic giants are altogether suitable to number amongst Herakles' more monstrous opponents.[6]

The Molione twins

According to Apollodoros (2.7.2), Herakles' first deed on returning to the Peloponnese after his sack of Troy was to mount a campaign against Augeias, in revenge for his failure to pay for the cleansing of his stables. Augeias enlisted as generals his two nephews Eurytos and Kteatos, sons of Augeias' brother Aktor (or Poseidon) and Molione, who are often referred to as 'the Molione', after their mother, rather than by the more usual patronymic 'Aktorione'. These two are referred to by Homer (*Iliad* 23.641) as twins (*didymoi*), but a number of later authors seem to indicate that they are Siamese twins, thought of as sharing a single torso, but usually with a full complement of limbs: for example Ibykos (285 *PMG*²), writing in the second half of the sixth century, has someone (presumably Herakles) boast that he has overcome the Molione, who are 'of the same age, equal-headed, one in limbs'. Because of their unusual physical appearance, the Molione are the most promising candidates for identification in Geometric art. Some scholars recognize them in a figure with a single body but two heads and two sets of limbs, which appears on a dozen late eighth- and early seventh-century pots and two bronze fibulae; others, however, have argued that the double figure is just a convention for representing two men fighting side by side. On balance, the case for identifying at least some of the images as the Molione is strong, but in none is there anything to indicate that the warrior against whom they fight is Herakles, and it should be noted that they are also supposed to have fought against Nestor.[7]

Kyknos

One of the last great battles of Herakles' career is that with Kyknos, the fierce warrior who used to haunt the sanctuary of Apollo at Pagasai in Thessaly and steal sacrificial victims before they could reach the god. Our most extensive source for the story is the *Shield of Herakles*, a poem attributed to Hesiod but probably dating to around 570 BC. Herakles is prompted by Apollo to attack this nuisance, and eventually overcomes him despite the efforts of Ares to support his son Kyknos; Herakles himself has the help of Athena as well as his nephew Iolaos. More than a third of the poem is taken up by the elaborate description of Herakles' shield, which gives the poem its name (ll.139–43):

In his hands he took his all-sparkling shield; no one ever broke this with blows or crushed it, and it was a wonder to see. For its whole circumference was shiny with enamel and white ivory and electrum, and radiant with gleaming gold, and zones of cyanus were drawn upon it . . .

Noting the high profile of Thebes in the poem, and some athletic scenes in the description of the shield (ll.301–11), Janko (1986) makes a good case for the *Shield* having originally been written for performance at the Theban festival in honour of Herakles and his sons (pp. 182–3). The encounter was also the subject of a poem by Stesichoros entitled *Kyknos*, of which only a brief summary survives (fr. 207 *PMG*), but which seems to have told a version of the story in which Herakles is at first beaten by the combined forces of Kyknos and his father Ares, but later returns and defeats Kyknos alone. A detail included in the summary is that Kyknos would use the skulls of his victims to build a temple to Apollo, rather as Pindar supposed Antaios to have roofed Poseidon's temple, as we have seen.

Both the single combat and the version in which the protagonists have divine assistance are reflected in the archaic visual arts from around 560 BC onwards. The episode features in only a handful of non-Athenian contexts, but is popular in Attic vase-painting, with over a hundred examples, the majority in black-figure and dating to the second half of the sixth century. These include a fine black-figure oinochoe by Lydos, c.530 BC (Berlin 1732), on which Herakles fights Ares over the dead body of Kyknos, their chariots standing by, driven by figures identified by inscription as Iolaos and Fear (Phobos), just as in the *Shield*; unlike the poem, however, the scene also includes Zeus, apparently on the point of intervening between the combatants. On a vivid red-figure krater fragment signed by Euphronios, c.510–500 BC (New York, private collection), Athena rather than Zeus occupies the centre of the scene, much as the *Shield* (ll.443–4) describes: 'But Athena, daughter of aegis-bearing Zeus, came against Ares, wearing her dark aegis . . .' The particularly active role taken by Athena in the story may explain why it was chosen as the subject of as many as three ceramic dedications to the goddess on the Athenian Akropolis.[8]

Prometheus

One final 'transgressor' encountered by Herakles is Prometheus. His deeds were only transgressive from the gods' point of view, however, and positively beneficial to mankind, so it is appropriate that Herakles' role here should be to help, rather than fighting against him. Prometheus' crimes were to cheat the gods of an equal share with man in the meat from sacrifices, and to steal fire from the gods; his punishment was to be chained up and have his liver pecked out every day by Zeus' eagle, regenerating every night ready for the punishment to continue indefinitely. The story of the punishment and Prometheus' subsequent rescue by Herakles goes back to Hesiod (*Theogony* 521–34), who explains that Zeus allowed it partly in order to increase his son's glory, partly because he was no longer angry with Prometheus. Herakles kills the eagle, but it is not entirely clear whether he actually releases Prometheus from his bonds, since Hesiod's account of his career ends (1.616) with the statement that 'great bonds confine him' still. His release is certainly established, however, in the fifth century, when it is the subject of the play *Prometheus Unbound*, sometimes attributed to Aeschylus, fragments of which suggest that Herakles is the agent of his freedom (p. 80). Pherekydes (fr. 17 F) only mentions the killing of the eagle, not the release, but locates the story after that of Bousiris on Herakles' way to the Hesperides' garden, with Prometheus advising Herakles to send Atlas to fetch the apples. One might expect the geographical location of the story to be in north Africa, on the way to the Hesperides' western abode, but sources from the *Prometheus Unbound* onwards seem to be united in placing it in the Caucasus mountains, north of the Black Sea.

In art, the rescue appears as early as c.620 BC on a fragmentary Attic black-figure krater by the Nessos Painter (Athens 16384): here Herakles has his bow drawn shooting arrows past Prometheus, who is bound to a stake, at an enormous bird behind him which appears to be wounded and dying. There are only a few other Attic representations of the story, all sixth-century black-figure and all with more or less exactly the same composition, with Herakles crouching, Prometheus slumped against the stake in a sitting position, and then the over-size bird. Herakles is perhaps alluded to, despite his physical absence, by the combination of figures on a Lakonian cup by the Arkesilas Painter, c.560 BC (Vatican 16592), on which Prometheus is bound to a column, bleeding profusely from the attack of a bird, while Atlas holds up the heavens. The two Titans are of course genealogically linked as brothers, but their pairing here inevitably calls to mind their mutual involvement with the Hesperides story.

The actual release of Prometheus was, according to Pausanias (5.11.6), represented alongside many other mythological scenes in a painting by the fifth-century painter Panainos on barriers at the foot of the statue of Zeus in his temple at Olympia. The release occurs just once more on an Apulian krater of c.350 attributed to the Suessula Painter (Berlin 1969.9), on which a young Herakles seems to be in the very process of undoing the bonds; Prometheus is framed by the roughly painted edges of the arch-shaped rock to which he is bound, below which the eagle plummets to join Persephone and a Fury in the Underworld. A small-scale sculptural group from the sanctuary of Athena at Pergamon of c.100 BC (Berlin 168) returns to the archaic scheme, with Herakles firing his bow, although Prometheus is now bound to a rock and accompanied by a personification of the Caucasus mountains; it has been suggested that Herakles here has the features of Mithradates VI of Pontus (p. 150), and that the whole group is an allegorical representation of Mithradates' liberation of the hellenistic world from Roman oppression.[9]

STRANGE BEASTS

The centaurs of Mount Pholoe

In the course of his career Herakles encounters a number of centaurs, creatures which appear in some of our earliest Greek art, easily recognizable by their hybrid form, half man half horse. There is a shadowy figure who shares the name of Geryon's cowherd, Eurytion, whom Herakles kills in order to rescue the daughter of Dexamenos, king of the Achaian city Olenos, from his unwanted attentions; the story is first attested in the first half of the fifth century in Bakchylides (fr. 44 SM) and on a handful of Attic vases, though the details are slightly unclear. We will return to the much better-known Nessos shortly, but should first consider Herakles' encounter with Pholos and the centaurs of Mount Pholoe, an episode which out-does many of the labours in its popularity as a theme for visual representation. Mount Pholoe is just south of Mount Erymanthos in Arkadia, and the story is usually placed on Herakles' way to fetch the Erymanthian boar.

In literature, first mention of the episode is made in a fragment of Stesichoros' *Geryoneis* (fr.181 *PMG*), in which Pholos serves Herakles a cup of wine, but for a full account we have to turn to Diodoros (4.12.3–8) and Apollodoros (2.5.4). These tell substantially the same story: Herakles was visiting Pholos as a guest, and in the course of entertaining him Pholos opened a jar of wine, either at Herakles' request or because Pholos recalled that Dionysos had left the wine with the centaurs specifically for this purpose; the smell of the wine attracted the notice of all the other centaurs on the mountain, who rushed in and tried to steal it, at which a fight ensued, the centaurs wielding pine trees and rocks; many of the centaurs were killed, and while Pholos was tending the dead, he was accidentally wounded by one of Herakles' arrows and died himself.

The encounter is well attested in archaic art, featuring amongst other Heraklean exploits on metopes of the Heraion at Foce del Sele and on the Throne of Bathykles. Earlier than both these and Stesichoros, however, it is first seen on a Protocorinthian lekythos of c.650 BC (Berlin F336), and appears in some detail on a Corinthian skyphos of c.580 BC (Louvre MNC 677): here Pholos, holding a cup, stands at the mouth of his cave beside a wine-bowl, while Herakles chases the other centaurs away with fire brands. Also notable is the Lakonian dinos by the Rider Painter, c.540 BC (Figure 2.2), on which Herakles is greeted by Pholos, differentiated from the other centaurs who rampage around the frieze by the fact that he has human front legs. Human and horse front legs feature indiscriminately in the scene's sculptural representation on the temple of Athena at Assos in the Troad, of c.530 BC. Though mainly of the Doric order, the temple bore an Ionic frieze, of which over half the surviving slabs depict Herakles scenes, including the fight with Triton. The lively Centauromachy is marked out as being the encounter on Mount Pholoe by the inclusion of Herakles himself with a bow, and behind him a centaur holding a cup, who is presumably Pholos. This scene is juxtaposed with one of a regular human symposium, in which four men recline on couches, one having his cup replenished by a serving boy from a krater nearby. It has been suggested that this feast might be in honour of Herakles, or that a deliberate contrast is being drawn between the disrupted hospitality of Pholos and the practices of a civilized society.

In Attic vase-painting, Herakles can be seen fighting groups of centaurs

Figure 2.2 Pholos and the centaurs of Mount Pholoe. Lakonian black-figure dinos, by the Rider Painter, c.550 BC (Paris E662). Photo: RMN © Hervé Lewandowski.

from the early sixth century, but these are not necessarily the inhabitants of Mount Pholoe. The particular episode only becomes securely identifiable from the last third of the century, when the focus shifts from the violent aftermath to the peaceful beginnings of the encounter – the meeting with Pholos, the opening of the wine, guest and host reclining for its consumption – and versions of the scene are popular in both black- and red-figure between about 540 and 470 BC. Pholos himself is usually distinguished by the holding of a cup, and emphasis is nearly always given to the *pithos*, the large storage jar of wine set into the ground. Sometimes attention is drawn to the *pithos* by its central position in the composition, sometimes by the fact that either Herakles or his host is dipping a cup directly into it. The latter motif suggests that the wine is being drunk neat, rather than following the proper Greek practice of being mixed with water in a krater before serving, a hint that all is not quite right. This uneasy combination of civilized and barbaric practices is highlighted in a dozen examples by the fact that Herakles is depicted reclining as though at a regular symposium, but on the ground rather than on a couch, in some cases even propped up directly against the *pithos*. It has been suggested that the focus on the *pithos* may be a reflection of the Pithoigia ritual of the Athenian Anthesteria, a festival of Dionysos on the first day of which the new vintage was opened.[10]

Hesione, the sea-monster and the first sack of Troy

Just one of Herakles' *parerga* brings him into conflict with a completely inhuman-shaped monster, the sea-monster which menaced the Trojan princess Hesione. The motif of the distressed damsel rescued from a monster, though familiar to a modern audience from its post-classical elaborations, is only otherwise found in Greek tradition in the better-known story of Perseus and Andromeda. Herakles' own sea-monster story is part of the complex of adventures which link the hero with Troy a generation before the famous Trojan War, in the time of Priam's father, king Laomedon. Reference is made in the *Iliad* (20.144–8) to the 'lofty stronghold of godlike Herakles, earth piled around it, which Pallas Athena and the Trojans once made, as a place of refuge from the sea-monster (*ketos*) when it pursued him from the seashore onto the plain'. Earlier in the poem we hear that Herakles once came with just six ships and a few men, and sacked Troy, 'for the sake of Laomedon's horses' (*Iliad* 5.640), an attack brought about by 'the senselessness of one man, the haughty Laomedon, who repaid Herakles, who had done him good service, with an evil word and would not give up the horses, for the sake of which he had come from afar' (5.649–51).

The background to these allusions is filled in by a substantial fragment of the fifth-century historian Hellanikos (*FGrH* 4F26b), preserved in paraphrase by an ancient commentator on the *Iliad* passage: Poseidon, angry with Laomedon for his failure to pay for his and Apollo's labour in building the walls of Troy, had sent a sea-monster to ravage the land; instructed by an oracle that he must give the monster his daughter Hesione, Laomedon duly offered her up, but also proclaimed that he would reward anyone who killed the beast with the immortal horses once given to his ancestor Tros by Zeus in return for Ganymede; Herakles was helped in the task by Athena, who built a protective wall around him, after which he got inside the monster and destroyed it from within; Laomedon, however, substituted mortal horses, and when Herakles later discovered the trick, he returned to sack Troy and claim the immortal horses.

This story is followed quite closely by Diodoros, although he has chosen to make the rescue part of the outward voyage of the Argonauts' expedition (4.42.1–7), with the sack happening some time later (4.32.1–5). Apollodoros likewise allows some time to elapse between the rescue, which he places on Herakles' return journey from the Amazons (2.5.9), and the sack of Troy, which he postpones until after Herakles' servitude to Omphale (2.6.4). According to both authors the expedition was on a larger scale than Homer had indicated, his six ships being increased to eighteen, and a prominent role was played by the Aiginetan hero Telamon; Laomedon and all but one of his sons were killed, and Hesione became Telamon's prize. Rather confusingly, Diodoros (4.49.3–7) also offers an alternative version in which the sack is placed on the Argo's return journey from Colchis, but the tradition of a separate expedition is clearly older. Indeed, Telamon's involvement in the story is attested already in a fragment of Peisandros (fr. 11 *PEG*), which mentions that Herakles awarded him a goblet for his part in the campaign.

Herakles' sack of Troy is depicted on the east pediments of the temple of Aphaia on Aigina, c.500–480 BC, the subject presumably chosen because of the involvement of the local hero Telamon; the crouching figure of Herakles is clearly recognizable by his lionskin helmet and bow. The earlier stage of the story, however, first appears in art on a Corinthian krater of c.560 BC (Boston 63.420), where Herakles shoots arrows and a far-from-helpless Hesione pelts the monster with stones; the monster itself is of rather bizarre appearance, looking like a horse's skull protruding from a cliff. It has been plausibly argued that this is a relatively accurate representation of the kind of fossils of prehistoric creatures found on the coast of the Troad, and that ancient attempts to explain such fossils are the origin of the sea-monster idea in Greek myth. More usually, however, the archaic *ketos* is depicted with a gaping scaly head with lion-like mane attached to a fishy tail, as on the exterior of an Attic black-figure cup of c.540 BC (Taranto 52155), where

Herakles ventures into the creature's jaws to grasp its tongue, perhaps reflecting the idea we saw in Hellanikos of the monster being destroyed from within, while Hesione stands anxiously by. Artists of the classical period establish a more elegant type for the monster, with an elongated head, tall ears, flippers, and spines or scales all over a long fishy body and tail.

A particularly evocative description of the monster is supplied by the first-century AD Roman writer Valerius Flaccus (*Argonautica* 2.451–578), who, like Diodoros, makes the rescuing of Hesione a stop on the Argo's itinerary (ll.499–505):

> . . . its starry eyes quiver through the blue-grey mist, and a thundering roar shakes the mouth circled with a triple-row of fangs, and its tail stretches back over the already-measured sea and its lofty neck hurries the spreading coils on. The sea escorts it as it lies heavily across a thousand waves, lapping its sides, and the storm drives it rushing upon the terrified shore.

Hercules at first attempts to bring down the enormous beast with his arrows, but when these have no effect he resorts to more primitive weapons (ll.530–6):

> And now the sea-monster is here with full momentum, now it gapes very close to its wretched prey. Alcides [*i.e. Hercules*] stands proud in the midst of the waters and awaits its onset, and strikes with a rock before the neck can rise. He doubles the great blows of his knotty club. The beast sinks to the bottom of the waves, now lying slack all through the shallows.

As we have noted (p. 30), Hesione's rescue was still being depicted c.AD 300 in the Piazza Armerina mosaic, which attests to the long-lasting popularity of the motif of the monster and the maiden.[11]

Nereus and Triton

If sea-monsters are challenging opponents, sea-gods can also be difficult to deal with, not least because of their capacity for shape-shifting. The particular deity encountered by Herakles is consistently named by our literary sources as Nereus, though he is variously met en route for Geryon's Erytheia or for the Hesperides' garden. A fragment of Pherekydes (fr. 16 F) has Herakles advised by the Nymphs who live by the river Eridanos to 'learn from Nereus where the golden apples were; he caught Nereus by force, for at first he kept turning into water and fire . . .'. Apollodoros (2.5.11) follows this story, specifying that Herakles managed to catch him while he was asleep and tied him up, despite his transformations, until he divulged the required information. The episode is strongly reminiscent of Menelaus' encounter with Proteus in the *Odyssey* (4.382–470), where again it is a question of compelling a reluctant sea-god to give information by holding on while he undergoes a series of metamorphoses.

The visual record suggests that Herakles' fight with a sea-god was a favourite theme in the archaic period – on a par with some of the more popular labours – but things are complicated by the changing identity of the deity concerned. Nereus can usually be recognized by his representation as an old man, with a receding hairline and/or white hair, either with a fish's tail instead of legs, or entirely human in form but carrying a fish. He occasionally appears outside Athens, for example wrestling with Herakles on a shield-band from Olympia of c.550 BC (Olympia B1881d), where the half-fish sea-god is accompanied by the inscription 'Old Man of the Sea', and his transformations are represented by a snake's head and flames coming from his head.

The same conception of Nereus first appears in Attic black-figure on a lekythos in the manner of the Gorgon Painter, c.580 BC (Louvre CA 823), where the god has a snake and a lion protruding from his fish-tail. After c.560 BC, however, the sea-god with whom Herakles wrestles is more often Triton, distinguishable from Nereus by his younger appearance and a generally longer fish-tail; the shape-shifting motif is also absent from images of Triton, and the match is sometimes watched by Nereus. The Triton scene proves extremely popular, appearing on at least 200 Attic vases between c.560 and 470 BC, the images perhaps influenced by the episode's very public presence on the pediment of Athena's mid-sixth-century temple on the Athenian Akropolis. Here the left corner of the pedimental triangle is conveniently filled by Triton's long tail, with Herakles kneeling alongside as he leans forward to grapple with Triton's human torso; the figure which fills the opposite corner of the pediment, with three bodies attached to a single tail, has sometimes been identified as Nereus looking on.

It is possible that the Triton scenes represent a separate story, but there is no mention of such a fight in literature, and it is more likely simply to be a variation of the Nereus episode, prompted by an artistic desire to show Herakles pitted against a suitably brawny opponent, rather than wrestling an old man. The change is variously accounted for by modern scholars as reflecting Peisistratos' introduction of the Panathenaic Games, which included wrestling, or his victories over Megara and Salamis in the 560s BC, or more broadly symbolizing Athens' overcoming of political unrest. The composition of the Akropolis' Herakles and Triton group is repeated on the frieze of Athena's temple at Assos, where the large scale of the wrestling pair is contrasted to half a dozen small Nereids who flee the scene with gestures of alarm. This section of the frieze could have been directly inspired by the Athenian pediment, since Assos had trading links with Athens in the late sixth century, or the episode could simply have been chosen as another good example of Herakles' civilizing influence to set alongside the Centauromachy we have already considered.[12]

Another shape-shifter encountered by Herakles is Periklymenos, one of the sons of Neleus who is killed in the course of Herakles' attack on Pylos. A full description of his powers happens to survive in a fragment of the *Catalogue of Women* (fr. 33a MW ll.12–17):

> . . . and lordly Periklymenos, the fortunate, to whom Poseidon the Earthshaker had given all kinds of gifts, for he could appear now as an eagle amongst birds, now he might become an ant, a wonder to behold, now again a shimmering swarm of bees, now a terrible, implacable serpent.

The *Catalogue* goes on to relate that only when Periklymenos is dead will Pylos fall, and that Herakles succeeds in killing him when he has changed into some animal form and is perched on Herakles' chariot. In his Herakles narrative Apollodoros (2.7.3) merely notes that Periklymenos used to 'fight by changing shape', but in an earlier account of Neleus' family (1.9.9) he details his transformations on this occasion as being into a lion, a snake and a bee. Ovid unsurprisingly makes more of the episode in his *Metamorphoses* (12.536–76), putting into Nestor's mouth an account of battle, during which Periclymenus concludes his repertoire of shapes by turning into an eagle, only to be shot down by Hercules' arrows.

Acheloos

Herakles' marriage to Deianeira is usually placed towards the end of his career, although their son Hyllos is supposed to be more or less an adult by the time of Herakles' death. Deianeira is daughter of Oineus, king of Kalydon, a city situated beside the river Euenos in south-west Aitolia and not far from the Acheloos, Greece's largest river, whom Herakles has to fight as a rival suitor. The seventh-century lyric poet Archilochos seems to have put an account of the fight into Deianeira's mouth, who 'recites to Herakles, reminding him of Acheloos' suitorship and what happened on that occasion', while she is being attacked by Nessos (fr. 286 W); another fragment (fr. 287 W) specifies that Acheloos fought in the form of a bull. A fine description of Acheloos is provided at the beginning of Sophokles' *Women of Trachis*, where Deianeira herself is again the speaker, explaining how she had lived in dread of marriage (ll.9–14):

For my suitor was the river, I mean Acheloos, who demanded me from my father in three shapes, coming in the visible form of a bull, then as a gleaming, twisting snake, then in a man's shape but bull-headed, and from his bushy beard flowed down streams of spring-water.

It should be said that river-gods are not generally sinister characters in Greek myth, but Sophokles is establishing Deianeira as a sympathetic character here, as we shall see (pp. 81–2); she goes on to express her joy at Herakles' intervention, but cannot describe the battle itself because she was too frightened to watch (ll.15–27). This gap in the story is made good later in the play (ll.503–28), where the chorus conjures up a vivid picture of the fight between bull and hero as an example of the power of Aphrodite.

In later literature, too, Acheloos is sometimes described as a shape-shifter, but his most abiding form is that of a bull, and this is crucial to an element of the story first seen in a fragment of Pindar (fr. 249a SM), that in the course of the fight Herakles broke off one of Acheloos' horns. According to some Acheloos' horn itself became the horn of Amaltheia, the horn of plenty, while others follow Pindar in having Acheloos get back his own horn by offering in its place the cornucopia he had obtained from Amaltheia. The missing horn provides the starting point for a slightly humorous version of the fight in Ovid's *Metamorphoses* (9.1–100) related by Acheloos, who explains ruefully how Herakles overcame him in each of his three forms, the hero adding insult to injury by comparing his snake incarnation unfavourably to the Lernaian hydra. The horn-of-plenty element is crucial to the rationalizing interpretation of the episode provided by Diodoros (4.34.3–4), who suggests that in fact what Herakles did, rather than fighting with Acheloos, was to divert the river and create a quantity of well-irrigated land, the horn symbolizing the diverted stream. In similar vein, Strabo (10.2.19) proposes that the idea of Acheloos' bull shape arose from the echoing sound of the river, his snake form and horns from the river's winding course, with the fight (again) representing Herakles' management of the river to produce richly cultivable land.[13]

In the visual arts Acheloos is most commonly represented as having the body of a bull and a man's head with bull's horns, though there are variations on the theme. The scene's earliest appearance is on a Corinthian cup, c.590–580 BC (Brussels A 1374), where Herakles wrestles with a centaur-like Acheloos, watched by figures who may be Deianeira and her father, and the fight is appropriately paired with that of Theseus against the Minotaur. In the later sixth century the episode is one of the many on the Throne of Bathykles at Amyklai, and Pausanias (6.19.12–14) also reports seeing a dedication in the Megarian Treasury at Olympia consisting of 'little figures of cedar-wood decorated with gold' representing Herakles wrestling with

Acheloos, the group apparently by the Spartan sculptor Dontas. In Attic art the scene appears more than twenty times, but the most striking depiction is on a red-figure stamnos by Oltos, c.520 BC (London E437), where Acheloos has a human torso, a long, sinuous fish's tail, and his satyr-like human head has a large bull's horn, which Herakles is about to break off.

Nessos

Finally, the best-known hybrid opponent of Herakles is the centaur Nessos, whom he kills in defence of Deianeira's honour, and whose death indirectly causes Herakles' own. The first extant literary source to give details of how the dying Nessos fooled Deianeira into believing that his blood, poisoned by the blood of the hydra with which Herakles tipped his arrows, would act as a love philtre is Sophokles' *Women of Trachis* (ll.555–77), which we will be considering in Chapter 3. As we have noted, Archilochos had already told the story of Nessos' attempted rape of Deianeira (fr. 286 W), and another fragment (fr. 288 W) assures us that Herakles, 'setting out with his wife, killed the centaur Nessos at the river Euenos'. No explicit connection is made here, however, between Nessos and Herakles' death, and our earliest source for the latter event, the *Catalogue of Women* (fr. 25.20–5 MW), makes no mention of the Nessos episode:

> Deianeira . . . did a terrible thing, greatly deluded in her mind, when she sprinkled poison on the tunic and gave it to the herald Lichas to take, and he gave it to lord Herakles, son of Amphitryon, sacker of cities; on receiving it, death's end came quickly upon him, and he died and came to the mournful house of Hades.

The passage is certainly not incompatible with Sophokles' version of the story, and interestingly already includes a role for the herald Lichas, but it would be equally consistent with a version in which the murder was deliberate on the part of Deianeira, 'deluded' perhaps simply by jealousy.

A definite link between Nessos and Herakles' death is finally provided by Bakchylides 16, which relates how, having left Oichalia 'devoured by fire', Herakles was about to make sacrifices on Cape Kenaion in Euboia when Deianeira heard the news that he intended marrying Iole: 'Mighty jealousy destroyed her, and the dusky veil over future events, when beside the rosy river Lykormas she received from Nessos the fateful monstrosity' (ll.31–5). The combination of details here is very similar to what we find in the *Women of Trachis*, but since neither the poem nor the play is precisely dated, it is impossible to say which influenced the other. Literary sources from Sophokles onwards show some concern with the logistics of the episode, placing Nessos' attempted rape either in the middle of the river (usually the Euenos) or on the opposite bank from Herakles, putting sufficient space between them for the assault and subsequent private conversation with Deianeira to seem plausible, and making Herakles' only possible weapon here his bow and arrow.

In archaic art, however, the moment most often chosen for depiction is a combat at close quarters between Herakles and Nessos, the former using his sword or club rather than arrows. Although slightly at odds with the logic of the story, this scenario is more in keeping with the archaic conception of a good fight, as well as suiting the limited canvas offered by most Greek media. There are a few remarkably early candidates for identification with the story: the first is a bronze statuette group from Olympia, c.740 BC (New York 17.190.2072), where a man is plunging his sword into a centaur; then there is an intriguing seal of c.700 BC (Munich Münzsammlung A1293), which shows a centaur leading off a small female figure, which could be an earlier stage of the story; and finally an ivory relief of c.660 BC (Sparta Museum), from the Spartan sanctuary of Artemis Orthia, shows a hero grabbing a centaur by the hair, about to plunge a sword into his back. The last is particularly interesting because its composition almost exactly matches the well-known scene on the Nessos Painter's amphora, c.620 BC (Athens NM 1002), where the identities of Herakles and Nessos are guaranteed by inscriptions. What may be Herakles' earliest appearance in Athenian vase-painting is in another version of this scene, on a Protoattic amphora of c.660 BC (New York 11.210.1), which depicts a hero attacking a centaur while a woman watches from a chariot; there are no inscriptions, but the narrative context is fairly clear.

The subject subsequently appears amongst other Heraklean deeds, as we have noted (pp. 27–8), on the Heraion at Foce del Sele and on the Throne of Bathykles at Amyklai. Independently, the story features on nearly a hundred Attic black-figure vases, with various combinations of the three principle characters, with or without onlookers. The episode is seen on only a handful of red-figure vases, but a striking instance is the tondo by the Ambrosios Painter, c.520 BC (London E42), which reduces the scene to just Deianeira riding on Nessos' back, reluctantly submitting to his embraces; the choice of moment here, shifting the focus away from the physicality of the fight towards the emotionally fraught relationship between would-be rapist and victim, is ahead of its time. The scene resurfaces in Roman wall-painting, where it can finally be given some sort of landscape setting. In the House of Menander at Pompeii (I.10.4, *in situ*), a painting of c.20 BC depicts Herakles aiming his bow at Nessos who, with Deianeira in his arms, is cantering off through the shallows of a river, in which the river-god Euenos reclines.

OVERVIEW

Monster-fighting is not confined to the labours, but also characterizes much of the rest of Herakles' career. The majority of these battles are attested in art and/or literature of the archaic period, and some appear with a frequency which suggests that they were at least as well known as the labours, if not better. Notable in this respect are the wrestling match with Triton, at more than two hundred examples, and the one hundred or so examples of the battles with Kyknos and with the centaurs of Mount Pholoe. The absence of references to the exploits of Herakles' youth and to the Syleus episode pre-500 BC may be simply an accident of survival, but in both cases there are elements which may have appealed more to classical than archaic sensibilities. The Cacus story is certainly a Roman creation, but may date considerably earlier than its first attestations in the first century BC, given its close association with Rome's oldest cult of Hercules. One or two episodes are hardly seen after the classical period, but several are memorably recreated by writers and artists of the hellenistic and early Roman imperial periods. Herakles himself occasionally oversteps the mark of civilized behaviour, as in his treatment of his music teacher Linos or the heralds of Erginos. Some motifs are repeated in different episodes, like the shape-shifting employed by Nereus, Periklymenos and Acheloos, and there are some common themes, like the punishment of offences against the laws of hospitality. Each encounter, however, has something distinctive about it, which is testimony to the inventive powers of the Greek myth-making imagination.

3

THE TRAGIC HERO

> The suffering Heracles, as a project for tragedy, is exceptionally sensitive material,
> almost too disturbing, almost taboo. And when tragedy does, eventually, dare to
> focus on this anomaly, disturbance is conspicuous.
>
> (Silk 1985, 7)

A COMPLEX CHARACTER

So far we have been considering Herakles the monster-slayer, the most
long-lasting side to his character, although it particularly dominates his
image in the archaic period. Herakles is, however, much more than a
one-dimensional muscle-man. In this and the next chapter we will consider other aspects of his character which come to the fore in the classical period, when they are developed in a variety of media, though most
especially in drama. To begin with, we look at Herakles' treatment by the
great fifth-century Athenian tragedians Sophokles and Euripides. In addition to the plays themselves, some reflections of their themes in the visual
arts of the classical period are worth brief comment, before we turn to the
revival of the tragic Herakles in first-century BC/AD Rome, especially in the
tragedies of Seneca. Herakles is not, in fact, a frequent hero of the tragic
stage, but the works under consideration here have had a disproportion-
ately significant influence on the development of his image. Some of the
elements of Herakles' story which are dealt with are in themselves tragic,
like the fit of madness in which he kills his first wife Megara and their children, or his death at the unwitting hands of his second wife Deianeira. Others are perhaps less obvious subjects for tragic elaboration, like his rescu-
ings of Alkestis, Theseus and Peirithous from the Underworld, or his rape
of Auge.

EARLY TRAGEDY

Herakles appeared in some of the earliest tragedies of which we have any record. As we shall see (p. 120), the early fifth-century tragedian Phrynichos produced an *Alkestis* which may have featured Herakles, and the same writer's *Antaios* must have given the hero a central role. Thereafter we have a little information about Aeschylus' treatment of Herakles, who must have been a major character in lost tragedies entitled *Alkmene* and *Children of Herakles*. The former presumably concerned Herakles' birth, while the latter title might indicate the story later covered by Euripides, or might refer to a chorus consisting of Herakles' offspring in a play about his death. Herakles also had an important role in the Prometheus plays which ancient commentators attributed to Aeschylus, although their authorship, date, and whether they formed part of a thematically unified trilogy, has been the subject of much modern debate. In the *Prometheus Bound* (ll.871–4), Prometheus himself reports the oracle given by his mother Themis that he will one day be freed from his bonds by 'a courageous one famed for his bow', i.e. Herakles. This release must have been accomplished in the *Prometheus Unbound*, fragments of which show that Herakles appeared as a character on stage, had a conversation with Prometheus about his career past and future, and that at some point he shot the eagle and later undid Prometheus' bonds. Herakles has no direct connection with Aeschylus' other plays, but he is mentioned briefly in the *Agamemnon* (458 BC), when Klytamnestra urges the captive Kassandra to accept her fate, 'for even Alkmene's son, they say, once endured being sold, in spite of the slave's barley-cake rations' (ll.1040–1).[1]

SOPHOKLES: DEATH AND DEIFICATION

Amongst Sophokles' lost plays, Herakles only certainly appeared on stage in the *Athamas*, towards the end of which he rescues the young Phrixos from sacrifice, although he must have been at least a background presence in the *Children of Aleos*, to which we will return in connection with Euripides' *Auge*, and in the *Amphitryon*. It is, however, above all the extant *Women of Trachis* that provides our most complete account of the hero's death, while a brief appearance in the *Philoktetes* offers a rare glimpse of Herakles the god.

Women of Trachis

Some commentators have placed the *Women of Trachis* early in Sophokles' career, in the 450s BC, but we do not have the evidence to establish a date with any certainty. The play is called after its chorus, women of the central Greek city of Trachis, to which Herakles has been exiled after his murder of Iphitos. It tells how Deianeira hears news of Herakles' sack of the Euboian city of Oichalia, but, on discovering that he is bringing home Eurytos' daughter Iole as a concubine, she recalls the 'love potion' she had received from Nessos and determines to use it on her husband. She sends a tunic impregnated with the centaur's blood to Herakles, who is celebrating his victory with a great sacrifice on Kenaion, the north-western headland of Euboia. The tunic causes him such great agony that he kills the herald Lichas who had delivered it, before being carried back to Trachis, where Deianeira has meanwhile discovered her mistake and committed suicide. The play ends with Hyllos reluctantly agreeing to carry out his father's wishes, that he should marry Iole and place Herakles on a pyre to die on the summit of the nearby Mount Oita.

As is the case with most tragedies, the story was not new, but Sophokles transformed it in a number of ways. The most immediately striking thing about the play is its treatment of Deianeira. She could easily have been por-trayed unsympathetically, like the Klytamnestra of Aeschylus' *Agamemnon*, who reacts to a similar predicament by murdering both her errant husband and the concubine he has brought home. Deianeira's very name means 'man-slayer', and scholars have suggested that there was an alternative tra-dition to the one that involves Nessos, in which her murder of Herakles was deliberate. As we have seen (pp. 76–7), we can trace the tale of Herakles' encounter with Nessos back as far as the seventh century BC in literature, and possibly even earlier in art, but the sixth-century *Catalogue of Women* makes no mention of Nessos, and may imply that the poisoned tunic was entirely Deianeira's idea. Apart from this there is some small support for the idea of an independently minded Deianeira in Bakchylides 5, an Olym-pic victory ode of 476 BC, which reports an encounter between Herakles, in the Underworld on his way to fetch Kerberos, and the shade of Deianeira's brother Meleager. In the course of their conversation, Meleager tells the story of his own death and Deianeira is referred to as a potential wife for Herakles, 'equal to you (Meleager) in stature' (l.168). The comparison of brother and sister here has been taken to indicate a feisty Deianeira, while recollection of Meleager's murder by their mother, Althaia, might point to a dangerous ruthlessness in the family's women-folk. One could also adduce Apollodoros' statement (1.8.1) that Deianeira 'drove a chariot and trained in the arts of war', a description which some have linked with the Deianeira who appears holding the reins of the chariot in one or two early vase-paint-ings of the Nessos episode.[2]

Sophokles' audience, therefore, may not have known which kind of a Deianeira to expect. From the very outset of the play, however, her character is established as essentially passive and easily frightened, with her account of rescue from marriage to Acheloos (pp. 74–5) and a scene-setting lament for her absent husband; sympathy is elicited for a dutiful wife left at home worrying, and the audience is primed to see the rest of the story from Deianeira's point of view. She has apparently been quite tolerant of Herakles' infidelities in the past, and expresses remarkable forebearance in the current situation (ll.443–8):

> DEIANEIRA: Love rules even the gods however he likes, and me too, so why not another woman such as I? So I am crazy if I throw any blame upon my husband, seized by this sickness, or upon the woman, accessory to something which is no disgrace and no reproach to me.

Once she is alone with the chorus, however, Deianeira cannot tolerate the prospect of having Iole actually in the house, although she continues to regard Herakles as in the grip of a disease rather than being angry with him (ll.536–53).

Her account of how she came by the love-charm with which she proposes to win Herakles back is detailed (ll.555–81), the narrative of events at the river Euenos making it very clear that Nessos is to blame for the imminent tragedy. Deianeira's lack of malice aforethought is further emphasized by her immediate horror and acceptance of the truth when she discovers the effect the potion has had on a piece of wool (ll.663–730); she clearly regards herself as guilty, however, and remains silent in the face of Hyllos' bitter denunciation as he recounts Herakles' suffering (ll.734–820). As is conventional in Greek tragedy, Deianeira's suicide occurs off-stage, but it is reported in heart-rending detail by the Nurse (ll.899–946). The location of the suicide on the marital bed, which Deianeira takes care to make up, both recalls her previously happy relationship with Herakles and underlines the perversion of her role as wife. This echoes a theme already apparent in the centrality to the plot of the tunic, a garment quite properly woven by the good woman of a well-run household, but put to such improper use. Deianeira's choice of death by stabbing with a 'two-edged sword' (l.930), rather than the hanging more usually adopted by women in tragedy, further subverts her femininity, but also leaves the audience with the image of a much more resolute figure than the one who opens the play.[3]

Allied to the issue of Deianeira's role in his death is the question of Herakles' motivation for the attack on Oichalia. This element of the story, too, has some precedent in archaic tradition, as does the murder of Iphitos, although the two are never explicitly linked as they are in the herald Lichas' tale in the play. Already in the *Odyssey* (21.11–41) we hear that Iphitos met his death when he was staying as a guest in Herakles' house, on account of some stolen horses he had retrieved on an expedition to Messene with Odysseus; Herakles' motive is not spelt out, but he is said to have kept the horses, the impiety of the murder is stressed, and the obvious inference is that he killed Iphitos in the ignoble pursuit of gain. A little later than the *Odyssey*, Herakles' quarrel with Eurytos and his subsequent attack on the city must have been the subject of Kreophylos' *Capture of Oichalia*. Very little of this survives, but one line (fr. 1 W) is addressed by Herakles to Iole, and according to Kallimachos (*Epigramme* 6.2–3 Pfeiffer) the poem cele-brated 'what Eurytos suffered and fair-haired Iole', which strongly suggests that the girl was central to the story. Iole's role as motivating factor is con-firmed in a fragment of the *Catalogue of Women* (fr. 26.29–33 MW), which lists Eurytos' four sons, including Iphitos, 'and after these he begat fair-haired Iole, on whose account the son of Amphitryon [. . .] Oichalia'; a few words are missing here, but the crucial point is clear. A version of the story involving Iole is also attested a little earlier by a Corinthian krater of c.600 BC (Louvre E632), on which Herakles reclines in the company of Eurytos, Iphitos and four other brothers, with Iole standing between the couches of Herakles and her father (all figures are named); this scene would have to be set at a stage in the story before Iphitos' death, and while relations between Eurytos and Herakles were still friendly.

A further strand to the story, not fully elucidated until Apollodoros (2.6.1), tells of an archery contest for Iole's hand in marriage, which Herakles won, but the family refused to let him claim his prize. That Eurytos' skill with the bow was on a par with that of Herakles is alluded to in the *Odyssey*, where Eurytos is said to have been killed by Apollo for challenging him to an archery contest (8.223–8), but the contest for Iole is not attested until c.500 BC, when it appears on a handful of late archaic Attic vases. The earliest of these is a black-figure amphora attributed to the Sappho Painter (Madrid 10916), which shows a distraught Eurytos trying to prevent Herakles from shooting an arrow at his son Antiphonos, while two other sons lie dead or dying at his feet; to the far right, Iole stands beside a target from which five arrows protrude.

The audience's attention is drawn to the question of Herakles' absence by the multiple explanations offered in the early part of the play, which cumu-latively present Herakles in a less than favourable light. Hyllos knows of Herakles' enslavement to Omphale and the war against Eurytos (ll.69–75), but not of the causes. Lichas cleverly spins all the elements into a single train of cause and effect (ll.248–90) in which the initial offence was not Herakles', but that of Eurytos and his sons, who denigrated his prowess at archery when he was a guest in their house, and subsequently threw him out of a banquet when he was drunk; it was in revenge for this insult that Herakles murdered Iphitos, and for his consequent period of slavery to

Omphale that he sacked Oichalia. Given the tradition we have outlined, the audience would probably have recognized Lichas' tale quite readily as false, though including some true details and others, like the mention of a falling out over archery, which contain a distorted reference to events with which the audience might have been familiar. The Messenger, however, quickly dismantles this tidy tale (ll.351–74), labelling Iphitos' demise uncompromisingly as 'death by hurling' (l.357), and making Herakles' sole motivation for the war the fact that Eurytos had refused his request for Iole as a concubine. This presents both events in the worst possible light, and further condemnation can be found even in Deianeira's loving references, which indicate that Herakles is hardly the ideal husband: he never sees his children (ll.31–3), he has had countless lovers (ll.459–60), and of course he is now threatening the stability of the household by introducing a second 'wife' (ll.427–9 and 536–42).

The focus of the play finally shifts from Deianeira and Trachis with Hyllos' report of events at Cape Kenaion, where Herakles was making thank-offerings to Zeus when Lichas arrived with the tunic (ll.749–812). Hyllos' description of the poison's effect once activated by the heat of the sacrificial fire is horrifying (ll.767–71):

> HYLLOS: . . . sweat broke out on his skin and the tunic clung to his sides, fitting close to his whole body, as though moulded by a sculptor; a convulsive pain bit into his bones; then a poison consumed him like that of some hateful, murderous viper.

The audience's sympathy for Herakles may be tempered, however, by his violent treatment of Lichas, who is on this occasion quite blameless (ll.779–82):

> HYLLOS: Seizing him at the turn of the ankle-joint, he hurled him onto a rock washed on both sides by the sea; the middle of his head was broken in pieces, and white marrow mixed with blood dribbled out of his hair.

Altogether, by the time Herakles finally makes his entrance at line 971, the audience is expecting quite a brutish figure, and the hero does little to soften his image in the protracted final scene. His physical torment is kept constantly in view in the text, his current state sadly contrasted to the former glorious achievements of his labours. Audience sympathy is again likely to be tempered, however, by Herakles' attitude towards those around him. The moment he learns that Deianeira, against whom he has been threatening bitter revenge, had acted in error, he completely loses interest in her. He assumes that his mother and other sons are on hand in Trachis, apparently unaware that they live elsewhere (ll.1146–54), a detail that corroborates Deianeira's account of his detachment from his family. And lastly the demands he makes of Hyllos are both unreasonable and hedged around with emotional blackmail: Hyllos is to place Herakles on a pyre on Mount Oita and light it, thus killing him and incurring the blood-guilt of patricide, or else he will be cursed (ll.1193–1202); then he is to marry Iole, a 'small thing' according to Herakles, or else lose his father's gratitude (ll.1221–9). Hyllos does in fact manage to negotiate his way out of lighting the pyre, but cannot avoid the latter request, despite the fact that he would 'rather die than live together with my worst enemy' (ll.1236–7).

Some commentators have accounted for Herakles' savagery during the time-span of the play as the flip side of his former civilizing role in ridding the world of monsters, itself the product of a violent nature. Others have suggested that Herakles should be understood as acting like the god he will become, and in particular like his father Zeus, in his selfish high-handed-ness and lack of interest in ordinary human concerns. An ancient audience may indeed have been more receptive to such ideas than a modern one, but it is clear from the reactions of the other characters that Sophokles' Herakles would have struck a fifth-century Athenian as at best ambiguous, perhaps even repellent.

Three other aspects which deserve mention even in such a brief account of the play as this are the division of parts amongst the three actors, the role of the Zeus, and the implications of the final scene. Firstly, it is clear from the combinations of characters who appear on stage at any one time that Deianeira and Herakles must have been played by the same actor. This would have made the play extraordinarily demanding for the protagonist, who would have spoken over 40 per cent of the play's 1,278 lines, and have had to switch between such very contrasting roles. The fact that Deianeira and Herakles never actually meet, despite the expectation of a meeting in a 'home-coming' story like this, and that there is an abrupt shift in the play's focus from the one figure to the other, has sometimes been regarded as a weakness, but it can equally well be understood as a deliberate reflection of the breakdown in the main characters' relationship.

Secondly, Zeus is prominent in the play – he is referred to more than thirty times – not only by virtue of being Herakles' father, and as recipient of Herakles' sacrifices at Kenaion, but also as the ultimate source of divine authority. It is no accident, therefore, that the written oracle which Her-akles left with Deianeira before he went away is said to have come from Dodona, a sanctuary of Zeus, rather than the more usual source of tragic oracles, Apollo's Delphi. This first oracle specifies that at the end of the fif-teen-month period for which Herakles has been absent he will find rest from his labours. Deianeira has evidently been worried by the possibility that this might mean Herakles will die (ll.46–8, 79–82 and 155–74), but fails to take it into consideration when making her fateful decision to send the tunic. Only when he is dying does Herakles himself finally understand both this and another oracle revealed to him by Zeus, which had foretold that his death would be brought about by one already dead, i.e. Nessos (ll.1159–73). The note of fatalism which these references to oracles impart is picked up by the very last line of the play (l.1278) – 'And nothing of this is not Zeus' – a reminder of the inescapability of divine will.

Finally, the end of the play has no *deus ex machina* to predict the future and therefore offer some lightening of the sombre mood. Whether or not the play alludes to Herakles' deification in other ways is a matter of debate, but the audience would certainly have known the tradition of a 'happy ending' for Herakles – as we shall see, the apotheosis story was widely known from at least 600 BC, and there was a cult on Mount Oita celebrating Herakles' resurrection from at least the sixth century (pp. 172–4 and 184–5). That the idea of Herakles' entry to Olympos was current specifically in fifth-century Athens can also be demonstrated by the appearance of his wedding to Hebe in contemporary vase-painting and on the comic stage, and by his status as a god in Attic cult (pp. 176–80).[4]

Philoktetes

The fact that Herakles in the end releases Hyllos from the obligation to light the pyre (*Women of Trachis* ll.1206–16) points to the tradition that this act was performed by Philoktetes, son of Poias, king of the neighbouring Thessalian city of Meliboia, who was rewarded by receiving Herakles' bow. This story underlies Sophokles' play *Philoktetes*, produced at the City Dionysia of 409 BC, a date which puts it very close to the end of Sophokles' career and almost certainly later than the *Women of Trachis*. The focus of the play is a later stage in Philoktetes' life, when he has spent ten years living in misery on the island of Lemnos, where he was abandoned by the Greeks on their way to Troy, disgusted by the incurable wound on his foot inflicted by the serpent guarding the sacred precinct of the goddess Chryse. The Greek army has now discovered, via the captured Trojan seer Helenos, that Troy will only fall with the help of Herakles' weapons, so Odysseus has come to Lemnos with Achilles' son Neoptolemos to fetch Philoktetes. The bow and arrows are referred to frequently throughout the play, as the object of Odysseus' mission and as the only means Philoktetes has had for acquiring food throughout his time on the island. Philoktetes makes explicit mention of how he came by them when begging that Neoptolemos will put him out of his misery by throwing him into the fire of Lemnos: 'I too once steeled myself to do this for the son of Zeus in return for these weapons which you are now holding' (ll.799–803). He calls the bow 'sacred' (ll.942–3), and addresses it as if it were a person, his companion in suffering (ll.1128–39).

These small reminders of Herakles foreshadow the appearance of Herakles himself on stage at the end of the play (ll.1409–51), where he fulfils the role of *deus ex machina*, solving the impasse the plot has reached by ordering Philoktetes to go to Troy, where he will be cured as well as winning glory. This is a very different Herakles from the suffering hero of the *Women of Trachis*: he is now a god, come from his 'heavenly seat' (ll.1413–14), who has won 'immortal *aretê*' by his great toils (ll.1418–20). There is perhaps reference to contemporary ritual practice, too, in Herakles' instruction that, after sacking Troy, Philoktetes should return home to Mount Oita and, 'whatever spoils you receive from this army, dedicate on my pyre a memorial of my bow' (ll.1431–3). And just in case the audience has forgotten Herakles' own connection with Troy, he remarks: 'for a second time the city will be destroyed by my bow' (ll.1439–40). Some commentators have suggested that Herakles here is in fact merely Odysseus in disguise (both parts would have been played by the same actor), cunningly playing on Philoktetes' longing for a father-figure. Most, however, see the intervention of the divine Herakles as re-asserting the value of collaborative action over individual honour, allowing Philoktetes to regain a place in society.[5]

EURIPIDES: MADNESS AND FAMILY VALUES

Three of Euripides' surviving tragedies feature Herakles as a major character, either on stage (*Alkestis* and *Herakles*) or as a pervading background presence (*Children of Herakles*). He also appeared in the lost *Auge*, the plot of which can be reconstructed with some confidence, and in the *Peirithous*, Euripides' authorship of which is disputed.

Alkestis

The *Alkestis* is one of Euripides' earliest plays, produced in 438 BC. We have also considered its dramatic setting on Herakles' way to tackle the mares of Diomedes (p. 40), and we will be returning to the central encounter between Herakles and Death (p. 120), but some comment on the hero's characterization is in order here. This is affected by the play's overall tone, which is a slightly uncomfortable mixture of the tragic and the comic, perhaps because it was produced as the fourth play in a tetralogy, in the place more often occupied by a satyr play after a trilogy of tragedies.

The overall story is certainly tragic, despite the happy ending, with much lamentation over Alkestis' untimely death and plenty of melancholy reflection on the consequences of bereavement for the family left behind. The theme of guest-friendship (*xenia*), too, is one which an ancient Greek audience would have taken seriously. While the situation may seem a little contrived to a modern audience, Admetos does in fact face a genuine dilemma when his old friend arrives just after Alkestis' death: should the demands of *xenia* take precedence over those of death ritual? His attempt to compromise, however, by entertaining Herakles in one part of the house out of earshot of the mourning in another, is comically doomed to failure, and provides the setting for Herakles to do a turn very much in his comic persona. A servant reports that he has never seen a worse guest, that Herakles is rude, greedy, drinking his wine unmixed, and singing out of tune (ll.750–60); Herakles himself then appears, clearly drunk, berating the servant for his solemn face and philosophizing in a maudlin fashion that drink and love are the only answer to human mortality (ll.773–802). When he finally discovers that the household's mourning is for Alkestis, however, rather than a mere formality for a stranger as Admetos has given him to understand, he quickly sobers up and sets out to tackle Death. When he reappears at the end of the play with the silent and veiled Alkestis, he prolongs the process of reunion with some typically tragic prevarication, and his rehabilitation as the heroic man of action is sealed by a hasty exit to 'go and perform the prescribed task for the royal son of Sthenelos' (ll.1149–50).[6]

Herakles

More clearly tragic is the eponymous hero of Euripides' *Herakles*, which was probably produced sometime between 425 and 416 BC. The play opens with Herakles' father Amphitryon, his wife Megara and three unnamed sons sitting as suppliants at an altar of Zeus the Saviour. Herakles himself is absent, engaged in his final labour in the Underworld, but presumed dead by Lykos, the new tyrant who has seized control of Thebes after killing Megara's father Kreon and is now attempting to put Herakles' children to death. The chorus of elderly Thebans can only protest feebly, and the family, having given up hope of rescue, have dressed themselves in funeral clothes when Herakles returns, reporting success in his mission to fetch Kerberos and explaining the delay in his return as due to his rescue of Theseus. Just when the day appears to have been saved, however, the goddesses Iris and Madness appear, on a mission from Hera to destroy Herakles' family, and a few lines later a Messenger reports the terrible effect of their intervention: in a fit of madness, Herakles has killed his wife and children, and only Amphitryon has escaped. Herakles' awakening from the sleep which follows his madness, to horrified realization of what he has done, is interrupted by the arrival of Theseus, who has come, too late, to help him fight against Lykos. Despite being a regular, mortal character, he performs something of the function of a *deus ex machina* in predicting that Herakles will be greatly honoured at Athens, where the hero reluctantly agrees to follow him into exile.

The story of Herakles' madness was not new, but Euripides' treatment of it is full of surprises. An ancient summary of the mid-sixth-century epic the *Kypria* includes the briefest mention of the story being told 'in a digression' by Nestor (*Argumentum* ll.28–9 *PEG*), and Pausanias (9.11.2) suggests that it was related by Stesichoros and Panyassis, while Pherekydes (fr. 14 F) gives the names of five boys 'thrown into the fire by their father'. None of these fragments is substantial enough to locate the story in relation to the rest of Herakles' career, but Diodoros (4.11.1–2) and Apollodoros (2.4.12) agree in placing it *before* his servitude to Eurystheus, and they may well be reflecting an older tradition. Placing Herakles' madness at the very *end* of the labours, however, allows Euripides to present Herakles at the height of his achievements, making his fall all the more dramatic. The figure of Lykos also appears to be an innovation on Euripides' part, although his persecution of Herakles' family is a motif borrowed from the *Children of Herakles* story.

Altogether, then, Euripides' audience would have been less easily able to predict the play's course than usual, and Amphitryon's prologue is restricted to a summary of the story so far, rather than forecasting events to come. A general knowledge of typical plots would lead one to anticipate Herakles' return in the nick of time, but Euripides confounds expectation with the swift despatch of Lykos only halfway through the play (ll.701–62). The madness story is then rather abruptly introduced by the dramatic entrance of Iris and Madness. This delegation of action to two minor deities adds a twist to the familiar motif of Hera's enmity, and the chorus' description of their appearance as 'above the house' (l.817) suggests that they are on top of the stage building, possibly 'flown in' by use of the crane. There is adaptation, too, of Athena's traditional role as Herakles' supporter when, according to the Messenger, she intervenes in Herakles' killing spree by hurling a boulder (ll.1002–6).[7]

Unlike the absent Herakles of the *Women of Trachis*, Euripides' hero is spoken of in very positive terms from the outset. Amphitryon presents the labours as the price Herakles, with proper filial piety, is prepared to pay to get him (Amphitryon) restored from exile to his home in Argos (ll.13–20). Both before and after his return, Herakles' exploits are explicitly characterized as making the world a more civilized place (ll.697–700):

CHORUS: But surpassing even his nobility of birth in virtue, he has made life calm for mortals by his labours, by destroying fearful beasts.

As Madness points out, Herakles' activities have benefited the gods, too (ll.851–3):

MADNESS: He has tamed the trackless land and savage sea, and single-handedly restored the gods' honours when they had been destroyed by sacrilegious men.

The point is further emphasized by three references to the Gigantomachy (ll.177–80, 1190–2, 1272), and Herakles is described no fewer than eight times as 'fair-conquering' (*kallinikos*), an adjective widely used as a cult title (p. 176). In particularly sharp contrast to Sophokles, Euripides presents Herakles as a family man who has an affectionate relationship with his wife and children. This is highlighted during the scene of Herakles' return, when he dismisses the labours as worthless in comparison to the protection of his family (ll.574–82), and when he is very gentle to the boys as they refuse to let go of his clothes, declaring that he will 'take them by the hand and lead these little boats, towing them like a ship; for I do not refuse the care of children' (ll.631–3). The image is sadly echoed at the very end of the play, when the devastated Herakles himself agrees to follow Theseus to Athens like a 'little boat' (l.1424).

This positive image of Herakles makes his downfall all the more shocking, and invites debate as to its causes. At a superficial level, the appalling turn of events is entirely governed by Hera's anger at Zeus' infidelity. As Iris presents the matter, Herakles must 'pay the penalty' in order that the proper precedence of gods over mortals be maintained (l.841–2), but Madness' reluctance to carry out the task demonstrates that it is not generally approved by the gods. The audience might very well sympathize, rather, with Herakles' own view of Hera (ll.1307–10):

HERAKLES: Would anyone pray to this sort of goddess? Out of jealousy because of a woman's bedding with Zeus, she has destroyed those who do good works for Greece and are not guilty of anything.

One ancient explanation, outlined in the *Problems* attributed to Aristotle (30.935a), attributes Herakles' frenzy to a fit of epilepsy, a disease supposed to be caused by an excess of black bile, and referred to in the Hippocratic *Diseases of Women* (7.23–4) as 'the Heraklean sickness'. Modern commentators have pointed out that violent strength is an inherent part of even the Euripidean Herakles' character, and suggested that it is almost inevitable that the monster-slayer's might should at some point be directed against innocent victims. Certainly we might criticize Herakles for the brutality of the action he plans against Lykos and his supporters (ll.565–73), and it is striking that the slaughter of his own sons seems to be justified by the delusion that they are Eurystheus' children (ll.970–1000). Lykos has already rehearsed the pragmatic justification for eliminating an enemy's child, i.e. because he might grow up to avenge his parents (ll.165–9), an idea which contributes to his tyrannical characterization. Herakles' madness, then, is shocking, but may well consist in a kind of optical delusion which deflects him into attacking the wrong targets, rather than in the killing *per se*; this is just the kind of misconception which constitutes the madness of Ajax in Sophokles' play of the same name and Pentheus in Euripides' *Bakchae*. In effect, Herakles accomplishes the threat which hangs over his family in the first half of the play, and the irony of the situation is heightened by the fact that the same actor would have played the parts of both Herakles and Lykos.[8]

The *Herakles* is typically Euripidean in problematizing other traditional elements, too. In an attempt to denigrate his achievements, Lykos calls into question the fact that Herakles uses a bow, 'most cowardly of weapons' (ll.160–1) rather than fighting with a sword and shield like a proper hoplite soldier. This passage, along with Amphitryon's defence of the weapon (ll.188–205) has prompted much discussion. It is true that other archers are regarded with suspicion in Greek literature, notably Pandaros in *Iliad* Book 5, but then it is prowess in archery which proves Odysseus' mettle in the *Odyssey*, and, as we have seen, it is Herakles' bow which will bring about the fall of Troy. The bow is foregrounded by its use in the killing of the children, and in Herakles' agonized musing towards the end of the play as to whether he should abandon the murderous weapon or keep it for the sake of the past glories it has achieved. Also highlighted is the issue of Herakles' double parentage. In the very first line of the play Amphitryon introduces himself as 'bed-partner of Zeus', apparently proud of the association, although he later denounces it in the face of Zeus' lack of assistance to the family (ll.339–47). Herakles himself blames Zeus for bringing Hera's hatred upon him, and quite daringly pronounces, 'I consider you (Amphitryon) to be my father, not Zeus' (1265).

The final scene of the play brings to the fore two other important issues, that of friendship and (again) Herakles' mortal or divine status; we will return to Herakles' contemplation of suicide in the next chapter (pp. 127–8). Friendship (*philia*) is a theme flagged up already in the prologue (ll.55–9), where Amphitryon muses that the family's plight has revealed their friends to be unreliable, and the motif continues right up to the very last line of the play, where the Chorus lament the loss of 'the greatest of friends' in Herakles. It is Herakles' relationship with Theseus, however, which particularly embodies the Greek ideal of reciprocal friendship, each helping the other in his hour of greatest need. Herakles greets Theseus on his entrance as 'my friend and relative' (l.1154), evoking both their blood relationship and the set of social obligations which bind them. Theseus expands on the theme when, intent on helping, he alludes to his own recent rescue from the land of the dead by Herakles and expresses contempt for fair-weather friends (ll.1220–5), and again when he concludes his offer of a home for Herakles in Athens 'for you are in need of friends at the moment' (l.1337). Herakles in turn declares, as he puts his arm round Theseus' neck for support, that they are a 'friendly pair' and that Theseus is 'the kind of man one should have as a friend' (ll.1403–4), before finally pronouncing that 'anyone who wants to have wealth or strength rather than good friends is a fool' (ll.1425–6).

Theseus' offer of a house and a share in his own wealth is already generous, but he forecasts even greater benefits (ll.1328–33):

> THESEUS: Everywhere in my land they have given me precincts; they shall be yours henceforth, and, while you live, they will be called by your name amongst mortals; when you are dead and have gone to Hades, the whole city of Athens will honour you, with sacrifices (*thusiai*) and monuments in stone.

This is clearly an aetiology, of a kind common in Euripides, designed to explain why real-life Athenians of Euripides' day worshipped Herakles. It is noteworthy that Theseus here makes no mention of Herakles' deification, and quite explicitly places him after his death in the Underworld. As we saw in the case of the *Women of Trachis*, however, there is no question but that the audience was aware of the apotheosis story, and the kind of sacrifices Theseus is promising are the *thusiai* regularly offered to the gods (pp. 174–5). There is also indirect reference to Herakles' happy eventual fate in the aged Chorus' hymn to youth halfway through the play, particularly in their idea that the gods ought to reward men by granting them 'a second youth (*hêbê*) as a clear mark of their virtue (*aretê*)' (ll.655–64).[9]

Children of Herakles

In Euripides' earlier play the *Children of Herakles*, produced c.430 BC, Theseus' role as embodiment of the civilized values of classical Athens is taken by his son Demophon. The play is set after Herakles' death, when his surviving children have been forced to travel all over Greece in search of sanctuary from their father's old enemy Eurystheus, with only the now elderly Alkmene and Iolaos to accompany them. As in the *Herakles*, the opening scene finds the family gathered at an altar of Zeus, this time in the Attic deme of Marathon, an area where Herakles' cult was particularly important (pp. 179–80). The main point of the play seems to be promotion of Athens' self-image as stalwart defender of suppliants, a theme seen elsewhere in tragedy in the city's provision of sanctuary for the Seven against Thebes, Oedipus and Medea. Iolaos is able to draw on this reputation in support of the case he puts to Demophon (ll.181–231), as well as alluding to Herakles' rescue of Theseus from the Underworld and spelling out the precise family relationship between the two – both are great-grandsons of Pelops via their mothers, making them second cousins. Herakles' own reputation is at stake in the next stage of the plot, when Demophon discovers an oracle predicting that Eurystheus' army will only be defeated if a maiden from a noble family is sacrificed to Demeter: an unnamed daughter of Herakles shows herself to be 'worthy of her father, worthy of her noble birth' (l.626–7) in volunteering to die for the good of the community.

The theme of old age versus youth is very apparent throughout the play, with the chorus, Alkmene and Iolaos (despite being Alkmene's grandson) all explicitly characterized as aged, and an almost comic exchange ensues between Iolaos and the Servant when the former decides to take to the battlefield, with much questioning of his ability to fight (ll.680–747). Herakles' current status as Youth's husband might already be in some of the audience's minds by the time the chorus says to Iolaos, 'There is no way you will ever get youth (*hêbê*) back again' (ll.707–8), a line which neatly prepares the way for news of Iolaos' rejuvenation (l.796). The Messenger contrasts Eurystheus' cowardice with the bravery of Hyllos, who has arrived with an army, before relating the miracle: in answer to Iolaos' prayers, Herakles and Hebe appeared as stars over his chariot, and Iolaos himself emerged from the gloom in 'youthful (*hêbêtes*) shape' (ll.849–58). Herakles' fate is spelt out by the chorus a few lines later (ll.910–18), when they reassure Alkmene that, rather than having gone to Hades on his death, her son is 'established in heaven' where he 'touches Hebe's bed of love in a golden chamber'.

The play does not end on this positive note, however, as an extraordinary exchange between Alkmene and the captured Eurystheus recalls Herakles' servitude. Alkmene rails at Eurystheus for having sent her son off 'to destroy hydras and lions' (l.950) and even down to Hades (l.949), while a surprisingly sympathetic Eurystheus explains that he had no choice in the matter, but 'Hera made me suffer this illness' (l.990). Alkmene's vindictive insistence that Eurystheus be put to death, flouting Athenian customs concerning the treatment of prisoners of war, is every bit as problematic as the issues raised by the character of Herakles himself in the other tragedies we have considered.[10]

Auge

Probably the latest of Euripides' plays to feature Herakles was the *Auge*, of which we have an outline of the plot and some thirty or so lines preserved (frs 264a–281 *TrGF*). The tradition Euripides was drawing on dates back at least as far as the *Catalogue of Women*, of which a substantial fragment (fr.165 MW) tells how Auge, adopted daughter of king Teuthras of Mysia, was impregnated by Herakles on his way to Troy and bore Telephos, future king of the Mysians. Around 500 BC Hekataios (*FGrH* 1F29) told a slightly different story, in which Herakles met Auge when he came to Tegea, where she was daughter of king Aleos; when she gave birth, Aleos cast her and the baby out to sea in a chest, which eventually washed up in Mysia, where she married Teuthras. Tegea remains the location of Herakles' meeting with Auge in all other extant versions, but there is some variation in Aleos' actions.

The story was the subject of Sophokles' *Children of Aleos* (frs 77–91 *TrGF*), the first play in a whole trilogy concerning Telephos, the plot of which can be tentatively reconstructed with the help of a passage from *Odysseus Against the Treachery of Palamedes* (14–16), a speech by the fourth-century rhetorician Alkidamas. According to this, Aleos is informed by an oracle that a child of Auge will cause the death of her brothers, so he makes her a priestess of Athena; she is nonetheless made pregnant by Herakles, and subsequently both she and the baby only escape a death sentence when Nauplios, the ferryman deputed to drown them, instead takes them to Mysia and sells them to Teuthras, who marries Auge and adopts Telephos. The usual conventions of tragic plotting would suggest that the original oracle was eventually fulfilled despite Aleos' attempts to circumvent it, and a much later source (Hyginus, *Fabula* 244) does mention that Telephos killed his uncles, presumably once he had reached adulthood. The action of Sophokles' play could only have covered part of the extensive time-frame involved, the title and extant fragments suggesting that it treated Telephos' return, in which case Herakles probably did not actually appear on stage.

Euripides' version, however, focused closely on Auge's plight and Herakles was certainly amongst the *dramatis personae*. The play would have begun with a prologue outlining preceding events, which do not seem to have included any oracle: Auge had been performing a night-time ritual for Athena at a spring near the temple when Herakles raped her while drunk, leaving behind a ring; the birth of the resulting baby has now brought pollution to the temple, where the child is concealed. The action then would have centred on Aleos' search for the cause of the pollution, discovery and exposure of the baby and Auge's condemnation to death. Herakles happens to return to the area, finds the child being suckled by a deer and, recognizing the ring which Auge has left with him, realizes what must have happened. Herakles is repentant and persuades Aleos to relent, and the play may well have ended with a god instructing Auge to take the child to Mysia where they will both find sanctuary with Teuthras.

The plot has similarities to Euripides' *Ion*, where the eponymous hero is the result of a god's rape of a mortal, and metrical characteristics of both plays suggest a date late in Euripides' career, between 414 and his death in 406 BC. The surviving lines give some indication of its melodramatic and romantic nature, including a statement from one character concerning the power of Love (fr. 269):

> Anyone who does not judge Eros to be a great god and highest of all powers is either stupid or, being inexperienced in his pleasures, does not know mankind's greatest god.

Herakles himself is presented in a remarkably positive light. Two lines probably spoken by him suggest that he treats the baby affectionately, much as the family man of Euripides' *Herakles* would have done (frs 272–272a): 'Who does not delight in childish playthings?', 'I'm playing; I always love a change from my toils.' More striking still is the fact that Herakles explicitly refers to the rape as wrongdoing, even if he does resort to the perennial excuse of drunkenness (fr. 272b): 'The wine drove me out of my senses; I admit that I did you an injustice, but the injustice was not intentional.'[11]

Peirithous

Finally, the *Peirithous* is of uncertain date. Its authorship is disputed, with some scholars both ancient and modern attributing it to the late fifth-century Kritias, although there is a fairly strong case for regarding it as Euripides'. More of this play survives than of the *Auge*, including a hypothesis (plot summary), some forty lines quoted by later authors, and around ninety lines, many incomplete, preserved on papyri (presented in *TrGF* as 'Critias' frs 1–14). The action is not entirely easy to reconstruct, however, and resonances with Aristophanes' *Frogs* have suggested to some that it was a satyr play rather than a tragedy, or perhaps a hybrid like Euripides' *Alkestis*.

The play is set in the Underworld and probably opened with Peirithous, already chained up in punishment for his presumption in attempting to abduct Persephone, in conversation with Theseus, who has stayed with him voluntarily. After the entry of the chorus Herakles would have arrived on the scene, calmly explaining to Hades' gatekeeper Aiakos that he has come in search of Kerberos, at Eurystheus' command. An exchange between Herakles and Peirithous about the latter's predicament seems to have followed, and a dialogue in which Herakles declines Theseus' offer of help in capturing Kerberos, since any assistance would diminish his achievement and make Eurystheus discount the labour. This conversation may have continued with Theseus requesting Herakles' help for himself and his friend. Later it is likely that an off-stage fight between Herakles and Kerberos was reported and either Hades himself or Persephone may have appeared to grant Theseus' and Peirithous' release, but we have no detail on how these latter stages of the story were dramatized. Friendship was clearly an important theme of the play, with Peirithous describing Theseus as joined to him 'in the unforged fetters of respect' (fr. 6), and Theseus in return declaring it shameful 'to betray a faithful man and friend who has been hostilely seized' (fr. 7.6–7). Also reminiscent of Euripides' *Herakles* and *Children of Herakles* is a reference to Theseus and Athens being 'always an ally for the unfortunate' (fr. 7.8–10).

VISUAL REFLECTIONS OF TRAGEDY

Herakles' death was never represented in archaic art, which focused rather on his apotheosis as we shall see (pp. 173–4), but it is alluded to on a small handful of classical red-figure vases. An intriguing image on an Attic pelike of c.420 BC, in the manner of the Washing Painter (London E370), is sometimes interpreted as the handing over of the poisoned tunic: on one side, a nude male figure is holding out a lionskin to a woman who is proffering a folded garment in return; on the other side stands a woman whose outstretched hand suggests she is giving orders. While not corresponding precisely to Sophokles' plot, this would retain the idea of Deianeira sending the tunic to Herakles via an intermediary, although some have preferred to identify the dominant woman as Omphale. Two or three Attic images dating from c.460–450 BC represent Herakles on his funerary pyre at a stage in the story between Sophokles' two plays. The best preserved is a psykter (New York, private collection) on which a still living Herakles reclines on his lionskin, spread on top of a pile of wood and foliage, and hands his bow and quiver over to a young man who is presumably Philoktetes. In the later fifth and early fourth centuries the pyre appears on three or four Attic and South Italian vases without Herakles, who appears in an upper register flying heavenward in a chariot driven by Athena – as this scene may be linked with a satyr play, we will return to it in the next chapter (pp. 110–11).[12]

One or two foreshadowings of the Euripidean Herakles can be found in classical vase-painting. The image of Herakles the family man can be seen, for example, some fifty years earlier than Euripides on an Attic red-figure pelike by the Siren Painter, c.480 BC (Louvre G229), on which all the figures are named by inscriptions. Here Herakles has his usual lionskin, club and bow, but is domesticated by wearing the standard male garb of chiton and full-length himation; the infant Hyllos, held on Deianeira's lap, reaches out towards Herakles, while Deianeira's own father Oineus looks on, balancing the watching Athena. A similar desire to humanize the great hero is also apparent in scenes depicting the young Herakles and his brother Iphikles attending music lessons, just like good Athenian boys, as on a red-figure skyphos by the Pistoxenos Painter, c.470 BC (Schwerin KG 708).

One image which may be more directly connected with Euripides' *Herakles* is the much-debated scene on a Paestan krater of c.340 BC signed by the painter Asteas (Figure 3.1). This shows Herakles about to throw an infant onto a bonfire of household furniture, while Megara runs away to the right; looking down from a colonnade above are a number of figures, including Mania, 'Madness' herself, with a whip in her hand, to the far left. This would have to have been inspired by a provincial revival of Euripides' play, some seventy to eighty years later than the original Athenian production, and some argue that it cannot be an illustration of the drama: there is no explicit indication of staging or costume, the action depicted is only reported in the play rather than being staged, Euripides' Messenger describes Herakles as killing the children with arrows rather than burning them, and the goddess involved is called Lyssa in Euripides rather than Mania. However, the architectural detail on the vase is at least suggestive of a fourth-century theatre set, and the differences could be accounted for by the painter not remembering details exactly (he is unlikely to have had

Figure 3.1 Herakles' madness. South Italian (Paestan) red-figure bell krater signed by the painter Asteas, c.340 BC (Madrid 11094). Inscribed figures: Herakles, Megara; (on upper level) Mania (Madness), Iolaos, Alkmene. Photo: Museo Arqueológico Nacional, Madrid.

access to a script), or simply using artistic licence in translating the spoken word to visual form. I would not entirely dismiss the possibility of a connection here, then, though the sceptics may be right in seeing this simply as an illustration of the myth rather than of a particular play. Half a dozen other South Italian vases, all dating c.340–320 BC, include Megara and two or three children alongside other traditional occupants of the Underworld, sometimes depicting one or more of the children wearing a bandage, as though now recovering from the mortal wounds inflicted by their father.[13]

ROMAN ADAPTATIONS

Ovid

The tragic Hercules of Latin literature appears first in two works by Ovid, both clearly indebted to Sophokles' *Women of Trachis*. The first is *Heroides* 9, one of a set of letters purporting to be from mythological heroines to their more or less feckless lovers, probably written fairly early in Ovid's career between around 25 and 16 BC. Deianira writes to Hercules complaining that the great conquerer of Oechalia has himself been conquered by his love for Iole, the latest in a succession of infidelities to have brought the hero into disrepute. The premise is humorous, and Ovid dwells on the incongruous image of Hercules enslaved to Omphale, dressed in her clothes and reduced to working wool while telling of his former monster-slaying exploits. The story remains essentially tragic, however, the letter ending with Deianira receiving news of Hercules' impending death and resolving to die in a manner befitting Hercules' wife and Meleager's sister. In a number of places Ovid provides a kind of commentary on Sophokles' play by a shift of emphasis, such as Deianira's description of Iole parading proudly through the city, perhaps soon to usurp her own position as Hercules' wife (ll.125–34), which is a more explicit expression of the Sophoklean heroine's fears.[14]

A more straightforward narrative appears in Ovid's *Metamorphoses*. Completed by AD 8, this fifteen-book epic begins with the creation of the universe and proceeds through practically the whole of Greek and Roman myth, telling stories loosely linked by the theme of transformation. As we have already seen (pp. 74–5), Hercules' battles with the shape-shifting Achelous and Periclymenus are included, but the story of Hercules' death is made germane by the 'metamorphosis' involved in his deification (9.101–273). This follows Sophokles' version of the Nessos story quite closely, but with added emphasis on Hercules' foolhardiness in leaping into the river without pausing to locate the safest crossing point. Ovid's Deianira explicitly compares herself to her brother Meleager when deciding to undertake such a daring deed as administering the 'love charm', although in fact her task is made even easier than that of Sophokles' heroine by the fact that Nessus has given her his own garment ready-soaked in blood. The effect of the poison is described in terms which verge on the melodramatic (ll.166–71):

> Without delay he tried to tear off the death-bearing garment: wherever it was pulled away, it in turn pulled away his skin, and, hideous to tell, it either stuck to his limbs despite all attempts to remove it, or it laid bare the huge bones in his lacerated body. His blood, just as a blade dipped in a cold tank will burn white-hot, hissed and boiled with the fiery poison.

A link with the transformation theme is created by Ovid's version of Lichas' death, which has the herald turning to stone as he hurtles through the air, and landing in the Euboean sea as a reef.

In order to reach Hercules' own metamorphosis, and justify the inclusion of the story, Ovid has to go beyond the point where *Women of Trachis* ends. Hercules on the pyre is described as being like a banqueter, reclining on his lionskin 'amongst the full winecups, crowned with garlands' (l.238), an image that immediately evokes the hero of comedy and of ritual. Also potentially comic is the pompous speech made by Jupiter explaining Hercules' fate, which concludes with a remark clearly aimed at Juno (ll.256–8):

> But if there is anyone, anyone at all, who perhaps will be aggrieved by Hercules as a god, who begrudges the rewards given, he will know that Hercules has deserved the gift, and will unwillingly approve.

Hercules is duly divested of his mortal elements by the fire, rejuvenated and swept up to the heavens. Ovid does not finish here, but continues as if he is going to relate the *Children of Herakles* story (ll.273–5), and indeed he does briefly tell of Iolaus' rejuvenation by Hebe (ll.397–401). In between, however, there is a lengthy digression in which Alcmena tells the tale of Hercules' birth, the metamorphosis involved being that of her maid-servant Galinthis, who tricked the birth-goddess Lucina into letting the delivery go ahead – a role celebrated in ritual at Thebes (p. 182) – and was turned into a weasel as her punishment. In response to this story, Iole recounts her sister Dryope's transformation into an oak tree.

Seneca

In contrast to Ovid's relatively light-hearted treatments, the *Hercules Furens* of Seneca the Younger is formally a tragedy, freely adapted from Euripides' *Herakles*. Also attributed to Seneca, though now generally thought to be by an imitator, is the *Hercules Oetaeus*, an adaptation of Sophokles' *Women of Trachis*. The former may have been written when Seneca was acting as tutor to Nero (AD 50–4) or when he served as a political advisor to the young emperor (AD 54–62), and is informed by the same Stoic ideas as his philosophical writings. We will return to Herakles as incarnation of Stoic values in the next chapter (pp. 127–8), but particularly relevant are Seneca's treatises *On Anger, On Clemency*, and *On the Brevity of Life* which discuss the merits of self-control, moderate government and fortitude in the face of death, major themes of the dramas. There is some debate as to whether Seneca's plays were actually intended for the theatre, for performance in private homes by a single speaker, or simply to be read, as a vehicle for Stoic teaching – there is no positive evidence that any of his tragedies was ever staged, though recent discussions make a plausible case for performance of some sort.[15]

The *Hercules Furens* differs from Euripides' *Herakles* in a number of ways, most significantly in its presentation of the central madness scene. Rather than having divine external agents appearing on stage just prior to the actual madness happening behind the scenes, Seneca shows Hercules descending into madness before our very eyes. There is still a strong divine element, since, in another radical departure from Euripides, Juno delivers a lengthy prologue, in which she invokes the assistance of a whole team of suitable personifications – Discord, Crime, Impiety, Error and Madness (ll.92–9). The absence of gods from the scene itself, however, combines with the audience's direct view of Hercules' actions to create the impression of a frightening psychological disintegration. The killing still seems to be performed off-stage, since Amphitryon's comments amount to a narration of the events not unlike a messenger speech, though in short sections interspersed with cries from Hercules and Megara. Here Hercules imagines he is killing the children of Lycus, rather than Eurystheus, and their deaths are even more gory and melodramatic than those described by Euripides (ll.1002–7):

> AMPHITRYON: See how he pleads with pitiful voice, holding out winsome hands to his father's knees – impious crime, grim and terrible to behold! Hercules has seized the pleading boy in his right hand and turning him twice, three times, has thrown him; his head has crashed, the house is drenched with scattered brains.

Another important change in emphasis from Euripides' version is signalled by the fact that Theseus accompanies Hercules on his return to Thebes, direct from Hades, and they seem to have Cerberus with them. Theseus is thus available to conduct a lengthy conversation with Amphitryon while Hercules is dealing with Lycus off-stage (ll.640–829), during which time he gives a very colourful description of the Underworld, and indeed the labour (p. 48). The extension here is compensated for by truncation of the final scene, which makes much less of the role of Theseus and Athens, playing to a Roman rather than an Athenian audience: it is Amphitryon who persuades Hercules not to commit suicide, and while Theseus still ends up leading Hercules away, there is no indication of the reception the Athenians will give him. Although the theme of reciprocal friendship is still present, then, it is subordinated to the theme of Hades' power, over which Hercules' triumph is only temporary as far as the play is concerned, and altogether the play ends on a less hopeful note than Euripides'.

The *Hercules Oetaeus* likewise makes significant changes to its model. Whereas Sophokles' *Women of Trachis* immediately invites sympathy with Deianeira and postpones Herakles' entry until the final quarter of the play, here the action in Trachis is prefaced by a prologue spoken by Hercules (ll.1–103), apparently on his way to Cape Cenaeum. This makes our first sight of Hercules that of the victorious hero, as he lists many of his labours and other monster-slaying activities in support of his claim to a place in the heavens. We do not see Hercules again until l.1131, now reduced to agony by the poisoned tunic, but this is only just beyond the halfway-point of the extravagantly long play, and the action continues well past Sophokles' ending to encompass both Hercules' death and his apotheosis. The whole structure of the play thus presents the story in a more positive light than Sophokles' version.

There are a number of changes to individual characters' roles, too. Lichas is reduced to a non-speaking part, and the false-reporting of Sophokles' herald is in any case precluded by the early appearance of Iole alongside other captive Oechalian women, who here function as an extra chorus, lamenting their unhappy fate. Iole, no longer silent, makes it explicit that the sack of her city was caused by her own beauty, and her father's refusal of Hercules' suit (ll.219–23). Seneca's Deianira, far from being timid or sympathetic, is initially mad with anger, threatening to kill Iole and any unborn child, as well as Hercules himself. Against this background her use of Nessus' blood perhaps seems less innocent, although she tells the same story as Sophokles' heroine about her acquisition of the 'love charm', and appears genuinely horrified on discovering its effects. Her suicide is here prefaced by Hyllus' entrance with news of Hercules' suffering, and attempts by Hyllus and the Nurse to dissuade her from such a course of action, on the grounds that she is not really guilty. Hercules' on-stage suffering is now witnessed by his mother, Alcmena, as well as Hyllus, and her presence prompts a striking insult to his arch-enemy Juno: 'By my virtue I have made my step-mother seem the concubine' (ll.1499–500) while Alcmena is worthy to be called Jupiter's wife.

Hercules' death on the pyre is reported by none other than Philoctetes, who includes some splendid detail of the hero's bravery and Stoic refusal to give way to emotion (ll.1740–6):

> PHILOCTETES: Placed amidst heat and threatening flames, unmoved, unshaken, turning his burning limbs to neither side, he encourages, instructs, administers though all on fire. To all his servants he gives a brave heart; you would think him on fire to burn. The whole crowd is stunned, the flames are scarcely believable, so calm is his brow, such majesty does the man have.

In due course Alcmena reappears with her son's ashes, giving vent to the lamentation which, according to Philoctetes, Hercules had forbidden while he was on the pyre. An almost comic note is sounded by the sudden interruption of Hercules' disembodied voice bidding her forebear her wailing now that he has attained a place in heaven (ll.1940–3), followed by a brief appearance in which he assures her that 'once again I, Alcides, have conquered the realms below' (l.1976). By way of postscript, Alcmena announces her intention to proclaim Hercules 'a new divinity to be added to the temples' of Thebes (ll.1980–1), to which the Chorus adds a prayer that Hercules will defend them against any strange monster that should threaten them.[16]

Pantomime and 'fatal charades'

Another performance genre in which the tragic Herakles seems to have been popular in the Roman imperial period is pantomime. We have no surviving scripts for these entertainments, but various references suggest that they usually consisted of a solo dancer, accompanied by one or more singers and instrumentalists, performing a mythological story with much athleticism and lavish spectacle. The *Madness of Hercules* was a favourite theme, and it evidently provided scope for bravura performances: Macrobius (*Saturnalia* 2.7.16–17) relates an anecdote about Pylades, a freedman of Augustus and well-known pantomime dancer, getting so carried away by the part that he shot arrows into the audience. Playing the part of the mad Hercules is also supposed to have been one of the emperor Nero's theatrical eccentricities (Suetonius, *Nero* 21):

> He sang tragedies representing heroes and gods, and even heroines and goddesses, having the masks made in the likeness of his own face and of whatever women he happened to fancy. Amongst other themes he sang *Canace in Labour, Orestes the Matricide, The Blinding of Oedipus* and *The Mad Hercules*. At this last performance, they say that a young soldier on sentry duty at the entrance, when he saw Nero dressed and bound in chains as the subject required, ran forward to bring help.

A final type of 'performance' worth mentioning here is the mythological role-play forced on condemned criminals in the first and second centuries AD, aptly dubbed 'fatal charades' in Coleman's comprehensive study of the practice (1990). One such method of execution seems to have involved burning a man alive as Hercules, by either dressing him in an inflammable garment or throwing him onto a pyre, in emulation of Hercules' final moments. This is first attested by an epigram of Lucillius (*Greek Anthology* 11.184), written under the reign of Nero, in which one Meniscus is cremated alive 'like Hercules before him' for stealing apples. Martial (*On Spectacles*) gives an account of various similar executions carried out during the 100-day festival which celebrated the dedication of the Colosseum at Rome in AD 80, including Pasiphae mounted by a bull, and both Orpheus and Daedalus savaged by bears. The specifically Herculean charade is twice referred to by the Christian Tertullian, writing in late second-century AD north Africa, who says he has witnessed a man being castrated as the god Attis while 'one who was being burnt alive had taken on the role of Hercules' (*Ad Nationes* 1.10.47, *Apology* 15.4).

OVERVIEW

Tragedy takes the monster-slaying Herakles of archaic tradition and explores the potential for disaster when he returns to the confines of the everyday domestic world. It is above all Euripides' version of his madness and Sophokles' of his death which define Herakles as a tragic hero, excessive in both his life and his suffering but nonetheless human. Both writers, however, are well aware of his status as a god in the Athenian pantheon, in which guise he is called upon to resolve the crises of the *Philoktetes* and the *Children of Herakles*. The mortal Herakles, too, can act as saviour in the *Peirithous* and in Euripides' *Auge* and bring about relatively happy endings. As will become clear in the next chapter, Herakles featured more commonly on the comic than the tragic stage, and there seem to be elements of comedy in Euripides' *Alkestis, Children of Herakles, Auge* and perhaps the *Peirithous*, long before Ovid's re-working of the death and apotheosis story. The Senecan Hercules takes its Greek models a step on from tragedy to melodrama, a tendency which was doubtless taken even further by pantomime performances of the Madness.

4

VICE OR VIRTUE INCARNATE

Concerning Herakles, now, everyone else keeps on celebrating his courage and counting out his labours; and no one, no poet nor historian, can be found to have made mention of his other good qualities, those belonging to the spirit . . .

(Isokrates, *To Philip* 109)

FROM MONSTER-SLAYING TO COMEDY, PHILOSOPHY AND ROMANCE

At the same time that Herakles was developing as a tragic hero, other sides to his character were also being explored and elaborated. In this chapter we will look at three broad trends in Herakles' treatment in literature and art of the classical period and later, his presentation as: (i) a figure of comedy; (ii) a player in philosophical discourse; and (iii) a romantic hero. These are quite distinct areas, but have in common a tendency to cast Herakles as the incarnation of either vice or virtue, taking to extremes particular elements of his character and suppressing others. They also all focus not on Herakles' famous monster-slaying exploits but rather on internal qualities, of the intellect, appetites and emotions.

We start with the comic Herakles, a hero of many self-indulgent vices, discussing his appearances in the extant plays of Aristophanes before considering what can be reconstructed of the many lost comedies and satyr plays of the fifth and fourth centuries which were based on Heraklean themes; we will also take a look at some later comic treatments of Herakles, in works by diverse authors including the Roman comic writer Plautus. The next section encompasses a variety of material relating to the 'intellectualization' of Herakles. At a simple level this involves the hero in allegorical encounters with personified abstractions, playing out variations on the basic theme of good against evil. More complex is the tradition of regarding Herakles as the embodiment of virtue, first seen in connection with athlet-

ics but later broadening out to include more intellectual and moral qualities, which eventually leads to Herakles donning the unlikely guise of the
philosopher. Finally, we consider Herakles as a romantic hero: although we
have already noted the existence of two wives and a number of lovers, we
have yet to see the elaboration of these relationships, which is especially a
feature of hellenistic and later literature.

THE COMIC HERO

Silk (1985) argues that Herakles is generally avoided as a subject for tragedy
because of his inherently disturbing character, whereas disturbance is grist
to comedy's mill, and it certainly seems to be the case that Herakles featured
far more commonly on the comic than the tragic stage. Unfortunately only
a very small proportion of Herakles' comic appearances survive, but there
as enough material to demonstrate that he was generally characterized as
a cheerfully promiscuous glutton, always on the look out for more food,
drink and lovers.

This aspect of Herakles' persona was not a fifth-century innovation. We
will return to lovers below, but as we saw in Chapter 2 consumption of wine
is a central feature of the Pholos story, the *pithos* involved in many archaic
representations indicating that large quantities are involved. As for food,
feasting is an important feature of Herakles' cult, as we shall see in Chapter
6, with evidence from Athens, Rhodes and Thasos especially suggesting
that worshippers understood their ritual eating as a reflection of Herakles'
own behaviour. What was expected of the archaic Herakles is summed up
by a line from the epic poem the *Wedding of Keyx*: 'Good men of their own
accord go to other men's feasts!' (Hesiod fr. 264 MW). As Merkelbach and
West (1965) demonstrate, this poem, in addition to narrating the actual wedding, may well have included accounts of Herakles eating Theiodamas' ox,
a story which recurs as the aetiology for Herakles' cult at Lindos (pp. 186–7),
and of his eating contest with Lepreus, which again involved consumption
of a whole ox, according to later sources such as Aelian (*Miscellany* 1.24).
There is no doubt, however, but that the classical period saw an elaboration of a character which was so very well suited to the developing genres
of comedy and satyr-drama.

Old Comedy

The origins of comedy, as of tragedy, are obscure, but Herakles seems to
have been an important character from an early stage, alongside Odysseus,

providing plenty of scope for mythological parody. As we have noted in Chapters 1–2, the early fifth-century Syracusan comedian Epicharmos wrote a *Herakles After the Girdle* and a *Bousiris*, and we also hear of an *Alkyoneus*, a *Herakles with Pholos* and a *Marriage of Hebe* by the same writer. As comedy becomes important at Athens in the second half of the century, we encounter further plays on Herakles themes, such as Hermippos' *Kerkopes*, and a *Bousiris* by each of Kratinos and the comic writer Plato, the latter also responsible for a *Long Night* (i.e. the occasion of Herakles' conception). Again likely to concern Herakles' birth are the two versions of an *Amphitryon* attributed to Archippos, who also wrote a *Herakles Marrying*, while Pherekrates was responsible for the intriguing titles *Man-Herakles* and *Pseudo-Herakles*. Also of note are two titles attributed to Nikochares, *Herakles the Producer* and *Herakles Being Married*, the grammatical formulation of the latter suggestive of a plot in which the hero takes the woman's role in a wedding, perhaps a version of the Omphale story. A *Zopyros Burning* by Strattis seems to have been an extended parody of the tragedy *Herakles Burning* by Spintharos, which must have taken Herakles' death story a step further than Sophokles had.[1]

The only comedies that survive in more than fragmentary form, however, are eleven plays by Aristophanes, no more than a quarter of his total output. Herakles actually appears on stage in two of these, and his name comes up in nearly all of the rest, even if only for characters to swear by.[2] That his prodigious appetite was a standard comic theme is indicated by a line in the *Wasps*, where a character assures the audience that this play is *not* going to feature 'Herakles being tricked out of his dinner' (l.60). In the *Peace*, likewise, a catalogue of cheap comic tricks, which Aristophanes is supposed to have expelled, includes 'those Herakleses kneading dough and being hungry' (l.741). Both plays also equate Aristophanes himself with Herakles, victorious over the political leader Kleon, described as a roaring, foul-smelling 'monster' (*Wasps* 1030–7 = *Peace* 752–60). Another aspect of the comic Herakles is alluded to in the *Clouds* (1045–54), where Wrong disproves Right's contention that hot baths make men cowardly by citing the example of Herakles, bravest of men and performer of most labours, whose baths are never cold. We will encounter this perhaps unexpected characteristic again in connection with Herakles' activities as founder and with his cult in Chapters 5 and 6.

The *Birds* won second prize at the City Dionysia festival of 414 BC. The plot is an escapist fantasy in which two Athenian citizens, Euelpides and Peisthetairos, leave Athens and set up an alternative republic in the sky, 'Cloud Cuckoo Land', with the help of the birds. Herakles appears towards the end of the play, after a succession of visitors to the new state have been sent on their way, as part of an embassy from the gods, alongside Poseidon and the god of the Thracian Triballoi tribe, representative of barbarian deities. Their mission is to initiate peace talks, because with the foundation of Cloud Cuckoo Land mortals have started making sacrifices to the birds, and the Olympian gods are going hungry. This conceit provides the perfect excuse for introducing Herakles, who is fixated on food throughout the scene – he is ready to agree to any terms when he hears mention of lunch, for which Poseidon upbraids him as 'stupid and a glutton' (l.1604), and takes a lively interest in the culinary details of Peisthetairos' roasting of some rebel birds. He is also presented as something of a thug, his first words being a threat to strangle whoever is responsible for walling off the gods, and later bullying the Triballian into agreeing.

Aside from such standard jokes, in a particularly interesting exchange (ll.1649–70) Peisthetairos exploits Herakles' status as a bastard (*nothos*) in an attempt to confuse and distract him from siding with the gods. The precise status of *nothoi* at Athens has been much debated, but in the latter half of the fifth century the category certainly included the sons of citizen men by any non-Athenian woman, and Herakles fits the bill because, as Peisthetairos explains, the mortal Alkmene is a 'foreigner' as far as the gods are concerned. Peisthetairos goes on to cite a law of Solon in support of his assertion that Herakles cannot expect to inherit anything if Zeus dies, because Athena will have a prior claim as his fully legitimate offspring. The assumption that the immortal Zeus might die and that the gods should be subject to Athenian law is of course absurd, but the idea of Herakles being of a status somewhere in-between god and mortal is important to his cult in some locations, as we shall see in Chapter 6.[3]

Herakles has an even higher profile in the *Frogs*, which won first prize at the Lenaia festival of 405 BC. The play opens with the god Dionysos disguised as Herakles, wearing a lionskin over his yellow festival-going tunic and carrying a club, on his way to Hades with his slave Xanthias in search of the recently dead Euripides, whom he plans to bring back to Athens because none of his successors can write a decent tragedy. The disguise has been explained by some commentators as signifying Dionysos' loss of identity, the first stage in a transformation of his character which will be brought about by the initiatory nature of his descent to the Underworld. Dionysos himself, however, indicates a more pragmatic reason for the disguise early on in the play, when he calls on Herakles (ll.108–15):

DIONYSOS: But the reason I've come wearing your outfit, looking like you, is so that you can tell me who the friends of yours are who you made use of when you came for Kerberos, in case I need them. Tell me about them, about the harbours, bakeries, brothels, inns, rest-stops, springs, roads, towns, rooms, the landladies, where there are fewest bedbugs.

The disguise evokes Herakles' famous journey to the Underworld, and Aristophanes plays on the audience's knowledge of the alternative traditions, which have him take Kerberos either by force or aided by a friendly Persephone. The assumption inherent in Dionysos' choice of disguise is that Herakles would be received favourably a second time round, suggesting the 'friendly' version, in which his initiation into the Eleusinian Mysteries plays a part. As soon as the protagonists actually set foot in the Underworld, however, Dionysos is terrified by mention of the shape-shifting monster Empousa, and promptly forbids Xanthias to call him Herakles (ll.298–9). Their reception by Aiakos, gate-keeper of Hades, confirms that Herakles is in fact far from welcome – 'You loathsome, shameless, reckless, foul, utterly foul, foulest creature . . .!' (ll.465–6) – and the cowardly Dionysos quickly passes his disguise over to Xanthias in the hope of avoiding the punishment Aiakos threatens. He resumes it briefly when 'Herakles' is more warmly welcomed by Persephone's maid, but immediately hands it back to Xanthias as soon as 'Herakles' comes under attack from a disgruntled landlady, and remains in his own persona for the rest of the play.

The standard comic theme of Herakles' appetite is evident in the passage quoted above, in Dionysos' supposition that Herakles will be able to supply tips for a traveller concerned with physical comforts. His gluttony is evoked a few lines earlier when Dionysos finally succeeds in communicating his longing for Euripides by likening it to a desire for pea soup, for which Herakles declares himself to have had cravings 'ten-thousand times in my life' (l.63), and again in Dionysos' impatient dismissal of Herakles' literary views: 'Just teach me about feasting!' (l.107). The theme recurs at the entrance to Hades, when Persephone's maid tries to entice 'Herakles' (Xanthias) to enter with a catalogue of the food her mistress has been currently preparing: 'she was baking bread, boiling two or three pots of ground-pea soup, grilling a whole ox, baking flat-cakes and rolls' (ll.505–6), 'she was also stewing bird-meat, and roasting sweatmeats, and mixing the sweetest wine' (ll.509–10). What finally persuades him, however, is an appeal to Herakles' other famous appetite, with mention of a girl pipe-player and three dancing girls. Food is again the issue for the Landlady who, a few lines later, recognizes 'Herakles' (now Dionysos) and seeks recompense for an unpaid bill in respect of sixteen loaves, twenty half-obol portions of stewed meat, much garlic, salted fish, fresh cheese, and sausages, not to mention a stolen mattress.

There is indirect reference to the issue of Herakles' status as a god during the scene in which Aiakos administers a whipping. Originally intended as a punishment for the 'dog-thief' (l.605), Dionysos' and Xanthias-Herakles' attempts to pass the buck turn the whipping into a competition to prove which of them is a god, during which Xanthias explains away one of his exclamations of pain as a musing on 'when the Herakles festival at Diomeia is due' (ll.650–1). This is a reference to the cult at Kynosarges (pp. 178–9), adding an extra dimension to the more general humour provided by the fact that one of the 'gods' is simply a slave in disguise.[4]

As we saw with the tragic Herakles, the hero of the comic stage is occasionally reflected in vase-painting. Just one Attic vase is in question here, an oinochoe of c.410 BC by the Nikias Painter (Paris, Louvre N3408), which depicts Herakles in a chariot driven by the winged goddess Victory and pulled by four unruly centaurs. Both Herakles and Victory have peculiarly ugly faces, which may well reflect contemporary comic masks, but are not obviously wearing actors' costumes, and the centaurs are the 'real' thing, with the human torsos attached to proper horse-bodies, rather than any kind of stage-animal. The link with comedy is confirmed, however, by the torch-bearer who precedes the chariot, who is 'stage nude' in the comic costume of mask, padded torso, baggy tights and floppy phallus. As we will see in Chapters 5–6, the image of Herakles in a chariot would immediately call to mind his ascension to Olympos, especially for an Athenian audience, and the substitution of Victory for the more usual Athena as driver is in keeping with the idea of Herakles' deification representing a final victory over death. The image here is clearly not a literal illustration of a play, but it could easily have been inspired by one of the comedies mentioned above which featured Herakles' apotheosis and/or his marriage to Hebe.

Satyr plays

Another comic genre contemporary with Old Comedy is the satyr play. This is distinct from comedy proper, because it was closely bound with tragedy, being written by the same poets and performed as part of the same competition at Athens' City Dionysia festival, a satyr play following directly on after each trilogy of tragedies. Only one complete text of a satyr play on any subject survives, Euripides' *Cyclops*, from which it is clear that the basic format was for a mythological story to be played out by three actors, with elements of parody, and with much humour being supplied by the antics of a chorus of satyrs. These half-man half-goat creatures were traditionally Dionysos' companions, renowned for their love of wine and lechery, the latter characteristic emphasized on the stage by the standard satyr-costume, which consisted of a bearded mask and a leather loincloth with perkily erect phallus. It is not surprising that Herakles was a popular figure in this genre, given the features he shares with the satyrs, and we have fragments of quite a number of plays on Heraklean themes. In Chapters 1–2 we have already noted satyr plays entitled *Kerberos*, *Herakles at Tainaron*,

Linos, Bousiris and *Syleus*. We have little more than the titles of two further satyr plays by Sophokles, a *Herakles* and a *Little Herakles*, the latter presumably dealing with the snake-strangling episode.

In a few instances the textual evidence is complemented by visual testimonia. There is a case to be made, for example, for linking Aeschylus's satyr play *The Lion* with early fifth-century vase-paintings of satyrs stealing Herakles' weapons, which he has to lay aside before wrestling with the Nemean lion. Likewise, two black-figure images of satyrs in fetters, being driven by Herakles himself or by a herald, may be linked with Aeschylus' *Heralds*. As we have seen (p. 54), this told the story of Herakles' treatment of the heralds of King Erginos of Orchomenos, although the play seems to have presented a less violent version than the one we know from later sources. None of these images gives specific indication of a theatrical setting – the satyrs are presented as the 'real' thing rather than as men in costume – so that we are at best seeing only an indirect reflection of the play.

There is, however, one explicit representation of a satyr play involving Herakles, on the so-called 'Pronomos Vase' of c.410–400 BC (Naples H3240). This depicts Dionysos and his consort Ariadne presiding over the humans involved in a real production: the tragic poet Demetrios, the *aulos*-player Pronomos and a lyre-player are surrounded by a troop of actors in costume, most of whom are holding rather than wearing their masks. Eight are dressed as satyrs, and a ninth wears the furry body-suit of Silenos, father of the satyrs, while the remaining three figures must be the main actors, all in tragic costume. To either side of the divine couple are actors in elaborate Oriental costume, a mature man with a bearded mask to the left, to the right a youth dressed as a woman, while further right again is an actor in the costume of Herakles, complete with club and lionskin, apparently in conversation with Silenos. The combination of characters makes it a plausible conjecture that this represents the cast of an *Omphale*, and we do indeed have fragments of satyr plays of this title by the mid-fifth-century tragic poets Achaios of Eretria and Ion of Chios, to which we will return.

Some images may illustrate satyr plays for which we have no textual evidence. For example, as mentioned previously (p. 96), a handful of late fifth-century Attic and fourth-century South Italian vases depict Herakles' ascension from the pyre. On the Attic example, a pelike of c.410 BC (Munich 2360), a youthful Herakles is whisked skywards in a chariot driven by Athena, while below nymphs named Premnousia and Arethousa try to douse the flames of the pyre with water, and satyrs named Hybris and Skopas seem to be making off with Herakles' spear and club, after a final inspection of the pyre. In this and the South Italian examples, the pyre has resting on it a human torso, which is usually identified as Herakles' corselet, with reference to Diodoros' account (4.38.3) in which Herakles sends to Delphi for advice on how to deal with his suffering, and is told to go to Oita 'with his war equipment'. However, Herakles is not usually depicted in body-armour, and an attractive alternative idea is that the torso represents a kind of imprint or memory of Herakles' mortal body, left behind as he becomes a god.

Other images again *may* reflect lost satyr plays, but are just as likely to be straightforward visual jokes, relying on the viewer's familiarity with satyrs' tendency to burlesque. On an Attic oinochoe of c.460 BC (London E539), for example, the only figure is a satyr wearing a lionskin and brandishing a club at a serpent which is guarding a tree bearing, not apples, but wine-jugs. This could be an illustration of a satyr play in which the humour was provided by the (notoriously cowardly) satyrs appropriating Herakles' costume and attempting to perform the Hesperides labour. A further level of

Figure 4.1 Drunken Herakles and Pans. Apulian oinochoe of the Bucrane Group, c.360–350 BC, private collection Taranto (Ragusa 126). Photo: Museo Nazionale Archaeologico di Taranto.

humour, however, is specific to the image's context: the wine-jugs in the tree *could* have been part of the joke on stage, drawing on the audience's familiarity with the habitual drunkenness of both satyrs and Herakles himself, but the joke makes even better sense when the tree is actually depicted on a wine-jug, implicating the user in the satyr's desire for drink. In a similar vein, the image on an Apulian wine-jug of c.350 BC (Figure 4.1) does not require more than a general appreciation of the conventional characterization of Herakles, and the topos of satyrs stealing his equipment, for its humour to be appreciated: a corpulent Herakles lies naked on his lionskin, asleep amidst the debris of a party – an amphora, a krater, what look like chicken-legs – while his bow and a large container are removed. The perpetrators here have full goats' legs, rather than just the tail and ears which generally identify satyrs, and so are usually labelled as baby versions of the half-goat god Pan.[5]

Middle Comedy and 'phlyax' plays

After Aristophanes, Herakles continued to be a subject for the Middle Comedy of the fourth century. As we noted in Chapter 2, known titles include Alexis' *Linos*, a *Bousiris* by each of Kratinos the younger, Antiphanes, Ephippos and Mnesimachos, and a *Kerkopes* by each of Euboulos and Menippos. We also hear of an *Antaios* and an *Omphale* by Antiphanes, an *Omphale* by Kratinos the younger, and an *Auge* and a *Herakles* by Philyllios; the latter includes a character called Dorpeia, 'Feast-day', a name sometimes used of the first day of the Anthesteria festival in honour of Dionysos. The occasional lines preserved from these plays are enough to indicate that Herakles' appetites were still a major part of his comic persona.

These plays were all written for performance at Athens, but the fourth-century visual evidence available to us largely comprises South Italian vases, which makes comparison with the textual evidence difficult. The issue is complicated by the possibility that the images may reflect local South Italian forms of drama, such as the 'phlyax' plays referred to by ancient writers. We have very little evidence for the content and form of this genre, and there is much debate about the extent to which it may have shared features with or been influenced by Attic comedy, but we do know that the phlyax-writer Rhinthon, active in Taras c.300 BC, wrote a *Herakles* and an *Amphitryon*. Despite uncertainties about the genre, modern scholars persist in using the term 'phlyax vase' to refer to *any* South Italian pot featuring actors in comic padded costume, sometimes with some indication of the stage setting. A dozen or so of these depict Herakles, identifiable by lionskin headdress and club, several making obvious allusion to his established comic characteristics. For example, on an Apulian wine-jug of c.370–350 BC (London F99), Herakles holds a large loaf of bread and pursues a woman carrying a wine-jug: he may be chasing her purely for the wine, or have more lusty pleasures in mind.

Just occasionally a good case can in fact be made for linking a 'phlyax' scene with a known Attic comedy, and an interesting example relevant to Herakles is the image on an Apulian bell-krater of c.375–350 BC (Figure 4.2). To the left, an actor in full padded costume, with a lionskin hanging from his shoulder, uses a club to hammer at a column which may be meant to represent a doorway; to the right, he is followed by another actor riding a donkey but carrying a large bundle on his shoulder. The combination of elements coincides so nearly with the scene of the disguised Dionysos and his grumbling slave arriving at Herakles' house that is difficult to escape the conclusion that this represents the opening of Aristophanes' *Frogs*. If so, the production which inspired the painter would have to have been a provincial revival some thirty to fifty years after the play was originally staged in Athens, but this is not entirely implausible. Furthermore, even where it is impossible to identify a comic scene with any known play, the images

Figure 4.2 'Phlyax' vase depicting Dionysus (with club and lion-skin) and Xanthias (on donkey) at Herakles' door – scene from *Frogs*? Apulian bell-krater, c.375–350 BC (Berlin F3046, now lost). Photo: after M. Bieber, *Die Denkmäler zum Theaterwessen im Altertum*, Berlin 1920, pl. 86.

do reinforce the evidence of the textual fragments for Herakles' continuing popularity on the comic stage in the fourth century.

Less commonly discussed in connection with comedy than the vases are a number of fourth-century scenes depicted in relief on items of metalware. An unusual silver dish of c.400–350 BC from Rogozen (Figure 4.3) depicts a naked Auge, her name inscribed above her head, and Herakles, identifiable by his usual lionskin, bow and quiver, and labelled with the word *dêladê*, which roughly translates 'You know who!' The scene has been interpreted as depicting the story as related in Euripides' play (pp. 94–5), with Auge very much the victim, her clothes already more or less ripped off, about to be raped by the drunken Herakles. However, in similar scenes found on two bronze mirror-cases of the late fourth century, the woman (not named here) seems more clearly to be taking a proactive role, trying to pull Herakles up from his slumped position on the lionskin. I would suggest that the same thing is happening in Figure 4.3, where it is not clear who

Figure 4.3 Auge and 'You know who'! Silver bowl from the Rogozen Treasure (Vratsa). Photo: Regional Historical Museum, Vratsa.

is pulling whom, but Herakles appears to be in no fit state to rape anyone: he is wearing a banqueter's wreath, leaning back unsteadily, and posed in such a way as to leave no ambiguity about his impotent state. This would be a clear reversal of the story presented in tragedy, but in keeping with comedy's stereotyping of women as insatiable for sex, and the rather frivolous tone of the *dêladê* inscription would better fit a comic interpretation. Although there is no direct link between the images and a specific play, they do at least provide some clue as to how the story might have been treated in comedies such as that of Philyllios.[6]

Later comic treatments

Herakles continues to be the subject of comic representation in the hellenistic and Roman imperial periods. As far as drama is concerned, Middle Comedy gave way to New Comedy around 300 BC, its foremost Greek exponent being Menander, and from around 200 BC a Roman version of the genre is developed by writers like Plautus, adapting its plots from Greek prototypes. One of the characteristics of New Comedy is that mythological subjects are no longer common, and divine figures are usually limited to speaking prologues rather than playing a part in the main action. Nonetheless, Herakles does still manage to feature, albeit in a more limited way than in earlier comedy. Writing in the first century AD, Dio Chrysostom comments (32.94):

> . . . in comedies and theatrical performances they do not raise much laughter by bringing on a drunk Karion or Davus [*typical comic cook and slave names*], but it does seem funny when they see a Herakles like this, staggering and, just as usual, in a yellow dress . . .

In the works of Menander, characters swear quite frequently 'by Herakles', as they did in Aristophanes, a reminder that this was a continuing feature of everyday speech, and we have some lines of a lost play entitled *Pseudo-Herakles*. We have already seen this title used by the Old Comedy writer Pherekrates, but it is not clear what the plot of his version was. The preserved lines of Menander's play include (fr. 409 *PCG*) a brief exchange between a cook and another speaker about declining standards in the serving of food, a stock element of Middle and New Comedy, while a passing reference to the play by Plutarch (*Moralia* 59c) suggests that the eponymous hero carried, not a proper club, but a hollow fake.

More directly concerned with Herakles, however, is Plautus' *Amphitryon*, produced c.195 BC, which provides a farcical account of Herakles' birth. As we have noted (p. 24), the story was already alluded to in the *Iliad*, and it is recounted in some detail in a long fragment of the *Catalogue of Women* (fr. 195.8–63 MW) which was recycled as a preface to the *Shield of Herakles'* account of the Kyknos myth. The story has obvious comic potential, and was treated once or twice in Old Comedy and in a phlyax play. Plautus' version, however, is very much in keeping with the conventions of New Comedy, starting with a prologue in which Mercury even comments on the genre-bending nature of the play: 'Let me make it a mixture: a tragi-comedy. For I don't really suppose I can make it completely a comedy, with kings and gods coming on stage' (ll.59–61).

Much of the preposterous plot is taken up with the comic business pro-duced by two sets of doubles, with Jupiter disguised as Amphitryon and Mercury as his slave Sosia, the latter being especially determined to make mischief for their real human counterparts. The climax of the sequence of mistaken identity gags is interrupted by a messenger speech, a borrow-ing from tragedy, delivered by the nurse Bromia. She recounts Alcmena's miraculously quick labour and the arrival of twin baby boys, one of whom 'was so big and strong that no one could get his swaddling clothes done up!' (ll.1103–4). She goes on to tell the familiar story of the snake-stran-gling, and how Jupiter finally proclaimed his role as Alcmena's lover and acknowledged paternity of the stronger child; as would befit the situation in real life, neither of the babies yet has a name, but their identities are obvious.

The Herakles of comedy occasionally makes an appearance in other lit-erary genres, too. In the third century BC, for example, Kallimachos' *Hymn to Artemis* (144–61) includes a vivid representation of Herakles loitering at the gates to Zeus' house, waiting for Artemis to return from her hunting trips, exhorting her to leave smaller prey in favour of boar and oxen – still a glutton despite his apotheosis. He appears later amongst a cast of gods in Seneca's *Apocolocyntosis* ('Pumpkinification') *of the Divine Claudius*, published in AD 54 shortly after the death and deification of this emperor. This satirical piece paints a ludicrous picture of Claudius' arrival in heaven and the gods' debate as to whether he should be allowed in. The Hercules who is sent by Jupiter to interrogate Claudius is characterized as 'the much travelled, monster-slaying Greekling, shockable, gullible, blustering, cow-ardly and ridiculously prone to believe in his own tragic image' (Eden 1984, 84), very much along the lines of the figure in Aristophanes' *Frogs*. Claudius manages to gain Hercules' support by recalling how he used to dispense justice in front of his temple (7.4–5), a reference perhaps to the temple of Hercules Victor near the Palatine (p. 196), where he used to deal with 'much more bullshit' than the hero had cleaned out of Augeas' stables. The day is won, however, by the deified Augustus who reminds the assembly of Claudius' many crimes, and Claudius is eventually condemned to an afterlife of eternal punishment in the Underworld.[7] During the discussion Hercules recognizes that his own claim to deity may be at stake (9.6), and indeed there was a long-running philosophical debate about his divine status (p. 174), which is further parodied in two works by the second-century AD writer Lucian. In his *Assembly of the Gods*, Momos ('Reproach' personified) is complaining about the many unworthy characters passing themselves off as gods, including various 'half-gods' of semi-mortal parentage, but Zeus defends Herakles as having earnt his place by means of the 'not few trials' he has undergone (§6); in *Zeus the Tragic Actor* (21), meanwhile, Herakles and others with mortal mothers are glossed as being 'resident aliens' amongst the gods.

In the visual arts, we find a comic Herakles persisting in sculpture. The stage figure, with mask and comic costume, is seen in terracotta figurines throughout the fourth century and later, occasionally performing a labour or falling asleep, but more often simply standing with his club over his shoulder. Also on a fairly small scale was the *Herakles Epitrapezios*, 'Herakles at table', a foot-high bronze statue attributed to the late fourth-century sculptor Lysippos, depicting the hero seated with his club in one hand, a wine-cup in the other. The original is described by Martial (9.44) and Statius (*Silvae* 4.6.32–47), both writing in the first century AD, as being currently in the possession of the art collector Novius Vindex but having once belonged to Alexander the Great; both writers comment on the idea of such a great god being presented in such a compact form. Numerous copies of the statue at its original small scale survive, as well as a colossal version over two metres high of the second or first centuries BC (Chieti 6029), found in the central Italian town of Alba Fucens. The type would certainly appear to play on Herakles's comic reputation as a glutton, although some have suggested that a more serious reference to the deified Herakles' feasting on Olympos is meant. Indisputably comic, however, is the hellenistic type of the drunk Herakles, either staggering or urinating (*mingens*), which is reproduced in a variety of media. A particularly fine rendering of the subject as a marble statue served as a fountain in the garden of the Casa dei Cervi at Herculaneum (Naples).[8]

HERAKLES INTELLECTUALIZED

With the vices of the comic hero in mind it may be difficult to imagine Herakles as the incarnation of virtue, but it is to this aspect of his multifaceted character that we now turn, beginning with a number of allegorical encounters. As we have seen in Chapters 1–2, a number of Herakles' exploits have at various times been interpreted as representing his triumph over death, but the idea begins to be made explicit at the very end of the archaic period when poets or artists pit the hero against a personification of Death himself, or the related figures of Sleep and Old Age. Such encounters are relatively uncommon in Greek myth, and have something of a folk-tale feel about them.[9]

Allegorical encounters: Sleep, Old Age and Death

The personification of Sleep (Hypnos) has a significant mythological pedigree, appearing already in Homer and Hesiod primarily as the twin brother of Death. He does, however, also appear without his brother in one or two other mythological contexts, the most common being Herakles' killing of the giant Alkyoneus. Our extant literary versions of the encounter are meagre, and make no mention of Hypnos: Pindar records that Telamon was with Herakles when he killed Alkyoneus (*Nemean* 4.25–30, *Isthmian* 6.31–5), while Apollodoros (1.6.1) places the encounter in the context of the battle of the gods against the giants, adding the detail that Alkyoneus was invulnerable so long as he remained on his own territory of Pallene, so that Herakles could only overcome him by dragging him beyond its boundaries.

A group of Attic vase-paintings, however, ranging in date from c.510 to 470 BC, depict Alkyoneus asleep, and in a number of cases the condition is apparent not only from the giant's recumbent posture and closed eyes but also by the presence of Sleep himself. One of the earliest examples is a cup attributed to the Nikosthenes Painter, c.510 BC (Melbourne 1730.4), where Hypnos, a small nude boy with wings, looks as if he has just parachuted down onto Alkyoneus' hip. The vase representations suggest that a version of the story in which Alkyoneus' sleep was an important feature was current in early fifth-century Athens, and the restricted chronological range may suggest a specific literary source, unknown to us. The fact that Sleep himself is not always present, however, suggests that the inclusion of the personification is an addition made by the vase-painters: the figure is a visual device to draw attention to the giant's state, equivalent to the verbal articulation possible in a poem or play of sleep's significance to the plot. Hypnos is depicted as asleep himself in one or two examples, self-reflexively characterized by the state he personifies, a feature common to personifications of physical states.[10]

There are no extant literary sources at all for Herakles' encounter with Old Age (Geras), but the story is known from a handful of Attic vases from the first half of the fifth century, on two of which Geras' identity is guaranteed by an inscription. It has been suggested that a lost drama might have provided inspiration for the images, but there is no evidence to make this more than a conjecture. These vases present three types of scene: Herakles and Geras talking, a fight in which Herakles clearly has the upper hand, and Geras running away with Herakles in pursuit. The story can thus be reconstructed as consisting of an initially amicable conversation which disintegrates into a fight and Geras' flight, or a pursuit followed by the capture of Geras and his imparting of some kind of knowledge, on the model of Herakles' encounter with Nereus. The scene in Figure 4.4 suggests that the former scenario is more likely, as it has a kind of speech bubble coming from Herakles' mouth saying *klausei*, 'you will weep', a threat which might plausibly be followed by a fight. The representation of Geras here is notable for the characterization of Old Age as bald, hunchbacked, leaning on a walking-stick, and with ugly, over-sized genitalia – this is very much in keeping with the Greeks' generally negative view of old age. The idea of Old

Figure 4.4 Herakles and Old Age (inscription: *klausei*, 'you will weep'). Attic red-figure pelike, name vase of the Geras Painter, c.480 BC (Paris G234). Photo: RMN © Hervé Lewandowski.

Age overcome calls to mind Herakles' ultimate happy fate, being promoted to immortality and marrying Youth – Hesiod even makes it explicit that he lives 'free from trouble and unaging (*ageraos*)' in the halls of Olympos (*Theogony* 955).[11]

In contrast to the Geras story, Herakles' encounter with Death (Thanatos) is attested only in literature, and specifically in tragedy. The plot of Euripides' *Alkestis*, which we have already encountered (pp. 40 and 87–8), centres on Herakles' rescue of the eponymous heroine after she has voluntarily died in place of her husband, Admetos. The story of Alkestis' selfless act is certainly older than the play, but it is not entirely clear whether the resolution always involved a wrestling match between Herakles and Death. The one possible archaic attestation of the rescue is an Attic black-figure amphora of c.540 BC by the Swing Painter (Louvre F60), which features Herakles (identifiable only by his club) leading a veiled woman, watched by Hermes, although Death himself is not depicted. In the first quarter of the fifth century the tragedian Phrynichos put Death on stage in his *Alkestis*, a fragment of which (frs 1c–3 *TGrF*) features Thanatos cutting off a lock of the heroine's hair, as though she were a sacrificial victim, a detail picked up in Euripides' version (ll.74–6); Sophokles presumably also dealt with the story in his *Admetos*, but nothing survives of this beyond its title.

In Euripides' version, Death sounds more like a bogey-man of popular folk-belief than a god, even of the Underworld. He appears in the opening scene in conversation with Apollo, who refers to him as 'priest of the dead' (l.24) and his ways as 'hated by mortals and abhorred by the gods' (l.62). Later Herakles gives a vivid description of how he intends wresting Alkestis from Death's grasp (843–54):

> HERAKLES: I shall go and lie in wait for the black-winged lord of the dead, Death, and I expect to find him drinking sacrificial offerings near the tomb. Then if I see him from my hiding place and seize him, throwing my arms around him in a circle, no one will be able to free him, as his rib-cage suffers, until he gives up the woman to me. But if I miss my prey and he does not come for his bloody offerings, I shall go below, to the sunless halls of Kore and her lord, and I shall demand to bring Alkestis back up, and prevail, and so I shall place her in the arms of my host . . .

In the event the fight takes place beside Alkestis' tomb, as Herakles reports very briefly (ll.1140–2), and his literal victory over Death here does away with the need for a journey to the Underworld to represent the overcoming of death. We can only surmise what Death would have looked like, but Thanatos is mentioned by the second-century AD grammarian Pollux (*Onomastikon* 4.141–2) as one of a number of tragic characters who required a 'special mask', alongside various other personifications and characters with physical peculiarities.[12]

The *exemplum virtutis*

In parallel with this allegorization of the hero, from the early fifth century we can also see the development of Herakles as the *exemplum virtutis*. This traditional Latin term means something like 'model of virtue', *virtus* being a translation of the Greek *aretê*, which encompasses physical and intellectual, as well as moral, qualities and is sometimes rendered more broadly as 'excellence'. The role is foreshadowed to some extent in late archaic art, where Herakles is sometimes depicted as the ideal athlete, with short curly hair rather than the long hair typical of other male figures. This characterization of Herakles as the prototypical athlete is apparent in the early classical metopes of the temple of Zeus at Olympia, too, as we saw in Chapter 1. Herakles' position as role-model for athletes is elaborated in anecdotes reported by later writers. According to Diodoros (12.9.6), the famous sixth-century wrestler Milon of Kroton went into competition 'dressed in Herakles' outfit, with lionskin and club'. The Thasian athlete Theagenes, who won an Olympic victory in 480 BC, was thought by some to have been fathered by Herakles (pp. 188–9). The late fifth-century pankratiast Poulydamas killed a lion on the slopes of mount Olympos 'in emulation of Herakles' deeds' (Pausanias 6.5.5), a feat commemorated by a statue on the base of which Poulydamas is depicted wrestling with the lion, indeed just like Herakles (Olympia 45).[13]

It is, however, in the poems of the early fifth-century Pindar and his contemporary Bakchylides that we see the first real interest in qualities other than the purely physical, and attempts to 'clean up' Herakles' image. A large proportion of their surviving work consists in odes written to celebrate the victory of athletes at the panhellenic games of Olympia, Delphi, Nemea and Isthmia, in which context Herakles offers an ideal role model and vehicle for praise of the victor. Herakles' particular role as founder of the games at Olympia (pp. 160–3) adds further point to his inclusion in odes for victories there.

Pindar was himself from Thebes, so his attachment to the Theban Herakles is perhaps not surprising. *Pythian* 9 written for Telesikrates of Kyrene, winner of the race in armour of 474 BC, makes reference to an earlier victory in the games at Thebes, most likely those of Herakleia festival described in *Isthmian* 4 (p. 182). This leads on to brief mention of Herakles' birth story (ll.84–6) and to the exclamation 'Any man who does not embrace Herakles in his speech is a fool!' (l.87). We have already mentioned *Nemean* 1 for its account of the snake-strangling episode, but the whole poem can be read as a profession of faith in Herakles. The story of the infant hero is prefaced by what is almost a prayer to the hero to assist the poet in singing of Chromios' achievements: 'For my part, I readily cling to Herakles on the subject of great heights of *aretê*, as I rouse up the ancient tale . . .' (ll.33–4). Later in the poem, Teiresias' prophecy (ll.62–72) emphasizes the justice of Herakles' victories by making his enemies 'lawless' monsters, men characterized by 'crooked excess', and the notoriously insolent giants, before predicting his eventual reward of marriage to Hebe.

In a similar vein, a fragmentary poem (fr.140a SM) which tells the story of Herakles' revenge on Laomedon, underscores the hero's righteousness by describing his enemies as 'overbearing' and Laomedon himself as 'guest-murdering', his actions 'shameful' (ll.54–9); by contrast, Herakles' piety is demonstrated by his establishment of altars to Zeus and Apollo (ll.62–4). Another fragmentary poem (fr. 169a SM), already referred to in connection with the mares of Diomedes, uses Herakles' deeds as proof of the maxim that 'Law, king of all mortals and immortals, guides while justifying (or bringing to justice?) the greatest violence with lofty hand'. Pindar's exact meaning here has been disputed since antiquity, and it is not entirely clear whether the violence is that of Herakles, the end justifying the means, or his opponents, which would show the hero in a better light.

Elsewhere Herakles' less admirable exploits or personal traits are played down. In *Olympian* 9 (ll.30–9), celebrating the victory of Epharmostos of Opous in the wrestling of 468 BC, Pindar seems to justify Herakles' violence, in three different stories, against Poseidon, Apollo and Hades as divinely sanctioned, although he hastens to 'cast the story away from my mouth', distancing himself from possible impiety. In two odes for Aiginetan victors, Herakles is cast as the beneficent friend to Aigina's local heroes, with no hint of the problematic behaviour, which is a feature of his other guest–host relationships. *Nemean* 7, for the boys' pentathlon winner Sogenes, refers to Herakles (ll.86–92) as 'kindly guest-friend' of Aiakos, and 'subduer of giants', invoking him as a patron for the young victor. The friendship extends to Aiakos' son Telamon in *Isthmian* 6, for the boys' pankration winner Phylakidas, which includes (ll.27–56) an extensive narration of Herakles' visit to Aigina to recruit Telamon for his expedition against Troy, 'on account of Laomedon's offence'. His arrival coincides with Telamon's wedding, at which Herakles proves to be a well-mannered guest, praying that the union should produce a son with his own virtues of strength and courage; Zeus instantly answers by sending the good omen of an eagle, which Herakles 'like a seer' interprets as predicting the birth of the great warrior Ajax.

Altogether, then, Pindar's Herakles is usually a paragon of piety and punisher of evil-doers, and we will return to his role as founder of the Olympic Games in Chapter 5. Much less of Bakchylides' work survives, but here Herakles is again the upholder of justice. In the fragmentary Nemean ode 13 an unidentified speaker, perhaps Athena or the nymph Nemea, is watching Herakles wrestle with the lion (p. 31) and predicts that the hero will put a stop to men's 'haughty violence' (ll.44–5). The lion-slaying is implicitly made into the model for the all-in wrestling competition at the end of the speech (ll.54–7): 'Truly I say that one day there will be sweat and toil amongst Greeks here for the garlands of the *pankration*'. A softer side to the hero is presented in the Olympic ode 5, which we have seen in connection with the characterization of Deianeira (p. 81), where Herakles' reaction to the dead Meleager's account of his own murder is surprisingly humane and philosophical. He sheds tears, 'pitying the fate of the long-suffering man' (ll.157–8), and utters the well-known saying, 'Best for mortals not to be born, nor to see the light of the sun' (ll.160–2).[14]

The 'intellectualization' of Herakles picks up pace towards the end of the fifth and into the fourth century BC. As we have seen in the previous chapter, the tragedians explored the extremes of the hero's nature, Euripides in particular highlighting Herakles' *aretê* as a foil to the disaster of his madness. A further step in the process is represented by the story of 'The Choice of Herakles' told by a contemporary of Euripides, the sophist Prodikos, which presents the hero in contemplative mode and explicitly makes *aretê* the motivation for his deeds. We do not have a text by Prodikos himself, but the story is preserved by a re-telling (in the mouth of Sokrates) in Xenophon's *Memorabilia* (2.1.21–34):

> They say that when Herakles was setting out from childhood into his prime, a time when the young, now becoming their own masters, show whether they will take the path of virtue (*aretê*) in life or the path of vice (*kakia*), he went out to a quiet place and sat not knowing which of the roads to take. There appeared two tall women approaching him . . .

The women turn out to be Virtue (*aretê*) and Vice (*kakia*) personified, characterized by their appearance: Virtue is 'pretty to look at and of free-born nature, her body adorned with purity, her eyes with modesty, her figure with reserve, and with white clothes', while Vice is 'grown into plumpness and softness, her face made up so that it looked whiter and rosier in appearance than it actually was . . . .' Each outlines to Herakles a different road he might take in life. The way offered by Vice is suitably appealing, and for a fifth-century Athenian audience must have immediately have evoked the Herakles of the comic stage:

> '. . . you will always be considering what tasty food or drink you can find, what sight or sound may please you, what scent or touch you may enjoy, which boyfriend's society will gratify you most, how you can sleep most comfortably, and how you can come by all these with the least trouble.'

The road of Virtue is predictably more like hard work, and includes a long list of prerequisites for winning the good opinion of gods and men, such as 'if you expect to be admired for your virtue by the whole of Greece, you must strive to benefit Greece . . . .' We are not given Herakles' reaction to either speech, but the conclusion – 'such, as Prodikos tells it, was Virtue's education of Herakles' – suggests that Herakles chose to follow the path of *aretê*.[15]

Prodikos apparently performed his 'speech on Herakles' to very large audiences, and the story's appeal would prove to be long-lasting, with variations appearing in Roman writers and in post-classical art, as we shall see. More broadly, too, Herakles' virtue would continue to be extolled as exemplary throughout the fourth century and beyond. Isokrates' address *To Demonikos*, probably written in the late 370s BC, cites the labours of Herakles alongside Theseus' exploits as models of *aretê* for the young man to emulate (7–8), and asserts that it was because of his *aretê* that Zeus made Herakles immortal (50). The internal qualities which make up this *aretê* are expanded upon in Isokrates' speech *To Philip* of 346 BC, in a lengthy aside which presents Herakles as a role model for the Makedonian king, partially quoted at the start of this chapter (110):

> If I had applied myself to the subject when younger, I could easily have shown that your ancestor was superior to all his predecessors in wisdom, honour and justice even more than in physical strength.

The choice of Herakles as *exemplum* here is governed partly by the fact that the Makedonian royal family claimed descent from Herakles, as we shall see (pp. 142–6), but the specific exploit which Isokrates relates (111–12) is his expedition against Troy, a model for Philip's intended campaign against the Persians. The aside concludes (114) that Philip should imitate Herakles not so much in his actions, which would be beyond the power even of many gods, as 'in the qualities of the spirit, love of humanity, and the goodwill he held towards the Hellenes'.

Just a few years later Herakles is again associated with the beautiful personification of *aretê* in Aristotle's *Hymn to Virtue* (*PMG* 842). This was written in praise of Hermeias, tyrant of Atarneus, who had been tortured and executed by the Persians in 341 BC, and his sufferings are compared to those of Herakles, Kastor and Polydeukes. All three heroes had 'endured much in their exploits hunting after your (Virtue's) power' (ll.9–12) and subsequently been immortalized, just as Hermeias himself will be in Aristotle's song.[16]

The proto-philosopher

Alongside this tradition of Herakles as a general *exemplum virtutis* there developed a trend for casting Herakles more specifically as a role-model for the philosopher. At a fairly light-hearted level, Plato's Sokrates declares himself inferior to Herakles, since even the arrival of an Iolaos would not allow him to vanquish the many heads of argument produced by the 'she-sophist hydra' and the bites of her 'crab sophist' assistant (*Euthydemos* 297b9–d2). Elsewhere, Plato's Phaedo casts himself as Iolaos to Sokrates' Herakles as they do battle against two argumentative interlocutors (*Phaedo* 89c5–10). This is a humorous reflection of the allegorization of Herakles' exploits which was already developing in contemporary mythographical writing, such as Herodoros' rationalizing account of the Hesperides episode which we have already noted (p. 9). More systematic use was made of Herakles, however, by the Cynics and later by the Stoics, both of which schools regarded him as an archetype of the philosophical struggle for *aretê*, and in particular the virtue of endurance.

The traditional founder of Cynicism was Sokrates' pupil Antisthenes, who taught at the Kynosarges gymnasium in Athens. As we shall see in Chapter 6, the sanctuary to which this was attached was sacred to Herakles, and was a well-known meeting place for *nothoi*, making it an appropriate venue for Antisthenes who, because of his Thracian mother, was himself a *nothos*. According to Diogenes Laertius' *Philosophers' Lives* (6.2), Antisthenes learnt 'patient endurance and disregard for feeling' from Sokrates, and demonstrated 'that suffering was a good thing' by the example of Herakles. Only fragments of his three or four works on Herakles survive, but these suggest that anecdotes about Herakles were related in support of the tenets that 'the chief good is to live according to *aretê*' and that '*aretê* can be taught . . . the wise man is worthy of love and a friend to his like, and nothing should be entrusted to chance' (frs 22–3 Caizzi). The stories in question included one about Herakles visiting Cheiron, 'the only one of the centaurs he did not kill, but listened to' (frs 24a–c Caizzi), and another in which Prometheus exhorted him to eschew worldly concerns and strive for knowledge of what is higher than mankind (fr. 27 Caizzi). In both of these cases the point seems to be that Herakles was prepared to learn from a wise tutor, but in another Herakles himself is the teacher, 'instructing his children to thank no one for praising them', i.e. to avoid the twin evils of false modesty or responding to flattery (fr. 26 Caizzi).[17]

Antisthenes' successor Diogenes of Sinope is supposed to have written a tragedy entitled *Herakles* (fr. 1c *TrGF*), and to have declared that the characteristic mark of his life was that, like Herakles, 'he put nothing before freedom' (Diogenes Laertius, *Philosophers' Lives* 6.71). A colourful picture of Diogenes giving a public speech at the Isthmian Games is painted by Dio Chrysostom (*Diogenes or On Virtue* 8.27–35), a philosopher himself influenced by both Cynic and Stoic ideas. In this speech Diogenes apparently compared his own philosophical struggle, which involved remaining unmoved by either pleasure or hardship, with Herakles' labours, recounting half a dozen of the hero's exploits. After suggesting that Herakles committed suicide because he had become weak and perhaps ill, he back-tracked to say that the hero's final labour was to clean the dung from Augeias' stables, demonstrating that he was not above such a humble deed. Ignoring the audience's favourable response, Diogenes then, 'perhaps with this deed of Herakles in mind', squatted down and defecated. Dio indicates no other motivation for this strange finale, but it would accord with the Cynics' general disdain for social conventions. Diogenes' follower Krates, too, is compared by several writers to Herakles, most elaborately in a passage of Apuleius (*Florida* 22.3–4):

> Just as the poets say that Hercules subdued the savage monsters amongst men and beasts by his virtue and cleansed the world, in the same way this our philosopher was a Hercules against quick temper, envy, avarice, lust and other monsters and crimes of the human spirit; he drove all these pestilences from their minds, purged households and tamed badness; he too was half-naked and distinguished by a club, besides being sprung from Thebes, where Hercules is said to come from.

The authors who preserve these anecdotes about the early Cynics all belong to the Roman imperial period, and Herakles evidently retained his significant role for the school until the end of antiquity. In a discourse written for the emperor Trajan in the early second century AD (*On Kingship* 1.52–84), Dio Chrysostom tells a story supposedly related to him during his wanderings in exile in the Peloponnese, when he chanced upon a rural shrine of Herakles. He encountered a wise woman there who told of Herakles being taken as a young man to a mountain, which had two peaks, one the seat of Royalty, the other of Tyranny. The paths to each peak and the appearance of each woman are described in elaborate detail, making it abundantly clear which represents which of Prodikos' Vice and Virtue – Tyranny's courtiers, for example, are Cruelty, Insolence, Lawlessness, Faction and Flattery, in contrast to Royalty's company of Justice, Peace, Civic Order and Law. Herakles of course eventually made the virtuous choice of Royalty, and proceeded to destroy tyranny wherever he found it, thus earning his title of 'saviour of mankind', and incidentally providing a suitable patron for Trajan. Elsewhere (*Oration* 60), Dio presents a rationalizing version of the Deianeira–Nessos story, in which Herakles is depicted as the Cynic philosopher corrupted: he is persuaded to abandon his lionskin for normal clothes, to sleep in comfort and eat refined food, as a result of which he becomes weak and flabby, and eventually sets fire to himself in disgust at his own self-indulgence.

Around the same time our earliest systematic description of the Cynic life, included in Arrian's collection of teachings of the Stoic philosopher

Epiktetos, cites Herakles first in a list of Cynic heroes (*Discourse* 3.22.57). Likewise, later in the second century, the eponymous philosopher of the dialogue *The Cynic* (13), sometimes attributed to Lucian, cites Herakles as being 'the best of men', his virtues including steadfastness, patience and rejection of luxury. The Cynic who appears in Lucian's *Philosophies for Sale* (8) similarly claims Herakles as the hero he emulates, carrying a club and wearing a short, threadbare cloak in lieu of a lionskin, 'campaigning against pleasures just like him . . . undertaking to cleanse life'. Lucian paints a more substantial portrait of the ideal Cynic in his *Demonax*, in the preface to which he notes that Demonax shared with the Boiotian Sostratos a striking combination of physical strength and a philosophical mind, because of which Sostratos had been nicknamed 'Herakles'. Less positively, Lucian devotes an entire essay to denigrating the antics of Peregrinos, a Cynic philosopher whom he evidently regarded as a shallow self-publicist. *The Death of Peregrinos* tells how Peregrinos advertised his intention to cremate himself, and proceeded to carry the deed out at the end of the Olympic Games of AD 165, declaring that 'one who had lived like Herakles must die like Herakles' (33). While the Cynics do seem to have favoured suicide in certain circumstances, this is the only instance of a link being made with Herakles' death, and Lucian contemptuously alleges that Peregrinos had not actually intended to go through with the act, although another source (Philostratos, *Lives of the Sophists* 563) presents his death as demonstrating philosophical courage.

Later still, the fourth-century emperor Julian could adduce Herakles as a role-model for the degenerate Cynics of his day, as having 'left the greatest example to mankind of this way of life' (*Oration* 6.187c–d). Elsewhere, Julian berates the Cynic Herakleios for irreverent use of myth, giving examples of the proper way to present stories about Herakles and adding a tale of his own which is yet another variation on Prodikos' allegory, casting Julian himself as the young man being educated by the gods (*Oration* 7.229c–34c).

Herakles' supposed self-control and fortitude in adversity were also admired by the Stoics. As we have already noted (pp. 99–102), the two Senecan Hercules plays are informed by Stoic values, although the picture is complicated by dramatic considerations and by the plays' relationship with their Greek models. In the *Hercules Furens*, for example, the hero's lengthy consideration of suicide (ll.1216–319) has been thought by some to reflect Seneca's own philosophical interest in the issue. The question is, however, already the subject of debate in Euripides' *Herakles*, where the hero ultimately rejects suicide (ll.1347–52) on the grounds that it might be seen as the cowardly option, quite unsuitable for a fearless warrior, and out of gratitude towards Theseus. Seneca's Hercules, by contrast, is motivated by less noble sentiments, only deciding to live when Amphitryon effectively blackmails him by threatening to kill himself. The Stoic hero is perhaps more apparent in the *Hercules Oetaeus* which, as we have seen, significantly expands on its Sophoklean model to include a death-scene in which Hercules displays unflinching self-control to the last on his pyre. Similarly, where Sophokles had represented Herakles' monster-slaying strength in an ambivalent light, the *Hercules Oetaeus* elaborates on the hero's civilizing role, his endurance and self-reliance.[18]

Elsewhere in Stoic writing, not only is Herakles a model to be emulated, but an explicitly virtuous motivation for his exploits is adduced. Seneca himself cites the hero alongside Odysseus as having been exemplars of Stoic wisdom to earlier generations 'because they were unconquered by toils, despised pleasure and were victors over all terrors' (*On Firmness* 2.1). He also contrasts the hero's altruism with Alexander the Great's selfishness in *On Benefits* (1.13.3):

> Hercules conquered nothing for himself; he crossed the world not desiring, but judging, what he would conquer, an enemy of evil men, champion of good, and bringer of peace to land and sea.

Epiktetos likewise declares, according to Arrian (*Discourse* 3.24.13–14), that Herakles 'went throughout the whole world "seeking out mankind's violence and lawfulness" (*Odyssey* 17.487), casting out and purging the one and introducing the other . . . .' He goes on to offer an astonishing exoneration of one of Herakles' more reprehensible traits, his tendency to beget and abandon children everywhere: the hero left them without regret because he knew 'that Zeus is father of mankind'. Herakleitos provides evidence of a more thorough-going Stoic intellectualization of Herakles' deeds in his *Homeric Problems*, an example of which we have already seen (p. 10). Just prior to that passage Herakleitos explains that (33.1):

> Herakles should be thought of not as someone so trained in bodily power that he was the strongest man of his time, but as a sensible man and an initiate of heavenly wisdom who brought to light philosophy which had been plunged into the depths of fog, as it were, as the most learned Stoics agree.

Stoic conceptions of Herakles may also underlie the hero's unexpected appearance in Orphic poetry of the late hellenistic or early Roman imperial periods. The Orphics proposed various alternatives to the traditional account of the creation of the universe, and according to one such cosmogony everything began with Water and Earth, who between them generated unaging Time, described as a serpent with wings and the extra heads of a bull and a lion, 'and a god's face in the middle', who is also known as

Herakles; Time/Herakles in turn generated an egg, from which the gods and ultimately the whole world are descended (Orphic fragment 54). As West (1983, 192–4) argues, the hero's equation with this Time accords with the Stoic identification of Herakles with an all-powerful God, 'because his strength is invincible, and whenever it will have become tired by carrying out its works, it will return into fire' (Seneca, *On Benefits* 4.8.1). There may also be a connection with the allegorical interpretation of Herakles' labours as representing the twelve months of the Stoic Great Year, the duration of the universe, at the end of which everything will be consumed by fire.

Images of the philosophical Herakles

This conception of Herakles as philosopher also finds some reflection in the visual arts. Several statue types originating in the fourth century BC and much copied during the hellenistic and Roman imperial periods depict Herakles not in mid-action, but rather at rest and contemplative. One such type is the 'Lansdowne Herakles', the original possibly by the early fourth-century sculptor Skopas, which depicts a young, beardless hero, holding the club in his left hand but resting it against his shoulder, while the lion-skin trails from his relaxed right arm. Another type is the 'Farnese Herakles' in which the mature (bearded), muscle-bound hero stands leaning on his club, with one hand behind his back holding two apples, presumably recently obtained form the garden of the Hesperides. The original is usually attributed to the late fourth-century Lysippos, and its appearance on a Corinthian coin of c.300 BC has led scholars to suggest that it was made for public display in Corinth, or for the neighbouring Sikyon, Lysippos' home town. Fifty or so copies are known, at various scales, the most famous being the colossal version Naples 6001, which is 3.17m in height and was probably commissioned for the Baths of Caracalla at Rome c.AD 215; unusually we even have the signature of the copyist, Glykon of Athens. In the context of the baths a celebration of the body beautiful would be appropriate, but the composition here adds a further dimension: the Hesperides episode was thought by some to be Herakles' final labour, and his contemplative stance would be appropriate for one reflecting on his imminent apotheosis; at the same time, his weariness makes the great hero seem just a little more human, a role model to whom the viewer could relate. These representations of the hero at rest are perhaps a natural development, in terms of sculptural style, from the classical Herakles of the Nemean lion metope at Olympia (p. 32). Their popularity in the hellenistic and Roman imperial periods, however, reflects the broader trend of Herakles' intellectualization.

Finally, an extraordinary allegorical painting of an intellectual Herakles is described by Lucian in his short piece *A Foreword: Herakles*. He claims to have seen this in a villa in the Rhône valley, where the local inhabitants identified Herakles with a Celtic hero called Ogmios. Herakles is depicted as a bald, wrinkled and sunburnt old man, though still recognizable by his trademark lionskin, club and bow; the 'most surprising thing' (§3) about the picture, however, is that he pulls a crowd of happy people behind him, their ears linked to Herakles' tongue by gold and amber chains. A Celt explains that they identify Herakles-Ogmios with eloquence, unlike the Greeks, who associate speech with Hermes, and that 'eloquence alone loves to show its full-grown bloom in old age' (§4). It is impossible to judge how much of this story is true – whether it is based on a real painting, and whether the interpretation is correct – especially since the elderly Lucian's agenda is to justify his coming out of retirement to address a large audience. It is also the case, as we have seen, that Lucian was familiar with the Cynic allegorization of Herakles, and thus with a conception of the hero which looked beyond his physical prowess. Nonetheless, the image presented here is a striking reflection of the intellectualization Herakles has undergone by the second century AD, and as summed up by the Celt (§6):[19]

> Altogether we consider the real Herakles to have accomplished everything by elo-quence, as a wise man, and to have exerted force principally by persuasion. His arrows, I think, are words, sharp, well-aimed and swift, wounding souls.

THE ROMANTIC HERO

Another aspect of this interest in Herakles' internal qualities is his representation as a romantic hero. An extensive love-life is, as we have seen, already a feature of Herakles' character explored in the classical period in both tragedy and comedy – it is love of Iole which ultimately brings about the hero's death, and Sophokles' Deianeira exclaims, 'Surely no one man has loved as many different women as Herakles!' (*Women of Trachis* 459–60). Much later, a speaker in Athenaios' *Sophists at Dinner* (13.556e) refers to Herakles as being a 'woman-lover', who had the greatest number of wives, but only one at a time. According to the lists compiled by Brommer (1984, 117–41), Herakles is recorded by one writer or another as having slept with an impressive total of ninety women, even without counting the fifty daughters of Thespios supposedly bedded by Herakles either in a single night or over fifty consecutive nights (pp. 183–4). These liaisons produced as many as one hundred and forty-one sons, again not counting Thespios' fifty grandsons, but a mere two daughters – Aristotle (*History of Animals*

585b22–4), who counts just one daughter and seventy-two sons, comments on this disparity, citing Herakles as an example of men and women whose nature is particularly to generate one sex or the other.

In addition to Herakles' women, we also hear of half a dozen or more young male lovers, including Philoktetes, Admetos and Abderos. According to Plutarch (*Erotikos* 761d) even Herakles' nephew Iolaos was one of his boyfriends:

> It is difficult to list the other loves of Herakles because of their great number; but lovers to this day worship and honour Iolaos, believing him to have been his beloved, and take oaths and pledges from their beloveds at his tomb.

There was indeed a cult of Iolaos at Thebes as well as one of Herakles (pp. 182–3) – Pausanias (9.23.1) mentions a gymnasium and stadium 'of Iolaos' near the Proitian Gates, where 'they show you a hero-shrine of Iolaos'. Thebes also had a strong tradition of homoeroticism, as the home of the mythical first homosexual Laios, and of the Sacred Band, an elite squadron made up entirely of lovers which enjoyed brief military success in the fourth century BC; Plutarch repeats his comments about Iolaos in connection with a discussion of the Band (*Pelopidas* 18). The association of Herakles and Iolaos in cult can be seen in Attika and Sicily, as we shall see in Chapter 6, and Plutarch is again our source for the more general comment that 'even now Iolaos is his altar-partner in many places, and people pray to them together, calling Iolaos Herakles' comrade' (*On Brotherly Love, Moralia* 492c).

It is possible to interpret Herakles' liaisons with young men as a reflection of the homosexual activities which form part of a warrior's initiation in many societies; the uncivilized 'outsider' status suggested by Herakles' lionskin and club, and his cattle-raiding activities, also suit a reading which casts Herakles as the archetypal initiator. These affairs can, however, just as easily be taken as yet another symptom of Herakles' voracious appetites. As we have seen earlier in this chapter, 'boyfriends' are part of the package offered by Prodikos' Vice, and an indiscriminate liking for both sexes is implied in an early fourth-century AD dialogue on the relative merits of homosexual and heterosexual love, set at a festival of Herakles. One of the protagonists urges the other not to omit mention of any affair with either a boy or a girl, because 'surely you know how keen the god was in matters of love; so I think he will very gladly receive your stories as offerings' (Pseudo-Lucian, *Affairs of the Heart* 1).[20]

Of all Herakles' lover-affairs, those which seem to have received the most extensive treatment in various genres of literature and art are with Omphale and with the youth Hylas, so we will look at them in a little more detail.

Omphale

The story of Herakles' enslavement to Omphale is briefly alluded to in tragic contexts, as we have seen, as part of the background to the Deianeira story, in explanation of the hero's absence from home. It was also subject to comic treatment – as already noted, *Omphale* was the title of two satyr plays and at least three comedies – but the surviving fragments do not give much indication of the plots involved. Food and drink is mentioned, as we might expect; Ion's Omphale (fr. 22 *TrGF*) tells her 'Lydian harpists and singers of ancient hymns' to 'honour the stranger', establishing a general impression of eastern opulence; Kratinos the younger (fr. 4 *PCG*) refers to a 'little horse', apparently a woman's hair-ornament, but not who is wearing it. Systematic accounts must have been provided by our fifth-century mythographers, but we only have paraphrases, again providing less than full detail of the narrative: according to Pherekydes (fr. 82 F), Zeus instructed Hermes to sell Herakles in payment for Iphitos' murder, and the Lydian queen Omphale bought him for three talents; Herodoros (fr.33 F) specifies that the period of servitude was three years, rather than the one year mentioned by Sophokles (*Women of Trachis* 252–3).

It is likely that the story involved an erotic relationship with Omphale at least in its comic versions, given Herakles' usual characterization, but this is not explicit in surviving literature until the late fourth century, when the rationalizing explanation we saw in Palaiphatos (p. 10) has Herakles 'enslaved' by love rather than literally in the queen's power, and mentions that he fathered a son. Our usual later informants are surprisingly short on details about the relationship: both Diodoros (4.31.5–8) and Apollodoros (2.6.2–3) have Herakles falling ill after his murder of Iphitos, and being advised by the Delphic oracle to be sold as a slave, the money to be paid to Eurytos as compensation for his son's murder; Diodoros describes Omphale as daughter of Iardanos, 'still unmarried' and queen of the Lydians; Apollodoros has her reigning over Lydia as widow of Tmolos, and specifies that Eurytos refused the blood-money; both authors then recount the Kerkopes and Syleus episodes. Apollodoros makes no mention at all of any romantic liaison, and Diodoros says only that Omphale was so impressed by Herakles' courage in vanquishing the Itonoi that she 'set him free, and having married him bore him Lamos'.

For more detail on the love affair, including the much-discussed element of the couple's exchange of clothes, we have to turn to Latin literature. The story seems to have appealed to the Augustan poets as providing a mythological *exemplum* for the modern lover metaphorically enslaved by his mistress. Omphale appears in a list of women famous for their dominance over men in Propertius 3.11 (17–20), with Hercules described as 'spinning his soft weight of wool with so hardened a hand'. This detail is elaborated upon in Propertius' account of the Cacus episode (4.9.47–50), during which Hercules adduces his experience with Omphale as he begs for admittance to the exclusively female grove of Bona Dea: 'I have carried out servile duties in a Sidonian dress and worked my daily weight of wool for the Lydian; her soft breast-band held my hairy chest captive, and I was a proper girl with hard hands.'

Ovid cites Herakles' endurance of servitude as a model for the patience required by a serious lover (*Ars Amatoria* 2.215–22), but elsewhere treats the episode at length. In *Heroides* 9, as we have seen (p. 98), Deianira's complaint includes a humorous vignette (ll.73–118) of Hercules dressed in his mistress' 'Sidonian gown', recounting his former labours as he helps with the wool-work, while Omphale herself has his lionskin and arms. Even more emphasis is placed on the exchange of clothes in Ovid's other telling of the story, which is adduced as one of several explanations for the nudity of worshippers at the Roman Lupercalia (*Fasti* 2.303–58). Hercules and Omphale have a feast and spend the night in a cave on the eve of a festival of Bacchus, swapping clothes before they dine. Hercules puts on Omphale's 'delicate tunics dyed with Gaetulan purple', but her 'elegant belt' is too small for him, her bracelets are broken by his large arms, and his big feet split her shoes. While they sleep, the lecherous god Faunus enters the cave in search of Omphale and, feeling his way in the gloom, carefully avoids the couch draped with the lionskin, climbing instead onto the one with soft drapes – where his intended assault is abruptly cut short when he encounters hairy legs, and Hercules throws him to the floor. The story fits a tradition of the interrupted rape, which both Greek and Roman audiences seem to have found amusing, and the internal audience of Ovid's account all laugh at the discomfited Faunus: 'thus ridiculed, the god does not love clothes which deceive the eye, and calls people to attend his rites naked'.

The visual arts may provide much earlier evidence for the clothes-swapping motif. Instances of Omphale's identification in Greek vase-painting are all contested, but there is a good case for recognizing her on a fragmentary Attic black-figure amphora of c.540 BC (Malibu 77.AE.45). Here we see a seated figure wearing a lionskin and holding a bow; the figure is clearly a woman, as her skin is painted white and she is wearing fine-strapped sandals; in front of her stands a male figure, holding a plectrum and kithara. There are no inscriptions, and the state of the vase makes it impossible to see if the man is wearing female clothing, but Omphale and Herakles are by far the most likely candidates. The only really plausible case for identifying the story in fifth-century art is on the Pronomos vase (above), but there are a few more possible candidates in South Italian vase-painting of the fourth century. For example, on a Lucanian pelike of around 350 BC (Louvre

K545) a young Herakles leans on his club, apparently in conversation with a woman who holds a spindle and distaff; the case for identifying her as Omphale rests on the combination of her wool-working equipment with the regal appearance imparted by her crown.

The story is altogether more popular in Roman art, as in literature, with the clothes-swapping motif making it readily identifiable. Omphale is a common subject for late Republican gems, depicted either alone with Hercules' lionskin and club, or in the very act of making love with Hercules on the lionskin, as on a mid-first-century carnelian in Vienna (Kunsthistorisches Museum IX B 1364). As we shall see (pp. 152–3), images of the couple may have political overtones at the end of the Republic and in the early empire, when they were associated with Antony and Cleopatra, and the ridiculous element of Hercules' enslavement is often emphasized. A wall-painting of c.AD 70, for example, from the House of M. Lucretius in Pompeii (IX 3.5, Naples 8992) depicts a drunken Hercules half-draped in a diaphanous dress, leaning on an old man for support and surrounded by three Cupids, while Omphale leans casually on his club, wearing the lionskin over a dress which leaves one breast exposed. A century later Lucian alludes to paintings, with which he assumes his reader will be familiar, in which Herakles is 'dressed in the most outlandish costume . . . in saffron and purple, carding wool and being struck by Omphale's sandal . . . the masculinity of the god made shamefully feminine' (*How to Write History* 10).

Alongside this kind of image, however, in the second century the couple begin to be depicted in more serious contexts, where the negative overtones of oriental decadence and the hero 'unmanned' are not obviously relevant. For example, a series of silver coins minted in Lydia Minor c.AD 150–250 feature Omphale with the lionkskin and/or club, and presumably celebrate her as a famous figure of the area's past. A positive reading of the Lydian queen is also presupposed by her appearance on one or two third-century sarcophagi, and by the striking statue of c.AD 200 (Vatican), which combines the portrait head of a contemporary Roman woman with the nude body of Omphale, holding the club and with the lionskin draped over her head and shoulders, its forepaws resting on her breasts and the rear paws half-concealing her pudenda.[21]

Hylas

There is, then, a romantic element to Herakles' affair with Omphale, but this is frequently overshadowed by the role reversal motif; for unequivocal romance we must turn to his homosexual relationship with Hylas. Our first and fullest accounts, in Apollonios' epic *Argonautika* and Theokritos' pastoral *Idyll* 13, were both written in the third century BC although their relative dates are debated. As we noted in Chapter 2 (p. 55), Apollonios has Herakles join the expedition immediately after his delivery of the Erymanthian boar, and generally characterizes him as a hefty, old-fashioned strong man. He kills an ox with a single blow of his club (*Argonautika* 1.427–8), he makes the *Argo* sink low in the water (1.531–3), he can row the ship single-handed (1.1161–3), and when he needs a new oar he simply uproots an entire tree (1187–206). This physical strength is coupled with moral rectitude, evidenced in his refusal to take command away from Jason when the opportunity is offered (1.341–9), and his abstention from the hospitality of the Lemnian women, which leaves him alone in a position to recall the Argonauts to their objective (1.854–78).

Hylas is introduced as an 'excellent squire, in the prime of youth' (1.131–2), attending Herakles when he joins the expedition. Although Hylas' youth and beauty is emphasized, the relationship is never explicitly described as erotic, but is presented almost as that of father and son, Herakles being said to have brought Hylas up after killing his father (1.1211–20). Hylas is in search of water for Herakles' dinner when the nymph of the spring Pegai, captivated by his beauty, pulls him into her waters, never to be seen again. Herakles' anguished reaction to the news of Hylas' loss is described in physical terms (1.1261–4):

> Hearing this, the salt sweat gushed down his forehead, and his dark blood seethed in his innards. Angry, he threw a fir-tree to the ground, and ran wildly on whichever path his feet carried him.

Herakles' efforts to find Hylas are in vain, but he forces the local people of Mysia to continue looking by taking their finest sons hostage, whom he eventually settles in Trachis (1.1347–57). Apollonios comments that 'the Kians still search for Hylas even now' (1.1354), and the Mysian city of Kios on the Propontis (modern Gemlik, Turkey), does indeed seem to have had an important cult of Hylas, the ritual for which included an annual search for the youth, in which the city's priest of Herakles may have played a part.

For Theokritos, the story provides the main substance of a pastoral poem on the power of Love. The story is very close to Apollonios' version, and here again the pair are briefly compared to a father and son (l.8), but the Greek vocabulary used to say that Herakles 'loved a boy' (l.6) makes it clear that an erotic relationship is in question. The poem paints an incongruous picture of the macho hero of epic in love, playing with traditional myth in a way that is typical of the hellenistic period in general, and of the genre of pastoral poetry in particular. Hylas is described as 'graceful, wearing long locks' (l.7), 'golden-haired' (l.36), 'most handsome (l.72), and in a moving simile his fall into the spring is likened to a shooting star falling into the sea (ll.49–51). Herakles' reaction to his loss is again extreme. He is compared to a hungry lion pursuing its prey (ll.61–2), driven to distraction and forgetful of his duty (64–71):

> So did Herakles traverse much land, through untrodden thorn-bushes, shaken by long-ing for the boy. Those who love are wretched; how greatly he suffered as he roamed over mountains and through forests . . . He wandered, frenzied, wherever his feet led; for a cruel god had lacerated his heart.

Although Herakles is again left behind, he makes his way to Kolchis on foot, rather than completely dropping out of the expedition as in Apollonios, but the Argonauts are nonetheless scornful of him as a deserter (ll.73–5). Local religious practice may again be obliquely referred to in lines 58–60, where Herakles cries 'Hylas!' three times, and three times the boy attempts to reply from beneath the water: it has been suggested that this detail reflects the ritual lament of the Kian cult.[22]

OVERVIEW

From the fifth century BC onwards a complex inner life was developed and elaborated for Herakles. The same audiences which viewed the sufferings of the tragic hero were familiar with Herakles as a stock figure of comedy and satyr play, a by-word for gluttony, drunkenness and lust. Our knowl-edge of the comic Herakles is limited by the poor survival rate of the dramas in question, but consideration of visual evidence alongside the few extant plays and fragments provides a good general indication of his character-istics. Alongside the loutish hero, the classical period also saw the more surprising development of an intellectualized Herakles. The potential for allegory inherent in Herakles' monster-slaying activities begins to be exploited in his more explicit encounters with Sleep, Old Age and Death, while Pindar and Bakchylides associated him with the physical excellence of the ideal athlete and further ethical qualities. Prodikos' *Choice of Herakles* is a significant work in this strand of the hero's development, explicitly seal-ing his association with *aretê* and laying firm foundations for his allegorical interpretation as role-model for the Cynics and Stoic. Finally, an interest in Herakles' persona as lover first appears in the classical period, but is more thoroughly explored in the hellenistic and Roman imperial periods, when he is portrayed as distraught over the loss of Hylas or hopelessly infatuated by Omphale. All of this takes Herakles a long way beyond the simple mon-ster-slayer of Chapters 1–2, while there are both continuities and contrasts with the tragic hero of Chapter 3.

5

POLITICAL HERAKLES

There has been no end of candidates willing to cast themselves as the 'new Hercules'. Of course, such claims require a certain self-belief. However, this hasn't stopped many of history's greatest egoists . . . from attempting to claim his lion skin.

(Blanshard 2005, xvii)

THE ART OF POLITICAL LEGITIMATION

The many sides we have already seen to Herakles' image, and the great range of stories attached to him, show the versatility of his character, which could be adapted to suit very different literary genres and visual media. A further aspect to this versatility can be seen in the ways in which Herakles was appropriated throughout antiquity for political ends, especially as a means of legitimating people's claims to territory or political power. In this chapter we will look first at Herakles' role as alleged ancestor of, and role-model for, the ruler – a guise in which he was claimed by the two Spartan royal families, by Alexander the Great's family, by the hellenistic kings who succeeded him, and by various Roman republican generals and emperors. Next we will we will turn to Herakles' role as founder and patron, of cities and cultural institutions; here we will consider his relationship with a variety of Greek colonies, before turning to his role in relation to the panhellenic games. Finally, we will consider some less direct uses of Herakles' image in archaic and classical Athens, where, some argue, he was invoked in support of the tyranny of Peisitrastos and his sons, and was later displaced by the more 'democratic' hero Theseus.[1]

HERAKLES AS ANCESTOR AND IDEAL RULER

The return of the Herakleidai

Various claims to descent from Herakles are bound up with the story of the 'Return of the Herakleidai', which outlines how the Peloponnese came under the control of an invading force comprised of Dorians and descendants of Herakles. As we noted in the Introduction (p. 11), the historical reality of any kind of invasion remains disputed, but the ancient tradition strongly asserts the role of Herakles as ancestor to royal households of a large part of the Peloponnese (see Figure 5.1). The story was told at some length already in the *Catalogue of Women* (frs 10a.1–19 and 233 MW), and various elements of it must have been explored in late fifth-century Athens in tragedies named after its protagonists, but since these have only survived in fragmentary form we have to turn to later sources for the full details.

In the first place, Herakles came to the aid of Aigimios, king of the small state of Doris in north-west Thessaly, in return for which Aigimios promised him a third share of Dorian land, which Herakles asked him to hold in trust for his descendants (Diodoros 4.37.3). After Herakles' death, and the death of Eurystheus, his son Hyllos led a campaign against the Peloponnese, having misinterpreted an oracle that he could return there safely after 'the third harvest' to mean 'in three years': he was killed at the Isthmos in single combat with the king of Tegea (Herodotus 9.26, Diodoros 4.58.1–4). Many years later, Hyllos' grandson Aristomachos again misinterpreted an oracle, as a result of which he too was killed at the Isthmos, but finally *his* sons discovered the true meaning of the original oracle: three *generations* had to pass before the Herakleidai could return. They set out in alliance with Aigimios' sons Pamphylos and Dymas, and successfully gained control of the Peloponnese, although the two Dorian princes were killed in the process; the Herakleids divided their new land by lot, Temenos becoming king of Argos, Kresphontes of Messenia, and Aristodemos (or his twin sons) of Sparta (Apollodoros 2.8).

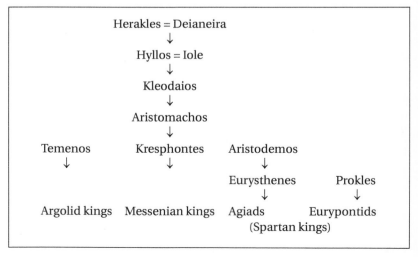

Figure 5.1 The Dorians and the sons of Herakles.

There are all sorts of problems with the details of this myth, which seem to be designed to make sense of some awkward mythological chronology – the Trojan War and a number of Argolid kings have to be fitted in between Herakles' death and the invasion – but the overarching theme of 'return' from exile implies a right of possession. Only the Herakleids themselves strictly have a claim to be returning, and only to the Argolid, whence Herakles' father Amphitryon went into exile in Thebes after accidentally killing his uncle Elektryon, and his power in Argos and Mycenae was usurped by Eurystheus' father. The claim seems to be extended, however, to cover most of the Peloponnese and to include the Dorians under the Herakleids' leadership, too. Indeed, ruling families in several different regions of the Peloponnese exploited the tradition to legitimize their position. A genealogical link with Herakles via Temenos was claimed by the early kings of Argos, including Pheidon, who ruled when the city was at the height of her power in the Peloponnese in the early seventh century. According to Strabo (8.3.33), Pheidon 'attacked the cities captured by Herakles and claimed for himself the right to put on the games which Herakles had established'. Corinth's link with the Herakleids is less straightforward, but descent from Herakles was claimed by the oligarchic group known as the Bakchiads, who ruled c.750–650 BC, via their eponymous ancestor Bakchis (Diodoros 7 fr.9), and later Corinthian families, too, may have traced similar genealogies: Thucydides (1.24.1–2) names as founder of Epidamnos, c.627 BC, one Phalios, son of Eratokelides, 'of the family of Herakles' descendants'.[2]

The Spartans

It is Sparta, however, which provides the earliest and most abundant evidence of exploitation of the association with Herakles. The return is alluded to as early as the seventh century BC in the works of the Spartan poet Tyrtaios (fr. 2.12–15 W):

> For Zeus himself, son of Kronos, husband of fair-crowned Hera, gave this city to the Herakleidai, with whom we left windy Erineos and came to the broad Peloponnese.

Elsewhere Tyrtaios urges his audience to take heart, 'for you are the race of Herakles the unconquered' (fr. 11 West), presenting the hero as an apt role-model for a city-state which had been aggressively expanding its territory during the eighth century and was fighting to maintain its position in Tyrtaios' time. The same poet also attests (fr. 19 W) the names of Sparta's three tribes, the Pamphyloi, Dymaneis and Hylleis, addressing them as distinct sections of the fighting force. The return myth provides eponymous heroes for the tribes in the two Dorian princes and Herakles' son Hyllos, although the link is weak, given that none of these characters plays a significant part in the conquest. Herakles' general prominence in archaic Sparta can be seen by his appearances in the region's visual arts. As we have seen in previous chapters, groups of Herakles' exploits featured in the decorative schemes of the sixth-century temple of Athena of the Bronze House on the city's akropolis and the Throne of Bathykles at Amyklai, while individual exploits appear on a high proportion of our few surviving Lakonian vases, c.570–540 BC. We will return to Herakles' cult at Sparta in Chapter 6.

In classical and later sources the return myth's most prominent role is in providing the foundation of the Spartan 'king-lists', which outline the descent of the two royal families from Herakles' great-great-great-grandsons Eurysthenes (the Agiads) and Prokles (the Eurypontids). The earliest extant versions of these lists are found in Herodotus, who adduces them in connection with the Agiad king Leonidas I, supreme commander of the Greek army at Thermopylai in 480 BC (7.204), and the Eurypontid Leotychides II, admiral of the Greek fleet which mustered against Mardonios the following spring (8.131). In each case this is not the first time that the character has been mentioned, but the genealogy is introduced at this point to provide him with a pedigree when he is about to play a significant part. More commonly, however, the genealogy is telescoped into a direct reference to the kings' descent from Herakles. Elsewhere in Herodotus (7.220), for example, the Delphic oracle which is supposed to have informed Leonidas' decision to take the final stand at Thermopylai proclaims that the only alternative to the sack of Sparta itself is the death of 'a king of Herakles' stock'. Occasionally the connection is commented on, as in the introduction to Xenophon's biography of Agesilaos II (400–360 BC): the 'greatest and finest thing' he can say about the noble birth of his subject is the fact that even in his own day the king's descent from Herakles is remembered (*Agesilaos* 1.2).[3]

The genealogical link could also be claimed by others at Sparta. In his life of Lysander, a Spartan general who enjoyed a particularly high profile towards the end of the Peloponnesian War (d.395 BC), Plutarch explains that his subject belonged to one of the many Herakleid families who were not Eurypontids or Agiads and therefore had no right to the throne. His overly ambitious, and ultimately unsuccessful, plan was to open up the kingship to all Herakleids, or even all Spartiates (*Lysander* 24.5):

> . . . so that the prerogative should be that not only of the descendants of Herakles, but of those judged like Herakles in the excellence (*aretē*) which had raised him to divine honours.

Writing c.AD 100, Plutarch's account here is informed by his familiarity with conceptions of the hero as *exemplum virtutis*, but there is some independent evidence to suggest that Lysander may have invoked Herakles for political ends. A much-discussed series of coins minted by eight Greek cities in Asia Minor and Rhodes bears the image of the infant Herakles strangling the snakes, sometimes with the legend SYN (conventional abbreviation for *symmachia*, 'alliance'). Traditional interpretations have seen these as representing an anti-Spartan alliance of the 390s or 380s BC, but Karwiese (1985) plausibly back-dates the coins to 405/4 BC and sees them as celebrating Lysander's liberation of the cities in question from the oppression of Athenian dominance.

Herakles' image was revived in the hellenistic period, when Sparta was struggling to regain the dominant position she had lost following the disastrous battle of Leuktra. The first Spartan coinage was minted under Areus I (reigned 309–265 BC), its introduction prompted by the need to pay foreign mercenaries and its imagery taking inspiration in part from the coinage of Alexander and his Successors (see below). Amongst the earliest types is one featuring the head of Herakles, with lionskin, on the obverse, and his club on the reverse, with a star either side symbolizing Kastor and Polydeukes. The same combination of Herakles and Dioskouroi imagery is found again on coins produced under Kleomenes III (235–222 BC), the reforming king whom Plutarch describes as so exemplary in his modest lifestyle and philanthropy that impressed petitioners declared 'him alone to be Herakles' descendant' (*Kleomenes* 13.5). Other third-century types depicted a head of either Apollo or Athena on the obverse, with Herakles seated on his lionskin on the reverse, holding his club and bow, sometimes accompanied by the letters LA for 'Lakedaimonia' (i.e. Sparta). Also from this period is a head of Herakles in the Sparta Museum (no. 52) from a colossal seated statue, its scale suggesting royal patronage although its original context is uncertain. It is possible that Herakles became favoured over the Dioskouroi because of his panhellenic appeal, as against the Dioskouroi's more local associations, in the context of a general hellenistic trend towards internationalization. The Dioskouroi may also have been downplayed because they provided a paradigm for the dual kingship, while Herakles suited the monarchical ambitions of Areus and Kleomenes.

This idea is borne out by the appearance of Herakles on a coin of Nabis (c.207–192 BC): on the obverse is his own portrait-head, on the reverse a seated Herakles with the legend *basileos Nabis*, 'king Nabis'. Nabis may have been of Eurypontid stock, providing him with some claim to royal power, but he ruled alone and his bold tactics earned him the label 'tyrant' from the contemporary historian Polybios (4.81), our major source for his reign. He was certainly faced with tremendous political pressures both within

Sparta itself and externally, first from the Achaian League and then from the growing power of Rome: in this context Nabis needed all the legitimizing help which Herakles' image could provide.[4]

The Makedonians

The return of the Herakleidai also, if indirectly, provided the kings of Makedonia with a genealogical link to Herakles. The association is first elaborated in connection with Alexander I (reigned c.498–454 BC), the earliest member of the Argead dynasty to play a significant part in Greek history, via his involvement in the Persian Wars. According to Herodotus (5.22), Alexander wished to compete in the Olympic Games but attempts were made to have him excluded on the grounds that he was a barbarian. He persuaded the officials of his Greekness, and therefore right to compete, by demonstrating his Argive descent, and promptly came equal-first in the foot-race. Herodotus later (8.137–9) fleshes the story out when he gives details of a genealogy which makes Alexander seventh in line from Perdikkas, a descendant of Temenos who had been expelled from Argos along with two brothers, and become the first king of Makedon. The anecdote is unlikely to be true – the first Makedonian king to appear in Olympia's records is Philip II in 356 BC – but suggests that the Greekness of the Argeads was still an issue when Herodotus was writing (c.430 BC), and gives an indication of the importance of ancestry in establishing a leader's credentials. The Herakles connection may be alluded to in Alexander's coinage, which included a type featuring the head and one paw of a lion in an incuse square.[5]

More explicit reference appears later in the century, when a head of Herakles wearing the lionskin cap is found in the coinage of Archelaos (413–399 BC). Son of Perdikkas II by a slave woman, Archelaos had only come to power after murdering his half-brother, uncle and cousin, so he was in particular need of a positive press, which was provided by a version of Makedonia's foundation myth in which the hero is suspiciously conveniently called 'Archelaos'. This story was promoted via a tragedy commissioned from the Athenian Euripides, who spent time as a guest at the newly developed Makedonian court in Pella during the last years before his death in 406 BC. A fragment from the beginning of the play (fr. 228 *TrGF*) has Archelaos himself outlining his genealogy, which shortens the usual sequence of generations to make Temenos a son of Hyllos, linking Archelaos with Herakles as closely as possible. The plot of the *Archelaos* can be reconstructed from the surviving fragments and from a later summary (Hyginus, *Fabulae* 219): Archelaos was cheated of the Argive throne by his brothers and sent into exile; the Thessalian king Kisseos promised Archaelaos his daughter and his kingdom in return for assistance against an enemy, but was subsequently persuaded to kill Archelaos, and ordered the construction of a hidden fiery pit; a servant revealed the plot to Archelaos, who turned the tables on Kisseos by throwing him into the pit instead; on instruction from Apollo, Archelaos fled northwards from Thessaly until he reached a place to which he was led by a goat, where he founded the city of Aigai, the ancient capital of Makedonia. It has been suggested that the play was actually originally performed at Aigai (modern Vergina), since it provides an aetiology for the city's name – 'goat' is *aix, aigos* in Greek – although it could equally likely have been produced at Dion, where Archelaos established a major dramatic and athletic festival. In either case the play would have functioned as a celebration of the king's connection to his mythological forebears, including Herakles, helping to support his claim to the throne.[6]

The head of Herakles in his lionskin appears again in the coinage of Amyntas III (393–370 BC) and Perdikkas III (365–359). The question of the Makedonians' Greekness became even more of an issue in the mid-fourth century, however, as Philip II (359–336 BC) began the expansionist policy which would soon see most of Greece under Makedonian control. While there is little evidence of Philip himself promoting the family link to Herakles, it was certainly picked up on by others who were anxious to gain his favour, as in the Isokrates passage we saw in the previous chapter (p. 124). In a much later source (Clement of Alexandria, *Protrepsis* 4.54.5) we hear of the Athenians voting to 'prostrate themselves before Philip at Kynosarges', suggesting that a statue of the king was set up in Herakles' major Athenian sanctuary (pp. 178–9), as the focus of some form of ruler-cult. There is debate amongst scholars as to the implications of such a dedication, some seeing it as complimentary acknowledgement of Philip's descent from Herakles, others as an insulting reference to allegations of the king's illegitimacy, given Kynosarges' association with *nothoi*. It is perfectly plausible, however, that the pro-Makedonian faction in Athens could have erected such a statue in the 330s, its location at the marginal Kynosarges being genealogically appropriate but also making it less offensive to the wider population, for whom the idea of worshipping a living human being was still something of a joke at this period.[7]

It is with Philip's son Alexander III ('the Great', 336–323 BC) that we see more systematic exploitation of Herakles. This was part of a broader programme of political propaganda, which made extensive use of the power of images to support Alexander's extraordinary acquisition of empire. In addition to his family's supposed genealogical link, Herakles may have appealed to Alexander because of the 'divine bastard' status which we have already seen alluded to in comedy (p. 107). Just as Herakles could be said to be the son of both Amphitryon and Zeus, Alexander seems to have promoted the idea of his own double-paternity: the mortal Philip's paternity legitimized his succession to the Makedonian throne, but Alexander's visit to the oracle of Zeus Ammon at Siwa in Egypt in 331 BC provided impetus for the idea that he was simultaneously son of the king of the gods. The idea of Alexander's divinity was highly controversial in his own lifetime and the extent to which he believed in it himself continues to be debated in modern scholarship. More mundanely, Herakles' expeditions against Troy and against the Amazons provided a model for Alexander's campaigns in the east.[8]

Arrian, one of our major sources on Alexander, provides some good examples of the way in which his subject expressed his association with Herakles, or at least how the association was reported. Alexander is portrayed as making sacrifices to Herakles alongside Zeus and other deities at several crucial points in the story: after safely crossing the Ister and defeating the Getai in 335 BC (*Anabasis* 1.4.5); before and after crossing the Hellespont into Asia Minor in 334 BC (*Anabasis* 1.11.7); before crossing the Hydaspes at the end of his Indian campaign in 326 BC (*Anabasis* 6.3.2); and again in 325 BC to celebrate the safe arrival of the naval force which had sailed up the Persian Gulf under Nearchos' command (*Indica* 36.3). More elaborate rituals in Herakles' honour are recorded in connection with Alexander's capture of Tyre in 332 BC. He had been refused entry to the city when he announced his desire to make sacrifices at the ancient sanctuary of Herakles-Melqart (pp. 191–3), so decided to attack, and was inspired by a dream in which Herakles himself led him into the city; the dream was interpreted as meaning that Tyre would be captured but with effort, 'since Herakles' deeds involved effort' (*Anabasis* 2.15.7–18). When the city eventually fell, Alexander granted amnesty to those who had taken refuge in the temple, and honoured Herakles with sacrifices, a procession, a naval review and athletic games, and a similar festival was celebrated when Alexander visited Tyre the following year (*Anabasis* 2.24.5–6 and 3.6.1).

In addition to these ritual attentions, Arrian presents several other events as undertaken by Alexander in a spirit of emulation of his great ancestor. The visit to Siwa, for example, imitates consultation of the oracle there by Perseus, on his way to kill the Gorgon, and by Herakles, en route for his encounters with Antaios and Bousiris (*Anabasis* 3.2.1–2). Likewise, in the winter of 327–326 BC, Alexander embarked on the last great siege of his campaign, of the rock Aornos (in what is now northern Pakistan), because of a tradition that Herakles had failed in the attempt – and Arrian has Alexander making reference to having surpassed Herakles in this exploit when trying to persuade his army to advance into India (*Anabasis* 4.28–30 and 5.26.6).[9]

The historical accuracy of Arrian, like all our textual sources on Alexander, is debatable, but fortunately we have contemporary visual evidence to confirm that Alexander put his association with Herakles to political use. Images of Herakles appear on coins of a variety of denominations, like Figure 5.2, first produced in Pella and Amphipolis in the early years of his reign and soon taken up by other mints. This type, depicting the head of Herakles in his lionskin on the obverse, and the enthroned Olympian Zeus on the reverse, with the legend 'of Alexander' becomes one of a standard set used throughout his career. The combination of images conveys Alexander's genealogical link with Herakles and perhaps with Zeus too, at the same time associating him with Herakles' martial prowess and Zeus' royal authority. A further detail, which could easily be missed by a modern viewer, is the knot in which the lion's paws are tied below Herakles' chin: its careful depiction suggests that this is quite deliberately included, evoking the apotropaic power of the Herakles knot (p. 31). There is some debate as to whether the beardless head wearing the lionskin should be taken as a portrait of Alexander himself, both on the coins and in the case of a statue fragment of c.330–320 BC said to be from Sparta (Boston 52.1741), but the message is not in doubt.[10]

Alexander's fondness for the hero-god may also be reflected in the naming of his son 'Herakles', born c.327 BC, by Barsine, daughter of the Persian noble Artabazos. While names which included that of a god were already common in Greek families, straightforward theonomy (calling a child directly after a god) is rarely seen before the hellenistic period, and 'Herakles' is only attested as a historical name in a few other instances, mostly from the Roman imperial period. As this Herakles would have been Alexander's first-born, and the only son alive at the time of his death in 323 BC, it is surprising that he did not have a higher profile in the bitter contest for

Figure 5.2 Head of Alexander/Herakles and seated Zeus: silver tetradrachm of Alexander the Great, from the mint at Alexandria, 326/5–318 BC. Illustration: Sheila Bewley.

succession. Although his claim was supported by Nearchos, according to Curtius (10.6.11) his Persian maternity counted against him, and he was passed over. He may already have been living in Pergamon in 323 BC (Justin 13.2.6), and Diodoros (20.20) mentions that he had been brought up there, in his account of Herakles' fate as a teenager, when he was reintroduced as a pawn in the contest for power between Alexander's former generals. In 309 BC Polyperchon briefly championed Herakles' claim to be Alexander's true heir, but on receipt of substantial bribes from his rival Kassander he promptly murdered both the boy and his mother.[11]

Non-Greek neighbours and hellenistic kings

The idea of claiming a genealogical link and using Herakles' image can also be seen from time to time amongst Greece's neighbours in the fifth and fourth centuries BC. For example, according to Herodotus (1.7), the Lydian king Kandaules was the last of a dynasty descended from Herakles and a slave-girl of Iardanos, which had been in power for 505 years down to 716 BC. The 'slave girl' in question must be Omphale, later billed as Iardanos' daughter (p. 132). Herodotus is likely to have been drawing on a local tradition of the Lydian capital Sardis, which had hellenizing ambitions at the time he was writing c.430 BC, however far back the story of the association really went.

Herodotus (4.8–10) is also our source for an account of the origins of the kings of Scythia, which he says he heard from Greeks who lived in the Black Sea area. On his way back from fetching the cattle of Geryon, Herakles is supposed to have had his horses stolen while he slept by a monstrous female, half-woman half-snake, who demanded that he sleep with her as the price for their return. He complied for long enough to father three sons, before leaving the viper-woman with a bow and a special belt, the stringing and correct putting-on of which were to be a test for the boys when they grew up. The youngest, Scythes, was the only one to succeed in the task, thus becoming the first in the line of Scythian kings, while his brothers Agathyrsos and Gelonos were sent into exile to become ancestors of the Agathyrsoi and Gelonoi tribes north-west of Scythia. Even Herodotus concedes that this is not the most likely account of Scythia's origins, but the idea of the monstrous mother makes sense in mythological terms as an explanation for the (in Greek eyes) barbaric nature of Scythians.

In a more conventional fashion, Maussolos of Halikarnassos, ruler of Karia 377–353 BC, associated himself with both Herakles and Zeus Labraundeus, an epithet derived from *labrys*, the axe Herakles is supposed to have obtained from the Amazon queen Hippolyte. Coins from the island of Kos

– where Herakles had a significant place in cult as we shall see in Chapter 6, and which was under Maussolos' control for a few years in the 350s – depict a head of Herakles with Maussolos' features. Political connections with Maussolos may also lie behind the renaming of the Karian city of Latmos, which became 'Herakleia' at this period. Finally, images of Herakles occur several times amongst the sculptures that decorated Maussolos' famous funerary monument, the Maussoleion, one of the Seven Wonders of the ancient world. He fights in the Amazonomachy which adorns one of the main friezes, a clear reference to the story of the *labrys*, while some have reconstructed the very fragmentary coffers as representing his labours; it has even been suggested that the pyramidal shape of the Maussoleion and its crowning chariot-group was meant to draw a parallel with Herakles' pyre and triumphal ascent to Olympos.[12]

After Alexander, use of Herakles' image is often explicable as direct imitation of his example. The wars of the Diadochoi, 'Successors', lasted for around forty years after Alexander's death, but by c.280 BC some stability had been established, with the former vast empire now divided into three major parts – mainland Greece and Makedonia under the Antigonids, Egypt under the Ptolemies, much of Asia Minor and the Middle East under the Seleukids – and the small kingdom of Pergamon under the Attalids. In all four cases the maintenance of power was bound up with the establishment of a ruling dynasty with a strong identity, their right to rule being asserted in propaganda which made use both of Alexander's own image and of the images he himself had used, including that of Herakles. The success of this strategy is evident in the dynasties' own longevity, and in the fact that it was imitated by a number of non-Greek kings from neighbouring areas.

In the first few years after Alexander's death, the Figure 5.2 type of silver tetradrachm was produced for Philip III Arrhidaios (323–317 BC), the last Argead to rule Makedonia, and it was soon taken up by Antigonos I Monophthalmos (306–301 BC), founder of the Antigonid dynasty. Contemporary political interest in Herakles may also be indicated by an inscription from the Makedonian palace at Aigai built around this time, significantly positioned in the throne-room, making a dedication to Herakles Patroos, 'ancestor'. The coinage of Antigonos' successors sometimes combined the Herakles-head with a horse and rider, and introduced the motif of the hero's trademark club, seen for example on the reverse of a gold coin of Philip V (220–179 BC) with the legend *basileos Philippou*. Another popular type of silver tetradrachm is the one we have already seen used by Nabis at Sparta, with the king's portrait-head on the obverse and Herakles seated on his lionskin on the reverse, with the *basileos* legend. This can be found, for example, in the coinage of the Seleukid Antiochos II (261–246 BC), featuring the portrait of his predecessor Antiochos I.[13]

Originally part of the Seleukid empire, Baktria gained its independence under Euthydemos (c.208–200 BC), who promptly produced this same type of tetradrachm with the seated Herakles. His son and successor Demetrios (c.200–180 BC) issued a coin type which featured his own portrait head on one side wearing an elephant-scalp cap, and on the other a youthful Herakles, with club and lionskin in his left hand, crowning himself like a victorious athlete with his right hand, accompanied by the legend *basileos Demetriou*. A few years later, Agathokles of Baktria (c.190–170 BC) minted a series of 'pedigree coins' bearing the portraits of Antiochos I and various Baktrian kings, in an attempt to assert his contested right to the Baktrian throne. These included a tetradrachm of the Figure 5.2 type, on which the head that wears the lionskin is clearly a portrait of Alexander, accompanied by the legend 'Alexander son of Philip', while the reverse bears the legend 'in the reign of Agothokles the Just'. Later still, the powerful Alexander-Herakles combination is invoked again by Mithradates VI of Pontus (112–63 BC), who briefly extended his realm from a small kingdom on the shores of the Black Sea to encompass most of Asia Minor, before his defeat by Pompey. His coinage included several versions of the Figure 5.2 type, in some of which the head in the lionskin cap may be a portrait of Mithradates himself; more clearly a portrait, with distinctive long sideburns, is a marble bust (Louvre MA 2321), which presents Mithradates again with the lionskin cap.[14]

Ptolemy I (323–282 BC) had established himself in Egypt almost immediately after Alexander's death, and as early as c.320 BC began to mint a new type of silver tetradrachm. This makes clever use of a combination of motifs: the portrait head of Alexander has the rams-horns of Zeus Ammon tucked under an elephant-scalp cap, proclaiming both his divine paternity and his conquest of distant India, while beneath his chin the Herakles knot is frequently visible. Both Alexander's and Ptolemy's own descent from Herakles is explicitly asserted in Theokritos' encomium (*Idyll* 17) of his successor, Ptolemy II Philadelphos (282–246 BC). The opening lines present Ptolemy I as enthroned in the halls of Zeus alongside Alexander and Herakles himself, who rejoices at his descendants' deification. The genealogy is insisted on, and an evocative picture is painted of Herakles' domestic life on Olympos (ll.28–33):[15]

> For the mighty son of Herakles is ancestor to both (Alexander and Ptolemy), and both can trace their lineage ultimately to Herakles; who, when he has sated himself with fragrant nectar and goes from the feast to the home of his beloved wife, gives the bow and quiver slung under his elbow to one man, and to another his iron club with jagged knots; and they take the weapons and the bearded son of Zeus himself to the ambrosial bed-chamber of white-ankled Hebe.

The Attalids at Pergamon promoted not one but two foundation-myths for their kingdom, both of which were designed to reinforce their claim to be Alexander's legitimate heirs. One built on a connection possibly elaborated previously by those surrounding Barsine's son Herakles, and alluding to Alexander's supposed descent from Achilles via his mother Olympias. According to tradition, after the fall of Troy Achilles' son Neoptolemos had taken Hektor's widow Andromache back to Epiros (Olympias' home region); a new twist provided the couple with a son called Pergamos, who migrated to Mysia where he founded the city of Pergamon. The other drew on the better-established story we have already seen portrayed in tragedy of Auge and her son by Herakles, Telephos, who grew up to become king of Mysia, fighting in the Trojan War as an ally of the Trojans. These stories provided Pergamon with a mixture of Greek and Trojan forebears, reflecting the ethnic mix of the historical population, and distracting attention from the lowly origins of the Attalids themselves. Myth and history are intertwined in Lykophron's *Alexandra*, an extraordinary poem, which, it has been plausibly argued, was produced at the Attalid court early in the reign of Eumenes II (197–159 BC). This relates the prophecies of Kassandra, daughter of Priam, king of Troy, which encompass the whole of the Trojan War and its aftermath, right up to the eventual rise to power of the Romans (as descended from the Trojans). An allusion to the tragic death of Barsine's son makes explicit the genealogical link between this historical character and his mythological ancestors (ll.801–4):

> . . . where one day hereafter the Tymphaian dragon, chief of the Aithikes (i.e. Polyperchon, king of Epiros) shall destroy at a feast Herakles, the seed of Aiakos and Perseus and not far from the blood of Temenos.

Perhaps from this period too is an epigram, which invokes the mythological Herakles as the hero of various of the labours, calling upon him to 'come down to the acropolis of unravaged Pergamon and save the great descendants of Telephos' (*Greek Anthology* 16.91).[16]

Eumenes II is also credited by most scholars as having commissioned the grandiose Altar of Zeus at Pergamon, as part of an extensive building programme begun in the late 180s BC. As we have seen, the exterior of the enclosure included Herakles in its extensive sculptural Gigantomachy, but the interior of the court celebrated the more locally significant story of his son in the 'Telephos Frieze'. Although fragmentary, enough of this frieze survives to make it clear that it is a remarkable work, being the earliest example of continuous narrative in Greek art and experimenting with landscape and spatial depth in a way not previously seen in relief sculpture. The very detailed story it tells combines elements which are not found together anywhere in extant literature, but which may have been told in epic form at the Attalid court, and could certainly have been researched in Pergamon's library, which was second only to that at Alexandria. Herakles himself appears near the beginning of the north frieze, meeting Auge and her father in Tegea, but then Auge is set adrift on a raft immediately after Telephos' exposure, coming to Mysia alone. Herakles reappears on the east frieze discovering the infant suckled by a lioness, after which the next extant scene has Telephos as a youth arriving in Mysia, presumably having been brought up back in the Peloponnese. The frieze is the earliest visual rendering of Herakles with the baby Telephos, a scene which would become popular in Roman art, including a striking wall-painting from Herculaneum, in which Arkadia personified looks on as Herakles notices his infant son being suckled by a deer (Naples 9008).

A late example of Herakles' image being put to political use by a hellenistic king comes from the small state of Kommagene in eastern Anatolia, which had seceded from Seleukid control c.163 BC and maintained its independence from Rome as late as AD 17. Antiochos I Theos (c.70–30 BC) established the worship of himself and a group of hybrid Greek–Persian deities – Zeus–Oromades, Apollo–Helios–Mithras, Artagnes–Herakles–Ares – celebrating his supposed descent from both Makedonian and Achaemenid royal families. The syncretism is reflected in the extraordinary style of the monuments erected at a number of sites across the kingdom, which combines Greek traits with approximations of ancient Persian dress, apparently at the king's express command. A particularly fine relief from the tomb-sanctuary of Antiochos' father Mithradates at Arsameia depicts Antiochos himself in Oriental costume, though clean-shaven, shaking hands with Artagnes–Herakles–Ares, the motif conveying that both figures are of the same divine status. The Herakles is bearded and nude apart from the lionskin tied around his neck, holding a club, in conventional Greek style; his anatomy, however, is heavily stylized, in marked contrast to the naturalism that was prevalent in contemporary Greek sculpture.

Roman generals and emperors

The political exploitation of Herakles by Alexander and later hellenistic kings was continued by leaders at Rome. Some of the earlier examples may have been inspired directly by the Hercules of Italian cult – for example, the ancient patrician family the Fabii claimed descent from Hercules and a nymph associated with the river Tiber (Plutarch, *Fabius Maximus* 1) – but generals of the later republican period and emperors could hardly have failed to be influenced by the success of this kind of propaganda amongst their eastern neighbours.

The leaders on both sides of the Second Punic War (218–202 BC) were associated with Hercules to some extent. Scipio Africanus is presented at various points in Silius Italicus' *Punica* as following in Hercules' footsteps: during a visit to the Underworld he finds his mother in company with Alkmene and learns that Jupiter is his father (13.615–49); he is presented with a choice between Virtue and Pleasure (15.18–128); as he celebrates the triumph awarded for his final victory over Hannibal, he looks like Hercules when he had conquered the giants (17.649–50). In Lucan (*Civil War* 4.656–60), the local peasant who recounts the Antaeus story (p. 56) comments that even greater fame was brought to the location when Scipio camped there in the course of his conquest of Hannibal. The extent to which Scipio himself promoted the link with Hercules is difficult to assess, though he is said to have invited his friends to a feast celebrating the dedication of a sanctuary of Hercules (Plutarch, *Rules for Politicians* 20).

There is a stronger case for seeing deliberate exploitation of such an association by Scipio's Carthaginian rival Hannibal. Evidence is provided by a series of coins issued in Spain during the period of Punic occupation under various members of Hannibal's family (237–207 BC), which feature portrait-heads of Hannibal or his father Hamilcar as Herakles-Melqart, wearing a laurel crown and holding a club over his shoulder. The connection is elaborated in various accounts of the Second Punic War. Livy, for example, portrays Hannibal making vows at the temple of Herakles-Melqart at Gades (pp. 191–3) before mustering his troops for the march on Italy (21.21); has Scipio's father challenge Hannibal's own assertion to be Hercules' rival (21.41); lets Hannibal advance as far as the temple of Hercules inside the Colline Gate when he invades Rome itself (26.10). Silius Italicus likewise has Hannibal dedicating spoils from his sack of Saguntum to Hercules at Gades (*Punica* 3.14–16), and characterizes his crossing of the Alps as an exploit rivalling the labours of Hercules (4.4, 11.135–7).[17]

In the second and first centuries BC a number of temples to Hercules were established at Rome by military leaders, as we shall see in Chapter 6. Any such public religious display has the potential to be a political statement, and in some cases we can clearly see an individual manipulating personal links with Hercules for political ends. In 78 BC, for example, after his victories over Mithradates, Sulla founded a temple of Hercules Magnus Custos ('the Great Guardian') in the Circus Flaminius and celebrated games for Hercules on a grand scale – the extravagant feast he provided for the people supposedly went on for days, with forty-year-old wine and such an excess of food that large amounts of meat were thrown into the river every day (Plutarch, *Sulla* 35). A series of coins commemorating these games features the head of Hercules on the obverse and the Erymanthian boar on the reverse, a reference to Sulla's home town of Cumae, where a pair of tusks in the temple of Apollo were said to be those of the Erymanthian boar (Pausanias 8.24.5).

A few years later, offerings to Hercules become a focus for rivalry between the two consuls of 70 BC. Crassus celebrated a lavish festival for Hercules Invictus (Plutarch, *Crassus* 2.2), probably by way of compensation for having only been granted an 'ovation' (rather than a full-scale triumph) at the end of 71 BC for his victory over Spartacus. Pompey had celebrated a full triumph at the same time in recognition of his victories in Spain, and at some point in his career dedicated a temple of Hercules Pompeianus near the Circus Maximus, the title suggesting an appropriation of the god as his personal protector. Such a connection might explain the choice of 12th August for the dedication of Pompey's theatre and temple of Venus Victrix in the Campus Martius in 55 BC, since this was the festival day of Hercules Invictus. The dedication of the temple may have been a direct challenge to Julius Caesar, who had begun promoting the idea of his family's descent from Venus as early as 69 BC (Suetonius, *Julius Caesar* 6). The opposition between the two men's patron deities is nicely set up in Appian's account (*Civil War* 2.76) of preparations at Pharsalos in 48 BC: when encouraging their soldiers before the battle, Pompey's watchword was Hercules Invictus, Caesar's Venus Victrix.[18]

The opposition continued into the next generation, with Augustus inheriting Caesar's association with Venus and Mark Antony claiming a direct genealogical relationship with Hercules. According to Plutarch (*Antony* 4 and 36), his subject was descended from an otherwise unheard-of son of Hercules named Anton; Antony himself thought he resembled statues of Hercules, and justified his extra-marital procreation of children with Cleopatra by reference to Hercules' example. Even in Plutarch's account it is clear that the link might not be entirely positive: he cites the destruction of the god's sanctuary at Patrai while Antony was staying in the town as a portent of his downfall (*Antony* 60). Elsewhere he draws an explicit parallel between Omphale's appropriation of Hercules' club and lionskin and Cleopatra's 'disarming and bewitching' of Antony, which caused him to abandon his military duties while he played with her (*Comparison of Demetrius and Antony* 3.3). As we saw in Chapter 4, such negative views of Antony's affair may have coloured the way Hercules and Omphale were depicted in contemporary art, and the situation parallels Aspasia's treatment in classical Athenian comedy as 'a new Omphale' to Perikles (Plutarch, *Perikles* 24). Antony's association with Hercules also seems to have been invoked in depictions of the struggle over the Delphic tripod, which cast Augustus as Apollo. The most public instance of this is a terracotta relief (Palatine

Antiquarium) from the temple which Augustus dedicated to Apollo on the Palatine Hill in 28 BC in thanks for his victory at Actium in 31 BC: the image asserts Augustus' rightful claim to power, and ultimate triumph over the impious Anthony.

More prominent than this negative use of Hercules' image, however, is the positive analogy drawn by contemporary poets between the hero and Augustus. Horace, for example, imagines a deified Augustus reclining with Hercules and Pollux on Olympos drinking nectar (*Odes* 3.3.9–12), and in his 'Letter to Augustus' (*Epistles* 2.1.10–12) equates the emperor's achievements with Hercules' labours. In Virgil's *Aeneid* the prophecy of Augustus' glorious future suggests that he will surpass his role-model (6.801–3):

> Nor indeed did Hercules travel over so much of the earth, though he pierced the bronze-footed deer, pacified the Erymanthian groves and shook Lerna with his bow.

The most extensive treatment of Hercules himself comes in the Cacus episode in *Aeneid* 8, which we considered briefly in Chapter 2, and this has been read by some as a deliberate allegory of Augustus' victories over various enemies of Rome. What is clearer, however, is the way in which both this episode and the poem as a whole present Aeneas as a second Hercules: Aeneas is hounded by Juno, his deeds are repeatedly referred to as 'labours', his descent to the Underworld parallels Hercules' as well as Odysseus' adventures, and much is made of his *virtus*. Since Aeneas is Augustus' ancestor and himself provides a model for Augustus' 'refoundation' of Rome, the link between Hercules and the emperor is still strong, if made at one remove.[19]

After Augustus, association with Hercules is picked up as part of the bad press surrounding the more autocratic emperors of the first century AD. Philo of Alexandria (*Embassy to Gaius* 78–9) accuses Caligula of arrogantly comparing himself with Hercules and other demi-gods, dressing up in a gilded lionskin and club. As we saw in Chapter 3, Nero is supposed to have taken the title role in performances of *The Mad Hercules*, and was perhaps influenced by Seneca's philosophical conception of the hero. Both Suetonius (*Nero* 6) and Tacitus (*Annals* 11.11) report an incident in Nero's childhood when a snake is supposed to have appeared in his cot, an obvious parallel with the infant Hercules. The adult Nero is said to have wanted to emulate his hero by killing a lion in the amphitheatre (Suetonius, *Nero* 53), and to have been hailed as Apollo and Hercules on his return to Rome as a victor in the Pythian and Olympic Games in AD 68 (Cassius Dio 53.20). According to Philostratos (*Nero* 5), he inaugurated the cutting of a canal through the Isthmos of Corinth by digging with a golden pitchfork, and returned to Corinth 'believing he had surpassed all the deeds of Hercules'.

It may be this event which is commemorated by a rock-cut relief of a Farnese-type Hercules in the wall of the canal, 5m above water level and 200m east of the Corinth–Loutraki road.[20]

In the last two decades of the first century Domitian seems to have equated himself with Hercules in more conventional ways. A colossal statue of Hercules in green basalt (Parma) stood three and a half metres tall in Domitian's throne-room in the Domus Augustana; the face has sideburns, and may be an idealized portrait of the emperor. The cult statue of a new temple of Hercules on the Appian Way certainly was, as celebrated in two epigrams by Martial (9.64–5); the poet flatteringly suggests that important prayers are addressed to Domitian while Hercules deals with lesser requests, and that had Hercules born Domitian's features when alive he would never have been subject to Eurystheus.

The official cult of Hercules enjoyed particular favour in the first few decades of the second century AD under Trajan and Hadrian, both born in Baetica (south-west Spain) and influenced by the cult of Herakles–Melqart at Gades. As we saw in Chapter 4, Dio Chrysostom elaborated a version of the Choice of Herakles as a model for Trajan, and Pliny the Younger explicitly compares the emperor with Hercules in his *Panegyric* (14–15), 'un-bowed and un-wearied' by his labours. Hercules appears on some of Trajan's coin-types, standing with his lionskin and club or just the head with lionskin cap; one type features Trajan's column in the form of a club, with lionskins draped at its base; and yet another shows just the club on the reverse. Hadrian made more extensive use of Hercules in his coinage. One type, minted at Rome c.AD 134–8, depicts the emperor himself as Hercules, a lionskin knotted around his neck; others characterize Hercules as Gaditanus by the apples he holds, a reference to the hero's travels to the far west.[21]

Later in the second century the Herculean excesses of Caligula and Nero are repeated and surpassed by Commodus. According to Cassius Dio (73.15–20) Commodus styled himself the 'Roman Hercules'; he renamed the months after epithets he had adopted for himself, including the Hercules-related 'Invictus', 'Amazonius' and 'Herculeus'; he had a club and lionskin carried before him everywhere he went; a rumour that he intended to shoot members of the audience like the Stymphalian birds kept people away from the amphitheatre; and once he rounded up men who were missing their lower legs, fitted them with serpent's tails, and had them clubbed to death as giants in a recreation of the Gigantomachy. Dio also reports (73.22) that Commodus had the head of the Colossus – a statue erected by Nero and already altered by Vespasian – replaced with his own portrait and made it look like Hercules by giving it a club and adding a bronze lion at its feet. Much of this is related also in the anonymous *Augustan History of Commodus*, which adds the details that the emperor changed the name of his African fleet to 'Commodiana Herculea'; that amongst many prodigies which appeared during Commodus' reign a bronze statue of Hercules sweated for several days; and that, after his death and deification, the priest assigned to his cult was entitled 'Herculaneus Commodianus'.

While these accounts are highly coloured, Commodus' appropriation of Hercules can be clearly traced in the more sobre medium of his coinage. Issues from early in his reign depict Hercules with the legend *comes*, identifying him as the emperor's 'guardian'; later the figure becomes *Hercules Commodianus*, the emperor's personalized version of the god, or *Hercules Romanus Augustus*, a complete assimilation between emperor and god as 'the Roman Hercules Augustus'. The portrait-head of Commodus on the later coins wears the lionskin, and the reverse sometimes features the Farnese-type Hercules or the bow, club and quiver. A well-known portrait bust of Commodus on the Capitoline (Conservatori 1120) likewise represents him wearing the lionskin, holding the club and the apples of the Hesperides, supported by a pedestal flanked by two Amazons and elaborately decorated with zodiacal symbols, reinforcing the Herculean connection by referring to the month October ('Herculeus'). The association must have taken hold in the popular imagination, because long after Commodus's death images of a Farnese-type Hercules on coins of some later emperors bear Commodus' portrait head.[22]

Commodus was murdered in AD 193, and there ensued a struggle for imperial power, with Septimius Severus eventually emerging victorious. In order to legitimize his rule, Severus needed to associate himself with the preceding Antonine emperors, and Hercules had an important place in the pantheon of Severus' birthplace, Lepcis Magna in North Africa, as did Bacchus. The two deities were jointly honoured in a huge temple, which Severus built on the Quirinal (Cassius Dio 77.16.3), and they appear side by side on the reverse of a gold coin of AD 194. The unreliable *Augustan History of Caracalla* (5) asserts that Severus' son and heir Caracalla rejected attempts to call him 'Hercules' when he had killed a lion and other wild beasts, but the Hercules association can still be seen in the coinage of several of the emperors who succeeded him, e.g. of Elagabalus, Alexander Severus and of Gordian III. Postumus (AD 260–9), originator of the breakaway 'Gallic Empire', made particularly prolific use of Hercules' image, for example producing a series which depicted all twelve of the labours.

In the mid-280s, the joint emperors Diocletian and Maximian adopted the informal titles 'Jovius' and 'Herculius', associating themselves with Jupiter and Hercules respectively. Maximian's association with Hercules is exploited for example in *Panegyric* 10, delivered in AD 289 at Trier, and images of Hercules feature frequently on his coins; both the speech and legends on the coins celebrate Maximian–Hercules as 'victor', 'uncon-quered' and 'peace-bringer'. When the Tetrarchy was formed in AD 293, the titles were extended to the two junior emperors, Galerius 'Jovius' and Constantius 'Herculius', and they were passed on to Severus II and Maxentius when they succeeded to places in the tetrarchy. The practice was soon abandoned, under the Christian emperors from Constantine onwards, having been roundly criticized by the Christian writer Lactantius in AD 314–15 (*On the Deaths of the Persecutors* 52.3):[23]

> Where are those surnames of the *Jovii* and the *Herculii*, just now so splendid and renowned amongst the nations, which flourished, having first been insolently assumed by Diocles and Maximian and afterwards transferred to their successors? The Lord has surely annihilated them and erased them from the earth.

HERAKLES THE FOUNDER

Colonies

The extensive travel involved in Herakles' myth made him an ideal role-model for the Greeks who took to their ships to found colonies overseas, especially in the archaic period, and in a few cases his patronage is explicit in the name 'Herakleia'. According to the sixth-century AD geographical dictionary by Stephanus of Byzantium (*Ethnika* 303–4), as many as twenty-three cities were so called:

> Herakleia: i) a conspicuous city of Thrace on the Pontos; ii) of Sicily; iii) of Lydia; iv) of Libya; v) of Sardinia; vi) of Italy; vii) of Gaul; viii) of Thessaly; ix) of Karia; x) in the Lydian Tauros; xi) between Skythia and India; xii) an island in the Karpathian sea; xiii) of Syria; xiv) of Phoenicia; xv) of Pieria; xvi) a city and island . . .; xvii) of Crete; xviii) of Elis; xix) of Karia, the one called Albakios, inland; xx) a city near Aiolian Kumaia; xxi) a city of Akarnania; xxii) an island in the Atlantic; xxiii) of Makedonia, founded by Philip II son of Amyntas.

A good number of these are known to us: Hansen and Nielsen (eds) 2004 catalogue nine cities called Herakleia, two smaller settlements of the same name, and two cities called Herakleion, and in one or two cases the name persists to the present day – (xii) may refer to the tiny Cycladic island of Irakleia, and (xvii) must be Crete's capital Iraklion. In several locations we have some indication that Herakles was an important figure in the ancient city's pantheon, especially from his appearance on coins.

In the eastern Mediterranean, a good example is Herakleia Pontike (modern Turkish Eregli) on the southern shore of the Black Sea. This colony was founded c.560 BC by the people of Megara and Tanagra in response, according to Justin (16.3), to a plague which was afflicting Boiotia: the Delphic oracle directed the Tanagrians to establish a new city and consecrate it to Herakles. The hero is a common figure on Herakleia Pontike's coins, his youthful head in the lionskin being the city's standard emblem, and a colossal statue of Herakles stood in the agora, according to the local historian Memnon (*FGrH* 434F52). One of the city's months was dedicated to Herakles, indicating that he held an important position in the local pantheon, and in the Roman period his annual festival included athletic contests. At some point the city dedicated representations of four of Herakles' labours at Olympia in celebration of a victory over their barbarian neighbours the Mariandynians (Pausanias 5.26.7). Herakleia Pontike was also the home of the Herodoros we noted in the Introduction (p. 4) as author of a substantial prose work on Herakles c.400 BC.[24]

Colonies in the west could make particular reference in their foundation-myths to the Geryon episode, which we know was being told in Sicily and southern Italy in the sixth century from the evidence of Stesichoros and Chalkidian vase-painting. On his way home with the cattle, Apollodoros (2.5.10) and, more elaborately, Diodoros (4.20–4) have Herakles passing through Italy and Sicily, his journey leaving various traces for future generations to remember him by. The Italian part of the itinerary encompasses the establishment of Herakles' cult at Rome (pp. 194–6), and some major construction work whereby he blocked Lake Avernus' outlet to the sea and built a coast road in Campania, referred to also by Propertius (3.18.4) and subsequently called 'Herakleia'. Other authors extend such a road all the way between Spain and Italy through Celtic territory, along which travellers were supposed to have safe conduct (Ps-Aristotle, *On Marvellous Things Heard* 85). On the Phlegraian Plain in Campania Diodoros reports a battle with giants, further to his earlier account of the Gigantomachy (p. 63), citing the third-century historian Timaios as his source. According to Dionysios (*Roman Antiquities* 1.44.1) he celebrated his victories in Italy by founding Herculaneum, a story that provides legitimation for Greek appropriation of the settlement in the sixth century BC. Similarly, Servius suggests in his commentary on Virgil's *Aeneid* (7.662) that Pompeii was named after Hercules' victory procession (*pompa*). The name is historically much more likely to derive from the Oscan word for 'five', referring to the amalgamation of five villages or to a group of five founders, but the Herculean explanation again provides some legitimation for Greek annexation of Pompeii around 500 BC.

Establishment of the late eighth-century BC Achaian colony of Kroton, on the southern coast of Lucania, is most often attributed to the city's eponymous hero. Herakles features in the city's coinage, however, including a mid-fourth-century type depicting the infant hero strangling the snakes.

More strikingly, another type portrays the adult hero seated before an altar with the legend *oikistes*, 'founder', which is the most explicit statement of Herakles' role as colonizer anywhere in the west. In what may be an attempt to harmonize two competing foundation myths, Diodoros (4.24.7) tells an awkward story whereby Herakles accidentally kills Kroton, raises a burial mound and predicts that there will later be a city on the spot. Further east along the Lucanian coast, the colony of Herakleia was founded in 433/2 BC jointly by neighbouring Tarentum, itself a Spartan colony of the late eighth century, and Thourioi, which had founded by a consortium of Greek cities as recently as 444/3 BC. The new city's name may well be a compromise between the Spartan and panhellenic identities of its founders, and is celebrated in its coinage, which from the outset frequently features images of Herakles, seated or standing, crowned by Victory, pouring a libation, or wrestling with the Nemean lion. Herakles' significance at Tarentum, too, is suggested by his appearance in the city's coinage in the fourth and third centuries BC, and by the existence of a colossal statue, which Plutarch (*Fabius Maximus* 22) reports was removed to the Roman Capitol by Fabius after his conquest of Tarentum in 209 BC.[25]

In Sicily, Diodoros (4.23) tells us that Nymphs caused warm baths to materialize for Herakles' refreshment at Segesta and Himera, the latter well known historically for its hot springs. Herakles instituted religious rituals at Agyrion for himself and Iolaos, as we shall see in Chapter 6; he also created a lake for the city and nearby both he and the cattle miraculously left permanent tracks along a rocky road. At Syracuse, Diodoros has Herakles establish a new festival for Persephone, and historically, worship of Herakles himself is attested in the city. Thucydides (7.73) mentions the Syracusan festival of Herakles in connection with the city's breaking of the Athenian siege in 413 BC, and Plutarch (*Nikias* 24–5) has the Syracusans actively encouraged by the diviners' interpretation of the sacrifices. The hero's youthful head in lionskin cap first appears on Syracusan coins at about this time, and early fourth-century types have him wrestling the lion.

In western Sicily, particularly interesting is the case of Eryx, where Herakles is supposed to have wrestled with king Eryx, the stakes being the cattle or local territory. This story must go back to the archaic period, because it is adduced around 508 BC, according to Herodotus (5.43–6), to encourage the Spartan prince Dorieus to found a city called Herakleia in Sicily: 'all the territory of Eryx belonged to the Herakleids, since it had been colonized by Herakles himself'. The expedition had the approval of the oracle at Delphi, but Dorieus was killed before reaching Eryx. A few of his followers, however, under the leadership of one Euryleon, went on to capture the city of Minoa on the south coast of Sicily, a colony of the neighbouring Selinous, itself a colony of Megara Hyblaia. The city was renamed Herakleia Minoa, perhaps by these Spartans although Herodotus does not make this explicit, and its association with the hero is reflected in his appearance on coins of the fifth and fourth centuries BC.[26]

According to Diodoros (4.29–30 and 5.15), a colony was founded in Sardinia by Iolaos, sent by Herakles, on the advice of the oracle, to accompany forty-one of his fifty young sons by the daughters of Thespios. Of the others, two remained in Thebes and seven in Thespiai, where they and their descendants became prominent citizens. Diodoros attributes to Iolaos the division of land amongst the settlers on Sardinia, and the building of temples and gymnasia, and maintains that the people of the island are called 'Iolaeis' to his day. The association is at first sight surprising, since historically there were no Greek colonies in Sardinia, but must reflect early Greek trading interests with the island and its flourishing cult of Herakles–Melqart. Enough iconographic evidence for the latter survives to have justified the mounting of an exhibition in Oristano in 2004 entitled *L'isola di Herakles*, accompanied by a conference. A more specific tradition attributes to Iolaos and the Thespiadai the construction of a particular form of prehistoric circular tower (*nuraghe*), which can be seen on Sardinia today, 'because Herakles was lord of all the land towards the evening star' (Ps-Aristotle, *On Marvellous Things Heard* 100).[27]

Finally, an unusual example of a colony within the Greek mainland is Herakleia Trachinia in Thessaly. This was founded by the Spartans in 426 BC, during the Peloponnesian War, according to Thucydides (3.92–3) in response to an embassy from the beleaguered people of Trachis and of nearby Doris, 'mother city of the Dorians', seeking help against attack from their neighbours of Mount Oita. The name Herakleia suited both the Spartan colonizers and the natives of Trachis who were amongst the first inhabitants, since the region was of course the site of Herakles' death. The link is made explicit by Diodoros (12.59.4–5), who explains that the Spartans were willing to help 'because Herakles, the Lakedaimonians' ancestor, had made his home in Trachis'. The new city was only a few miles from Thermopylai, and further impetus for its foundation may have come from a Spartan belief that Herakles had helped in the battle of 480 BC. There were good strategic reasons, too, as Thucydides explains: Herakleia was on the major land route to northern Greece, while its harbour on the Gulf of Malis would offer a base for patrolling the straits of Euboia, important to Athens as a route for the importation of grain. In practice, however, Spartan supremacy was short-lived, the city coming under constant attack by neighbouring Thessalians and the colonists being put off by the harsh regime of the Spartan governors. Forceable decolonization began in 395/4 BC when the city was taken by the Thebans and Argives, and by 370 it was firmly back under control of the Trachinians, with no trace of the Spartans left.

Herakles' mythological and cultic links with the region (pp. 184–5) certainly pre-date the colony, but there may be a shift in emphasis in treatments of the story correlating with the political fortunes of Herakleia Trachinia. The late fifth-century historian Skythinos (*FGrH* 13F1) asserts that Herakles himself founded the city after overcoming local brigands called the Kylikranes, emphasizing Sparta's role as civilizers of an unruly local population, whereas later writers make the Kylikranes friendly co-founders.[28]

The Games

Some of the institutions with which Herakles is credited are only associated with him by later writers. The tradition that he established the Olympic Games, however, is already firmly attested in the first half of the fifth century BC, and may well date back into the archaic period. In Chapter 4 we noted Herakles' role as model for the victorious athlete in Pindar, and there is particular reference to the hero's foundation of the relevant games in several of his *Olympian* odes. As we saw in Chapter 1, *Olympian* 10 (476 BC) provides the earliest attestation of the Augeian stables story and it is his victory here which Herakles is said to have celebrated by establishing the sanctuary of Zeus and its festival (ll.23–5, 43–9 and 55–9):

> The laws of Zeus urge me to sing of the special contest he founded beside Pelops' ancient tomb with its six altars . . . [*battle with the Molione twins*] But the strong son of Zeus, having drawn up his whole army and all their plunder in Pisa, measured out a sacred grove for his supreme father. He marked off the Altis in an open space by fencing it around, and made the encircling area a place for feasting, honouring the stream of Alpheos along with the twelve lord gods; and he called it the Hill of Kronos . . . Time moving forward clearly declared how, dividing the gifts of war, he sacrificed the best, and how he established the four-yearly festival with the first Olympic games and its victories.

The poem goes on to list the first victors in individual competitions before returning to direct praise of the current honorand, Hagesidamos. Establishment of the festival is likewise attributed to Herakles and characterized as 'the first-fruits of war' in *Olympian* 2 (ll.2–4), also of 476 BC, and in the same year *Olympian* 3 (ll.11–41) relates the origins of the Olympic olive crown: having founded the games, Herakles realized that Olympia was lacking in shade, so he travelled to the land of the Hyperboreans to fetch the olive trees he had noticed previously, when pursuing the Keryneian hind, to plant around the sanctuary. In *Olympian* 6 (66–71), of 472 or 468 BC, Herakles is said to have established for Zeus not only a festival and the 'greatest custom of games', but also an oracle, its seers being the descendants of Iamos.

Herakles' role as founder of the Olympic Games seems to be generally agreed. Around 400 BC, Lysias begins his *Olympic Oration* (*Speech* 33.1–2) by asserting that Herakles founded the contest 'out of good will towards Greece', envisaging the games as conducive to 'mutual friendship amongst the Greeks'. Polybios (12.26) quotes the third-century BC historian Timotheos for the idea that Herakles established the Olympic Games and the sacred truce 'making a proof of his own principle . . . never willingly to be the cause of evil to anyone'. Apollodoros (2.7.2) follows Pindar in placing the foundation of the games after Herakles' defeat of the Moliones and Augeias; Diodoros (4.13–14) inserts a very short account of the Cretan bull labour before explaining that Herakles decreed that the Olympic prize should be a simple crown 'because he himself had done good services to the race of men without receiving any payment'.

The idea of Herakles measuring out the sanctuary is nicely elaborated in an anecdote reported by Plutarch (fr. 7 Sandbach): the sixth-century mathematician Pythagoras calculated Herakles' height on the basis of the generally agreed fact that the stadium at Olympia measured 600 of his footsteps; the difference between this and other Greek stadia, 600 normal feet in length, indicated Herakles' size in relation to ordinary mortals (assuming a correlation between foot-length and height). In fact, while Olympia's stadium is indeed the longest in Greece at 192.3 metres, the difference between this and the 178-metre length of the stadia at (for example) Delphi and Nemea would make the Heraklean foot just 2.4cm longer than the ordinary one, suggesting that the hero was only a little taller than average. The statistics should not, of course, be taken so literally – the story reflects a popular impression of the Olympic stadium as being outsize, obviously the work of a super-human hero.

An odd variant on the tradition attributes the foundation of the games to a different Herakles, who was one of the Idaian Daktyloi ('Fingers'), a group of minor deities usually associated with the story of Zeus' secret upbringing in a cave on Mount Ida in Crete. Diodoros (5.64) comments on the conflation between this Daktyl Herakles and Herakles son of Alkmene, the former being the real founder of the Olympics. Pausanias (5.7.6–10) takes up this version, explaining that Herakles was the eldest of these Daktyloi, who set his brothers a race, the prize being a crown of wild olive, which he had brought back from the land of the Hyperboreans:

> To the Idaian Herakles, therefore, belongs the glory of having arranged the games at this time and first giving them the name 'Olympics'; he established that they should be held in every fifth year, because he and his brothers were five in number.

This Daktyl Herakles does occasionally surface elsewhere, for example as doorkeeper of a sanctuary of Demeter at Mykalessos in Boiotia (Pausanias

9.19.4), but remains rather obscure and an unlikely candidate as founder of such a significant, panhellenic institution. Pausanias cites local historians as his source for the tradition, and is plausible that the Eleans may have cultivated the idea of the Daktyl Herakles as a more palatable founder than the Herakles who had killed their legendary king Augeias and his nephews the Moliones. Indeed, a little earlier Pausanias (5.4.6) comments that the ancient Eleans had taken some persuading to worship Herakles son of Amphitryon, because they regarded him as an enemy. That there was some dispute even in antiquity is suggested by Strabo (8.3.30.50–5):

> We must let go the ancient stories about the foundation of the temple and the establishment of the games, some saying that Herakles one of the Idaian Daktyloi was their founder, others the son of Alkmene and Zeus, who was also the first to compete and be victorious. For such things are variously told, and not much to be credited.

In addition to the question of the Olympic Herakles' identity, there were one or two alternative foundation myths. Pausanias (5.7.10) briefly reports, again as local, the story that the games were first held to celebrate Zeus' victory over Kronos. A more serious contender is the hero Pelops, whose chariot race with the Elean king Oinomaos for his daughter Hippodameia's hand in marriage provides a fairly straightforward aetiology for one of the oldest events of the games. As we saw in Chapter 1, this story was prominent in the sculptural programme of the temple of Zeus, displayed in the east pediment over its entrance, although the metopes depicting the twelve labours give Herakles a substantial presence too. In yet another ode of 476 BC, Pindar tells the story of the chariot-race and concludes with mention of Pelops' cult at Olympia and the fame of the contests 'on the racecourse of Pelops' (*Olympian* 1.93–6), while an Olympian victory ode by Bakchylides (8.29–31) speaks of olive wreaths won 'in the famous games of Phrygian Pelops'. In terms of cult, Pelops is certainly more obviously prominent, his shrine consisting of a small, enclosed grove of great antiquity – indeed predating Herakles' foundation of the rest of the sanctuary in Pindar's account – which was embellished with a Doric portico in the fifth century BC. Herakles certainly had an altar at Olympia, near the Sikyonian Treasury according to Pausanias (5.14.9), and his attribution of the cult's inception to Iphitos, traditional reinstitutor of the games in 776 BC (5.4.6), suggests that it was regarded as ancient. This cult has left no firmly identifiable archaeological traces, however, and Pausanias is probably right in his assertion that Pelops is honoured much more highly at Olympia than any other hero (5.13.1). Elsewhere, Pausanias (5.16.4) cites Hippodameia's thanksgiving for her marriage to Pelops as the aetiology for the girls' games in honour of Hera, but for the main festival of Zeus his insistence on the Daktyl Herakles as founder means that both Pelops and Herakles son of Amphitryon are sub-ordinated to the status of memorable early competitors (5.8.2–4).

Less well attested is the tradition of Herakles founding the Nemean Games, which were historically established in 573 BC. There is an obvious potential link with Herakles via the story of his first labour, and indeed we noted in Chapter 1 that Bakchylides 13 links the lion-slaying with the *pan-kration* competition at Nemea. Pausanias (2.15.2–3) juxtaposes mention of 'the lion's cave', which was shown off to tourists in the mountains not far from Nemea, with his description of the sanctuary of Zeus, which was in a state of disrepair in his day, the games having been long since moved to Argos. However, there is another myth, according to which the contests originated as funeral games for the baby Opheltes, accidentally killed when Adrastos, king of Argos, and his companions paused at Nemea on their way to fight against Thebes. This story goes back to at least the early fifth cen-tury BC, when it was the subject of a play by Aeschylus and is related in Bakchylides 9, an ode for a Nemean victor which makes brief mention of the lion as 'the first of Herakles' famous labours' (ll.8–9), but does not make him a founder. By contrast, explicit attribution to Herakles of the games' foundation is not attested until much later, in the first-century AD Probus' commentary on Virgil's *Georgics* (3.19) and in a handful of ancient com-mentaries on Pindar's *Nemean Odes*. Neither Diodoros nor Apollodoros mentions the Nemean Games at all in connection with Herakles, and while there is evidence of a substantial hero shrine for Opheltes within the sanc-tuary, there is none for a cult of Herakles. Altogether, our hero's link with the Nemean Games seems weak: promotion of the Opheltes story would obviously have better suited Argive claims to control the games than an association with the panhellenic Herakles.[29]

TYRANNY AND DEMOCRACY AT ATHENS

Archaic Athens: Herakles and Peisistratos

There is considerable scholarly debate over the extent to which Herakles' image was put to political use in late archaic Athens. Herakles' prominence in the sixth-century city's visual arts is unquestionable: as we have seen in Chapters 1 and 2, the great majority of the hero's labours and other exploits can be found in Attic black-figure and early red-figure vase-painting, with popular scenes like the Nemean lion running to hundreds of extant exam-ples. Some of Herakles' earliest appearances in architectural sculpture, too, come from the Athenian Akropolis. In addition to the group of Herak-les fighting Triton on the mid-sixth-century temple of Athena (p. 73), two limestone pediments from smaller buildings of the same date show the Triton battle and the slaying of the hydra, the latter complete with Iolaos waiting in a chariot, and a crab. Also contemporary is the small-scale pedimental group representing Herakles' introduction to Olympos, the hero himself clearly recognizable by his lionskin, approaching the seated Zeus and Hera, escorted by Hermes.

This is one of two types of the introduction scene which are much elaborated in Attic black-figure around 550–500 BC: (i) we have around twenty-five examples of Herakles being escorted on foot by Athena to the enthroned Zeus; and (ii) over one hundred of Herakles riding in a chariot. The simplest example of type (i) is on a cup by the Phrynos Painter, c.540 BC (London B424), where the scene is reduced to just three figures, Athena leading Herakles by the wrist towards a seated Zeus; Athena's gesture here is one commonly seen in wedding processions, where the groom grips the bride's arm, making this a striking inversion of male–female roles. In type (ii) there are a few examples where an unidentified woman in the chariot may be Hebe, and she is actually named on one late sixth-century hydria (New York 14.105.10), but on the whole she seems not to be a particularly important feature of the apotheosis for sixth-century Attic painters. A further type of scene expressing promotion to Olympos is that of Herakles reclining amongst the gods, a good example being the much-cited bilingual vase by the Andokides Painter which has a black-figure scene of Athena standing by Herakles' couch one side, a red-figure version on the other (Munich 2301).

It is especially the introduction to Olympos scenes that have given rise to the suggestion of deliberate exploitation of Herakles' image by the tyrant Peisistratos. In an influential article, Boardman (1972) links the chariot-type scenes with Peisistratos' return to power in Athens in 546 BC, which he reportedly achieved by dressing up an unusually tall woman called Phye as Athena and riding with her in a chariot into the city, where she proclaimed him to have Athena's favour (Herodotus 1.60). The truth of this story has been questioned, and there are significant problems with any hypothesis that the vases represent a programme of self-promotion by Peisistratos. To start with, at this period an ordinary mortal who claimed close association with the gods would be regarded as impious, so for Peisistratos to identify himself as Herakles in the chariot alongside 'Athena' would have been risky – indeed Herodotus' account does not make such an identification explicit. Then it should be noted that the majority of the vases date from the last third of the century, some time after the event and for the most part after Peisistratos' death in 528/7 BC. A further difficulty is presented by the relatively humble status of vase-painting, which is not an obvious vehicle for political propaganda. As far as we can reconstruct the logistics of the trade, pots were commissioned by individual customers or bought 'off the peg', so that the choice of decorative image would have been dictated by individual whim rather than by any possible directive from those in political power.[30]

Boardman himself clarifies in a later article (1989b) that he sees the images as reflecting current ideas rather than deliberate propaganda. It is certainly reasonable to suggest that the broad fashion for depicting Herakles was based in part on his role as exemplar of aristocratic values, while his extraordinarily wide range of adventures offered scope for the painters to exercize their creativity. Against this background the particular popularity of the scenes expressive of Herakles' apotheosis is explicable, quite independently of the Peisistratids, in terms of the development of his cult at Athens. Most of our direct evidence dates from the fifth century BC and later, as we shall see in Chapter 6, but the late archaic visual record suggests a strong interest in Herakles' status as the hero who becomes a god. We might understand one or two other specific scenes as being given impetus in a general way by religious innovations of Peisistratos and his sons, without having to posit deliberate political manipulation. For example, the first appearance of Gigantomachy scenes featuring Athena and Herakles coincides with the reorganization of the Panathenaia in the mid-560s, early in Peisistratos' career, while later sixth-century scenes of Herakles playing the kithara might reflect the introduction of Homeric recitals to the festival by Peisistratos' son Hipparchos (Plato, *Hipparchos* 228b–c).

A more specific link, again proposed by Boardman (1975), concerns a change around 530 BC in the way the Kerberos labour is represented, when Herakles seems to be employing persuasion on the hound rather than brute force. Such persuasion is apparent in two very similar versions by the Andokides Painter at about this time, one red-figure (Paris F204), one black-figure (Moscow 70): with either Athena or Hermes standing by, Herakles crouches down and reaches out a pacifying hand towards Kerberos, who stands half inside a portico representing the gates of Hades; in the black-figure scene, Persephone stands within the porch. Boardman argues that these changes are linked with the creation of the Lesser Mysteries, a festival celebrated within Athens and serving as a preliminary for those wishing to be initiated at the Greater Mysteries of Eleusis. The festival's mythological charter was provided by the story that Herakles had to be initiated before journeying to the Underworld, in order to gain Persephone's favour and assure his safe return. Whether or not Boardman is right, Herakles' connection with the Mysteries was certainly made political later. Xenophon (*Hellenika* 6.3.6) recounts a peace-making embassy at Sparta, shortly before the battle of Leuktra in 371 BC, in which the Athenian Kallias, an official of the Eleusinian cult, regrets that the two cities should have ever been at war with one another when Herakles 'your founder', along with the Spartan heroes

Kastor and Polydeukes, had been the first 'foreigners' granted admission to the Eleusinian Mysteries.[31]

A final type of scene where Peisistratos has sometimes been identified with Herakles is the struggle over the Delphic tripod. This became popular in Attic vase-painting around 520 BC, and the Andokides Painter's version (Figure 5.3) adopts a common format, with Herakles striding off to the left grasping the tripod while Apollo, identifiable by his bow, pulls at the tripod; Athena and Artemis stand by in support of their favourites. Interpretations are complicated in this case, though, by the possible influence on the scene's iconography of the pediment of the Siphnian Treasury at Delphi, built c.525 BC, where Zeus intervenes between Apollo and Herakles. The pediment has been interpreted as reflecting contemporary rivalry between Delphi (Apollo) and Peisistratos (Herakles), who had his own collection of written oracles in Athens (Herodotus 5.90), the myth ultimately legitimating Delphi's authority. A similar approach sees the scene as a reference back to the 'First Sacred War' of the early sixth century, when the Delphic Amphictyony (a league to which Athens belonged) wrested control of the oracle away from the city of Kirrha, which had been mistreating visitors on their way to the sanctuary; Herakles here would be representing

Figure 5.3 Herakles and Apollo struggle over the Delphic tripod: Attic red-figure amphora by the Andokides Painter, c.530–20 BC (Berlin F2159). Photo: © bpk, Antikensammlung, Staatliche Museen zu Berlin.

the impious Kirrhans, Apollo the proper order of things restored by the Amphictyony.

Both of these readings make sense in terms of the story as we know it from Apollodoros (2.6.2) – that Herakles tried to carry off the tripod in anger at the Pythia's refusal to grant him a response to his request for purification from his murder of Iphitos – and Pausanias (10.13.8), who relates it as a specifically Delphic story. However, a more positive role for Herakles is offered by a reading of the scene which considers the end of the story: either voluntarily or because of Zeus' intervention, Herakles gives the tripod back and is granted an audience with the Pythia. The scene thus offers a model of civilized conflict resolution, while emphasizing Delphi's openness to all comers, the tripod standing both for the oracle and for the panhellenic Pythian Games (in which tripods were a traditional prize). This interpretation works well for the pediment, on very public display beside the Sacred Way leading up to Apollo's temple and the stadium beyond it at Delphi. A viewer of Figure 5.3 and the other Attic vases, however, most likely seeing the pot in the context of a symposium, might not have read so many layers of meaning into the image, but simply have enjoyed the idea of the popular hero's challenge to divine authority.[32]

Classical Athens: Herakles, Theseus and democracy

If a specific connection between Herakles and Peisistratos' family is difficult to pin down, the hero's broader association with archaic aristocratic values is not in question. It is also incontrovertible that the start of the fifth century sees a steep decline in the frequency with which Herakles is depicted in Attic art, while images of Theseus increase in popularity. This has often been explained as reflecting a shift from sixth-century aristocracy and tyranny to a growing concern with democracy after Kleisthenes' reforms of 508/7 BC. As a legendary king of Athens Theseus is an unlikely champion of the new political system, but the anomaly is explained away by the supposition that he voluntarily handed over power to the people (Plutarch, *Theseus* 24–5). As a local hero, Theseus is also much better suited than the panhellenic Herakles to represent an increasing sense of Athenian identity. The shift from one hero to another is not as neat as some have supposed, however: a number of instances where the two are juxtaposed seem rather to celebrate their common monster-slaying prowess, and one or two later fifth-century images of Herakles suggest that he could be made to adapt to a democratic setting.[33]

Theseus is credited with a series of victories over monsters, encountered on his journey around the Saronic Gulf from Troizen in the Argolid to Athens:

Periphetes the Club-Man; the pine-bending Sinis; the wild sow of Krom-myon; Skiron who made travellers wash his feet before kicking them off the cliffs; the wrestler Kerkyon; and Prokrustes who stretched or cut travellers to size to fit his guest-bed. A further deed performed after his arrival in Athens is the capture of the Marathonian Bull, supposed by some to be the same creature previously captured by Herakles, and the crowning achievement of his career was the slaying of the Minotaur. Once established as king of Athens, Theseus mounted an expedition against the Amazons and brought back Antiope or Hippolyta as his queen, and at his friend Peirithoos' wedding he fought against the unruly centaurs. The similarities with Herakles are obvious, and the fact that the cycle of 'Saronic Deeds' only begins to appear in art and literature from around 500 BC makes it plausible that Theseus' story was strongly influenced by that of Herakles. The tradition that Herakles rescued Theseus from the Underworld was a theme particularly explored in Euripidean tragedy, as we saw in Chapter 3, which also provides our earliest evidence for the idea that Theseus handed over his cult sites to Herakles; the third-century BC Athenian historian Philochoros (*FGrH* 328F18) specifies that Theseus retained just four shrines for himself. There are a few juxtapositions of the two heroes' deeds in Attic vase-painting of the late sixth and early fifth centuries. For example, a stamnos by the Kleophrades Painter (Philadelphia L64.185) features Herakles and the lion on one side, Theseus and the Minotaur on the other. The comparison is more fully explored, however, on two important buildings, the Athenian Treasury at Delphi and the temple of Hephaistos in the Athenian Agora.[34]

The Athenian Treasury was dedicated after the Battle of Marathon in 490 BC – the style of the extant sculpture suggests a slightly earlier date, but Pausanias' explicit comment that it was built with Persian spoils (10.11.4) is corroborated by epigraphic and archaeological evidence. It has a total of thirty metopes, those from the north side being devoted to individual encounters of Herakles, with the Nemean lion, the Keryneian hind, the horses of Diomedes, a centaur, and Kyknos; those from the west side make up a group of six depicting Geryon, his dog Orthos and his cattle. Metopes from the south side feature five of Theseus' early deeds (the sow and Skiron are not included) and the Minotaur, while a series of eight or nine metopes, probably placed on the prominent east side of the building, depict a battle with the Amazons which involves both heroes; this theme is continued in akroteria (roof decorations) in the form of Amazons on horseback. It is notable that the Herakles scenes occupy the less conspicuous sides of the building – its rear and the side which gives onto the steep terrace of the temple of Apollo above – while Theseus' victories on the south side would have been clearly visible to visitors toiling up the Sacred Way. Immediately below the Theseus metopes stood a monument, dedicated at the same time as the treasury, representing the eponymous heroes of the ten tribes on which Kleisthenes' democratic system was based. Altogether, then, the treasury's sculptural programme is an apt celebration of Athens' victory over the barbarous Persians, while the prominence of Theseus asserts the distinct identity of a newly democratic Athens in the panhellenic context of Delphi.

Back in Athens itself, the mid-fifth-century temple of Hephaistos was designed with a predominantly Athenian audience in mind. As noted in Chapter 1, nine labours of Herakles are spread over ten metopes on the east side of the building, conspicuous from the Agora below. The first four metopes on each of the north and south sides, at the east end of the building, depict all seven of Theseus' early deeds plus his fight with the Minotaur. Theseus appears again inside the west porch, where a continuous frieze depicts the Centauromachy, and probably also in the unidentified battle scene which adorns the east porch. The close juxtaposition and similarity in composition of the two hero's monster-slayings invites comparison between them, and would have reminded a fifth-century viewer of the tradition of their friendship which articulates Athens' special relationship with Herakles. The three labours missing here, which had been portrayed on the temple of Zeus at Olympia only a few years previously, are the Cretan bull, the Stymphalian birds and the Augeian stables: the first has probably been left out in order to avoid duplication with the Theseus and bull metope, while the absence of the other two reduces the number of Peloponnesian references. Here, then, the emphasis is on an Athenian Herakles, who joins with Theseus in providing a model of heroism in the political centre of the city.

The substantial role played by Herakles in the decorative scheme of both buildings may be further explained as recognition of his part in helping the Athenians at Marathon. The battle was more explicitly commemorated in the Stoa Poikile, below and a little way to the north-east of the temple of Hephaistos in the Agora, in a painting by Mikon and Panainos of c.460 BC. Pausanias (1.15.3) describes this as depicting many of the Persians fleeing towards their ships, pursued by Greeks, and 'the hero Marathon is painted there, after whom the plain is named, and Theseus rising out of the earth, and Athena and Herakles'.[35]

While it is true that Herakles' image has a lower profile in fifth-century Athens than in the previous century, the two examples from the Agora show that it was still alive and well in the public consciousness. As we saw in Chapter 2, Herakles also played a part in the Gigantomachy of the Parthenon's east metopes, and some scholars identify him more prominently as the youthful figure D in the pediment above, reclining on his lionskin (others see this as Dionysos on a panther-skin). Less directly, the hero may have been called to mind by the north frieze of the temple of Athena Nike, completed in the late 420s BC, which has recently been interpreted as representing the victory of the Herakleidai over Eurystheus. Various details in the frieze correspond well to the story as told by Euripides (pp. 92–3), and the image would have provided a suitable celebration of recent Athenian victories over their Peloponnesian enemies in 426/5 BC. Later again, an Athenian dedication set up at Thebes makes Herakles himself a champion of democracy: Thrasyboulos and the supporters who had helped him put an end to the oligarchic government of the Thirty Tyrants in 404 BC are said to have dedicated a colossal statue group of Athena and Herakles in the Theban sanctuary of Herakles, as a thank-offering for Thebes' support of the democrats (Pausanias 9.11.6).[36]

OVERVIEW

Herakles' career as a political figure is long and geographically wide-ranging. Most clearly political is Herakles' adoption as ancestor and role-model by a great many leaders. Of various regions that claimed descent from Herakles, especially via the myth of the return of the Herakleidai, Sparta produces the most evidence, with the genealogical link being assumed throughout antiquity and sometimes deliberately evoked, especially in the politically turbulent hellenistic period. Use of Herakles' image as a political tool is particularly developed by the family of Alexander the Great, which had much to prove as Makedonian power rapidly expanded in the fourth century BC. The copious imitation of Alexander's deployment of Herakles-imagery amongst later hellenistic kings demonstrates its continuing efficacy, its legitimizing power now enhanced by the association with Alexander himself. The take-up of Herakles-imagery by non-Greek neighbours is testimony at once to an increasingly international outlook during the hellenistic and Roman imperial periods, and to Herakles' cross-cultural appeal. For Roman generals and emperors, cultivation of Hercules as a personal saviour-god and use of his image could sometimes be taken to extremes, but the deployment of the title 'Herculius' even in late antiquity demonstrates the enduring power of the hero's image. For many ordinary people in antiquity, however, the most memorable thing about Herakles would have been his role as founder of their own city, while his role as founder of the panhellenic institution of the Olympic Games made Herakles significant to all Greeks. The idea that institutions of the present day, from cities and concrete local landmarks to rituals, were a result of Herakles having once passed through is a clear indicator of the power of the past in the ancient consciousness. Finally, specific links with the Peisistratids at Athens remain difficult to prove, although there is no doubt about his status more generally as role-model for the aristocratic classes in the archaic period.

WORSHIP OF THE HERO-GOD

Herakles contained the potential to shatter the limits of Greek religion.
(Burkert 1985, 211)

HERAKLES *HEROS-THEOS*

So far we have seen Herakles the monster-fighting strong man, Herakles the tragic or comic hero, Herakles the incarnation of vice or virtue, and Herakles embroiled in politics. From a twenty-first century perspective he would seem too ambivalent a character to be an obvious candidate for worship. In keeping with the ethical complexity of ancient Greece's polytheistic religion, however, there is widespread evidence in the ancient world for ritual practices carried out in Herakles' honour.

In cult as well as in myth the many-sidedness of Herakles' character is further complicated by his ambiguous status as both hero and god, summed up in Pindar's striking appellation *heros theos*, 'hero god' (*Nemean* 3.22). Most Greek heroes, however great their deeds in life, eventually die and spend the rest of eternity in the Underworld or on the Isles of the Blessed. They may be thought of as continuing to exercize power, and can be offered sacrifices and prayers by the living in the hope of some practical benefit, but they remain decidedly dead. In mythological terms, Herakles really ought to be a hero, since he has a god for a father but a mortal mother – this is a very common pattern of mixed parentage for heroes, like Perseus (divine father Zeus, mortal mother Danae) or Achilles (mortal father Peleus, goddess mother Thetis). A parallel for Herakles' ambiguous status is provided, however, by the healing hero-god Asklepios: he is the product of a union between Apollo and the mortal woman Koronis, spends his life doing good as a physician, and in due course dies, struck down by Zeus' thunderbolt for attempting to raise someone from the dead. Despite this heroic *curriculum vitae*, Asklepios seems to have been promoted to divine status in cult in the late sixth or early fifth century, and this is marked by the acquisition of several deified abstractions as daughters, such as Hygieia (Health), just as the divine Herakles acquires Hebe (Youth) as a wife. Asklepios' apotheosis, however, is never turned into a story like that of Herakles, and even the daughters are largely confined to representation in ritual contexts at Asklepios' sanctuaries rather than having any independent place in myth.[1]

The story of Herakles' apotheosis explains his ambivalent nature in terms of a change from one status to another, and some ancient writers even rationalized the promotion as being Herakles' reward for the twelve labours (Diodoros 4.10.7) or for helping the gods in their battle against the Giants (Pindar, *Nemean* 1.67–72). The idea that such a reward might lie at the end of all the toils and tribulations of human life is a powerful one, especially for a culture whose religion generally confined its aspirations to well-being in the here and now. Only the mystery cults held out any hope for happiness in the afterlife, and the story of Herakles' initiation at Eleusis shows that the overcoming-of-death theme apparent in several of his exploits was associated with this hope from at least the late sixth century. The many failings of Herakles' mortal character might serve to make him seem more human, and allow him to be perceived as a model for the common man hoping for a better afterlife. It is this aspect of Herakles which led to his later identification with Christ, and which prompts Burkert's arresting assessment of his significance quoted at the start of this chapter.

To an extent the myth of Herakles' deification may reflect a historical change in how he was perceived, which we can actually chart in our sources from the archaic period. In the *Iliad*, Achilles, contemplating his own imminent death, muses that 'not even mighty Herakles escaped his doom, even though he was much loved by lord Zeus, son of Kronos, but fate overcame him, and the bitter anger of Hera' (18.117–19). Clearly Herakles, like any other Homeric hero, is thought of here as dying at his appointed hour, however valiant the deeds of his life. The first time we see any suggestion of the promotion to Olympos comes in the *Odyssey*, when Odysseus meets Herakles in the Underworld, a fearsome figure equipped with bow, arrows and an elaborate gold breastplate. He complains of the servitude he suffered during his life to 'a lesser man', who inflicted difficult tasks on him, including the fetching of the hound of Hades, which he achieved with the help of Athena and Hermes. But the description is introduced rather oddly (11.601–4):

> Next I observed mighty Herakles,
> his image (*eidolon*); for he himself enjoys the feasts
> of the immortal gods, and has as his wife fair-ankled Hebe,
> child of great Zeus and golden-sandalled Hera.

The transition from the dead Herakles to his *eidolon* is abrupt linguistically, and the whole idea of a 'replacement' Herakles existing in Hades while the real one feasts on Olympos is awkward. Even in antiquity, Lucian made fun of the *eidolon* idea, when he presented the Cynic Diogenes in conversation with Herakles in Hades, 'laughing at Homer and such silly stories as this' (*Dialogues of the Dead* 16). Most commentators have suspected that the three lines 602–4 are a later interpolation, added to 'update' the Underworld scene once the idea of Herakles' apotheosis became standard. There is a similar problem with Herakles' appearance towards the end of Hesiod's *Theogony*, because this part of the poem is thought to have been added later. Here Herakles features in a list of gods born to Zeus, and a few lines later there is a reference to his marriage to Hebe and his happy life on Olympos, having performed 'a great deed amongst the gods' (950–5), perhaps a reference to his role in the Gigantomachy. The sixth-century *Catalogue of Women* (fr. 25 MW) has a kind of double version of Herakles' eventual fate: Herakles dies and goes down to Hades, 'but now he is a god', married to Hebe on Olympos and reconciled with Hera.[2]

Literature, then, gives us a heroic Herakles c.700 BC in the *Iliad*, while the earliest references to Herakles the god are not precisely dated. In this respect, representations of the apotheosis story in vase-painting are a vital source of information. We noted some sixth-century Athenian interpretations of Herakles' introduction to Olympos in Chapter 5, but even earlier is a Corinthian aryballos dating from around 600 BC (Figure 6.1): Herakles rides in a chariot with Hebe, their names inscribed just behind them, followed by a lyre-playing Apollo and the Muses; they are greeted by Athena, Aphrodite and two Graces, behind whom Zeus and Hera are enthroned, with Hermes standing between them. Though made in Corinth, this little perfume-bottle was found at Vulci in Etruria, which already suggests some geographical dissemination of the apotheosis story. The same scene also appears around this time on a krater from Samos and

Figure 6.1 Marriage of Herakles and Hebe. Corinthian aryballos from Vulci, Necropoli dell' Osteria, c.600 BC. Drawing: *Archeologia Nella Tuscia* II (Rome 1986, pl.48).

on a Parian amphora found on Melos (Athens 354); not much later is a cup from Sparta of c.570 BC (New York 50.11.7), which represents Herakles being led on foot by Athena to the seated Zeus.[3]

Altogether the artistic evidence would suggest that Herakles was deified in the late seventh century, and that the story of his apotheosis very quickly became popular all over the Greek world. Even with the invention of this neat explanation of Herakles' double status, however, there remained some doubt about the matter throughout antiquity. As we saw in Chapter 4, Aristophanes and others could joke about Herakles' status as a 'bastard' amongst the gods, and as late as the first century BC Cicero is one of a number of writers to group Herakles with Asklepios, Dionysos and the Dioskouroi as gods about whom one might 'have doubt' because of their mortal mothers (*On the Nature of the Gods* 3.18.45), and who have won their place in heaven by merit, alongside 'those qualities through which an ascent to heaven is granted to man: intellect, virtue, piety, faith' (*Laws* 2.19). Perhaps as a way of mitigating the problem, a tradition developed that the newborn Herakles was taken up to Olympos and suckled by an absent-minded Hera, until she noticed the baby and pushed him away, her spilt milk becoming the Milky Way. This tale appears in literary works of the hellenistic period, such as Pseudo-Eratosthenes' *Katasterismoi* 44, which explains that 'it is not possible for sons of Zeus to share in the honour of heaven unless any of them sucks Hera's breast', but must date to at least the fourth century BC, when the scene of the infant Herakles' nursing appears on an Apulian lekythos (London F107). On one Etruscan mirror of c.300 BC it is an adult, bearded Herakles who suckles, the scene accompanied by an inscription, which explains that 'this shows how the mortal Hercle became the legitimate son of Uni' (the Etruscan equivalent to Hera). This suggests a version of the story where the suckling is part of the apotheosis and Herakles' final reconciliation with Hera, rather than an early foreshadowing of his eventual divinity.

In the passage just mentioned from *On the Nature of the Gods*, Cicero concludes that the deciding factor in allowing the figures in question to count as gods is the wide extent of their worship, and it is in connection with cult practice that Herakles' ambiguity of status is most striking. Herodotus comments on the correctness of practice of those Greeks 'who have founded and maintain two Herakles-sanctuaries, in one of which they sacrifice as to an immortal, with an Olympian name, and in the other making offerings as to a hero' (2.44). This statement has long been understood as reflecting a basic distinction in Greek religious practice between the different kinds of worship offered, on the one hand to the Olympian gods, and on the other to heroes, the dead and certain other 'chthonic' (i.e. associated with the Underworld) powers. A god has a temple (*naos*), a cult statue and a raised altar (*bomos*), at which an animal is sacrificed with its head pulled back so that the throat is pointing heavenwards when cut; a hero usually has a shrine (*heroon*) at the site of his grave, with a low hearth (*eschara*) or pit (*bothros*), where the sacrificial victim's blood can flow directly down into the ground. To sacrifice to the Olympians is to 'fumigate' (*thuein*), because the gods were thought to enjoy the smell of the fatty smoke rising and, after the kill, meat from the sacrificial victim is shared in a communal feast; when sacrificing to chthonians, one had to 'devote' (*enagizein*) the victim, usually by burning it whole (a 'holocaust').

Recent scholarship, however, has tended to revise this traditional sharp opposition, preferring to think of individual cults as on a 'sliding scale' between the two extremes; significantly, it has been shown that many heroes received the kind of sacrifice which was followed by feasting, and that there is no clear distinction between types of altar before the Roman period. At the same time, studies of Herakles have questioned the extent to which Herodotus' idea of a dual cult was ever put into practice, pointing to the fact that the majority of the evidence seems rather to emphasize his divine nature. Nonetheless, there remain some notable features in Herakles' cult which cannot easily be explained unless we understand them as reflecting something of the ambiguous status he has in myth.[4]

RITUALS AND REMAINS

We have a good deal of information about Herakles' worship in locations all over the Greek world, starting with the widespread use of variations on his name. Just as 'Herakles' itself seems to derive from 'Hera', derivatives of 'Herakles' are attested in literature and inscriptions as the names of real people – most popular are Herakleides and Herakleitos (for men) and Herakleia (for women). Individual heroes rarely generate names, so this would suggest that Herakles was regarded as a god in the areas concerned. More directly, some evidence for sanctuaries, statues and rituals in Herakles' honour comes from prose writers who had an antiquarian interest in ancient customs, especially Plutarch and Pausanias. In a few cases these written accounts can be matched up with the archaeological remains of Herakles' sanctuaries. Most of our material evidence, however, consists of votive reliefs dedicated to Herakles, and inscriptions which attest his festivals or record local cult regulations and administrative matters.

What follows is by no means an exhaustive account, but rather a survey of instances where we have particularly interesting information to work with. There are all kinds of local peculiarities in practice, but three features appear again and again: the importance of feasting, a connection with youth and athletics, and the exclusion of women – there was even a traditional saying 'a woman does not go to a shrine of Herakles' (*CPG* 392, 88). Also commonly attested are the cult titles Alexikakos, 'Warding-off evil', and Kallinikos, 'Fair-conquering', which reflect Herakles' mythological prowess as slayer of monsters. The latter may also allude to success in athletic and other competitions, and appears already in a fragment of the seventh-century BC lyric poet Archilochos of Paros, in what seems to be the opening of a hymn to Herakles: 'Hail to the fair-conquering, hail lord Herakles!' (fr. 324 W). The title appears in several locations in what seems to have been a common formula for inscription over the doorway of private houses: 'Herakles Kallinikos lives here: let no evil enter'. This is attested as part of an anecdote concerning Diogenes the Cynic, who, on seeing such an inscription, is said to have made fun of the superstition by asking 'But how will the master of the house get in?' (Clement of Alexandria, *Stromata* 7.4.26.1).

At a similarly popular level women were thought to 'receive charms' from Herakles and make amulets from his image to ward off evil (Diodoros 5.64.7). This kind of protection was also invoked more publicly, for example at Ephesos, where Herakles reportedly earned the title Apotropaios ('Averting Evil') by destroying a plague-causing spirit (Philostratos, *Life of Apollonios of Tyre* 4.10 and 8.7). The hero-god's power as saviour and benefactor of mankind is similarly invoked in the hellenistic and Roman imperial periods in the naming of warships and merchantmen 'Herakles' or 'Hercules'.[5]

Athens and Attica

Despite his tenuous mythological connections with Attica, Herakles was clearly important to the Athenians. Diodoros (4.39.1) would have it that the Athenians were the first people to give Herakles divine worship, and their example persuaded 'all the Greeks, and after them everyone throughout the inhabited world, to honour Herakles as a god'. He was one of the major deities who had a monthly festival day, on the fourth, which he shared with Hermes and Aphrodite. Herakles' cult was celebrated at a number of sanctuaries within or just outside the city walls, including Kynosarges by the Ilissos river, as well as several sites in rural Attica. Some rituals were conducted by the city, but many more were financed at a local level by a variety of types of associations, some (such as the demes) part of the official Kleisthenic system of citizen associations, some (such as phratries and *gene*) well-established hereditary groups, and others (often called *thiasoi*) private religious groups whose main activity was feasting. Fourth-century votive reliefs from Athens also depict families making private sacrifices to Herakles: one (Athens EM 8793) shows a woman and children, with no man present, and bears the inscription 'Lysistrate dedicated [this] to Herakles on behalf of her children'; another, from Kynosarges (Athens EM 3942), shows a whole family leading an enormous ox.[6]

There are no substantial archaeological remains of any Athenian sanctuary of Herakles. Literary sources tell us that the 'very conspicuous' sanctuary in the deme of Melite had a statue of Herakles Alexikakos, reputedly by the Argive sculptor Hageladas and dedicated at the time of the great plague of the early 430s BC. Such a statue might imply a regular temple, but elsewhere the more common form of sacred building seems to have been an unusual structure consisting of four columns on a raised base, supporting an entablature sometimes temporarily roofed with foliage. This appears in a number of vase-paintings and votive reliefs, as in the early fourth-century relief depicted in Figure 6.2. A young Herakles stands beside the shrine, lionskin over his arm, and the words 'of Herakles Alexikakos' are inscribed on the structure's base. The pot on top of it may be a reference to the wine-offering which Hesychios (*s.v. oinisteria*) tells us was given to Herakles by 'those who were about to become ephebes [young men of around 18–20], before they cut off the lock of hair', a ritual which was enacted as part of the Apatouria festival. The connection with youth is further suggested here by the presence of Hermes, who shares Herakles' association with gymnasia and was worshipped alongside him at the Academy, where 'Hermes presides over reason, Herakles over physical strength' (Athenaios 13.561d). Herakles was also one of the deities invoked as witness to the Ephebic Oath

Figure 6.2 Hermes and Herakles Alexikakos by a four-column shrine. Attic votive relief, c.370 BC (Boston 96.696). Photo: © 2011 Museum of Fine Arts, Boston.

sworn by the youths during their two years' military service. A particular aspect of Herakles' protective powers is healing, seen most clearly in the cult of Herakles Menytes ('Bringing to light'), supposedly founded by the tragedian Sophokles in response to a dream where the god 'revealed' the whereabouts of a stolen wreath (*Life of Sophokles* 12). Whether or not this story is reliable, dedications to Herakles Menytes have been found at the sanctuary of Asklepios on the south slope of the Akropolis, of a type often made to healing deities, representing the part of the anatomy to be cured.[7]

The kind of sacrifice which was made to Herakles at his various Athenian sanctuaries is not always clear. Euripides' Theseus speaks of Herakles receiving *thusiai* (p. 92); Pausanias and others mention *bomoi*, altars of the raised variety, in connection with Kynosarges and the Academy, while the Melite sanctuary sounds like that of a god. Divine sacrifice seems to be in question in Theophrastos' parody of the 'Late-Learner' (*Characters* 27), who is eager to participate in various activities which are unsuitable for his advanced years: when invited to take part in a sacrifice at a Herakleion, he 'throws off his cloak and raises the bull to cut its throat'. This is part of our evidence that even such large animals as the ox were lifted up so that their blood could flow over the altar; in this case the task was presumably reserved for young men, the show of strength being particularly apt in Herakles' cult. Post-sacrifice feasting is widely attested – indeed, Aristophanes' first play the *Banqueters* (427 BC) was named after a group who 'dined in a shrine of Herakles and then got up and became the chorus'. Both sacrifice and feasting are reflected in images of Herakles himself: on sixth- and fifth-century Attic vases he leads an ox decorated with sacrificial garlands, or roasts meat over an altar; on an early fourth-century krater (Athens 14902), he reclines in the four-columned structure, roofed with foliage, while attendants bring him food and wine.[8]

We know most about such feasting at the Kynosarges sanctuary, founded, according to Pausanias (1.19.3), by a youth called Diomos, one of Herakles' lovers and eponymous hero of the deme of Diomeia. Here there was a gymnasium, and each month his twelve official 'table-companions' (*parasitoi*) held a sacrifice followed by a banquet. An unusual feature is that, at least in the classical period, these *parasitoi* were chosen from amongst the *nothoi* who frequented the sanctuary; Plutarch (*Themistokles* 1.2) explains that such company was suitable for Herakles, who was himself a bastard amongst the gods, an idea we have already seen exploited in comedy (p. 107). Once a year, however, in either Hekatombaion (June–July) or Metageitnion (July–August), a festival was celebrated in Herakles' honour at Kynosarges by the whole city, including women and children. Priests of Herakles and Diomos were also involved in another Herakleia, with a procession, ox-sacrifice and distribution of meat, which seems to have been a minor city festival, although it was administered by the *genos* of the Mesogeioi.[9]

It is possible, however, that a different kind of sacrifice is depicted on an Attic red-figure oinochoe of the late fifth century (Figure 6.3). The young Herakles himself stands to the right, identifiable as ever by his club; the youth to the left holds a lekythos for making libations, while the older man in the centre is wearing the elaborate unbelted tunic of a priest. There is no raised altar or any other kind of architectural structure, but rather a low mound at the foot of a tree, with just the skull of an ox visible on top. One scholar takes this to be the representation of a holocaust at a low hearth, arguing that in the Olympian kind of sacrifice, followed by feasting, the head of the victim would not normally belong to the portion burnt for the god. Another disagrees, citing finds at Isthmia of skull fragments burnt on the altar of Poseidon, and pointing to other examples of primitive altars used for sacrifices to the gods. Such conflicting interpretations demonstrate the difficulty of using images as evidence for ritual practice, but the scene does raise the possibility that Athenian ritual occasionally placed more emphasis on Herakles' mortal side.[10]

Outside Athens itself, there was an important cult of Herakles at Marathon. Pausanias reports that the Marathonians claimed to be the first to recognize Herakles' deity (1.15.3 and 32.4), and as we have seen (p. 169) Herakles was thought to have fought alongside the Athenians against the

Figure 6.3 Holocaust sacrifice to Herakles? Attic red-figure oinochoe, circle of the Kadmos Painter, c.420–400 BC (Kiel B55). Photo: by kind permission of Kiel, Antikensammlung – Kunsthalle zu Kiel.

Persians in 490 BC; in Herodotus' account of the battle (6.108), the Athenian army at Marathon set up camp in Herakles' sanctuary. This sanctuary is later mentioned in the sacred calendar of the Marathonian Tetrapolis, and its location has been identified by the discovery in the area of two fifth-century inscriptions, one recording a dedication to Herakles, the other regulations for his games. Marathon is mentioned in Pindar's odes as the site of some of his clients' former athletic victories, like Epharmostos, victor in the wrestling at Olympia in 468 BC: 'having left the beardless category, what a contest did he win among his elders at Marathon for the silver cups . . .' (*Olympian* 9.89–90). In addition, musical contests are attested by the image on a mid-fifth-century Attic pelike by the Epimenides Painter (Plovdiv Museum), which represents a kithara-player named 'Alkimachos' standing on a plinth surrounded by flying Victories, each named for the Games at which Alkimachos has been successful, at the Panathenaia, Nemea, Isthmia and Marathon. As at Kynosarges there were *parasitoi* of Herakles at Marathon (Athenaios 6.235d), and a fifth-century votive relief from the nearby deme of Rhamnous shows the feasting Herakles himself reclining on his lionskin, holding a cornucopia and a wine-cup.

Elsewhere in rural Attica an unusual feature of Herakles' cult is his strong association with members of his family, including his mother Alkmene, his divine wife Hebe, his nephew Iolaos and the children who outlived him, reflecting the local popularity of the Herakleidai myth. Sacrifices to the Herakleidai are listed in the sacred calendars of Erchia and Thorikos. An inscription provides detailed information on a sanctuary of Herakles at Porthmos, near Sounion, administered by the Attic *genos* of the Salaminioi: the biggest event of the year was probably the sacrifice in Mounichion (March–April) of an ox worth 70 drachmas, but smaller sacrifices of sheep worth 12–15 drachmas were made to Alkmene, Iolaos, and a 'nurse', perhaps of Herakles' children.[11]

The Peloponnese

In the Peloponnese, where so much of Herakles' myth takes place, there is a thin scattering of evidence for his worship in a number of locations in the Argolid, Arkadia, Lakonia, Messenia, and at Olympia (p. 162). It is particularly tempting to read significance into evidence for cult activity in locations associated with Herakles' myth – for example, we hear of a statue of Herakles at Tiryns by the sixth-century sculptors Dipoinis and Skyllis (Clement, *Protreptikos* 4.47.8) – but in only a few cases do we have enough information to establish anything about the nature of the cult.

Of particular interest is the case of Sikyon, near Corinth, where Pausanias (2.10.1) records that there was a sanctuary of Herakles with an ancient wooden idol and an unusual form of sacrifice. He explains that the Sikyonians had originally sacrificed (*enagizein*) to Herakles 'as to a hero', but then a Cretan called Phaistos taught them to sacrifice (*thuein*) to him 'as to a god': 'and even now the Sikyonians slaughter lambs and burn their thighs on the altar, and eat some of the meat as from a sacrificial victim, but sacrifice (*enagizein*) some of it as to a hero.' The story may have arisen simply to explain an unusual custom, rather than reflecting a real change of practice, but the form of sacrifice which Pausanias describes as current in his day corresponds well with the kind of 'compromise' sacrifices we shall see attested on Kos and Thasos. Also of note is Pausanias' account (7.25.10) of Boura in Achaia, a little west of Sikyon, where there was a cave dedicated to a local Herakles Bouraikos, in which a simple kind of dice oracle operated.

At Sparta, despite his political significance and prominence in archaic art, Herakles seems not to have had a festival to himself, but was honoured alongside other deities at a festival called Ergatia (Hesychios s.v. *Elakateia*), which may indicate that he was thought of as a craftsman god here, as seems to be the case also in Arkadian Megalopolis, where he was included amongst a group of deities called Ergatai, 'Workers' (Pausanias 8.32.4). Pausanias (3.15.3) describes Herakles' sanctuary at Sparta as being close to the city walls, with a statue of Herakles in hoplite armour, which may well be the statue which Cicero (*On Divination* 1.34) says streamed with sweat before the battle of Leuktra in 371 BC, a portent of the disastrous Spartan defeat. Two other statues associated Herakles with the Spartan ephebes: one received sacrifices from young men competing in the 'Ball-game', which appears to have been a rite of passage marking entry to adulthood, while another stood by an entrance to 'the Planes', site of an annual ritual combat amongst the ephebes (Pausanias 3.14.6–8).

Outside the city of Sparta, Herakles was supposed to have built a temple on the road to Therapne for 'Pelvic' Asklepios, in thanks for the cure of a hip-wound incurred in battle against Hippokoon and his sons (Pausanias 3.19.7). Popular reverence for Herakles amongst Spartan soldiers is suggested by two instances of the army's manoeuvres in neighbouring Arkadia. Thucydides (5.64–6) implies a causal link between Agis II's successful attack on Mantineia in 418 BC and the fact that his army was using an Arkadian sanctuary of Herakles as a base. A more explicit link is made in Xenophon's account (*Hellenika* 7.1.31) of the Spartans' encounter with other Peloponnesian forces at Arkadian Eutresis in 368 BC: a rousing speech by Archidamos III is followed by thunder and lightning, showing the gods' favour, and the fortuitous presence of a sanctuary and statue of Herakles on the army's right wing fills the soldiers with 'such strength and confidence that it was a job for their leaders to hold them back', resulting in a decisive victory.

The Battle of Leuktra features from a different perspective in a story about the Herakles worshipped at Messene, the city restored by Epaminondas and the Thebans after their victory of 371 BC. Here the sanctuary was known as that of Herakles Mantiklos after its supposedly ancient founder: a year before the battle a priest of Herakles in the Sicilian city of Messene dreamed that this Herakles Mantiklos had been invited to Mount Ithome for a festival of the gods (Pausanias 4.23.10 and 26.3). Like most of Pausanias' account of Messenian history, this story probably owes much to the new city's attempts to recreate a heroic past, but there is one piece of solid evidence for Herakles' cult, which reputedly comes from Ithome. This is a fourth-century votive relief (Athens NM 1404), which depicts Herakles standing beside the same kind of four-columned structure we saw at Athens (Figure 6.2), approached by a man with a sacrificial ox and a sheep.[12]

Central Greece

In central Greece there are many more links between Herakles' myth and ritual. At Thebes, the city of his birth, we have brief mention of sacrifices made in the past to Herakles as a hero (Diodoros 4.39.1), but most evidence indicates divine worship. Isokrates (*Philippos* 32) writes to Philip of Makedon that 'the Thebans honour the founder of your race more than the other gods with processions and sacrifices (*thusiai*)'. A festival is attested by the second-century AD Antoninus Liberalis (*Metamorphoses* 29), who tells the story of a Theban heroine called Galinthias, who was turned into a weasel (*gale*) by the Fates for assisting at Herakles' birth, concluding: 'even now the Thebans . . . sacrifice first to Galinthia before the festival of Herakles'. The main festival seems to be in honour of both Herakles and his sons and is referred to by Pindar, in an ode which may have been performed at the Herakleia, celebrating the victory of Melissos of Thebes in the *pankration* at Isthmia in 478 BC (*Isthmian* 4.61–79). The poem specifies that there are eight sons, 'whom Megara daughter of Kreon bore', which would seem to indicate the children killed by Herakles, although the number is greater than in other versions of the madness story (pp. 88–92). A feast is prepared for Herakles 'above the Elektran Gates', and many victims are sacrificed holocaust for the eight sons in an all-night ceremony; the following day there is 'the final event of the annual games, a deed of strength', in which Pindar's victor had previously been successful.

The site of this festival must have been the sanctuary of Herakles which Pausanias (9.11.1–7) locates just outside the Elektran Gates to the south-east of the city and describes in some detail. Mention of a rock known as 'the Moderator', supposed by the Thebans to be the very boulder thrown by Athena to bring an end to Herakles' rampage, provides a further link with the madness story. The sanctuary had a statue of Herakles the Champion (Promachos), suggestive of a warlike character, but also an ancient wooden statue supposedly dedicated by the legendary Cretan master-craftsman Daidalos himself; the historical fourth-century sculptor Praxiteles was responsible for the temple pediments depicting Herakles' labours (p. 28). The temple housed what were supposed to be Herakles' own weapons, and the strength of popular belief is suggested by the story that the arms mysteriously vanished before the battle of Leuktra, a portent interpreted as meaning that Herakles had already set out for the battle (Xenophon, *Hellenika* 6.4.7). Diodoros (15.53.4) elaborates on this, crediting the general Epaminondas with the stratagem of having the sacred weapons' disappearance reported in order to overcome his superstitious soldiers' reluctance to fight. Even more prosaically, Polyainos (*Stratagems* 2.3.8) simply has the rusty weapons polished up and shown off to the troops within the temple before their departure. The underlying assumption of all three versions, however, is that ordinary soldiers would have taken heart at the thought of Herakles leading the way. The sanctuary also had a gymnasium and stadium 'both named after the god', and presumably used for the games attached to Herakles' festival, associating the Theban Herakles with the young and athletics, as at Athens and Sparta. Elsewhere in the city, as we have seen (p. 131), was a shrine of Iolaos where lovers in the Sacred Band took their vows.

Religion and politics combine in Theban coinage, where Herakles begins to appear from the middle of the fifth century, reflecting the city's renewed self-assertion as it recovered from the mistake of collaboration with the Persians in 480–479 BC. Thebes' traditional numismatic motif was the figure-of-eight shaped shield, a type which seems to be associated with the heroic age rather than with the equipment of a contemporary hoplite. The shield continues to appear on the obverse of Theban coins, while the reverse now features images of Herakles striding into battle, stringing his bow, or as an infant strangling the snakes. It has been suggested that the weapons in Herakles' temple may have been the figure-of-eight shield and a sword, rather than the hero's club and bow. This is unprovable, as is the idea that such a shield is referred to in Theokritos' account of the snake-strangling, where Amphitryon puts Herakles and Iphikles to sleep 'on a bronze shield' (*Idyll* 24.4), although the shape would indeed be ideal as a cradle for twins.

Elsewhere in Boiotia, Herakles had a sanctuary at Thespiai served by a priestess who remained a virgin until her death. Although temporary chastity was often required for the performance of Greek rituals, life-long virginity was unusual, but Pausanias (9.27.6–8) offers an explanation in the shape of a local version of the story of king Thespios' fifty daughters. Herakles slept with forty-nine of them in the same night, but just one refused, and 'considering himself to have been insulted, he condemned her to remain a virgin all her life, serving as his priestess'. Pausanias himself, though, is reluctant to believe that Herakles could have behaved so arrogantly, and spots the problem that this story is set during Herakles' mortal life: 'he would hardly have set up a temple to himself, and a priestess, as though he were a god'. The story aside, though, the very existence of a priestess of Herakles is striking, given the usual masculinity of his cult, and the best guess is that the Thespians celebrated a 'sacred wedding' (*hieros gamos*) of Herakles in which the priestess was regarded as his bride. A virgin priestess is also attested at two other Boiotian sites, where Herakles seems to have been worshipped under the obscure title Charops. At Thisbe Pausanias reports (9.32.2) a sanctuary and festival of Herakles, while he identifies (9.34.5) a location on Mount Laphystion outside Koroneia as the place where Herakles brought Kerberos up from the Underworld. Some details of the cult at at the latter site are provided by inscriptions of c.250–150 BC recording the manumission of slaves, for whom the priestess of Herakles acted as guarantor.[13]

The only other place where we hear of celibacy required in Herakles' attendants is the case of the priest of Herakles Misogynes, 'the Woman-Hater', somewhere in Phokis, reported by Plutarch (*Why are Delphic oracles no longer in verse?* 403f–404a). Here, however, the terms were a great deal less strict, with the priest's celibacy only lasting for his year's service in the first place, and some relaxation of the rule being possible. A young priest once fell prey to temptation while drunk, but when he fled to Delphi for advice the oracle said, 'The god concedes all things that are necessary'. The title 'woman-hater' hardly fits with the lustful Herakles of Thespiai, but it has been quite plausibly suggests that it arose, like the general exclusion of women from Herakles' cult, from the widely attested idea that the presence of women impairs a warrior's energy.[14]

Just north of Boiotia is the region in which myth locates Herakles' death, as we have seen most fully recounted in Sophocles' *Women of Trachis* (pp. 80–6). The inhabitants of Mount Oita told Herodotus (7.198) that their river Dryas had miraculously arisen to cool Herakles' death-agonies, and a place on the mountain was called 'the Pyre, because there the mortal body of the god had been burned' (Livy 36.30.3). This can be linked with the report of an ancient commentator on Homer (on *Iliad* 22.159) that a quadrennial festival was held on Mount Oita for Herakles, which included games and an ox-sacrifice in which the victims were burnt whole. There is indeed archaeological evidence for cult on the mountain-top from the sixth century, including bronze figurines of Herakles, potsherds inscribed with simple dedications to him, and remains of bones consistent with the holocaust of oxen, pigs and sheep. Early interpretations of this evidence suggested that the myth of Herakles' fiery death was created as an aetio-logical explanation for a pre-existing ritual, but more recent work suggests that the myth came first. Such fire festivals with holocausts are characteris-tic of Semitic religion, which has led many to speculate about possible con-nections between the ritual on Mount Oita and the Phoenician god Melqart (see below), although no really plausible link has been established.[15]

A final aspect of Herakles in central Greece is the association with heal-ing which we have already seen at Athens. At Hyettos in Boiotia, Pausa-nias (9.24.3) reports a temple of Herakles, which had a crude statue 'of the ancient sort', where the sick were able to obtain cures. A similar concern may be reflected in Herakles' association with the hot springs in the pass at Thermopylai. We saw Herakles as founder of hot springs in Sicily in Chapter 5, and according to Athenaios (12.512f) all hot springs were sacred to Her-akles, but a particular link with Thermopylai is made as early as Peisandros' *Herakleia* (fr. 7 W): 'At Thermopylai the goddess grey-eyed Athena makes hot bathing-places for him beside the edge of the sea.' Herodotus (7.176) knew of an altar dedicated to Herakles at the Thermopylai springs, and Strabo (9.4.13) speaks of 'hot waters honoured as sacred to Herakles'.[16]

Kos and Rhodes

Beyond mainland Greece, we find cults of Herakles on the Dodecanese islands of Kos and Rhodes, both colonized by settlers from the Argolid in the tenth century BC. Herakles' mythological connections with Kos are already attested in the *Iliad*: after Herakles' sack of Troy, Hera stirred up the storm winds which destroyed his companions and blew the hero himself off course to Kos (14.249–56); Zeus eventually rescued Herakles and sent him home to Argos, having punished Hera by suspending her from Olym-pos with anvils tied to her feet (15.18–30); in the meantime Herakles must have had an amorous affair on the island, because the contingent from Kos who accompanied Agamemnon's expedition to Troy was led by two grandsons of Herakles, sons of Thessalos (2.676–9). The missing episode, in which Herakles sacked the city of Kos, was alluded to in the *Catalogue of Women* (fr. 43a W), and provides (fr. 78 F) the motivation that king Eury-polos, a son of Poseidon, had opposed Herakles, who responded violently, killing Eurypylos and his sons and making his daughter Chalkiope pregnant with Thessalos. These sources show that Herakles was well-established in Koan mythology at a relatively early date, and his general local importance is attested by his appearance on the island's coinage from the mid-fourth century: the obverse features his bearded head in a lionskin, the reverse his club and a crab (a symbol of Kos).

Plutarch (*Greek Questions* 304c–e) links the old stories to some remarkable features of Herakles' cult in the deme of Antimacheia in the centre of the island: during the conflict, Herakles disguised himself as a woman and hid in the house of a Thracian woman; once he had overcome the Koans, he married Chalkiope, wearing 'a bright-coloured dress'; this is why 'the priest of Herakles at Antimacheia puts on women's clothes and binds his head with a band before coming back from the sacrifice', and why bridegrooms are given 'a woman's dress' to wear. This inevitably calls to mind the clothes-swapping of the Omphale episode, but there are many anthropological parallels for cross-dressing during rites of passage, intended to confuse evil daimons at a dangerous time of transition, and there are comparable wedding customs reported by Plutarch within Greece: at Sparta the bride had her head shaved and was dressed in a man's clothes (*Lycurgus* 15), while at Argos the bride wore a false beard (*Virtues in Women* 245e–f). The cross-dressing of the priest might be explained if he was involved in a *hieros gamos* celebrating the marriage of Herakles and Hebe.

This connection with weddings can also be seen in epigraphic evidence for Herakles' cult in Kos town. An inscription of c.300 BC from a sanctuary of Herakles, Hebe and Hera, records various ritual regulations: the sanctuary was used for celebrations in honour of marriage, although men and women were kept separated in different rooms; Herakles himself was expected to visit, and *nothoi* could take part in the sacrifice but not be priests; unusually, fish were part of the sacrifice to Herakles. Another inscription, of c.350 BC, records part of a cult calendar, listing sacrifices for Herakles on the 28th of an unspecified month, which are to consist of a preliminary holocaust of a lamb followed by a regular ox sacrifice. As at Sikyon, it is tempting to interpret this as a kind of compromise sacrifice, reflecting Herakles' partial mortality.[17]

Herakles' Homeric connection with Rhodes is via his son Tlepolemos, who duels with Sarpedon (*Iliad* 5.628–55), and is named as leader of the contingent from Rhodes in the Catalogue of Ships; a digression here explains that Tlepolemos originally came to the island in search of refuge after he had killed Herakles' uncle Likymnios at Tiryns (2.653–70). Tlepolemos himself was worshipped by the Rhodians as their founder, with sacrifices and games 'as for a god' (Pindar, *Olympian* 7.77–80). For Herakles' cult, we have most information about Lindos, where an unusual annual sacrifice was held: one or two oxen were taken from the plough and slaughtered to the accompaniment of curses, and if anyone said a 'good word' or word of good omen throughout, the ritual was violated. This is an exact inversion of the usual belief that incorrect words or bad omens would nullify a ritual, and all the writers who report it offer an explanatory story: on arriving at the Rhodian port of Thermydrai, Herakles felt hungry and asked a farmer called Theiodamas to sell him one of the oxen yoked to his plough; when the farmer refused, Herakles took the ox by force, roasted and devoured it, while the farmer stood by helplessly cursing him; Herakles enjoyed the cursing so much that he instituted a permanent ox-sacrifice to himself in the place and made the farmer his priest.

This story obviously resonates with the comic image of Herakles as a cheerful glutton, but it also contains darker elements. Commentators have compared the cursing involved with the cheerfully abusive speaking (*aischrologia*) which was part of the worship of Demeter, in which context it was meant to promote fertility or ward off ill luck, or with the ritual cursing of 'scapegoats' to load them with the ills of the people before they were driven out of the city. Alternatively the cursing might reflect guilt at the shedding of the plough-oxen's blood, an idea seen in the Athenian Bouphonia ritual, where those involved in the sacrifice to Zeus Polieus were symbolically tried for murder. Herakles' high profile at Lindos is further suggested by the existence there of a painting *Herakles* by the fourth-century Parrhasios, who claimed that he had depicted the hero 'just as he often appeared in his dreams' (Pliny, *Natural History* 35.71–2). Both Herakles and Tlepolemos are amongst the mythical characters supposed to have made dedications at the temple of Athena at Lindos, according to a second-century BC inscription known as the 'Lindian Chronicle' (Copenhagen 7125).[18]

Thasos

On the northern Aegean island of Thasos, it is still possible today to visit the substantial sanctuary of Herakles, excavated in the 1930s, a few hundred metres southwest of the ancient agora in Thasos town. Herodotus (2.44), who visited Thasos in the mid-fifth century, thought that the sanctuary had been founded by the Phoenicians, and he had himself seen a temple of 'Thasian Herakles' in the Phoenician capital Tyre. Six hundred years later Pausanias, too, visited Thasos, where he was told that the islanders worshipped 'the same Herakles as the Tyrians' but in addition paid honours to 'Herakles son of Amphitryon' (5.25.12). The archaeological evidence, on the other hand, suggests that the sanctuary was established when the island was colonized by Greeks from Paros c.700 BC, and commentators have generally abandoned the idea of a pre-Greek phase. Recent work has identified two small sixth-century buildings in the sanctuary, but places a major monumentalization at the beginning of the fifth century, including a single-chamber temple and a complex of five dining rooms (Figure 6.4).

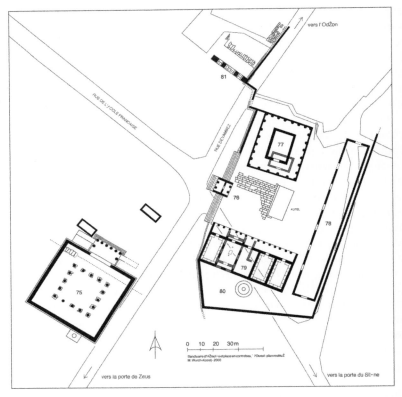

Figure 6.4 Plan of Herakles' sanctuary on Thasos. Plan: reproduced from Grandjean and Salviat (2000, fig. 94) by kind permission of the École Française d'Athènes, © EfA/ M. Wurch-Kozelij.

Directly south of the sanctuary is the 'Gate of Herakles and Dionysos' in the city walls, built in the early fifth century, decorated with reliefs of Herakles the archer and Dionysos, with niches for the offerings of passers-by and an inscription: 'The sons of Zeus, of long-veiled Semele and Alkmene, stand as guardians of this city' (*IG* XII 8.356).

Further evidence for Herakles' importance on Thasos is provided by Pausanias' description (5.25.12) of a fifteen-foot high bronze statue of the god dedicated by the Thasians at Olympia, by the early fifth-century sculptor Onatas of Aigina. Pausanias (6.11.2–9) also reports the case of the famous Thasian boxer and pancratiast Theagenes, who won the boxing competition at Olympia in 480 BC and many other prizes besides; his father Timosthenes was a priest of Herakles, but 'the Thasians say' that it was

Herakles himself who fathered Theagenes. The story may well have been inspired by Theagenes' prodigious athletic prowess, but Pausanias goes on to give the history of a statue of Theagenes to which the Thasians 'customarily sacrifice as to a god' – this was a rare honour for a historical figure. Towards the end of the fifth century, Hippokrates, who spent four years as a public doctor on the island, mentions Herakles' sanctuary as a point of reference when identifying the locations in which he had treated some of his patients. The Herakleion also features in Polyainos' memorable account (*Stratagems* 1.45.4) of events in 404 BC, at the end of the Peloponnesian War: the Spartan general Lysander rounded up the Athenian-supporting Thasians into the sanctuary, promising them an amnesty, and then proceeded to massacre them.

Images of Herakles were everywhere on the island. He appears on a Thasian vase in the mid-sixth century (Thasos 1703), and in the fourth century his head is stamped onto the amphoras used to export the island's celebrated wine. Most significantly, though, he featured on numerous Thasian coin-types, of all values, from c.400 BC until the early third century AD. The earliest type is clearly meant to remind the Thasians of the city's gate, since it features a head of Dionysos on one side, while on the reverse Herakles is bearded, wearing the lionskin and kneeling with drawn bow; the legend Thasiôn behind him is the usual way of indicating the coin belongs to the 'people of the Thasians', and the kantharos at his feet indicates the particular coin-issue. Later types have the head of Herakles (bearded or not) on the obverse, with his bow and club on the reverse, or return to the Dionysos-Herakles combination, but with both gods represented as beardless youths; the nude Herakles now stands, leaning on his club and with his lionskin slung over his arm, accompanied by the words 'of Herakles, Saviour of the Thasians'. This title 'Saviour' (Sôtêr) is used of Zeus and other deities to express their power to save humans from danger, and is first attested of the Thasian Herakles in an inscription of c.300 BC listing the official religious festivals of Thasos, which include a Soteria for Herakles Saviour in the month of Anthesterion (February–March) and a Great Herakleia in Thargelion (May–June); a decree of c.350 BC adds the detail that games were held at the Herakleia.

All of this suggests that Herakles was one of the island's principal deities, but there has been much discussion of the rituals performed in his honour and what they imply about his divine/heroic status. There is no doubt about the importance of feasting at his main sanctuary: at least one of the sixth-century buildings was a dining chamber, while the later dining complex consisted of five rooms each containing seventeen couches, and analysis of animal bones shows that sacrificial victims were cut into portions for distribution. This connection with feasting is also reflected in a hellenistic relief carved in the rocks of the ancient marble quarries at Saliari, a few kilometres southeast of Thasos town, which depicts Herakles reclining on his lionskin.

However, something other than the usual form of Olympian sacrifice seems to be indicated by two inscriptions which use an unusual verb *ena-teuein*, 'to pay a ninth-part', a term which Scullion (2000) interprets as a kind of partial destruction-sacrifice, as in Herakles' cult at Sikyon, in which a portion of the victim is holocaust but the majority is available for consumption. The first is a sacred law of c.450 BC concerning the cult of Herakles Thasios, found in the agora, which prohibits the sacrifice of goats and pigs, and bans women from Herakles' worship – '. . . nor is it right for a woman (to participate)' – reflecting the exclusivity to men we have seen in Herakles' cult elsewhere. Its final clauses stipulate that no ninth-parts shall be paid, no *gera* (perquisite portions for the priest) are to be cut, nor *athla* (portions given to winners of the Games), all of which suggests a holocaust sacrifice, with no meat available for consumption. The prohibitions are most easily explained as making an explicit contrast between the agora ritual and the kind of ritual usually performed for Herakles on Thasos, which clearly involved feasting. The second inscription, of c.300 BC, found in the sanctuary but concerning the lease of a 'garden of Herakles' nearby, seems to confirm that the ninth-part sacrifice was practised elsewhere: the text is fragmentary, but it indicates the sacrifice of an ox, with a ninth-part paid, and a ritual banquet in small dining-rooms within the garden. The compromise of the ninth-part sacrifice may in itself reflect Herakles' ambiguous status, while the contrast between sanctuary and agora rituals could explain why Herodotus and Pausanias insist on distinguishing two Thasian Herakleses, though the Phoenician connection complicates things.[19]

Erythrai

As on Thasos, Phoenician origins are claimed by Pausanias (7.5.5–8) for the Herakles worshipped at Erythrai on the Ionian coast (modern Turkish Ildırı, near Çeşme), though there is no archaeological evidence to prove or disprove the theory. He was clearly preeminent in the local pantheon, as he appears very frequently on coins as well as in inscriptions, and Pausanias assures the reader that 'you would be delighted with the Herakleion . . . for its antiquity'. He tells the story of how the god sailed from Tyre, in the form of a statue, on a raft which anchored halfway between Erythrai and the nearby island of Chios. The two communities competed over the statue, until it was revealed to an Erythraian fisherman in a dream that his city's women-folk should cut off their hair and twist it into a tow-rope. The

Erythraian women refused, but some Thracian women who happened to live in the city, both slaves and free, consented to having their hair cut, and the raft was duly hauled ashore. Ever afterwards the rope was kept as a relic, and the Thracians were the only women allowed into the Herakleion.

It is possible that this elaborate story was made up to explain the appearance of Herakles' cult statue, which Pausanias says was not like other Greek statues he had seen but 'exactly like the Egyptian'. This could just mean that the statue was indeed very old, given the rather 'Egyptian' appearance of the late seventh-century Daedalic style of Greek sculpture, or the statue might really have been of non-Greek origin. The curious detail of the Thracian women is reminiscent of the Thracian woman supposed to have hidden Herakles on Kos: one possible explanation is that slaves were allowed access to Herakles' cult in both cases, 'Thracian' being an imprecise reference to slave status. Alternatively, the women allowed into the Herakleion in historical times may have been the female members of a particular clan known as the Thrakidai, rather than ethnic Thracians. Either way, the crucial role of women (of any status) remains striking: their inclusion may signal that the ritual at Erythrai was one of reversal and the dissolution of prevailing order, like the Kronia at Athens and the Saturnalia at Rome. The story of the rope suggests that the ritual role played by the women included hair-offerings, as made by youths at Athens.[20]

The 'Tyrian Herakles'

The 'Tyrian Herakles' invoked in connection with Thasos and Erythrai is usually identified by modern scholars as the Phoenician god Melqart. Our knowledge of Phoenician mythology is limited, but Melqart seems to have shared a number of traits with Herakles, especially his function as colonist: Melqart, whose name means 'Lord of the city', was regarded as the founder and protector of Tyre, and by extension as patron of Phoenician foundations overseas. From at least the fifth century BC there was frequent conflation of the two in the minds of Greek writers, who use the name 'Herakles' even when the Phoenician context makes it clear that they must mean Melqart, and in some locations the complete assimilation of the two gods can be seen in cult practice.

A prime example of this syncretism can be seen at Gades (Cadiz), linked with Herakles in Greek myth from c.500 BC as the home of Geryon, but established as a Phoenician colony from at least the eighth century. The sanctuary of Melqart is identified by Greek writers as a Herakleion, and a detailed description of the cult there is provided towards the end of the first century AD by Silius Italicus (*Punica* 3.21–44). According to Silius, the wooden doors of the temple were carved with images of the Nemean lion, the Lernaian hydra, the Keryneian hind, the Erymanthian boar, the horses of Diomedes and the capture of Kerberos, along with Herakles' encounters with Antaios, Nessos and Acheloos, and his apotheosis on Mount Oita. He goes on to describe the interior: there was no image of the god, but a perpetual fire was kept alight on the altar; the priests, who were vowed to chastity, went barefoot, with shaven heads and wearing plain linen garments; no women or pigs were allowed to enter. We have seen the prohibition of women elsewhere in Herakles' cult, and even the barefoot priests have a Greek parallel in the priests of Zeus at Dodona, but other elements (the absence of an image, the ban on pigs) are characteristically Semitic and clearly belong to Melqart.

Whatever other traits the two deities shared, a major point of contact, which suggested their identity to the Greeks, seems to have been the belief that they had been burnt on a pyre and subsequently resurrected. We have seen the ritual reenactment of Herakles' death on Mount Oita, and what seems to be a confused report of something similar for Herakles–Melqart at Gades is relayed by Pausanias (10.4.4). A man called Kleon had been visiting Gades but he and 'all the rest of the crowd' left temporarily 'on the command of Herakles'; on his return, Kleon found a giant 'sea-man' spread over the ground, 'burning, struck with lightning by the god'. Frazer's interpretation remains plausible (1898 vol. 5, 222), that this is an outsider's misunderstanding of a ritual where Melqart was burnt in effigy beside the sea, a ritual from which our informant, as a foreign visitor, was excluded. A later stage of such a ritual, reflecting the god's resurrection, may be indicated for Melqart's ancient sanctuary at Tyre, where, according to Josephus (*Antiquities* 8.146), king Hiram, a contemporary of Solomon, 'built a temple of Herakles and Astarte, and was the first to perform the awakening (*egersis*) of Herakles, in the month of Perition'. Both burning and subsequent ascension to the heavens are found in the ritual of the Hittite god Sandan at Tarsos in Cilicia, who again was identified by the Greeks with Herakles. This has been reconstructed from the images on a series of coins from the city representing the burning of Sandan on a pyre followed by his ascension to the heavens in the form of an eagle. The complete assimilation of Sandan with Herakles can be seen an address to the people of Tarsos by Dio Chrysostom (*Oration* 33.47), who speaks of 'the very beautiful fire' prepared for 'your founder Herakles'.

The Phoenician cult of Melqart at Gades also suggests an ingenious explanation for the famous Pillars, first attested in Pindar: 'the Pillars of Herakles, which the hero-god set up as famous witnesses of the furthest limit of voyaging' (*Nemean* 3.21–3). Diodoros (4.18.2–5) goes into more detail: the Pillars were founded by Herakles after his expedition against Geryon, 'at the farthest points of the continents of Libya and Europe which lie beside the ocean' to commemorate his campaign; in order to make them as impressive as possible he built out the promontories on either side, which had the beneficial side-effect of making the passage too narrow and shallow for sea-monsters to enter the Mediterranean; some people say that the two continents were originally joined and Herakles cut the passage between them, causing 'the ocean to mingle with our sea'. The Pillars have been variously identified with the Rock of Gibraltar, on the European side, and at least three mountains in the region of Ceuta in Libya. None of the candidates is particularly columnar, but pillars are a striking feature of the cult of Melqart. According to Herodotus (2.44) the ancient temple he saw at Tyre 'dedicated to Herakles' was remarkable, amongst other wonders, for 'two pillars, one of pure gold, the other of emerald stone which shone brightly in the night'. Herakles–Melqart's sanctuary at Gades also had a pair of magnificent pillars, described by Strabo (3.5.5) as made of bronze and more than three metres tall; it is not difficult to imagine how travellers' reports of them might have become exaggerated. The idea of Herakles' Pillars might also have been promoted by his dealings with Atlas, who is described by Homer (*Odyssey* 1.52–5) as holding up the 'tall pillars which keep the earth and sky apart'.[21]

Sicily

Herakles' role as archetypal colonist gave him a special place in the Greek cities of the west, as we have seen (pp. 157–9). In Sicily his cult was widespread, but we have most information on Diodoros' small home city of Agyrion, where Herakles is supposed to have founded various rituals (Diodoros 4.24). At Agyrion Herakles was 'honoured on equal terms with the Olympian gods with festivals and splendid sacrifices', and instituted 'annual honours and sacrifices for Iolaos' at a 'notable sacred precinct', entered by a 'Herakleian Gate'. Diodoros talks of 'all those living in the city' growing their hair long in Iolaos' honour, 'until with rich sacrifices they have obtained good omens and made the god propitious'; boys who fail to perform the 'customary rites' are struck dumb until they undertake to make the appropriate sacrifices. This ritual growing of hair is paralleled elsewhere in Greece, and the eventual cutting may well have marked entry to adulthood, as at the Athenian Apatouria. It is not quite clear whether Iolaos, Herakles himself or both are the recipient of the annual Games, including gymnastic contests and horse-races, but the whole population, free and slaves, is involved in sacrificing to the god and feasting.

There are no archaeological remains to match Diodoros' enthusiastic account, but some way to the southwest of Agyrion are the fine ruins at

Figure 6.5 The temple of Herakles at Agrigento, Sicily. Photo: author's own.

Akragas (Agrigento), which include the only extant Greek temple of Herakles, situated on the ridge known as the 'Valley of the Temples', along with the temple of Hera and the huge, unfinished temple of Zeus. A few of the columns have been restored (Figure 6.5), though a better idea of the sturdy mid-fifth-century Doric style is given by the neighbouring temple of 'Concord', preserved by its conversion into a Christian church. Around 70 BC, Cicero (*Against Verres* 2.4.94–5) describes the temple of Herakles, 'not far from the forum', as especially sacred and beautiful, and notes that the bronze statue of Herakles had half its face worn away by the constant kissing of worshippers. One of the many crimes of which the Roman governor Verres stood accused was attempting to steal this statue, though he was unsuccessful; Cicero refers to his prosecution of the corrupt governor as 'a labour of Hercules', making fun of the fact that Verres' name means 'boar'.[22]

THE ROMAN CULT OF HERCULES

Herakles' presence in the Greek colonies meant that he was known in southern Italy from an early date, while, further north, the Etruscans imported Greek pots which bore his image throughout the sixth and fifth centuries BC, as well as creating images of their own. Some have attributed the Roman Hercules exclusively to this Greek origin, others have argued for his descent from the Phoenician Melqart, and others again have suggested the influence of native Italian traditions. The Phoenician theory has not found wide acceptance, but native Etruscan art certainly attests his adoption into local mythology as Hercle from the sixth century, and both Greek and Italian elements seem to be incorporated into Hercules' ritual. According to Livy (5.13.5–6), as early as 399 BC, when Rome was beset by plague, he was one of the six major deities propitiated with a *lectisternium*, a ritual where couches were set for the gods' feast.[23]

The most venerable site of Hercules' worship at Rome was the Ara Maxima in the Forum Boarium. The story of its foundation links it with Greek tradition by setting the event on Hercules' return journey with the cattle of Geryon, and by giving an important part to the local king Evander, an exile from Arkadia who had settled his followers in the area which would eventually become Rome. When Hercules had rid the vicinity of the monster Cacus, Evander, recognizing that he was destined for immortality, decided to offer him divine rites; the first sacrifice was made by Hercules himself, who ordered the Arkadians to repeat the sacrifice every year at the same 'Greatest Altar'. In historical times the cult was at first a private one, according to Livy (9.29.9–11), administered by the Potitii and Pinarii clans, the preeminent position of the former explained by the tradition that the Pinarii had arrived late for the original feast (Livy 1.7, Dionysios, *Roman Antiquities* 1.40). Control was transferred to the state in 312 BC, however, on the advice of the censor Appius; such tampering with established religious custom led to bad luck for both the clan, which entirely died out within a year, and for Appius, who was subsequently struck blind. From then on the annual festival, on 12th August, was presided over by the urban praetor.

Various details of historical practice are reflected in Virgil's account of the sacrifice Evander made in the company of Aeneas (*Aeneid* 8.268–305), and Livy's of the sacrifice made by Romulus when he founded Rome (1.6–7): the ritual followed Greek forms; women were excluded; the officiant wore nothing on his head except a wreath of laurel picked on the Aventine; the victim was sacrificed in the morning, but unusually there was then a break until evening, when the innards were burnt, after a torchlight procession and the singing of hymns celebrating Hercules' great deeds. The 'Greek rites' obviously reflect a perception of Greekness in the cult's origins, and one ancient explanation of the ban on women contrasts the cult with a very Roman one. We encountered Propertius' version of the story in Chapter 4 in connection with Omphale, but Macrobius (*Saturnalia* 1.12.28) adds some details: a woman refused Hercules permission to drink from a spring belonging to the Bona Dea, because it was her festival day when nothing of hers might be touched by a man; this led to a general exclusion of women from Hercules' cult throughout Italy. The exclusion of women reflects the

Greek Herakles' misogyny, whose gluttony, too, is paralleled at the Ara Maxima in the practice of consuming the sacrificial animal whole on the spot, even including its skin. A final notable element of the cult at the Ara Maxima is the tithe (*decuma Herculis*) expected of the worshippers: one tradition had it that this was done because Hercules himself dedicated a tenth of Geryon's oxen. Tithes may originally have been a pastoral form of offering, commuted into tithes of commercial profit as the Forum Boarium developed into a commercial centre.

Another side to Hercules' character comes to the fore in the temple founded in 187 BC near the Circus Flaminius by the general Marcus Fulvius Nobilior for Hercules and the Muses, adorned with statues brought back from his campaigns in north-west Greece. It is probably these same statues which are represented on a set of coins struck by Quintus Pomponius Musa around 66 BC, the choice presumably made in reference to Musa's own name: one features Hercules, nude except for his lionskin, playing the lyre and inscribed 'Hercules Musarum'; the others present the nine Muses, each identified by suitable attributes. Other Republican military leaders, however, chose to honour Hercules in his more obvious warrior aspect. After his conquests in Greece in the 140s BC, Mummius established a temple of Hercules Victor or Invictus ('Unconquered') on the Caelian and instituted the custom of dedicating a tithe of war spoils to Hercules. Also built in the latter part of the second century BC was the surviving round temple of Hercules Victor in the Forum Boarium, where Hercules sometimes has the obscure epithet Olivarius. The tithe was also paid by Sulla in 78 BC and by Crassus in 70 BC alongside other honours to Hercules after their victories, as we saw in Chapter 5. Under the Principate, Hercules' official cult was intricately bound up with political propaganda, its fortunes dependent on the whim of the emperor.

In popular religion, however, Hercules' worship remained important throughout the first to third centuries AD – according to Dionysios (*Roman Antiquities* 1.40), 'one could hardly find any place in Italy where the god Hercules is not honoured'. As we have noted (p. 45), Hercules was worshipped as protector of cattle on transhumance routes in central Italy, and other variations on his more general role as Alexikakos are attested too. For example, an inscription of AD 150–250 from Artena, just south of Rome, records a hymn-like poem which invokes Hercules as 'guardian of secure anchorage', praises him specifically as saviour of the shipwrecked and gives an apparently personal account of an instance of the god's intervention on behalf of seafarers in distress. Many 'colleges' were dedicated to Hercules, semi-official religious associations whose purpose was to meet regularly and fund sacrifices to their god; some colleges also financed common burial grounds. The best documented case is that of the worshippers of

Hercules Victor at Tibur, outside Rome, who were divided into two colleges, the *Herculanei Augustales*, incorporating imperial cult, and the *iuvenes Herculanei*, 'young men' of Hercules; several such colleges of *iuvenes* are known elsewhere in Italy, paralleling the Greek Herakles' association with youth. Epigraphic evidence shows that the membership of some colleges was drawn from the wealthy classes, but others included people of quite lowly status – poorer farmers, freedmen, and even slaves – a feature again reminiscent of the Greek Herakles. Outside Italy fewer colleges are attested, but the cult spread far and wide due to Hercules' popularity with the army. In some provinces he was assimilated to local deities, like the Celtic Ogmios (p. 130), invoked in lead curse-tablets found at Bregenz on Lake Constance. Hercules' popularity endured in the face of the growing appeal of Christianity, and even after Christianity became the official religion of the empire in the early fourth century, Hercules continues to be ubiquitous.[24]

OVERVIEW

Herakles was unusual in the ancient world for being both a hero and a god. This ambiguity of status reflects a real historical progression in how he was perceived, and is articulated in myth by the story of his ascension to Olympos and marriage to Hebe. Our most extensive evidence for his cult comes from Attica, but interesting rituals and remains are to be found in the Peloponnese and central Greece, on the islands of Kos, Rhodes and Thasos, at Erythrai and in Sicily. In several places he was identified with the Phoenician Melqart or the Hittite Sandan, with whom he shared a kind of fire ritual. In practice he was most often honoured with sacrifices followed by feasting and considered to be a god, but there are a number of instances where we see holocausts or partial destruction sacrifices, elements of ritual more commonly associated with worship of heroes and the dead. Notable features of Herakles' cult which recur are its exclusivity to men, an association with athletics, ephebes and initiation, the involvement of *nothoi* and slaves, the special form of shrine, a particular emphasis on feasting, and a sacred marriage with Hebe. His mythological warrior qualities are sometimes apparent, but most frequently he is a general averter of evils, including sickness. The Roman cult of Hercules has much in common with its Greek counterpart, especially the exclusion of women, association with youth and a cross-class appeal. The Ara Maxima might be regarded as its official centre, but at a popular level it was widespread all over the empire.

HERAKLES AFTERWARDS

POST-CLASSICAL VARIATIONS

> As each age has renegotiated its notion of the hero, Hercules has been there
> to mark that change. Stories about Hercules do far more than just recount
> amazing exploits, they take us into the heart of the culture that celebrates
> them.
>
> (Blanshard 2005, xviii)

THE AFTERLIFE OF A HERO

In the preceding chapters we have seen the extraordinary variety of
ways in which Herakles was represented in Greek and Roman literature
and art, his role in politics and the religious thought and practice of the
ancient world. Herakles' story continued to evolve, however, beyond the
end of classical antiquity. A systematic survey of the wealth of material
available is beyond the scope of this chapter. As detailed in the Further
Reading section and notes, however, there are a great many books and
articles dealing with specific aspects of Herakles' reception by later cultures, from representations of his Choice in Renaissance painting to modern productions of the Herakles tragedies by Sophokles and Euripides.
What I aim to do here is to whet the reader's appetite for further study
by picking out some major themes and providing a few examples from
different times, places and media. The problem of our hero's name is
especially acute in this chapter, but I shall continue my practice of using
'Herakles' when discussing Greek material and 'Hercules' for Latin contexts. Since Latin was the predominant language of the Renaissance, and
has continued to hold sway over subsequent reflections on antiquity,
'Hercules' is appropriate in much of the discussion, though I have tried
to respect modern writers' and artists' choice of name/spelling as far as
possible.[1]

HERAKLES/HERCULES AND THE CHRISTIANS

The ubiquity of Herakles/Hercules in the Roman empire made it inevitable that early Christians would encounter him wherever they went, and the popularity of his cult made him at first a rival to Christ. However, there are some obvious similarities between our hero and Christ – both gods born of mortal woman, who suffer, rid the earth of evil and overcome death – that provide scope for analogies to be drawn. As early as the second century AD, Justin Martyr (*Dialogue With Trypho* 69.3) could write:

> When it is said that Herakles was strong, that he travelled the whole world, that he was born of Zeus and Alkmene, that after his death he was taken up to heaven, do I not understand that this is an imitation of the Scripture which says about Christ that he runs his course as strong as a giant?

Whether or not such comparisons with pagan gods and heroes were useful was clearly a contentious issue for the Church Fathers. In the mid-third century, Origen pours scorn on the pagan philosopher Celsus' suggestion that Herakles (amongst others) would be a worthier subject of worship than Jesus, incidentally denigrating the Rhodian ritual we encountered in Chapter 6 (*Contra Celsum* 7.54):

> But since he refers us to Herakles, let him present us with examples of this man's sayings and justify his unholy servitude to Omphale, and let him demonstrate that he was worthy of divine honours who, having taken an ox from a farmer by force and like a brigand, feasted and delighted in the imprecations which the cursing farmer said to him as he ate; thus even to this day it is said that the demon Herakles receives sacrifice accompanied by curses.

In the early fourth century, Lactantius is similarly concerned with our hero's vices. A chapter in his *Divine Institutes* (1.9) is devoted to Hercules' life and death, beginning with comment on his unpropitious birth from Alcmena's adulterous union and questioning the divinity of one 'who, enslaved to his own vices, against all laws, treated both males and females with infamy, disgrace, and outrage'. He goes on to dismiss the labours in terms reminiscent of the allegorical interpretation, which we saw being used in the hero's favour by Stoic philosophers in Chapter 4:

> For he is not to be thought braver who overcomes a lion, than he who overcomes the violent wild beast shut up within himself, i.e. anger; or he who has brought down the most rapacious birds, than he who restrains most covetous desires . . .

On the other hand, writing only a little later than Lactantius, Saint Basil mounts a defence of the potential moral worth of pagan myth in *On the*

Value of Greek Literature, which includes a re-telling of Herakles' choice between Virtue and Vice (5.55–77) as an example for his young nephews to imitate. It is also likely that many ordinary Christians were less exercised about Herakles' shortcomings than the theologians, his status in popular pagan cult as warder-off of evil making him easy to assimilate with the new Saviour. This is suggested by his appearance amongst the wall-paintings which adorned the Christian catacombs of Via Latina at Rome, apparently quite at home alongside images from the Old Testament and the Gospels. Room N includes three images of Hercules: fighting the hydra, lionskin to one side; leading Alcestis towards a seated Admetus, grasping a three-headed Cerberus by the neck in his left hand for good measure; leaning on his club beside the snake-guarded apple-tree of the Hesperides. The second and third of these can easily be interpreted as symbolizing the over-coming-of-death, a theme perhaps even more relevant to the Christian hope of resurrection than it had been to pagan hopes for the afterlife. The hydra scene, though not so specifically apt for the funerary context, had already appeared on Roman sarcophagi, alongside other labours, as we saw in Chapter 1.[2]

In the early sixth century the mythographer Fulgentius provided Hercules with just the kind of allegorical 'make-over' he needed in order to become more thoroughly acceptable to a Christian audience. Throughout the *Mythologies*, Hercules is identified with virtue and his opponents with various vices, often with the help of contrived etymologies. Cacus, for example, is derived from the Greek *kakon* meaning 'evil' (2.3), while Omphale must be lust 'because *omphalos* in Greek means the navel; for lust is ruled in the navel by women' (2.2). Antaeus, too, is interpreted as a sort of lust, 'born of the earth, because lust alone is conceived of the flesh', and Hercules' tactic of holding him away from contact with the earth is explained in the same terms (2.4):

> For when virtue holds on high the whole mind and denies it the sight of flesh, it immediately emerges as victor. Thus too he is said to have sweated long in the contest, because hard is the battle which fights with desire and vices.

While not sophisticated, Fulgentius' work is important because of its influence on the development of Christian allegory in the Middle Ages, setting the scene for Renaissance elaborations. Fulgentius' contemporary Boethius made more restrained use of references to pagan mythology in his *Consolation of Philosophy*. In one of the poems which punctuate the work (book 4 poem 7.13–35) he lists twelve of Hercules' labours as a parallel for the moral struggle in which the sage must engage. Boethius' list is significant, because it is the deeds he details, rather than the twelve identified in antiquity, which would become predominant in the Renaissance. Seven of the canonical labours are included (the lion, hydra, boar, birds, mares, Hesperides, Cerberus), but the remaining five (hind, stables, bull, Amazons, Geryon) are replaced by battles with the centaurs, Achelous, Cacus and Antæus, and holding up heaven is billed as 'his final labour', which was rewarded with heaven, an example for all to follow. In earlier prose sections of the work individual exploits of Hercules are more briefly adduced as allegorical illustrations of the topics under discussion. For example, when discussing difficult themes like providence and fate (4.6.3):[3]

> . . . such is the subject-matter that, when one doubt has been cut away, innumerable others grow up, like the hydra's heads; and there can be no end unless a man controls them by the most lively fire of the mind.

A more thoroughgoing theological dimension was added to the allegorical understanding of Hercules' exploits in early fourteenth-century Italy in Dante's *Inferno*, which uses references to Hercules' descent to Hades and victory over various monstrous opponents to symbolize Christ's harrowing of hell. Cerberus guards the third circle of hell, in which freezing rain torments the gluttonous, described as a three-headed beast with red eyes, black beard and swollen belly, flaying the sinners with his claws (6.13–19); he is referred to as 'the great worm' (6.22), identifying him with the Devil, though Virgil is able to pacify him with a fistful of soil, which he chews on greedily like a mortal dog (25–33). Hercules is not named here, but there is clear allusion to his labour at 9.98–9, where a divine messenger reminds the fallen angels that 'your Cerberus still bears wounds around his chin and neck'. In the case of others of his traditional opponents the reference to Hercules is explicit; some are themselves being punished, others are employed to keep order in hell and help Virgil and Dante on their way, but all are associated with sins appropriate to their classical personas. The river of blood, which scalds the violent in the seventh circle, is patrolled by the centaurs Chiron, Pholus and Nessus, 'who died for the beautiful Deianira and made for himself his own revenge' (12.68–9); Nessus guides Dante safely to the other side (12.114–39). A winged Geryon appears at the end of Canto 16 and is extensively described in Canto 17, before he flies the protagonists down the steep cliff from the seventh to the eighth circle, where various types of fraud are punished; Geryon himself is 'the foul image of fraud', with the face of a righteous man but the brightly coloured body of a serpent with a venomous sting (17.7–27). Cacus, now a centaur with a fire-breathing dragon on his shoulders, guards the thieves in the seventh ditch of the eighth circle, his own wicked ways having been curtailed 'under the club of Hercules' (25.25–33). Antaeus, unchained amongst the giants, lowers the visitors into the ninth circle, the very bottom of Hell reserved for traitors, holding Virgil in 'the mighty grip once felt by Hercules (31.132).[4]

In France, meanwhile, Hercules' encounters with monsters were presented as Christ's battle against evil in Chrétien le Gouays' *Ovide Moralisé* (1340), a version of Ovid's *Metamorphoses* interpreted for a Christian readership. This approach was hugely influential on later French literature, for example informing Christine de Pizan's treatments of Hercules in her *Letter of Othea* (1401) and *Book of the Mutation of Fortune* (1403), as an exemplar of the virtue of strength. Even more overt is Pierre de Ronsard's hymn to 'the Christian Hercules' (1555), which identifies eighteen parallels between Hercules and Christ, from their half-mortal half-divine parentage to their triumph over death. Juno's attempt on the infant Hercules' life via the snakes is likened to Herod's massacre of the children, Hercules' marriage to Youth is matched by Christ's to Eternity, and as for their opponents (ll.173–82):

> Ah, what are these foul monsters, these dragons by Hercules defeated? What the thousand horrors, the thousand strange beasts, this terrible serpent with seven heads, this lion, the centaurs overcome, Geryon, Busiris, and Cacus, who all lived as misshapen monsters, if not the Vice and the enormous Sins which Jesus Christ, by the celestial effort of his great Cross, put to death at a single blow?

Ronsard's Hercules is not consistently a Christ-figure, however, appearing elsewhere in the contrastingly playful guise of romantic role-model (*Odes* 2.30):

> If I used to love a pretty maidservant, hey, who would dare to blame me for so lowly a love? Hercules, whose honour flies to heaven, loved Iole well, who, a prisoner, tamed he who was her master.

Between these extremes, Ronsard presents Hercules in his more traditional character as the archetypal monster-slayer, 'who astonished Lerna with his bow, who imprisoned the Hound of Hell' (*Elegy to Muret* ll.17–18), and as a suitable role-model for French kings, as we shall see.[5]

In England, Francis Bacon could comment in 1609 that the Hercules who crossed Ocean in a clay cup to save Prometheus (*On the Wisdom of the Ancients* ch. 26):

> . . . seems to represent an image of the divine Word, hastening in the flesh, as it were in a fragile vessel, to the redemption of the human race.

In 1648, the Scottish polymath Alexander Ross provides a fairly systematic list of analogies between the labours and the Christian's duties (*Mystagogus Poeticus*, s.v. 'Hercules'):

By Hercules may be meant every good Christian; who must be a valiant Champion to encounter against the Snakes of malice and envy, the Lion of anger, the Boar of Wantonness, and to subdue the Thespian daughters of Lust, the Centaurs and wild horses of Cruelty, the Hydra of Drunkenness, the Cacus of Theft and Robbery, the Busyris of Tyranny, yea Hell itself, and the Devil that great Dragon.

The parallel with Christ is drawn less obtrusively by Milton. In his early poem *On the Morning of Christ's Nativity* (1629) the infant Jesus' superiority to a catalogue of pagan deities is implicitly likened to Hercules strangling the snakes: 'Our Babe, to shew his Godhead true/ Can in his swadling bands controul the damned crew' (ll.227–8). Similarly, in *The Passion* (1630) the suffering Christ is spoken of in Herculean terms, as 'Most perfect Heroe, try'd in heaviest plight / Of labours huge and hard . . .' (ll.13–14). The most striking example, however, is an indirect one, which recalls Dante's deployment of Hercules' opponents, at a key moment of the much later work (1671) *Paradise Regained* (4.562–71):

> But Satan smitten with amazement fell
> As when Earths Son *Antaeus* (to compare
> Small things with greatest) in *Irassa* strove
> With *Joves Alcides* and oft foil'd still rose,
> Receiving from his mother Earth new strength,
> Fresh from his fall, and fiercer grapple joyn'd,
> Throttl'd at length in the Air, expir'd and fell;
> So after many a foil the Tempter proud,
> Renewing fresh assaults, amidst his pride
> Fell whence he stood to see his Victor fall.

TELLING HERCULES' STORY I: RENAISSANCE LITERATURE

In most of the foregoing Hercules is alluded to rather than being the focus of a narrative. The fourteenth to sixteenth centuries, however, see a revival of the idea of providing a systematic account of his exploits, which, as we saw at the very outset of this book, had been attempted in both poetry and prose in antiquity.

Petrarch included an unfinished chapter on Hercules in his set of biographies, *On Illustrious Men* (1337–8), beginning: 'While it is very easy to tell stories about Hercules, it is extremely difficult to compose a history', because there were probably many 'Herculean men' and hence the multitude of variations and uncertainties concerning Hercules, 'so that the reader, as if entangled in the windings of a labyrinth, cannot find his way out' (2.12.1–4). Petrarch calls Hercules 'that rather celebrated philosopher'

(2.12.5), but in fact goes on to emphasize his physical strength in a narrative which relates a selection of labours and other exploits in brief and relatively straightforward style. Boccaccio devotes a chapter of his *Genealogy of the Gods* (13.1) of 1360–74 to Hercules, recounting no fewer than thirty-one labours, before continuing to much briefer notices of seventeen named sons. Around the same time, Boccaccio's *Famous Women* includes an entry on Deianira (no. 24), in which he conflates Iole with Omphale, an error also apparent in his earlier *Amoroso Visione* (1342). Here the narrator is faced with a choice between a narrow door and a wide one, each leading to a different love, and halfway through the poem (canto 26) he sees a painting of Hercules working at Iole's loom, with Deianira exhorting him to return to her. Both the narrator's situation and its reflection in the painting look forward to the theme of Hercules' choice between Vice and Virtue which would become popular in Renaissance art (below), though here the narrator knowingly choses the 'wrong' wider door, a humorous inversion of the story's usual outcome.[6]

More extensive, and a great deal more complex, than either Petrarch or Boccaccio's works is Coluccio Salutati's monumental *On the Labours of Hercules* (1406). This runs to four substantial books, covering the story of Hercules' birth, youth, upwards of thirty labours and other exploits, death and deification. The work's stated aim is to explain how Seneca could have made Hercules a god in the *Oetaeus* after portraying the slaying of his wife and children in the *Furens*, but the discussion ranges far and wide, with copious reference to the extensive research which has informed the allegorical interpretations which Salutati offers of each episode. His Hercules is endowed with 'that excellence of all virtues, which raises him above the common condition of human virtues' (3.5.1), is repeatedly dubbed a 'philosopher', and is one of the first Renaissance Herculeses to face the choice between Vice and Virtue, as we shall see.[7]

Alongside these various Latin accounts, a number of writers offered versions of Hercules' story in their own languages. The Spanish theologian and poet Enrique de Villena, for example, wrote *The Twelve Labours of Hercules* (1417), which keeps strictly to twelve labours, if not the canonical ones, offering three readings of each in the medieval tradition of exegesis of the Scriptures. For example, Villena's account of the hydra story (his Chapter 7) locates the monster in a noxious marsh, which consumed animals and rendered the territory uninhabitable; it includes the details that for each of the hydra's head which was cut off another three would grow in its place, and that Hercules overcame the beast by surrounding it with fire. The labour is first interpreted allegorically, as the fight of the virtuous against the all-consuming 'delights of the flesh', the three heads being the vices of sloth, gluttony and extravagance, against which the only remedy is to surround oneself with the 'fire' of an ascetic life. Next, the historical 'truth' of the story is established as Hercules having used fire to drain and dry out a great lagoon, with many mouths, which had been making the surrounding territory impossible to cultivate. Finally, the tale is identified as being of particular moral and practical application to farmers, a group apparently especially prone to carnal vices.

No fewer than three Hercules narratives, two in Italian and one in Latin, came out of the court at Ferrara in the fifteenth and sixteenth centuries. The hero was important to the ruling d'Este family, at least three of whom were named after him, and the first of the three works was indeed commissioned in honour of Ercole, son of Nicolo d'Este, soon after his birth in 1431. Pietro Andrea de Bassi's *The Labours of Hercules* relates Hercules' whole life story, counting the infant snake-strangling episode as the first of around twenty labours; a fifteenth-century manuscript of the work heads each labour with a miniature illustration, number ten for example depicting Hercules leaning over the side of a ship as he plants his pillars in the sea. Amongst the spectacular elements of the adult Ercole's wedding in 1473 to Eleonora of Aragon, daughter of the king of Naples, were life-size sugar-sculptures representing Hercules' labours, and a dance featuring Hercules and Deianira, alongside other mythological lovers, attacked by centaurs whom the hero vanquished. A second Ercole d'Este (1534–59) was in power at Ferrara when Lilio Gregorio Giraldi produced his prose *Life of Hercules* (1539), narrating twenty-six labours, and Giambattista Giraldi Cintio wrote his epic poem *Twenty-Six Cantos on Hercules* (1557). Giraldi's work is in a similar vein to Salutati's, and colourfully damned for its lack of literary merit by Galinsky (1972, 201): 'both Herakles' moral monstrosity and the author's monotonously monumental erudition smother whatever *vita* there was left in Herakles by that time'. Ercole II was certainly conscious of his namesake, commissioning a gigantic statue of Hercules by Sansovino (1553) to stand in the Piazza Matteotti of Brescello, a town he proposed to rename Erculea when it came under Ferraran control.[8]

More readable than most of these works, however, is Raoul Le Fèvre's *Recueil des hystoires de Troyes* (1464), translated a few years later into English by William Caxton and reprinted numerous times as *The Ancient History of the Destruction of Troy* or just *The Destruction of Troy*. The Iliadic sack of Troy by Agamemnon in fact occupies only the third of the three books, the first two being taken up by the story of Hercules' dealings with Laomedon and an elaborate digression on Hercules' 'worthy deeds' and his death – an abridged version of the *Recueil* was indeed published as *The Book of the Strong Hercules*. Le Fèvre's Hercules is just as virtuous as the hero of contemporary allegorical literature, and like the ancient philosophical hero he faces intellectual as well as physical challenges, being a keen student of an academic version of Atlas, and later being sought after as teacher. He is, however, a much more flesh-and-blood character, owing much to the medieval tradition of the chivalrous knight. His relationship with Megara, for example, is romanticized by a lengthy courtship, and her death results, not from Hercules' senseless madness, but from his tragic reaction to a false accusation of adultery.

This conception of Hercules as a medieval knight resurfaces indirectly in Edmund Spenser's *Faerie Queen* (1590–6), where Arthur and his knights are often compared to Hercules, and the monsters they slay have features in common with those of the labours – the Blatant Beast of Book 6, for example, is described as offspring of Cerberus and the Chimaera (1.7). Book 5's theme of Justice especially invites such references, opening with an explicit comparison between the protagonist Artegall and Hercules (Canto 1.2):

> Who all the West with equal contest wonne,
> And monstrous tyrants with his club subdued:
> The club of Justice dread with kingly power endewed.

Artegall's imprisonment by the Amazon Radigund (Canto 5) is very obviously modelled on the Omphale episode, with Artegall dressing in women's clothes and an explicit parallel being drawn at 5.14 with Hercules, his club replaced by a distaff and 'his Lyons skin chaungd to a pall of gold'. The presumptuous Souldan in Canto 8 is compared to 'the Thracian tyrant' Diomedes, 'torn in pieces by Alcides great' (8.31), this characterization indirectly identifying his slayers Arthur and Artegall with Hercules. More extensively, the villain of Canto 10 is the tyrant Geryoneo, son of the Geryon killed by Hercules; the original slaying of Geryon is recounted in 10.9–11, foreshadowing Arthur's victory over Geryoneo in the following canto. Finally, the nameless Monster slain by Arthur in Canto 11 breathes out a noxious last breath and 'puddle of contagion' more hateful than Lerna or the Stygian lake (11.32); the reference once again equates the knight with Hercules, the hero already implicit in the description of the beast itself – a hybrid with dog's body, lion's claws, dragon's tail, eagle's wings and a maiden's face – perhaps born of Echidna (11.23), and certainly a match for the ancient monsters of Greek myth.

HERCULES' IMAGE REBORN: ART FROM THE RENAISSANCE ONWARDS

Images of Hercules had appeared throughout the Middle Ages in a variety of media. Manuscripts of texts featuring the hero, such as Boethius (above), might be illustrated with representations of his deeds, and relief carvings in stone decorate all kinds of structures, such as the Hercules at rest on the thirteenth-century baptistery pulpit in Pisa's cathedral. He could be found, too, on smaller-scale objects in metal, wood or ivory, for example performing a whole set of the twelve labours on the ivory panels which adorn the ninth-century wooden throne of St Peter's in Rome. In Renaissance Europe, however, Hercules' image becomes ubiquitous.[9]

Cycles

Just as in contemporary literature, groups of Herculean exploits appear in the Renaissance visual arts, the episodes chosen often following Boethius' list, rather than the canonical twelve of the ancient sources. Lucas Cranach the Elder, for example, painted a series of *Labours of Hercules*, seven of which survive (post-1537, Braunschweig). Groups of labours were popular in the medium of tapestry, too, a set having been made, for example, for Albrecht V of Bavaria's Dachau Palace, completed in 1577, while a single tapestry made for Pope Leo X (1513–21), *The Triumph of Hercules* (The Royal Collection), features seven labours in a central colonnade, with scenes from his life above and below.

In Rome, the brothers Annibale and Agostino Carracci painted frescoes depicting various labours for the Camerino of the Palazzo Farnese (1595–7), creating a suitable backdrop for the classical statue of the Farnese Herakles; they had previously executed a series of Hercules scenes, with a third brother Ludovico, for the Palazzo Sampieri in Bologna (c.1593–4). Later, for the Villa Doria Pamphili, Algardi produced a series of stucco reliefs to decorate the ceiling of a 'Galleria di Ercole' (1647), their designs modelled on a set of rock-crystal intaglios by Annibale Fontana illustrating half a dozen Herculean exploits, originally intended to adorn a casket (c.1560–70, Vienna). In Florence, Cosimo de Medici (below) commissioned an elaborate fountain from Vincenzo di Rossi in 1560, which was to be crowned with Hercules holding the celestial orb, with sculptural groups depicting eleven other labours below, and eight further exploits featuring in bronze reliefs decorating an octagonal balustrade around the base; although the project was never fully realized, seven sculptures were complete by 1584 and were installed in the Palazzo Vecchio in 1592.

In France, Toussaint Dubreuil adorned the Gallery of Diana at Fontainebleu with twenty-seven Herculean scenes in 1595, in honour of Henri IV's association with the hero (below). In Madrid, Francisco de Zurbarán painted a cycle of ten Hercules scenes for the Salón de Reinos in the Palacio del Buen Retiro (1634, Prado), including a *Hercules Fighting*

Cerberus featuring a splendid three-headed hell-hound, its black fur contrasted to the rather pallid flesh of the hero who drags him up from the fiery halls of Hades.[10]

Such Herculean cycles continue to be found in eighteenth- and nineteenth-century art, albeit less frequently. The Villa Borghese in Rome, for example, has a 'Sala di Ercole', with frescoes by Christoph Unterberger (1784) commissioned by Marcantonio Borghese; not one of the five subjects depicted is a traditional labour, but emphasis is placed rather on Hercules' apotheosis, this central image being surrounded by others representing the hero's death and events leading up to it (Hercules victorious over Achelous, Nessus and Deianira, the killing of Lichas). The Salon de la Paix of the Hôtel de Ville in Paris likewise had a set of eleven *Episodes From the Life of Hercules* by Eugène Delacroix (1851–2); the paintings were destroyed by fire in 1871, but surviving drawings and oil sketches by Delacroix and his assistant Pierre Andrieu indicate that the subjects included Hercules resting, his choice between Vice and Virtue, and such exploits as his rescue of Hesione and his fight against Cacus.

Individual exploits

More common than groups of deeds, however, are works focusing on individual labours or other battles, which offered suitable subjects for both sculpture and two-dimensional media, just as they had in antiquity. A particularly striking example is Dürer's painting *Hercules Killing the Stymphalian Birds* (1500, Nuremberg), which tackles this difficult subject by representing the birds as Harpies, with human (female) heads and torsos attached to lion-like forepaws and a serpentine tail. This conflation of the birds with the Harpies goes right back to the first century AD Hyginus (*Fabula* 20), who refers to Phineus' attackers as 'Stymphalides', and illustrators of Hercules texts from Boethius onwards seem to have found the hybrid creatures more satisfyingly monstrous than mere birds. Another unusual approach is taken in Hendrick Goltzius' engraving of *Hercules Victor* (Figure 7.1), which depicts the Farnese Hercules statue viewed from behind, so providing a clear view of the Hesperides' apples, with the heads and shoulders of two contemporary observers at the bottom right of the image to emphasize the sculpture's size. Beneath is a poem:

> I, Hercules, terror of the world, rest, weary after subduing the three-formed king of further Spain and after taking the apples from the turning-point of Hesperus, where the never-sleeping serpent had guarded them in gardens of gold.

Figure 7.1 Hendrick Goltzius, *Hercules Victor*, c.1592 but published and dated 1617 (New York 17.37.59). Photo: © SCALA, Florence, Metropolitan Museum of Art, New York, 2011.

Usually, however, the emphasis is firmly on Hercules as the ideal of physical strength tested to the limit. In Giambologna's sculptural group of Hercules and Nessus (1599), for example, made for the Loggia dei Lanzi on the Piazza della Signoria in Florence, the hero's strength is dramatically underscored by the centaur's contorted pose. In painting, Rubens' *Hercules Fighting the Nemean Lion* (c.1608, Bucharest) presents the naked hero grappling closely with the lion, one foot resting on an already vanquished leopard. The same artist's *Hercules in the Garden of the Hesperides* (c.1638, Turin) has the hero grasping the apples, urged on by a small *putto*, with one foot on the head of the conquered serpent Ladon. Especially in the more active battle scenes, Hercules' nudity and rippling muscles invite appreciation at an aesthetic level, and perhaps also at an erotic one. The wrestling match with Antaeus, in particular, has potential homoerotic overtones, as the two strongmen grapple with each other's naked bodies.[11]

The monster-slaying Hercules continues to be depicted in both painting and sculpture in the eighteenth and nineteenth centuries. Sir Joshua Reynolds, for example, produced an *Infant Hercules Strangling the Snakes* (1786, St Petersburg) for Catherine II of Russia, in which the brightly lit central babies are surrounded by a crowd which includes a Teiresias who looks like the writer Samuel Johnson and a Hera who resembles the tragic actress Sarah Siddons. Gustave Moreau painted several of the labours, including a *Hercules and the Lernaean Hydra* (1869–76, Chicago), in which a young, beardless hero stands before the towering seven-headed serpent, its menace emphasized by the presence of several human corpses, though all the figures are rather dwarfed by the rocky landscape.

Other subjects are introduced, too, such as Hercules' despatch of Lichas, most dramatically rendered in Canova's sculptural group (c.1795, Paris), which follows Sophokles' description (p. 84) in representing a diaphanous tunic clinging closely to the hero's torso, as he swings the unfortunate herald by his foot preparatory to hurling him to his death. In painting, Lord Frederic Leighton's *Hercules Fights Death for Alcestis* (1869–71, Hartford) is a study in colour contrasts: the centre of the painting is dominated by the recumbent white-clad form of the dead Alcestis; to the left, the grieving Admetus and servants wears reds and oranges; to the right, the warm brown flesh of a naked Hercules, seen from behind, stands out against the grey-black figure of Death, swathed in dark drapery. The story would particularly have appealed to the Victorian fascination with death and the afterlife, and indeed the painting is described by Leighton's friend Robert Browning at the end of his poem *Balaustrion's Adventure*, a version of the Alcestis story written in 1871.

Vice or Virtue revisited

The allegorical conception of Hercules so popular in Renaissance literature underlies many of his appearances in the visual arts. Overtly allegorical, for example, is Rubens' club-wielding *Heroic Virtue (Hercules) Overcoming Discord* on the ceiling of Banqueting House in Whitehall, London, paired with *Prudence (Minerva) Conquering Sedition* (1630–4).

Nowhere is the allegorical Hercules more apparent, however, than in representations of his choice between Virtue and Vice. During the medieval period battles between individual personified virtues and vices had been popularly depicted, notably in Prudentius' *Battle for Man's Soul* (c.AD 400), but representation of an all-encompassing Virtue seems to have been avoided before the fourteenth century, as incompatible with the idea of Christ as incarnation of God's supreme virtue. Prodikos' tale of Hercules at the crossroads was therefore not taken up until Petrarch alludes to it briefly twice in his *Life of Solitude* (1.4.2 and 2.9.4) of 1346, and the earliest Renaissance narration of any length comes at the beginning of the fifteenth century in Salutati's *On the Labours of Hercules* (3.7.1–4). Both scholars knew the story via Cicero's Latin version (*De Officiis* 1.118) rather than from a direct reading of Xenophon's Greek, and both combine it with the Pythagorean idea of a parting of the ways in life, symbolized by the letter Y. Subsequent visual and literary representations of the Choice, and modern scholarship thereon, have always placed Hercules *in bivium*, 'at the cross-roads', although the location is not quite explicit in the ancient accounts.[12]

We know of no representations of the Choice in the visual arts of Greece and Rome, despite the visual potential of the scene, but its popularity as a theme in the Renaissance and beyond is amply documented in Panofsky's influential study *Hercules at the Crossroads* (1930). The many variations in these post-Classical versions highlight the issue of how the two personifications can be characterized by their appearance. In Lucas Cranach the Elder's *Hercules at the Crossroads* (c.1500, Munich), for example, Virtue is dressed (albeit scantily) and has her hair decently arranged and covered in a veil, whereas Vice is completely naked and dishevelled, looking out of the picture with a most immodest gaze straight at the viewer; Virtue bears comparison with the title figure of Cranach's *Charity*, Vice with his many provocative-eyed Aphrodites.

In Veronese's *Allegory of Virtue and Vice* (c.1580, Frick Collection, New York), all three characters are in 'modern' dress, Hercules apparently about to embrace Virtue, but looking back over his shoulder towards the approaching Vice. Virtue wears the laurel crown of victory, while Vice's skirt is lifted to reveal the head and naked torso of a female, indicative of the true nature beneath her civilized exterior, and the painting's moral is made explicit by the inscription on an architectural feature in the background which proclaims that 'honour and virtue flourish after death'. Annibale Carracci's *Choice of Hercules*, commissioned for the Farnese Palace Camerino in 1595–7 (above, now in Naples), features a particularly muscular, nude Hercules seated on a rock beneath a palm tree. To the right, Vice's diaphanous drapery does little to hide her voluptuous body, and beside her an actor's mask and a musical instrument provide further characterization; to the left, a modestly attired Virtue holds a sheathed sword and points to a rocky path zigzagging upwards, at the bottom of which sits a poet ready to record Hercules' great deeds should he chose this way.

Carracci's version provided a model for Paolo de Matteis' *Choice of Hercules* in Temple Newsam House, Leeds (Figure 7.2). This was commissioned by Anthony Ashley-Cooper, third Earl of Shaftesbury, who had seen Carracci's painting in Rome and considered it a fitting illustration for his own philosophical treatise on the advantages of Virtue over Pleasure, the *Notion of the Historical Draught of Hercules* (1713). In other seventeenth- and eighteenth-century renderings of the subject the contrast between the

Figure 7.2 Paolo de Matteis, *The Choice of Hercules*, 1712 (Temple Newsam House, Leeds). Photo: Temple Newsam House (Leeds Museums and Art Galleries); Photographic Survey, The Courtauld Institute of Art, London.

two figures is developed further, with Virtue assuming Athena's armour, its hard surfaces contrasting magnificently with the voluptuous naked flesh of Vice, for example, in a Rubenesque *Choice of Hercules* in the Uffizi (c.1610, Florence). The format could also be used to represent other kinds of choice, for example in Joshua Reynolds' portrait of the famous actor David Garrick, *Garrick Between Tragedy and Comedy* (private collection, 1760–1).[13]

The eloquent 'Gallic Hercules'

Hercules' association with Virtue is further underlined in a number of influential sixteenth-century handbooks of myth and iconography. Natale Conti's ten-book *Mythologies* (1551) and Vincenzo Cartari's *Images of the Gods* (1556) both present Hercules as a moral principle, his monster-slaying representing the victory of virtue over various vices. The second edition of Cartari (1580) includes a woodcut and interpretation of the 'Gallic Hercules', an image based on Lucian's description of the Herakles Ogmios painting he claims to have seen in Gaul (p. 130), which depicts an aged

Hercules, still equipped with lionskin, club and bow, but attached to a crowd of followers by lines running from his tongue to their ears.

A similar image (Figure 7.3) appears in the first edition of Andrea Alciato's *Emblematum liber*, illustrating the entry 'Eloquence superior to strength' and accompanied by a description, which ends with the comment that 'by eloquence the powerful speaker pulls even the hardest heart where he will'. Another relatively unfamiliar story is alluded to in the entry 'On those who venture on what is beyond their power', in which the sleeping Hercules is attacked by pygmies, 'crushed like fleas' when the hero awakes. Later editions add further Heraclean images, such as the 1612 Padua edition's 'The Twelve Labours of Hercules', in which the woodcut squeezes in nine labours plus the funeral pyre around the hero, accompanying a text that is a general encomium of virtue. Geoffrey Whitney's *Choice of Emblems* (1586) includes an entry on 'The crossroads of virtue and vice' (no. 40), a woodcut of the Choice being accompanied by a poem which begins:

> When Hercules, was dowtfull of his waie,
> Inclosed rounde, with vertue, and with vice,
> With reasons firste, did virtue him assaie,
> The other, did with pleasures him entice . . .

In Cesare Ripa's *Iconologia* (1593), 'Heroic Virtue' (no. 317) is represented by the image of Hercules naked, but for the lionskin draped over his arms, leaning on his club and holding three apples of the Hesperides:

Figure 7.3 Andrea Alciato, *Emblematum liber*, Augsburg 1531, 'Eloquence superior to strength'. Photo: © Alciato at Glasgow project.

The Lion and Club denote the *Strength* of Virtue, that is immovable; secondly, the Apples, bridling Anger, *Temperance* in Riches; thirdly, the generous Despising of *Pleasure*, which is heroic. The Club is knotty, to shew the great *Difficulties* to be met with in living virtuously.

The eloquent Hercules seems to have appealed to Renaissance humanist sensibilities as an embodiment of the power of language. Erasmus likened his own and his friends' intellectual work to Hercules' labours at various points in his writings. The comparison is elaborated particularly in his early work *The Antibarbarians* (1520), where he presents Jacob Batt as boasting:

You yourself, a witness to those troubles, saw how far I have acted the Hercules – how many lions, how many boars, how many Stymphalian birds, how many bulls, how many Antaeuses, how many Geryons, how many Diomedes, how many Nessuses I slew; how I exposed Cerberus to the daylight, having dragged him out of his lair, where he was wont to terrorise the bloodless shades; by what great virtue I only just managed to overcome by Greek fire the Lernaean hydra, prolific in its deaths, and I do not know whether that once most dangerous pest yet breathes.

Hercules comes up frequently in the *Adages* (1500–36), most extensively in no. 2001, which is a 5,000-word essay on the Greek phrase *Herakleioi ponoi*, 'Herculean labours', interpreted in moralizing vein as a model for the good man's struggle to overcome vice, and for the scholar's efforts to get to grips with classical literature. A well-known portrait by Holbein (London, 1523) depicts Erasmus with his hands resting on a book which has 'the Herculean labours of Erasmus of Rotterdam' written in Greek on the gilded page-edges facing the viewer.

The association could, however, be turned around to the humanists' detriment. Dürer's engraving *Der Hercules* (1496), for example, introduces the Gallic Hercules (identifiable because he is wearing a type of winged hat more commonly worn by Mercury) into an unusual version of the Choice. Here, theoretical dispute between the two personifications has turned into an actual fight, in which Virtue, fully clothed, her head modestly covered, wields a sword against a suitably naked and voluptuous Vice, caught in the act of debauchery with a satyr. Hercules himself stands slightly aloof from the contest, holding up a stick but not obviously supporting one side or the other, and with his mouth slightly open as though speaking, while an infant boy stands to one side. It has been suggested that this is a parody of the humanist faith in words, the eloquent Hercules being ineffectual in a situation which demands action, the small boy referring to his penchant for pederasty, a vice considered especially prevalent amongst the ancient Gauls. If this reading is correct, the engraving constitutes a bitter indict-ment of Dürer's contemporary humanists, for their excesses and/or for their hypocrisy. A more blatant satire, sometimes attributed to Holbein (1522), which turns the 'Hercules Gallicus' title against a different subject, is a woodcut depicting the great reformer Luther as 'Hercules Germanicus'. The name appears on a plaque hanging from a tree, in front of which Luther, wearing Hercules' lionskin over his monk's habit and wielding a fearsome club, tramples such major figures of classical and Christian learning as Aristotle and Thomas Aquinas.[14]

The comic Hercules

Less elevated aspects of Hercules' story also appear. His sojourn with Omphale is perennially popular, produced by Lucas Cranach the Elder, for example, in at least ten versions of *Hercules and Omphale*. One of these (1537, Braunschweig) depicts the queen herself still holding a large spindle, but the hero has a loom-shuttle in his hand while servant-girls wrap his head in a wimple. Abraham Jenssens' version of the subject (1607, Copenhagen) takes inspiration from Ovid's *Fasti* (p. 133), as Hercules is kicking a goat-legged Pan/Faunus out of the bed he shares with the voluptuously naked Omphale. Lucas Cranach the Younger's pair of paintings *The Sleeping Hercules Beset by Pygmies* and *Hercules Awakes and Drives off the Pygmies* (Dresden, 1551) depicts the lionskin-clad hero surrounded by diminutive people in contemporary northern European dress, against a Germanic landscape. Lorenzo Lotto's portrait of Andrea Odoni (1527, Hampton Court) depicts the antiquities dealer surrounded by classical sculptures, including a Hercules wrestling Antaeus, a standing Hercules, and a small Hercules *mingens* apparently urinating into a bowl. Rubens' *Drunken Hercules* (c.1612, Dresden) has the naked hero staggering, his bulk scarcely supported by a voluptuous satyress and a satyr, wine-jug still in hand, the composition inspired by a Roman relief.[15]

HERCULEAN POLITICS

The 'virtuous' Hercules lent himself to political as well as moral allegory. As we have seen, Hercules was regarded as patron of the ruling d'Este family at Ferrara, and numerous other European aristocrats and monarchs likewise claimed him as role-model or even as supposed ancestor, just as Greek and Roman leaders had done before them.

At Florence the hero appears on the city's seal from the late thirteenth century onwards, with the motto 'Florence subdues depravity with a Herculean club'. Hercules appears in the sculptural decoration of Florence's cathedral, on the inner and outer door-jambs of the Porta della Mandorla (c.1391–1405), as a standing figure with lionskin and club, and in combat with the lion, the hydra and Antaeus. In 1409 a six-foot snowman of Hercules is said by a contemporary witness to have been made in the Piazza di San Michele Berteldi, along with 'a great quantity of beautiful lions'. It cannot be coincidence that the city's Herculean imagery was taken up by Medici family, who came to prominence in the 1430s. The cathedral's three labours were repeated around 1460 in large-scale paintings for the Sala Grande of the new Medici palace, produced by the brothers Antonio and Piero Pollaiuolo; the works themselves are lost, but the hydra and Antaeus scenes are reflected in small panels by Antonio (c.1475, Florence), and the latter in his bronze statuette-group of *Hercules and Antaeus* (c.1475–80, Florence). These Antaeus images depict the moment when Hercules has just succeeded in lifting his opponent away from the nourishing earth, and is squeezing the life out of him, and indeed an inventory of 1492 graphically describes the Medici palace Hercules as 'bursting Antaeus'.[16]

The death of Lorenzo de Medici, 'the Magnificent', in 1492 was marked by Michelangelo, according to Condivi's biography of the artist (Chapter 10), by the carving of a statue of Hercules over seven feet high. The Medici's return to power in 1530, after a period of exile, was likewise celebrated with a statue, this time a five-metre tall group of *Hercules and Cacus* (1534), originally commissioned as a pendant to Michelangelo's *David* though completed by Bandinelli, which is still conspicuous in the Piazza della Signoria. Around the same time Michelangelo reprised the Hercules scenes of the cathedral and the Medici palace in a red-chalk sketch of three *Labours of Hercules* (c.1530, Windsor), including a particularly fine lion straddled by Hercules who forces its jaws apart with visible effort. Cosimo I de Medici, who became Duke of Florence in 1537, personalized the city's traditional Hercules seal by replacing the legend with his own name, and was responsible for commissioning the *Fountain of the Twelve Labours* from Rossi (above). He also had a Sala d'Ercole created in his private apartments in the Palazzo Vecchio, its ceiling decorated with a selection of Hercules' labours by Vasari (1558); the artist's own commentary on the paintings (*Ragionamenti* 7) explicitly links the Medici with Hercules' virtues.

In Venice, too, Hercules occupies a prominent public position from an early date On the west façade of Saint Mark's Basilica, overlooking the piazza, is a set of six reliefs installed in 1267 consisting of three imported Byzantine works, each thematically paired with a contemporary piece: Saints George and Demetrius fight against evil, while the Archangel Gabriel pairs with the Virgin Mary to form an Annunciation; in the Hercules pair, a fifth-century AD struggle with the boar is matched by a thirteenth-century rendition of the hero trampling the hydra, carrying the hind on his shoulders for good measure. Although Herculean imagery is not taken up as extensively here as at Ferrara and Florence, the hero does reappear in a public context in two paintings produced around 1575 by Veronese for the Palazzo Ducale. Both feature a personification of the city together with our hero and another Greek deity, and the titles alone – *Venice with Hercules and Neptune* (Budapest) and *Venice Receives the Homage of Hercules and Ceres* (Venice) – make the political message hard to miss.[17]

Parts of Spain could claim particular connection with Hercules due to the hero's travels there in pursuit of the cattle of Geryon. The town hall of Seville, begun in 1527, is adorned with figures of its two founders Hercules and Julius Caesar, inspired by the triumphal entry into the city the previous year of Charles V complete with images of Hercules and his Pillars (below). Hercules likewise appears on the ornate sixteenth-century town hall of Tarrazona, a city whose coat of arms claims it to have been built by the Biblical Tubal-Cain and re-built by Hercules. Rubens sketched a painting of *The Apotheosis of Hercules* (1637–8, Brussels) for the hunting lodge of Philip IV of Spain near Madrid, in which a rather portly Hercules steps from his pyre into chariot drawn by four horses, driven by putto, while another crowns Hercules with a wreath. In 1682, Charles II of Spain was celebrated as Hercules' descendant in Juan Fernandez de Heredia's *Labours and Endeavours of Hercules*.

Moving away from the Mediterranean, the court of Duke Philip II of Burgundy (1419–67) saw the composition of Le Fèvre's influential story of Hercules (above). The lavish wedding of Philip's successor, Charles the Bold, to his third wife Margaret of York in 1468 included a performance of Hercules' labours in mime, the last being 'the carrying and erection of the Columns', featuring an elderly Hercules in a ship. The Burgundian tradition of association with Hercules was particularly exploited by Charles V, who inherited rule of Burgundy in 1506, at the tender age of six, before going on to become king of Spain in 1515, and Archduke of Austria and Holy Roman Emperor in 1519. As early as 1516 he adopted as his symbol a depiction of the Pillars of Hercules accompanied by the motto *plus ultra*, an inversion of the *ne plus ultra* (go 'no further') phrase supposedly written on the Pillars by Hercules himself, a warning to sailors against passing through the straits of Gibraltar to the dangers of the Atlantic. Charles' motto has been variously interpreted in geographical or ideological terms, expressing an interest in exploration of the recently discovered New World or an ambition to expand the Christian realm to the east, in conflict with the Ottoman Empire, and south to Africa. Whatever its original intent, however, the idea of 'going beyond' the limits of normal human endeavour seems apt for Charles V's extraordinarily extensive rule.[18]

Other central European rulers were presented as Hercules making his Choice, just as Trajan had been in Dio Chrysostom's discourse *On Kingship*

(p. 126). For example, a broadsheet commemorating Maximilian I's accession to the Electorship of Bavaria in 1595 included an engraving by Johann Sadeler depicting the young duke at the crossroads. The Cardinal-Infante Ferdinand of Austria was depicted in same role in one of the engravings by Theodor van Thulden in the *Pompa Introitus Ferdinandi* (Antwerp 1642), a set of designs by Rubens for the triumphal entry into Antwerp after the Battle of Nördlingen in 1634. Ferdinand appears dressed in Hercules' lionskin with a club, led away from Love and Pleasure by a fully armed Athena up the rocky path of virtue towards a temple of Virtue and Honour on top of a hill, while a cannon to the right alludes to the Nördlingen victory.[19]

Even northern European rulers might find a link with Hercules. In England, the anonymous poem *Les douze triomphes de Henry VII* (1497) systematically equates the king's achievements to the labours, his defeat of Richard III at Bosworth, for example, being likened to Hercules' victory over the Erymanthian boar. The Swedish king Gustavus Adolphus Magnus (1611–32), founder of the Swedish Empire, was represented as the Gallic Hercules in a German print, and during the reign of his daughter, Kristina, Georg Stjernhjelm produced an epic *Hercules* (1653), based on the Choice story. Towards the end of the seventeenth century, the academic Olaus Rudbeck identified the Öresund, the dangerous strait between Sweden and Denmark, as the true location of the Pillars of Hercules, and went on to argue in his massive *Atlantica* that Hercules himself had in fact been Swedish, his name originally being Härkolle, 'warrior chief', while Sweden was Atlantis and Swedish mankind's original language. In Denmark, meanwhile, king Christian IV (1588–1648) had the 'Giants' Tower' of his castle at Koldinghus adorned with colossal statues of classical heroes, each holding a shield with the coat of arms of territory under Danish control: Hercules represented Sweden, Hannibal Denmark itself, Scipio Norway, and Hector South Jutland. At the Rosenborg Castle in Copenhagen, Christian had a writing desk decorated with gilt illustrations of Hercules' labours, and was responsible for establishing the King's Gardens, where Frederik IV later (1709) installed a statue of Hercules wrestling with the lion by Giovanni Baratta, which in turn gave its name to the 'Hercules Pavilion' built in 1773.[20]

FROM MONARCH TO REVOLUTIONARY: HERCULES IN FRANCE

Hercules' particular significance for the French is based on a tradition dating back at least as far as the first century BC which makes him the ancestor of the Gauls. In Chapter 5 we saw how, in antiquity, a number of Italian and Sicilian cities gave themselves a mythological pedigree by attributing their foundation to the hero on his return journey with the cattle of Geryon. In the continuous narrative offered by Diodoros (4.19.1–2), before reaching Italy Herakles passes through Keltika, bringing peace and founding the city of Alesia in the north-east. Diodoros later (5.24.1–3) amplifies the account with the story of a Celtic princess who had scorned all previous suitors as unworthy, but 'wondering at Herakles' virtue and bodily superiority, she accepted his embraces with all enthusiasm'; in due course she bore a son, Galates, who had inherited his father's physical and mental excellence, and established the kingdom of Galatia. This idea of the Herculean ancestry existed alongside a medieval tradition of descent from the legendary Francus, eponymous king of the Franks, descended from the Trojans and sometimes identified with Aeneas' son Astyanax. A further link is provided by the Gallic Hercules, which as we have seen became a popular image in the Renaissance. The particular relevance of Lucian's tale to France is promoted in the sixteenth century by its translation into French in Geoffroy Tory's *Champfleury* (1529), a version told by Budé in *Institution du Prince* (1547), and its inclusion in French translations of mythological handbooks like those of Alciati and Cartari. In 1579, the historian Claude Fauchet's investigation into France's origins questioned the idea of Trojan ancestry, but accepted Hercules' foundation of Alesia as fact, and interpreted Lucian's tale as meaning 'that Hercules achieved his enterprises by fine language; and that being wise and prudent, he made great conquests' (*Collection of Gallic and French Antiquities* 2.35).

Both the general and the particular Herculean models were deployed in the service of Renaissance French monarchs. A statue of François I (1515–47) at Rouen depicted the king very much in the guise of Lucian's Hercules, according to his librarian Claude Chappuys (*The Great Gallic Hercules Who Fights Against Gods*, 1545):

> From his mouth issue four chains, two of gold two of silver, which lead to being attached to the ears of figures named below [Nobility, the Church, Advice, Labour]. But they are so loose that everyone can judge that they do not serve as constraints, and so that they are voluntarily pulled by the eloquence of the new Hercules . . .

François' son and successor Henri II (1547–59) was greeted on his triumphal entry into Paris in 1549 by a very similar statue, and a speech of welcome which cast Henri himself as 'a third Hercules', surpassing the hero-conqueror of Libya and the eloquent Hercules of the Celts. Ronsard likewise calls Henri II 'the Hercules of the French, who purges vices' (*Odes* V, *To King Henri II*), and urges his son Charles IX (1560–74) to 'imitate the deeds of this great prince: purge your domain of all error, then like him you will be amongst the gods' (*Sonets divers, To King Charles IX*). According to Ronsard, Charles' successor Henri III (1574–89) will also ultimately 'drink nectar at the table of the gods, like the valiant knight Hercules' (*Les Parques, To Henri III*). Ronsard takes up the image of the 'Gallic Hercules' as a flattering parallel for the same monarch's eloquence (*Panegyric of Fame*), having alluded to it more obliquely in earlier works in honour of Henri II, his patron Cardinal Charles de Lorraine and his teacher Dorat – in each case the honorand is said to 'pull by the ears' his audience.[21]

The association was promoted especially under Henri IV (1589–1610), who had a particular claim to descent from Hercules as a member of the House of Navarre. Indeed, a funerary oration by André Valladier explicitly commented on the king's use of Herculean imagery, noting it as being like Alexander the Great's imitation of the hero. Henri Pierre Matthieu made much of Henri's genealogy on the king's triumphal entry into Lyon in 1595, in the spectacle itself and in the commemorative booklet (*The Entry of the Very Great Prince Henri IV into his Fair City of Lyon*), quoting the first poem of du Bartas' *Pyrenean Muses*:

> Hercules having conquered the triple pride of Spain made himself the father of the king of this mountainous corner, which has always taken its law from the sons of his sons. Henri, unique terror of the land of the Hesperides, you could have no greater ancestor than Alcides; he could have no greater descendant than you.

Lyon also celebrated the occasion with a twelve-foot high statue of Hercules, with inscriptions on its pedestal identifying Henri as 'second son of the Thunder-throwing God, who valiantly purged the earth of wicked men', and 'king of the French by Herculean labours'. Henri himself was unable to make a planned entry to Avignon in 1600, but sent his new wife Marie de Medici, whose own family at Ferrara was also associated with Hercules, as we have seen. An elaborated account of the entry published a year later, Valladier's *Royal Labyrinth of the Trimphant French Hercules*, divides Henri's life into seven parts, each illustrated with an engraving of a triumphal arch, celebrating a labour of Hercules and a corresponding exploit of Henri.[22]

Later kings were less systematically identified with Hercules, but the association is still to be found. Louis XIII, for example, is represented in an engraving of 1635 by Abraham Bosse as *Hercules the Emperor*, the obligatory lionskin and club rather ill-assorted with the king's otherwise seventeenth-century attire; an image of the victorious Hercules also appears on Louis's elaborately decorated armour. Louis XIV was depicted at the crossroads in an engraving by Pierre Daret (1650), with an accompanying text in which Virtue exhorts him to 'imitate another young Alcides, keep far away from sensual pleasure'. More publicly, this Louis appears as Hercules on Paris' Porte Saint-Martin, in Étienne le Hongre's relief celebrating the king's victory over the Triple Alliance (of England, Holland and Sweden) in 1668: with lionskin slung over one arm, the other resting on his club, the nude Louis is crowned by Victory as he stands upon a vanquished foe. The same idea lay behind the statue of Louis XIV made by Martin Desjardins for the Place de la Victoire, in which the Triple Alliance is represented by a Cerberus at the king's feet. The Choice scenario was again applied to Louis XV in a pamphlet commemorating his coming of age and formal accession to the throne in 1723. He was later responsible for the completion of a 'Salon d'Hercule' at Versailles in 1736, with François Le Moyne's dizzying ceiling-painting of the *Apotheosis of Hercules*.

Hercules' association with sixteenth- and seventeenth-century monarchs makes him an unlikely hero of the French Revolution. Nonetheless, in the debates concerning imagery suitable for the new Republic, he was produced as a serious contender for the role of incarnation of the French people. In August 1793, a 24-foot-high plaster statue was produced for a festival, masterminded by Jacques-Louis David, celebrating the anniversary of the abolition of monarchy and the recent defeat of the Girondins, whose counter-revolutionary uprising had threatened the Republic's unity. The statue is reproduced in an engraving of *The French People Overwhelming the Hydra of Federalism*, in which a club-wielding nude male – a figure who could hardly escape identification as Hercules – tramples a half-human, half-serpentine monster. Three months later David proposed that a colossal statue, 46 feet high, of Hercules holding his club should be installed on the Pont Neuf, and that the figure should be reproduced for the official state seal. A sketch for the latter produced by the engraver Dupré depicts a nude male standing with a club in his left hand resting on the ground, and in his right hand two small, winged female figures representing Equality and Liberty. The base was to be made of rubble from the statues of kings which formerly adorned Nôtre Dame's porticoes, the statue itself of bronze, the forceful, virile figure well suited to the temperament of the Reign of Terror period. Beyond the statue's basic political symbolism, David's radical vision for the French people was spelt out in the words which were to be inscribed on its body: 'light' on its forehead, 'nature' and 'truth' on its chest, 'force' and 'courage' on its arms, and 'work' on its hands. The actual statue was never realized, but the engraving *View of the Mound of the Champ de la Réunion* depicts a plaster version as a prominent feature of the Festival of the Supreme Being in June 1794, and it probably appeared also at the Festival of Victory four months later.

With the fall of the radicals more abstract symbols were adopted, like the liberty cap, but Hercules persisted for a short while in the image approved by a law of 1795 for silver coins, of Hercules embracing Liberty and Equality, with the legend 'unity and force'. For bronze coins, however, the approved figure was 'Marianne', Liberty personified, with the legend 'Republique française'. It was this female image which triumphed as the embodiment of Republican France, remaining a standard symbol on French coins until the demise of the franc in 1999, and even surviving today on smaller denominations of the French Euro.[23]

TELLING HERCULES' STORY II: LITERATURE FROM THE SEVENTEENTH CENTURY ON

After the Renaissance, attempts to narrate systematic accounts of Hercules' life are rare, but individual episodes continue to be the subject of literary treatments in a variety of genres. The theatrical Hercules of antiquity reappears on stage in reinterpretations of the tragedies of Sophokles and Euripides, and other aspects of the hero's story have been dramatized, too, sometimes set to music. In poetry Hercules has been cast in various lights, and the occasional prose work has taken him as model for the hero of a narrative with a contemporary setting.[24]

Sophokles and Euripides revisited

Sophokles' *Women of Trachis* has not been the subject of anything like as many modern performances and adaptations as his other plays – the *Archive of Performances of Greek and Roman Drama* (*APGRD*) lists around eighty between 1635 and 2010, as against ten times that number for *Oedipus the King*. Two of the earliest versions appeared in seventeenth-century France. Jean de Rotrou's *The Dying Hercules* (1635) was dedicated to the influential Cardinal Richlieu, who identified himself with the hero and filled his residences with his image. Pier Francesco Cavalli's *Hercules in Love* (Paris 1662) was commissioned for Louis XIV's marriage to Maria Theresa of Spain, though not performed until two years later. In England, Handel's oratorio *Hercules* (1745) uses a libretto by Thomas Broughton, influenced by Seneca and Ovid as well as Sophokles and taking the story on to the hero's apotheosis. Senecan influence is also likely in a number of eighteenth-century ballets and other musical entertainments, such as Jean Favier's *The Apotheosis of Hercules* (Milan, 1768) and Francesco Clerico's *The Death of Hercules* (Florence, 1792).

The story is largely absent from the nineteenth-century stage, as far as we know, but sees a revival in the twentieth century, notably in Ezra Pound's free translation, broadcast on BBC radio in 1954. Controversial for its colloquialism and downplaying of Deianeira's role – or 'Daysair' as she is called here – this version nonetheless is thought by many to succeed in Pound's aim of making a classical text accessible to a modern audience. A German translation of Sophokles' play produced in Cologne by Hansgünther Heyme in 1976 strikingly drew attention to its theme of the destructiveness of desire by opening with the Chorus setting up a pair of straw puppets, one male one female, with exaggerated sexual attributes. More recently, the play is memorably translated into a modern setting in Martin Crimp's *Cruel and Tender* (2004–5), directed by Luc Bondy, who also directed a production of Handel's opera in the same years. Here Hercules becomes The General, leader of bloody anti-terrorist campaigns in Africa and suspected of crimes against humanity, who falls for the teenage African refugee Laela and is eventually brought down by a pillow, a gift from his wife Amelia, in which is secreted a phial of biochemical poison.[25]

Euripides' *Herakles* is one of the least frequently performed/adapted of his plays, the *APGRD* listing only around forty productions between 1657 and 2006. This paucity is certainly not due to distaste of the child-killing motif *per se*, since the *APGRD* has details of over nine hundred performances of Euripides' *Medea*. Rather, it may be the difficulty of interpreting the madness, for which, as we saw in Chapter 3, many explanations have been offered, and the particular issue of assigning such madness to the very masculine hero Herakles. The earliest known adaptation was a northern Italian musical entertainment, *Hercules Persecuted* (1657), with a score by Domenico Sciava, but there is then a long gap before an English performance of the original Greek text at Reading School in 1818, and just one other nineteenth-century production is known, in Greece in 1879. The appearance of Wilamowitz's edition of the ancient text in 1895 saw the beginning of the play's revival, however, and the scholar also produced a German translation, which was used for a production in Vienna in 1902. Frank Wedekind's *Herakles*, written in 1917 and first performed in Munich in 1919, is only loosely related to Euripides, consisting of twelve separate scenes in a structure reminiscent of the mystery play, and taking the story on to Herakles' apotheosis. A prologue spoken by Hermes sets the tone by declaring that the audience will not be subjected to a show of the labours, but rather will see a man's soul, and Herakles' own explanation for his madness is telling (Act 1, scene 2):

HERAKLES: The fury, unleashed in Herakles by ever more violent monsters, raged on.

We have already seen the idea of the madness as something internal to the hero, rather than an external force, in Seneca's *Hercules Furens* (p. 100), and the link between the monster-slaying and the domestic violence is further explored in later twentieth-century productions.

Two English-language adaptations of the madness story deserve particular mention. Archibald MacLeish's *Herakles* was first produced at Ann Arbor in 1965, as a one-act play under the auspices of the University of Michigan's Professional Theater Program. The scene is set at the modern archaeological site of Delphi, where three tourists – the American Mrs Hoadley, her daughter and an English governess – find the ancient myth brought to life before them. MacLeish published a revised version two years later, with a new first act which introduced the previously absent figure of Professor Hoadley, a Nobel-prize-winning physicist of great physical stature though in a wheelchair. The Professor's scientific achievements are meant to be analogous to the labours, while the Hoadleys' strained relationships parallel the disintegration of Herakles' family, and the whole is a parable warning against the temptation to 'play god' with modern technology.

More recently, the Yorkshire poet Simon Armitage's *Mister Heracles*, premiered at the Courtyard Theatre in Leeds in 2001, emphasizes the alienation of the warrior from the outset by presenting him as an astronaut returning from outer-space – a suitable twenty-first-century parallel for the ancient Underworld. Modernity is also apparent in Madness' use of an electronic device to activate Heracles' innate violence, and in the modern equivalents of the 'monsters' faced by the hero in the Chorus' account of the labours, such as flesh-eating viruses and nuclear explosions. The gods are largely replaced by an unspecified military organization from whose service Heracles has gone AWOL, and his madness is clearly portrayed as coming from within his own psyche, rooted in his experience as a warrior. Heracles himself exclaims (Armitage 2000, 54):

> Oh, my children and my wife, that your death
> Were in me all the time, waiting to hatch.

As Riley argues (2008, 312–37), the resurgence of interest in Euripides' play in the late 1990s and 2000s coincides precisely with an increasing popular understanding of the dangers of Post-Traumatic Stress Disorder in war veterans, and the public discussion of real-life cases of fathers – not just mothers – who kill their children.[26]

Of the ancient tragedies in which Hercules plays a 'cameo' role, only two have a significant post-classical performance history. Sophokles' *Philoktetes* has been reworked more frequently than *Women of Trachis* (the *APGRD* lists around one hundred and thirty productions, 1540–2009), but Hercules does not always appear on stage. Several influential modern versions choose to leave Hercules out altogether, such as André Gide's *Philoctetes* (1898), Heiner Müller's *Philoktet* (1968) and Seamus Heaney's *The Cure at Troy* (1990), although he does continue to play a *deus ex machina* role in Oscar Mandel's *The Summoning of Philoctetes* (1961).

More popular still is Euripides' *Alkestis*, the *APGRD* listing more than two hundred and sixty productions between 1539 and 2010. In the seventeenth and eighteenth centuries the story particularly attracts musical treatments, such as Jean-Baptiste Lully's opera *Alcestis, or the Triumph of Alcides* (Paris, 1674), with a libretto later translated into German for Georg Caspar Schürmann's *The Faithful Alcestis* (Hamburg, 1719). In England, Handel's *Admetus, King of Thessaly* (London, 1727) introduces a rival for Admetus' love in the form of a Trojan princess Antigona, inspired by the need to provide parts for two rival *prima donne* of the day. In Germany, in 1773, the influential German writer Christoph Martin Wieland produced the libretti for the operettas *Alcestis* and *The Choice of Hercules*, representing the hero in so relentlessly virtuous a light that Goethe famously retaliated with the farce *Gods, Heroes and Wieland*, towards the end of which a red-blooded Hercules laughs that, had he really met Virtue and Vice, he would have tucked them one under each arm and carried them off. Amongst twentieth-century treatments, notable is Thornton Wilder's *The Alcestiad, or A Life in the Sun*, produced at the Edinburgh Festival of 1955 and made into an opera a few years later with music by Louise Talma. This followed the success of T.S. Eliot's *The Cocktail Party*, premiered at Edinburgh in 1949, which takes the Alcestis story more loosely as a model, with Hercules' role taken by the character Sir Henry Harcourt-Reilly, the psychiatrist who brings about the husband and wife's reconciliation.

Other dramas

In addition to versions of the ancient tragedies, various aspects of the myth have been subject to other dramatic treatments, both tragic and comic. Though largely absent from the seventeenth-century English stage, Hercules arguably lies behind a number of other tragic characters, and appears in person in Thomas Heywood's *The Silver Age* and its sequel *The Bronze Age* (1613), which include several labours and the hero's death. A few years later a comic Hercules appears in company with the gluttonous Comus in Ben Jonson's masque *Pleasure Reconciled to Virtue*, performed at the court of James I over the Christmas season of 1617–18 and featuring the young prince Charles as chief masquer. Hercules' birth story was controversially dramatized later in the seventeenth century, with versions of Plautus' comedy *Amphitryon* produced in French by Molière (Paris, 1668) and in English by Dryden (London, 1690), the latter with incidental music by Purcell.

Other individual exploits appear from time to time, such as André Destouches' opera *Omphale* (Paris, 1701), in which Hercules has to compete for the Lydian queen's love. In the eighteenth century the Choice theme recurs in various musical genres, including J.S. Bach's cantata

Hercules at the Crossroads (Leipzig, 1733), written for the birthday of the crown prince Friedrich of Saxony, Handel's oratorio *The Choice of Hercules* (London, 1751), recycling incidental music written for a never-performed play *Alcestis*, and Vincenzo Righini's chamber opera *Alcides at the Crossroads* (Trier, 1790). Both the Choice and Omphale appear as subjects of symphonic poems by Camille Saint-Saëns: *The Youth of Hercules* (1877), and *Omphale's Spinning-Wheel* (1869), the latter based on a poem by Victor Hugo which juxtaposes an image of the domestic equipment with the ghosts of Hercules' monstrous opponents.[27]

On the twentieth-century stage, Jean Giraudoux's *Amphitryon 38* (Paris, 1929) takes up the birth story – 38 being an estimate of the number of earlier productions under the title – but otherwise the main competition to versions of the ancient tragedies have been portrayals of the labours. Claude Terrasse's comic operetta *Les Travaux d'Hercule* (Paris, 1901) presents Augias, in the course of running away with Hercules' wife Omphale, accidentally performing all the labours but perpetually cheated of glory as Hercules gets the credit for each achievement. Equally comic is Friedrich Dürrenmatt's *Hercules and the Augean Stables*, first produced as a radio-play on North West German Radio in 1954 and adapted for the stage in 1962, which presents Hercules, disenchanted with his status as national hero and heavily in debt, forced to accept a commission to clear Elis of years of accumulated dung. His proposal to use the rivers is thwarted by local factions with a vested interest in the *status quo*, who ensure that it is delayed in committee after committee – a satire on the bureaucracy of Dürrenmatt's native Switzerland – while Hercules kicks his heels, until he eventually departs on a commission to tackle the Stymphalian birds.

Still more loosely related to ancient myth is Tony Harrison's play *The Labourers of Herakles*, commissioned for a one-off performance at the eighth International Meeting on Ancient Greek Drama at Delphi in 1995. The chorus of five female builders appeared on a set representing the building-site of a theatre, dominated by a silo bearing the Herakles logo of the Greek cement company (Figure 7.6a). The hero's madness was violently enacted, before Labourer 1, in Herakles' persona, and narrated the terrible story of Miletos' destruction by the Persians in 494 BC, and the contemporary Athenian playwright Phrynichos' attempt to memorialize it in a tragedy which was immediately banned.[28]

Poetry and prose

Nineteenth- and early twentieth-century poetry features a relentlessly serious Hercules. The Philhellene German poet Friederich Hölderin regularly presents the hero's toils as allegories for man's, and especially his own, spiritual struggles. His *Hymn to Hercules* (1796) culminates in an exhortation to the hero to join him in claiming their reward of immortality, and in *The Only One* (1802) he even identities himself as Hercules' brother. One poem which focuses on a specific Herculean exploit is *Chiron* (1801), based on the story of the immortal centaur, accidentally wounded by Hercules, who eventually ends his potentially eternal suffering by helping him to die in Prometheus' place. The same episode was treated in the French poem *Chiron* (1852) by Leconte de Lisle, who like Hölderin was an experienced translator of Greek and Latin literature, and whose hymn to the *Solar Herakles* (1862) was influenced by contemporary scholarship on comparative mythology (pp. 11–12). A few years earlier Leconte had related Hercules' death in *The Centaur's Robe* (1845), the pyre allegorized as an expression of the hero's burning ambition, which ultimately makes him immortal. Here he is referred to as 'the ancient dispenser of justice' (l.1), a characterization elaborated in *The Childhood of Hercules* (1856), where the baby hero is exhorted (ll.45–6):

> Sleep, future dispenser of justice, tamer of ancient crimes,
> in the expectation and pride of your magnanimous deeds.

The subject of Sully Prudhomme's poem *The Stables of Augias* (1867) is an unusual one, but again presents an austerely ethical Hercules, who declares that true courage entails battling disgust. Two other labours are treated early in the cycle *The Trophies* (1893) by Leconte's pupil José Maria de Heredia, the early history of Greece being represented by half a dozen sonnets including 'Nemea' and 'Stymphale'.

The Swiss poet Carl Spitteler never fulfilled his intention of writing a Hercules epic, but the hero does play an important role at the end of his *Olympian Spring* (1900–10). Here Hercules is sent by Zeus to save a degenerate mankind, stripped of his divinity in the process and himself a model of ideal humanity, constantly struggling to overcome Hera's antagonism. Spitteler's imaginative recreation of Greek myth earned him the Nobel prize for literature; less successful is the interminable dramatic poem *Herakles* (1908) by his American contemporary George Cabot Lodge, an allegory of the soul's journey towards truth and freedom. There is a lengthy series of scenes in Thebes, where the hero rejects Creon's offer of the throne, before a visit to Delphi confirms the inevitability of his servitude to Eurystheus, which, in a twist to tradition, is the catalyst for Herakles' murder of his children. He emerges from his madness and departs determined to expiate his crime by performing the labours, which are then assumed to have occurred before a final scene in which Herakles frees Prometheus from his fetters by revealing the insubstantial nature of the God he had opposed. Much shorter – and arguably more effective – is Emile Verhaeren's *Hercule* (1910), which focuses on the end of the hero's life, presenting him as a lonely figure recalling his glorious labours and singing defiantly as the pyre blazes beneath him on Mount Oeta.

In prose, a notable reworking of Hercules' myth is Charlotte Yonge's novel *My Young Alcides* (1875). This tells the tale of Harold Alison, born in Australia son of a transportee, who returns to England wracked by guilt after accidentally killing his wife Meg and their two children in a drunken rage. Yonge creates inventive parallels for the twelve labours, via which Harold makes the arduous journey towards social rehabilitation and spiritual peace. The slaying of the hydra, for example, is represented by a chapter in which Harold buys up the Dragon's Head pub with a view to turning it into a temperance reading room, but numerous beer-shops immediately spring up in its place. Many characters are given names suitable to their roles, such as Hippolyta Horseman, from whom Harold wins the prize of an antique belt in an archery contest. In the end Harold meets an untimely death from smallpox, contracted via a lock of hair sent to him by his young sister Dora, who had herself caught the disease whilst out shopping with Ernest 'Nessy' Horseman. While some of the details of the story may sound a little contrived, Yonge is remarkably successful in building up a convincing overall narrative, replete with the varied cast of characters one would expect from a Victorian novel and reflecting social issues of its time. In her modest preface to the book, Yonge writes that her aim has been to show that Hercules 'and his labours belong in some form or other to all times and all surroundings'.[29]

In a lighter vein, Agatha Christie exploited the name of her best-known detective in a collection of short stories entitled *The Labours of Hercules: the legend of Poirot's retirement* (1947). The preface sets up the conceit, in a conversation between Poirot and a fellow of All Souls, Oxford, which draws the analogy between the ancient hero's monster-slaying and the detective's services in ridding society of criminal menaces, after which Poirot decides that his final cases will be chosen in emulation of his namesake. The degree to which each of the twelve mini-mysteries is modelled on the relevant labour varies. The link is rather tenuous, for example, in the case of 'The Nemean Lion', which involves the kidnap of a Pekingese dog humorously referred to as 'a veritable lion', or in 'The Augean Stables', which concerns political sleaze. Some of the later stories, however, contrive to make the parallel more systematic. For example, in 'The Apples of the Hesperides' Poirot retrieves a priceless golden goblet from a convent on the west coast of Ireland, while the final case involves a nightclub called Hell and a drug-smuggling guard-dog Cerberus.

HERCULES THE MOVIE STAR[30]

The *peplum* and after (1957–85)

Alongside his literary and theatrical incarnations, since the late 1950s Hercules has appeared as a hero of both the large and the small screen. The trend was set by the 1957 *Hercules*, originally produced in Italy as *Le fatiche di Ercole*, directed by Pietro Francisci, starring Steve Reeves and Sylvia Koscina. The film was marketed in the United States by Joseph E. Levine, who mounted a massive $1-million publicity campaign, the posters and billboards promising a 'cast of thousands' in 'the mighty saga of the world's mightiest man'. Interestingly, despite the wealth of stories provided by the ancient tradition, the film casts Hercules as the hero of the quest for the golden fleece. As we have seen (pp. 55 and 134–5), Hercules does have a role in the ancient Argonautika story, and indeed the well-known 1963 film *Jason and the Argonauts*, directed by Don Chaffey with animation by Ray Harryhausen, very properly features Nigel Green as an older Hercules. In *Hercules*, however, Jason's role is subordinated, and it is Hercules who plays the romantic lead, falling in love with the daughter of Pelias, king of 'Jolco'. There is a nod to the ancient tradition in the princess' naming as Iole, but the love story is very much a product of its time: at the outset of the film Hercules rescues the scantily clad Iole from a runaway chariot, the romantic nature of their relationship is confirmed by a passionate kiss within the first half hour, and the film concludes with the inevitable happy ending of their marriage.

If the romance was designed to appeal to the female audience, there is also plenty of action for the boys. Hercules throws a discus beyond the horizon, kills both the Nemean lion and the Cretan bull with his bare hands, and towards the end wraps chains around two pillars and pulls the entire palace down. This Samsonesque moment is typical of the tendency of 1950s and 60s films to conflate Hercules with other strongman figures, especially the Italian hero Maciste, who is often 'translated' into Hercules to appeal to a more international audience. Physical strength and monster-slaying prowess had of course been a feature of Hercules' character from his earliest appearances in ancient Greece, but the figure of the strongman had a particular appeal to the post-war Italian rural audience, while also playing to a view of bodybuilding as self-betterment, an important element of the American dream. The 'father of modern bodybuilding', Eugen Sandow, was photographed in 1897 posing as the Farnese Herakles, and Steve Reeves, star of both *Hercules* and its sequel *Hercules Unchained*, was the first of a succession of actors to play the part who began their careers as bodybuilders. At 6'1" Reeves was not the tallest of Herculeses, but he had already won the title 'Mr Pacific Coast' in Oregon at the age of twenty (1946), and he went on to become 'Mr Western America' and 'Mr America' (1947), 'Mr World' (1948), and ultimately 'Mr Universe' (1950).[31]

Hercules was not meant to be anything more than entertainment, but the film does make some attempt to deal with two important issues which we have already seen raised in ancient literature, and which become regular concerns of later Hercules movies The first is the idea of the flawed hero, which is flagged up in the opening titles: 'Even the greatest strength carries within it a measure of mortal weakness'. Hercules' impetuosity is blamed for the death of Iole's unpleasant brother Iphitus, and Hercules has to spend the rest of the film proving himself worthy. The second is the problem of Hercules' immortality: ancient myth marries the deified hero off to the goddess Hebe, but the conventions of modern storytelling require him to live happily ever after with the film's mortal heroine. *Hercules* solves the dilemma by having the hero renounce his divinity, a tactic which incidentally removes a major barrier to the audience's identification with him. Shortly after Iphitus' death the unhappy Hercules visits 'the Sibyl' in an anachronistically ruined Greek temple:

HERCULES: I can't stand being superior. Let me experience the real things – love, or hate.

SIBYL: Those are mortal states, Hercules.

HERCULES: If it's my immortality making me unhappy, then I'll do without it!

SIBYL: That's dangerous, Hercules. Don't you know how foolish you'd be to renounce it? To be born a man and see everything die is not to be immortal. Stay as you are, be a god – don't exchange immortality for fear, pain and sorrow.

HERCULES: I want to live like any other mortal man. It is my prayer to have a family. I want children of my own. . To see the children growing up.

The immortality problem is variously handled in later Hercules films, and one might compare its treatment in completely unrelated stories, such as Tolkien's *The Lord of the Rings*, in which the elf princess Arwen renounces her immortality for life with the mortal Aragorn.

The box-office success of *Hercules* laid the foundations for a whole genre of 'sword and sandal' films, sometimes referred to as the *peplum*, in reference to the short tunics of both make and female protagonists. Its immediate sequel was *Hercules Unchained* (1959), by the same director and with the same stars (Figure 7.4), again lavishly promoted in the States by Levine – a Hollywood garden party featured an ice statue of Hercules, and seven hundred guests went home with four-pound chocolate figurines of the hero. The film's framing narrative inserts Hercules into a myth with which he has no connection at all in antiquity, the Seven Against Thebes story, in which the brothers Eteocles and Polyneices fight over the kingship of Thebes. The

Figure 7.4 Steve Reeves in *Hercules Unchained* (1959). Photo: from http://www.
briansdriveintheater.com/stevereeves.html

film's status as a sequel is explicitly signalled at the outset by the presentation
of Hercules and Iole as newly-weds, but the unexciting prospect of a story
about domestic bliss is headed off by a substantial sub-plot concerning the
hero's enslavement to the Lydian queen Omphale, as reflected in the original Italian title *Ercole e la regina di Lidia*. While this is genuinely part of the
ancient Hercules' story, the film betrays no hint of the effeminizing motifs
of clothes-swapping and the hero wool-working, but develops the character
of Omphale as a seductive enchantress, played by the French model Sylvia
Lopez, rather reminiscent of Homer's Circe. There are several other nods to
the *Odyssey* story, as well, such as the fact that Omphale's kingdom of Lydia
seems to be an island (rather than a section of Asia Minor); there is a significant role for a young Ulysses, several brief shots of his home on Ithaca, and
his father Laertes leads the expedition which comes to Hercules' rescue.

When not in Omphale's clutches, Hercules is his usual strongman self.
His credentials are established early on in his fight with Anteus, an exploit

which we have seen to be popular in the post-classical tradition. The giant is played by Primo Carrera, an Italian heavyweight boxer who had won the world title in 1933, but quarter of a century later a less than formidable opponent. The 'fabulous feats of human power the screen has never shown before!' promised by the posters are more convincingly delivered, however, towards the end of the film, when Hercules battles with tigers in Eteocles' private amphitheatre (a feature borrowed from Hollywood's image of the evil Roman emperor) and topples siege-engines in the final spectacular battle outside Thebes. The romantic ethos of the first film reasserts itself at the very end of *Hercules Unchained*, despite everything, with Iole's rather improbable announcement that 'Somehow the gods will be kind if we just love one another', to the accompaniment of a sunset and soaring orchestral score.[32]

Over the next ten years around one hundred and twenty films were produced with Hercules as hero (in at least one version of the title). Some of these retain a vaguely ancient Greek setting, however far their plots may diverge from the mythological tradition, such as *Hercules and the Princess of Troy* (1965). In others, however, the figure of Hercules is completely divorced from his Greek context, such as *Hercules of the Desert* (a Western, 1960), *Hercules Against the Mongols* (the sons of Ghengis Khan, 1960), *Hercules and the Black Pirate* (set in seventeenth-century Spain, 1962), and even *Hercules Against the Moon Men* (1964). The title role is nearly always played by an actor with body-building credentials. Mark Forest, for example, star of *Mole Men against the Son of Hercules* (1961), *Hercules Against the Mongols* and *Hercules Against the Sons of the Sun* (1964), had been 'Mr Venice Beach' in 1954. Reg Lewis, star of *Fire Monsters Against the Son of Hercules* (1962), had been 'Junior Mr Olympics' at the age of seventeen and from 1954 performed in Mae West's Review, a nightclub act aimed at a female audience, before becoming 'Mr Olympics' (1956), 'Mr Universe' (1957), 'Mr America' (1963), and later briefly reviving his career in 1983 as 'Mr America Over Forty'.

The English (Leeds-born) Reg Parke, star of *Hercules Conquers Atlantis* (directed by Vittorio Cottafavi, 1961), had broken the American monopoly on body-building titles by winning the 1951 'Amateur Mr Universe' competition, going on to become 'Mr Universe' in 1958 and 1965. Posters for *Atlantis* hold out the prospect of 'unprecedented spectacle with a cast of thousands', while its protagonist will be 'pounding the screen with the tremendous power of violent action!' While conforming to the *peplum* genre in this respect, however, the film has some unusual features, notably in its presentation of Hercules as less than consistently virtuous, and in the anti-nuclear weapons message of its narrative concerning the danger 'out of the west'.[33]

Reg Parke was longstanding mentor to Arnold Schwarzenegger, who was 'Mr Universe' by the age of twenty (1967) and went on to win the 'Mr Olympia' contest as many as seven times. His very first movie part, long before Conan the Barbarian and the Teminator, was the title role in *Hercules in New York* (1972), directed by Arthur Allan Seidlemann. At this stage Schwarzenegger was billed as 'Arnold Strong' and his voice had to be dubbed because of his heavy Austrian accent. The film's premise is that Hercules, after a lightning-bolt accident on Olympus, finds himself in present-day New York, where his inexperience of the modern world gets him into all kinds of comic problems, while various gods attempt to bring him home.

Even more preposterous is the *Hercules* of 1983, directed by Luigi Cozzi, starring Lou Ferrigno, who had begun body-building at the tender age of thirteen, citing Steve Reeves as one of his role-models, and won the 'Mr America' and Mr Universe' titles in 1973 and 1974. At 6'5" he tops all the 1960s Herculeses, and had made his name in the late 1970s and early 80s as the Incredible Hulk. The plot bears little resemblance to any ancient myth, beginning in outer space and involving Hercules in thwarting the wizard Minos' attempts to take over the world, battling with giant robots and avoiding the seductive temptations of the luscious princess Arianna (Sybil Danning). Amongst other negative distinctions, Ferrigno and Danning won the year's Golden Raspberry Awards for worst new star and worst supporting actress, but the film nonetheless spawned a sequel, *The Adventures of Hercules* (1985), in which Hercules is on the trail of the Seven Mighty Thunderbolts which have been stolen from Zeus.[34]

A hero for the 1990s

The 1990s saw a revival of Hercules' fortunes on screen, beginning with the series *Hercules: the Legendary Journeys*. This consists of five feature-length made-for-TV films, produced in 1994, followed by six seasons of forty-five-minute episodes released between 1995 and 2000, starring Kevin Sorbo, directed by Bill Norton for NBC Universal, and filmed largely in New Zealand. So successful was the series that it spawned two spin-offs, *Xena, Warrior Princess* (1995–2001), in which the Kevin Sorbo Hercules makes regular appearances with his Amazon friends, and *The Young Hercules* (1998–9), in which a teenage version of Hercules is at 'Cheiron's Academy' for heroes. As with the earlier films, the plots of the *Legendary Journeys* combine episodes traditionally associated with Hercules with exploits borrowed from other Greek heroes and elements from other mythologies entirely, including several Norse gods. The fourth film, *Hercules in the Underworld*, for example, includes a wrestling match with the giant Eryx as well as featuring a splendid animatronic Cerberus in Hades, which Hercules eventually coaxes into submission rather than simply applying brute force, an approach we saw in some ancient representations of the labour, too (p. 165). The fifth film, *Hercules in the Maze of the Minotaur*, on the other hand, begins with the hero in retirement, working his farm with wife and children, before he is called away to fight a monstrous opponent traditionally associated with Theseus.

The feisty Deianeira first appears in the second film, *Hercules and the Lost Kingdom*, played by Renee O'Connor, where she has to compete with the distraction offered by Omphale; from the third film, *Hercules and the Circle of Fire*, onwards Tawny Kitaen's Deianeira has Hercules more firmly domesticated, until the beginning of the TV series, when Hera has destroyed the family. A seductive Iole briefly leads Hercules astray in *The Underworld*, the fifty daughters of Thespios pursue him in 'Eye of the Beholder', early in Season 1, and a second wife, Serena, appears for just two episodes in Season 3 before she too falls victim to Hera's hatred. As this list suggests, the 1990s Hercules is fairly firmly heterosexual, although there are occasional humorous hints of something beyond comradeship with Iolaus, the most explicit being in *Maze of the Minotaur*, when Deianeira interrupts a wrestling bout between the two of them, with torsos bare above their leather trousers, and the small child with her asks, 'Mommy, what's Daddy doing to Uncle Iolaus?'

While the *Legendary Journeys* is very light entertainment, it does an excellent job of 'translating' Hercules for a modern audience. Unlike the 1950s and 60s movies, it makes extensive use of the gods, with Anthony Quinn's Zeus an especially memorable character in the five films. The motif of Hera's hatred – part of the story since Homer – is well deployed, the goddess' presence frequently indicated by the appearance in the sky of just a pair of eyes and a peacock feather, to the accompaniment of a menacing musical theme. In addition to familiar Olympians like Apollo, Hephaestus, Artemis and Aphrodite, more minor deities and personifications also appear from time to time, like Nemesis, Discord, Fortune and Hope. The earlier films' focus on the body-building hero is wittily subverted in the casting of Cory Everson, a former Ms Olympia (1984–9), as Atalanta, a female Spartan blacksmith, in three episodes scattered across Seasons 1, 2 and 4. Kevin Sorbo's Hercules, on the other hand, is far from the muscle-bound heroes of the 1950s and 60s: at 6'3", and formerly a model, Sorbo is not implausible as a monster-slayer, but he is the long-haired, smooth-shaven romantic hero of the 1990s.[35]

The hero's revival received a boost in 1997 with the feature-length Disney animation *Hercules*. Though easy to criticize for its adherence to tried-and-tested formulae, and for its haphazard treatment of mythological characters, the film has a number of interesting features which provide further indication of Hercules' adaptability to changing social *mores*, and particularly the challenges involved in presenting him to a young audience. The opening voice-over (a cameo role for Charlton Heston) establishes the film's general ethos:

> NARRATOR: Long ago, in the faraway land of ancient Greece, there was a golden age of powerful gods and extraordinary heroes. And the greatest and strongest of all these heroes was the mighty Hercules. But what is the measure of a true hero? Ah, that is what our story is . . .

The focus is clearly on Hercules' internal, moral qualities, rather than on the display of mere monster-slaying prowess – though there must of course be an element of the latter to provide the kind of excitement the 1950–60s films had made synonymous with the hero. One of the film's major departures from tradition concerns Hercules' parentage: rather than being the result of an adulterous relationship between a god and a mortal woman, he is the true child of Zeus and Hera, cruelly snatched away by the villainous Hades, almost (but not quite) drained of his divinity, and brought up on earth by the kindly foster-parents Amphitryon and Alcmene. This not only removes a moral difficulty which might have undermined the film's qualification for a U Certificate (suitable for children of four and over), but also paves the way for a handling of the immortality issues not dissimilar to that of the 1957 *Hercules*. Despite having spent most of the film trying to regain his godhood, in the end Hercules rejects a life on Olympus in favour of human love:

> HERCULES: Father, this is the moment I've always dreamed of. But . . . A life without Meg, even an immortal life, would be . . . empty. I . . . I wish to stay on Earth with her. I finally know where I belong.

The casting of 'Meg' as an experienced older woman is an innovative twist, fitting her for an equally innovative role as Hades' accomplice, although she is ultimately redeemed by her love for Hercules. There is of course no reference to the child-killing story attached to Megara in the ancient sources, and she is assimilated to Deianeira by her first appearance in the clutches of Nessus. Other characters mix elements from Hercules' story or are borrowed from other myths entirely: the winged horse Pegasus properly belongs to the Corinthian hero Bellerophon, while the jovial satyr 'Phil' (voiced by Danny DeVito) takes his name from Philoctetes, traditionally recipient of Hercules' bow from the pyre, and his role as Hercules' teacher confounds him with another hybrid creature, the centaur Cheiron, traditional educator of Greek heroes. The delightfully villainous Hades (voiced by James Woods) and his realm are strongly influenced by popular conceptions of the Christian Devil and Hell, the sharp opposition between Olympus and the Underworld emphasized by contrasting colour schemes: warm oranges, yellow and pink characterize the former, the gods each surrounded by a glow, while the latter and its denizens are all in cold blues, greys and black.

The film is indeed remarkable for its overall 'look', masterminded by the eminent British cartoonist Gerald Scarfe, which makes imaginative use of Greek artistic prototypes to establish a plausible setting. The teenage Hercules' first show of careless strength topples a colonnade in the mode of an authentic Greek stoa, while the architecture of Thebes, the 'Big Olive', is created by a piling up of pillars and pediments Manhattan-style. Particularly original is the recurrent use of vases, both within the plot – the young Hercules nearly destroys a potter's shop – and in stylized comment on the proceedings, as when Hercules' image is displayed on various Attic black-figure amphoras and hydrias ('they slapped his face on every vase'). Most engagingly, a chorus of Muses steps off a vase at the outset of the film and reappears at intervals to provide sympathetic comment on the action, performing the role of a Greek tragic chorus though in the musical style of a Gospel choir. The humour here is matched by some nice moments of self-parody, as in the cameo 'appearance' of the directors John Musker and Ron Clements as stone-masons, or the strong resemblance of Hercules' lionskin to Scar, villain of *The Lion King*, Disney's hit of 1994. The serious business of merchandizing is likewise sent up by the image of crowds flocking into the 'Hercules Store', and by the comic turn by Hades' incompetent sidekicks Pain and Panic proudly exhibiting their 'Air-Herc' sandals and drinking from a Hercules ™ plastic cup.

Whatever liberties the film may have taken with the mythological tradition, it grossed a very respectable $250 million worldwide, a figure not as impressive as *The Lion King*'s $780 million in 1994, but placing it in the twenty top-grossing films of 1997. The song 'Go the distance', sung by Hercules as he grows up, was nominated for Academy and Golden Globe Awards for Best Original Song, and various aspects of the direction and animation won Annie Awards.[36]

CONCLUSION: HERAKLES/HERCULES NOW

Our hero's post-classical development has, then, taken him in an almost bewildering variety of directions. In the Middle Ages and the Renaissance he is the pre-figuration of Christ, the incarnation of Virtue, and generally an allegory for all things morally correct. A favourite subject for painters and sculptors, especially in the Renaissance but later too, he appears in this ethical guise, but also as monster-slayer *par excellence* and sometimes in his comic persona. At various times he has been a political symbol all over Europe, with particular significance in some Renaissance Italian city-states and both monarchical and revolutionary France. His story has been told and re-told, with tragic or comic emphasis, in poetry and prose, and especially in drama, on stage and screen.

What of Herakles/Hercules in the twenty-first century? Christian and moralizing allegory may no longer be in fashion, but the hero is alive and well in modern media. Jeanette Winterson's 2006 novella *Weight* focuses on the figure Atlas and his relationship to the universe he carries on his shoulders, a metaphor for the human condition, but gives Heracles a significant role. The hero is largely his comic self, a self-confessed braggart who in his youth 'killed everything, shagged what was left, and ate the rest' (Winterson 2006, 31–2). He has an erotically charged relationship with Hera, and experiences only a few qualms about cheating Atlas into resuming his burden once the Hesperides' apples have been collected. He nonetheless meets a properly tragic death in a close telling of the Sophoklean story.

In addition to the recent theatrical appearances of Hercules already noted, two plays produced in the north of England in 2010 further demonstrate our hero's continuing fascination for a modern audience, in both tragic and comic guise. In May, at the University of Leeds, George Rodosthenous and a team from the School of Performance and Cultural Industries presented *Heracles' Wife*, an updated reworking of the *Women of Trachis* which aptly cast the hero as a celebrity footballer, captain of an unspecified 'United'. The first act follows Sophokles in focusing on Deianira, here the independently minded owner of a hair salon, her gossipy girls playing the part of the chorus, their comic turns a foil to the mounting tension of Deianira's anxiety as we await Heracles' return. A radio announcement and conversation in the salon fill in the background that Heracles is to be questioned about the murder of his chauffeur Sam Nessus, and that his affair with Iole Gandenza has caused her father to withdraw his sponsorship from the team. The second act shifts attention to the hero, fresh from sporting triumph in Madrid, at a decadent party centred around a small swimming pool, where he is portrayed with all the callous self-indulgence modern culture associates with such stars. Here it is the teenage Hyllus who delivers the fatal gift from Deianira, in the shape of a bottle of foxglove liqueur, and Heracles dies in magnificent agony in the pool.

Two months later the comic hero returned in the opening season of Chester's Grosvenor Park Open Air Theatre, in Helen Eastman's *Hercules*, commissioned by Chester Performs. A Chorus of Rumours, a press-pack of journalists, follows Hercules and his practical nephew Iolaus as they work their way through the twelve labours. The monsters are imaginatively portrayed, some by means of puppetry, others commuted into human opponents, like the wrestler stage-named 'The Nemean Lion', whom Hercules strips of his lycra leotard. Particularly memorable is the 'Bore' from the university town of Erymanthia, an elderly Classics don sipping sherry as he recites the dullest bits of Homer, his sleep-inducing ramblings about academic publications finally outdone by Hercules' tedious account of his own column in *Men's Health*. Despite a billing as suitable for children of seven and upwards, the play hints at Hercules' murder of his family from the outset, and it is explicitly discussed when Hercules meets 'Meg' in the Underworld. Like some of his cinematic predecessors, this Hercules is tormented by his hybrid status and tempted to forsake the chance of immortality in exchange for human love. Eventually, however, the conflict is cleverly resolved as Hercules agrees to become a god 'who remembers how it feels to be mortal / and tries to look out for all those who have only a mortal life to live' (final scene).

As for film and related media, 2010–11 has seen the re-release of the *Legendary Journeys* series Seasons 1 and 2 on DVD. Marvel Comics' series *Incredible Hercules* ran from 2008 to 2010, building on a character who had first appeared in 1965, and was a regular in the adventures of *The Mighty Thor* in the 1960s and early 70s, before becoming a founding member of the superhero teams the Champions (1970s), the Avengers (1980s and 90s) and the Mighty Avengers (2000s). Despite being apparently killed off in issue 141 of *Incredible Hercules*, the hero briefly lived on in the 2010 mini-series *Fall of an Avenger, Twilight of a God* and *Heroic Age: Prince of Power*, and may yet return to save the world. The Marvel character's conformity to modern superhero norms of extraordinary strength, speed and immortality is not out of keeping with his ancient persona, nor is his weakness for women, although the storylines take him far from his traditional exploits.

A contemporary visual incarnation of the hero with more substantial links to his ancient Greek image is the protagonist of Marian Maguire's *The Labours of Herakles*. First exhibited in Blenheim in 2008, with a tour of regional galleries of New Zealand scheduled to continue well into 2012, this set of twelve lithographs and eight etchings aptly casts the hero as a European colonist. He is depicted engaged in the 'labours' of a historical settler, hunting, clearing and cultivating the land, in hostile encounters with the natives, writing home, and is even a signatory to the 1840 Treaty of Waitangi, as Queen Victoria's representative opposite a Maori chief. The series' success must be due in large part to Maguire's inventive fusion of art-historical models, reflective of the complex relationships of colonialism, seen for example in *Herakles Takes Up Dairy Farming* (Figure 7.5). The figures in the foreground are straight from a late sixth-century BC Attic

Figure 7.5 Marian Maguire, *Herakles Takes Up Dairy Farming*, lithograph 2006/7. Photo: by kind permission of the artist.

black-figure amphora attributed to the Lysippides Painter (Boston 99.538), the bull of the original made into a cow to fit the modern narrative, while the background image of Mount Taranaki references Charles Heaphy's watercolour of 1840, *Mount Egmont from the Southward* (Alexander Turnbull Library, Wellington C-025–008).[37]

And finally, at the end of our own 'Herculean task', we return to the name, which can be found today attached to the most unlikely variety of entities. We have already mentioned two modern Greek locations called Irakleia/ Iraklion (p. 156), but across the Atlantic can be found the small city of Hercules, California. This was incorporated in 1900, having started life as housing for the workers when the California Powder Works moved out of San Francisco in 1881 and became the Hercules Dynamite Company. The association with strength must also explain the choice of name of Greece's major cement company Iraklis, founded in 1911, whose logo with the stylized head of a lionskin-clad head of Herakles can be seen all over the country (Figure 7.6a). A similar conceit lies behind the name of its long-standing rival group Titan, though the lack of an instantly recognizable iconography for this unspecified god has left the company with an entirely abstract logo.

The use of 'Herakles' and 'Hercules' for Greek and Roman ships noted in Chapter 6 (p. 176) has a number of modern counterparts. The Lockheed Martin Super Hercules C130J transporter plane, still in production, is the most recent version of a family of military aircraft whose design dates back to the Second World War. The aircraft-carrier *HMS Hercules*, launched in 1945 and finally decommissioned in 1995, was the most recent ship to bear the name, in the tradition of the Hercules class of 74-gun ships of the line, designed for the British Navy by Sir Thomas Slade in the mid-eighteenth century. Less grandly, the Hercules Cycle and Motor Company founded in Birmingham in 1910 continued to produce bicycles until 2003, having apparently chosen the name for its association with durability and robustness.

The ancient hero's ability to see off all opponents presumably informs the naming of several football teams. Founded in 1908, Thessaloniki's first-division Iraklis is the oldest club in Greece, with an image of the Farnese Herakles as its logo (Figure 7.6b) – an idea imitated by its arch-rival in the city 'Aris', named after the god of war Ares, which makes similar use of a classical statue. The Iraklis club name also encompasses a whole host of sports besides football – basketball, track and field, swimming, cycling, ice hockey, water-polo, judo, fencing and table-tennis – being particularly successful in recent years in volleyball and wrestling. Even older is the Netherlands' second-division Heracles Almelo, founded in 1903, while in Spain, Alicante's second-division Hércules Club de Fútbol, founded in 1922, boasts a victory in the 2010–11 season over Barcelona FC.

The rationale behind the use of Hercules for red, white and rosé wines produced by Nemea Wines is presumably the hero's connection with the area via his first labour, though more obscure is any link justifying the Greek brand-name for tinned *gigantes* (broad-beans baked in a tomato sauce). The New York band *Hercules and Love Affair* has achieved both critical and

(a)   (b)

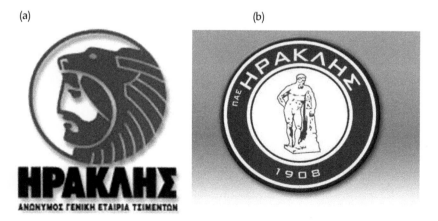

Figure 7.6 Herakles in modern Greece: logos of (a) the Greek cement company Iraklis, and (b) the Thessaloniki sports club of the same name.

popular success since its debut in 2008, its posters regularly featuring the hero of Greek myth. According to founder-member Andy Butler the name was carefully chosen, within a tradition of using Greek references in house music, inspired by the paradox of the world's strongest man vulnerable in respect of his young male lover Hylas: 'I was attracted by the Hercules story because it was about embracing the femine within the hyper masculine.'[38]

What is it, in the end, which has made Herakles such a long-lived and ubiquitous hero? The question is impossible to answer definitively, but the survey presented in this book suggests that there are two fundamental factors underlying his enduring popularity. First, Herakles is the original flawed superhero, a type that has never ceased to fascinate western audiences: by extraordinary feats of monster-slaying strength he is the reliable defender of civilization, but at the same time his excesses brings destruction on himself and others. These two sides to his character are in constant tension, but the balance between them is ultimately tipped towards the positive by the second factor: his apotheosis. In antiquity, those making sacrifice to Herakles the god would have been constantly aware of his mortal origins, and the stories about his weaknesses must have made him seem more approachable than the average Olympian – he was a model for the common man, who might ultimately hope to follow him into the company of the gods. When the pagan gods 'died' at the end of antiquity this hope could be translated into a Christian context by assimilating Herakles to Christ or Virtue, and even in the twenty-first century, when for many the expectation of an afterlife is faint, Herakles can still represent the triumph of good over evil in the here and now.

NOTES

FOREWORD

1 Exhibition: Edith C. Blum Art Institute, Bard College, Massachusetts, March–May 1986, accompanied by the catalogue Uhlenbrock 1986. Conference proceedings published as: Bonnet and Jourdain-Annequin (eds) 1992, Mastrocinque (ed.) 1993, Jourdain-Annequin and Bonnet (eds) 1996, Bonnet, Jourdain-Annequin and Pirenne-Delforge (eds) 1998, Rawlings (ed.) 2005, Bernardini and Zucca (eds) 2005.

2 Padilla 1998 covers the ancient Greek material; the discussion runs to just thirty-three pages, but the extensive notes act as a guide to previous scholarship.

INTRODUCING HERAKLES

1 We also hear of a *Herakleia* by the sixth-century epic poet Kinaithon of Lakedaimonia (*PEG* Cinaetho frs 6–7). Translations of the fragments of Peisandros' and Panyassis' epics: West 2003, 176–217. For an overview of Herakles in epic, see Huxley 1969, 99–112 and 177–88; Matthews 1974 discusses Panyassis at length.

2 Fragments of the early mythographers are collected in Fowler 2000 (for Herakles, s.v. Pherecydes Atheniensis frs 16–18 and 68–84, and Herodoros Heracleota frs 1–4 and 13–37). Cameron 2004 discusses Apollodoros in the context of the development of mythography in the Roman imperial period. Around AD 100 the biographer Plutarch wrote a life of Herakles (referred to in his *Theseus* 29) but only a few fragments survive.

3 The study of names has been greatly enhanced by the *LGPN* project, which is collecting and cataloguing the names of real people in ancient Greece, using the evidence of ancient writers and inscriptions.

4 Labours as water management: e.g. Schoo 1969, Bader 1985, Knauss 1990; on Herakles the hydraulic engineer see Saloway 1994. See Stern 1996 on Palaiphatos and the genre, or more briefly Stern 1999.

5 The Dorian Herakles: Müller 1830 vol. 1, 425–64 and Wilamowitz 1895 (though he later changed his mind: Wilamowitz 1932: 20–6); for an overview of the 'Dorian invasion' question, see Cartledge 2002, 65–87. The native Greek Herakles: Nilsson 1932: 187–220 (Mycenaean), Friedländer 1907 and 1914 (Argive). West (1985: 144–54) uses the *Catalogue of Women* to argue for a geographical expansion of myths surrounding Herakles' family from an early stage localized in the Argolid.

6 Puhvel 1987 provides an overview of the comparative approach (see especially 241–55). The classic discussion of Herakles' Indo-European dimension is Dumézil 1970a, 96–107; more recently, see e.g. Davidson 1980, and Bader 1985 and 1992.

7 Important early studies: von Schroeder 1914, Schweitzer 1922; Levy 1934; Brundage 1958; Fontenrose 1959. More recent studies include Burkert 1987 and 1992a, b; Hermary 1992; Boardman 1998b.

8 A chronological survey of Herakles' treatment in Greek literature was undertaken as early as 1871 by Emmanuel des Essarts. The growing popularity of this source-based approach can be seen in various surveys of Herakles' myth (cf. Further Reading): Brommer 1984 and 1986, Carpenter 1991, Schefold 1992, Gantz 1993, Shapiro 1994. An early forerunner of these is Flacelière and Devambez 1966; Kerényi's detailed telling of the story (1959, 125–206) is supported by extensive reference to the sources. A useful A–Z guide to ancient literary sources for Greek myth can be found in Hard 2004, 1–20.

9 Brommer (1985, 183) cites c.3500 as the number of Herakles images in extant Greek vase-painting as a whole; Boardman et al. (1998) catalogue 3520 Greek and Roman images, though many more are listed in the *LIMC* articles on other figures in the relevant scenes. Hampe 1936 discusses the fibulae (see especially 41–9) and other early Boiotian material, his chronology being refined by Fittschen 1969 (see 147–52 and 213–21); Kunze 1950 provides a full catalogue of the shield-bands; see Boardman 1992 for the Lakonian art statistic.

10 On the Etruscan material, see Schwarz 1988; Mastrocinque 1993 and McDonough 2002 discuss select examples; Ritter 1995 provides a systematic history of Hercules in Roman art to the time of Augustus; Moitrieux 2002 offers a detailed study of Hercules images from Gaul; Segura 1996 discusses images and inscriptions from Spain; Coralini 2001 catalogues images from domestic contexts in the Vesuviana area.

I MONSTERS AND THE HERO I: THE TWELVE LABOURS

1 Fontenrose 1959 analyses themes and plot components common to Greek and oriental dragon-slaying stories; see especially 321–64 on Herakles. Murgatroyd 2007 surveys mythical monsters in classical literature (see especially 131–45). Several papers in Bonnet et al. (eds) 1998 discuss aspects of Herakles' encounters with monsters: see especially Boardman, Verbanck-Piérard and Gilis, Schnapp-Gourbeillon, Parisi Presicce and Scarpi.

2   Ashmole and Yalouris (1967, 22–9, pls 143–211) provide detailed photo-graphs. Barringer 2005 presents a persuasive case for reading the temple's sculptures as a unified ensemble intended as a positive model for Olympic athletes. On the temple in its ritual context, see Barringer 2008, 8–58; see also Scott 2010, 181–7.

3   Haubold 2005 discusses the different presentations of Herakles in the *Theogony* and the *Catalogue of Women*.

4   The Chest of Kypselos is discussed by Pollitt 1990, 210–15, and Carter 1989. On the Throne of Bathykles, see Pollitt 1990, 23–6, and Martin 1976.

5   Detailed studies of the Heraion and its sculpture are supplied by van Keuren 1989, and Zancani Montuoro and Zanotti-Bianco 1954.

6   For a detailed discussion of the *Tabula Albana*, see Sadurska 1964. Jongste 1992 catalogues around seventy Roman sarcophagi which depict some or all of the labours; for a second-century relief depicting the twelve labours around Omphale and Hercules (Naples), see Grabar 1967, fig. 72. On the Piazza Armerina mosaic, see Carandini et al. 1982, 312–25 pls XLIX–LII 105–29. Coins: *BMC* Alexandria 1043–56. The 'Gryllos Papyrus' is *POxy* XXII 2331; see Roberts 1954, Maas 1958 and Nisbet 2002. Small (2003, 79–116) includes clay relief bowls and the 'Iliac Tablets' (reliefs with which the *Tabula Albana* is usually grouped), in her consideration of the developing relation-ship between image and text in the hellenistic and Roman periods, and see 138–41 on illustrated papyri.

7   See Nicgorski 2005 on the Herakles knot, and Cairns 2010, 129–49 on Bakchylides 13.

8   The Corinthian scenes are discussed in Amyx and Amandry 1982. Phaistos coin: Kraay and Hirmer 1966, no. 552.

9   This labour may be reflected in ritual at Athens: an inscription of c.AD 120 (*SEG* 31 no.122, 37f.) recording regulations concerning a group called 'the Herakliastai in the Marshes' specifies that once a year the treasurer must procure a boar for sacrifice to Herakles.

10 Zanker 1996 argues that the labour is indirectly conveyed by means of visual description, alongside the more explicit narration of the Nemean lion story.

11 Coins: Kraay and Hirmer 1966, no. 514; Kraay 1976, 101–2 no. 320.

12 Selinous coin: Kraay and Hirmer 1966, no. 187. Marconi (2007, 110–15) discusses competing identifications of the Selinous metope as Herakles' encounter with the bull or with Acheloos.

13 The earliest Amazonomachies to be securely identifiable as Theseus' exploit are those in the Stoa Poikile (p. 169) and the Theseion of c.460 BC (Pausanias 1. 17.2), and in contemporary Attic vase-painting. See Boardman 1982 on the influence of the Persian invasions on the imagery, and more broadly Tyrrell 1984 on Amazons in Athenian thought.

14 On Stesichoros' poem, see Page 1973 and Barrett 2007. The relationship between the poem and archaic art is discussed in detail by Brize 1980, and

more briefly by Robertson 1969 and Shapiro 1994, 71–7; see Brize 1985 on the bronze pectoral.

15 Cattle-raiding as a common Indo-European mythological motif is discussed by Lincoln 1976; see Burkert 1979 and 1998 on Herakles as ideal protector of cattle, and 1977 specifically on the Geryon myth; van Wonterghem 1998 discusses the evidence for worship of Hercules by cattle-herders in central Italy, though see Bradley 2005 for a more cautious approach. On folktale motifs, and especially on Nereus' involvement, see Davies 1988. Croon 1952 elaborates on the 'herdsman of the dead' motif.

16 Littlewood 1968 catalogues classical literary references to apples. Nearchos' Herakles *melapheres* is discussed by Jucker 1977. On the Meidias Painter's scene and Hygieia, see Stafford 2005a. I am indebted to Diana Burton for reference to the St Petersburg stamnos.

17 Greek and Roman images of Kerberos are conveniently categorized by the number of heads in Woodford and Spier 1992. On the Roman door motif, see Davies 1978, 206–7. The evolution of ideas about the afterlife is traced by Bremmer 2002; Edmonds 2004 looks in detail at selected fifth- and fourth-century re-workings of the *katabasis* tradition. Vermeule (E.T.) 1977 discusses oriental prototypes for the scene of Herakles leading a sphinx, another Greek symbol of death, found on a small handful of Attic vases of around 500 BC. Schoo (1969, 103–7) once again offers an implausible interpretation, that Kerberos represents a volcano such as Stromboli, the snake elements symbolizing lava flows.

2 MONSTERS AND THE HERO II: OTHER BATTLES

1 See Woodford 1983 for an overview of the episode's iconography; several examples appear in Neils and Oakley 2003, catalogue nos 10–12; the young Herakles features briefly also in Golden 1990. See Stern 1974 on Theokritos' *Idyll* 24.

2 On Zeus as protector of strangers, see Dowden 2005, 78–80; on human sacrifice as largely an *idea* rather than a reality in ancient Greece, see Hughes 1991 (83–5 on Iphigeneia, 187–8 on Bousiris). Livingstone (2001, 1–90) provides a thorough introduction to Isocrates' speech. The images are discussed as reflections of Greek ritual practice in Durand and Lissarrague 1983, and van Straten 1995, 46–9 figs 48–53.

3 Small 1982 discusses the evolution of Cacus' story in Etrusco-Roman myth; Virgil's impact on later versions is discussed in Green 2004, 247–50. Propertius 4.9's sophisticated manipulation of genre and refraction of contemporary politics and cult has been much discussed: see e.g. Anderson 1964, Cairns 1992, Spencer 2001; see below pp. 152–3 for political interpretations.

4 Nimmo Smith 2001 provides an accessible introduction, see especially 29–30. Rosen (2007, 43–66) discusses the myth's use of mockery and how

this relates to the humour of Old Comedy and other satirical genres. See also Kirkpatrick and Dunn 2002, especially 52–4 on the South Italian vases.

5 For the Gigantomachy from Zeus' point of view, see Dowden 2005, 35–9. I discuss the episode as part of the Greek creation myth in Stafford 2009.

6 Moore discusses Herakles' involvement in the archaic Gigantomachies in a series of articles: see 1979 on Lydos' dinos and 1977 on the Siphnian Treasury; her case for placing Herakles in the central group of the Akropolis Athena pediment (1995) is less convincing. The Siphnian Treasury frieze has most recently been discussed by Neer 2003, who proposes an interesting political reading. On the Parthenon metope, see Schwab 1996.

7 An early reference to the twins' conjoined form can also be found in the *Catalogue of Women* fr. 17a MW. See Snodgrass 1998, 26–33 and 82–4 for discussion of the images.

8 Akropolis dedications: black-figure plate by Lydos (Akropolis 2410) and two fragmentary pinakes (Akropolis 2545a–b and 2555). For discussion of the sources, see Shapiro 1984, Janko 1986 and Zardini 2009 (who provides a database of images); see also Martin 2005. Borg 2002, 143–5 considers images which include the figure of Fear.

9 On all aspects of Prometheus, see Dougherty 2005. On the Pergamon sculptures, see Pollitt 1986, 37 fig. 30.

10 Stupperich 1992 and Finster-Hotz 1984 provide detailed studies of the Assos temple's iconography. The Attic banqueting and meeting scenes are discussed, respectively, by Noel 1983 and Verbanck-Piérard 1982; see also Wolf 1993 on the reclining Herakles, especially 41–2, pls 118–30.

11 Boardman (2002, 36–8 figs 7–9, and 144–6 figs 117–19) reviews the fossil theory and alternative explanations. More generally, see Ahlberg-Cornell 1984.

12 Brommer 1983 considers the relationship between Nereus and the Old Man of the Sea. The political interpretations are discussed by Glynn 1981.

13 Ovid's version of the story is discussed in Secci 2009.

3 THE TRAGIC HERO

1 On the Aeschylean Prometheus, see Dougherty 2005, 66–78; see also Taplin (2007, 80–2) on an Apulian krater 'more than probably related' to the *Prometheus Unbound*, on which Herakles has fatally wounded the eagle.

2 Introductions to all aspects of the play are provided by Easterling 1982, 1–23 and Davies 1991, xvii–xxxix; the two scholars have differing views on key issues. On earlier treatments of the myths concerned and Sophokles' innovations, see also: March 1987, 47–77; Davies 1984; Pralon 1996. Kreophylos' *Capture of Oichalia* is discussed by Burkert 1972 and Friedländer 1914, 335–41. See Cairns (2010, 75–92) on Bakchylides 5, and Fisher (1992, 206–7 and 304–8) on the role of *hybris* in Herakles' quarrel with Eurytos in Panyassis' *Herakleia* and in *Women of Trachis*.

3 On Deianeira's culpability, see especially Faraone 1994 and Carawan 2000; Buxton (1988, 43–4) argues that no single character can be blamed for the play's outcome.

4 The debate about the play's ending is usefully summarized by Holt 1989, who argues that the apotheosis is presupposed. Finkelberg 1996 proposes a textual emendation which would make an explicit link between the play and the ritual performed on Mount Oita. Calame 2005 compares the Sophoklean Herakles' death with examples of heroic funerary ritual and sacrificial practice. Currie (2005, 369–81) reviews mythological and historical examples of voluntary death by fire associated with immortality. Liapis (2006, 56–9) reads the ending as a deliberate allusion to *Odyssey* 11's double version of Herakles' fate (pp. 172–3).

5 For Herakles as Odysseus in disguise, see Roisman 2001, 50–2. Greengard (1987, 88–99) discusses the choice of Herakles as champion of social values. According to Dio Chrysostom (*Speeches* 52 and 59), both Aeschylus and Euripides produced *Philoktetes* tragedies, too, but it is unclear whether Herakles appeared on stage in either.

6 Marshall 2000 suggests that *Alkestis* may have been a response to legislation of 440/39 BC restricting comic drama in some way, but the issue of the play's genre remains contentious. See Buxton 1985 on *xenia* and Herakles' characterization; Goldfarb 1992 focuses on the conflict of values; Fitzgerald 1991 offers a darker interpretation of the final scene.

7 Sources for the story before and after Euripides are discussed by Pache (2004, 49–65) and linked with the cult of Herakles' children at Thebes (p. 182). Papadopoulou 2005 provides a stimulating discussion of the play's presentation of Herakles.

8 Riley 2008 reviews representations of Herakles' madness and the scholarly debate concerning its nature (see 14–50 on Euripides); see also e.g. Pike 1978, Hartigan 1987 and Fitzgerald 1991. Silk 1985 argues that Herakles is being punished for his 'interstitial nature' which constitutes a threat to the established cosmic order; cf. Fisher 1992, 434–8. Griffiths 2002 suggests that the death of Herakles' children is a punishment counterbalancing his transgressive overcoming of death in other contexts. Buxton (1988, 46–8) suggests that the play does not fully explain Herakles' downfall.

9 See George 1994 on the archer v. hoplite debate and the stage-prop bow Herakles must have carried; see also Cohen 1994 on bow v. club in the visual arts, and Worman 1999 on interactions between the play's verbal imagery and visual elements of the performance. Kirkpatrick and Dunn 2002 discuss Herakles' striking personification of his weapons at ll.1376–82, arguing that this is an allusion to comic versions of the Kerkopes episode. Mikalson 1986 compares Euripides' and Sophokles' treatment of Herakles' relationship with Zeus, and see Padilla 1994 on paternity as a theme in Euripides' play. Dunn 1997 discusses the play's false endings and final lack of closure; Theseus' role here is discussed in Mills 1997, 129–59; see also Walker 1995, 127–41.

10 On the play in general, see Wilkins 1993 and Allan 2001. Wilkins 1990 examines the play's focus on youth, and see Fisher 1992, 424–7 on its presentation of Eurystheus' *hybris*.

11 For late fifth-century Athenian views on rape, see e.g. Harris 1990. Sutton 1984 provides an accessible account of Sophokles' lost plays; see 13–15 and 126 on the *Telephos* trilogy and 17–19 on the *Amphitryon*. Bauchhenss-Thüriedl 1971 traces the development of the Telephos myth in art (and see below pp. 149–50).

12 Against the identification of London E370 as Herakles swapping clothes with Omphale is the fact that the woman has none of the orientalizing attributes we might expect in depictions of a Lydian queen at this period: Llewellyn-Jones 2005, 51–2 figs 1–2.

13 Taplin 2007 discusses possible reflections of Euripides' plays in South Italian vase-painting, including *Children of Herakles* (126–30), *Herakles* (143–5) and *Alkmene* (170–4); see also 238–40 on an Apulian vase attributed to the Darius Painter (Princeton 1983, 13) which may be related to a play (otherwise unattested) in which Herakles and the goddesses of Eleusis come to the aid of Medea and her children; on this vase see also Griffiths 2006b, 50–1 fig. 2. For contrasting views on the relationship between drama and images, see Small 2003, 37–78 (especially 70 on Asteas' krater).

14 On *Heroides* 9 and its possible sources, see Jacobson 1974, 235–42.

15 Zanobi 2008 argues for the inclusion of pantomimic elements in Seneca's plays making them more appealing to a popular audience. Fitch (1987, 15–61) provides a useful introduction to all aspects of the *Hercules Furens*. For comparison of Euripides' and Seneca's treatments of the madness, see Papadopoulou 2004 and Riley 2008, 51–91; see also OKell 2005 on the play's didactic purpose.

16 Dupont 1989 argues that the last two scenes of the play constitute a re-writing of the *consecratio*, the ritual whereby Roman emperors were deified after their death. Stössl 1945 surveys all the literary accounts of Herakles/Hercules' death, and includes (119–22) a structural comparison of *Women of Trachis* and *Hercules Oetaeus*.

4 VICE OR VIRTUE INCARNATE

1 Bowie 2000 provides a useful overview of the mythological subject matter of Old Comedy other than Aristophanes. Long (1986, 55–7) discusses fragmentary comedies concerning the Antaios, Bousiris and Omphale episodes. Padilla 1998b is speculative, but includes useful lists of comedies and satyr plays featuring Herakles.

2 On oaths in Aristophanes, see Dillon 1995.

3 Under classical Athenian law not even a fully legitimate daughter could inherit in her own right, so it has been suggested that the reference here is to Epikleros ('heiress') as a cult title of Athena: Sommerstein 1987, 305 (*ad*

l.1653). On the law in question here and the status of *nothoi* more generally, see Ogden 1996, 31–212, and Patterson 1990.

4 Sommerstein 1996, 9–20 provides a convenient introduction to the play. Padilla 1992 argues that both Herakles and Aeschylus represent the good old-fashioned values that eventually win the day. The initiatory interpretation is discussed at length in Lada-Richards 1999; Edmonds (2003 and 2004, 111–58) raises some valid counter-arguments, focusing rather on Aristophanes' manipulation of myth.

5 On Figure 4.1 see McPhee 1979; Woodford 1989 discusses the iconographic tradition of the appropriation of Herakles' attributes. Simon (1982, 136–9) discusses possible reflections of the Aeschylus plays, while Wolf (1993, 143–54 pls 80–117) considers the broader question of links between satyr plays and scenes of satyrs with the reclining Herakles. See Laurens and Lissarrague 1989 on the imagery of Herakles' pyre.

6 See Taplin 1993 on the methodological issues at stake in comparing the South Italian vases and plays, especially 10–11 and 45–7 (pls 8.26a and 13.7). While Small (2003, 37–78) is rightly critical of identifications of tragedy in vase-painting, she does admit the possibility of painters being influenced by their experience of comedy in the theatre. On our Figure 4.2 and comparable images, see Shefton 1989, and Stewart 1996 and 1997, 171–4.

7 Binder 1974 discusses the influence of Virgil on Hercules' portrayal here.

8 On the Herakles Epitrapezios, see Bartman 1986; also Pollitt 1990, 102–3, and Ridgway 1997, 294–304.

9 I discuss Herakles' propensity for allegory in Stafford 2005a; on Greek personification more generally, see Stafford 2000 or (more briefly) 2007. Shapiro 1986 charts the earliest stages of allegorical expression in Greek art.

10 On Sleep, see Shapiro 1993, 148–55 and Stafford 2003. Andreae 1962 discusses images of the Alkyoneus encounter in detail; Borg 2002, 153–7 considers Hypnos' role in these scenes.

11 On the Geras scenes, see Shapiro 1988 and 1993, 89–94 figs 43–7; also Borg 2002, 88–95.

12 On Euripides' treatment of the myth, see Conacher 1988, 30–5. On Thanatos' appearance in late sixth- and fifth-century art, see Shapiro 1993, 132–47 and 159–65.

13 Mackay 2002 discusses the significance of Herakles' hairstyle in archaic vase-painting. Currie (2005, 133–9) discusses the anecdotes in the broader context of athletes' emulation of heroes; see also 307–12 on Pindar's *Nemean* 7. For Poulydamas' statue base, see Barringer 2008, 47–8 figs 35–7.

14 On the social context of Pindar's praise poetry, see e.g. Hornblower and Morgan eds 2007. Surveys of Pindar's treatment of Herakles are provided by Pike 1984, Vivante 1985 and (in most detail) Nieto Hernández 1993. The two fragmentary poems mentioned are preserved on papyri: fr. 140a on *POxy* 498, fr. 169a on *POxy* 2450 (on which see Pavese 1968). On the Aiginetan poems, see Burnett 2005, especially 53, 77–88 and 179–202. On Bakchylides,

see Cairns 2010; Fisher (1992, 229–35) discusses Pindar and Bakchylides' presentation of Herakles' relationship with *hybris*.

15 On *aretê* and the Euripidean Herakles, see Papadopoulou 2004, 129–89; cf. Murray 1946 on Sophokles' role in establishing Herakles' claim to the title 'best of men'. I discuss the 'Choice of Herakles' further in Stafford 2005a; see also Whitman 1987, 22–4 (who dubs this 'the first true personification allegory in the West', 22), Sansone 2004 (who argues that Xenophon keeps closely to Prodikos' own wording), Kuntz 1994 (on the tradition of heroic choice myths) and Rochette 1998 (on later versions of the story).

16 The Isocrates passage is discussed in Too 1995, 129–40. On Aristotle's hymn see Bowra 1938, Crossett 1967, Renehan 1982 and Bolonyai 2004.

17 Billot 1993 defends Antisthenes' debated connection with Kynosarges. Rankin (1986, 101–34) outlines Antisthenes teachings on the virtuous life. See Höistad 1948, 22–73 on the development of Herakles as a Cynic hero.

18 Fitch (1987, 40–4) offers a balanced account of the extent of Stoic idealism in the *Hercules Furens*; Rosenmeyer 1989 reviews the broader debate about Stoicism in Seneca's drama.

19 Howard 1978 is a detailed study of the Lansdowne Herakles. Vermeule 1975 surveys the Farnese Herakles type; see also Pollitt 1993, 101–2, Edwards 1996, 145–9, and Ridgway 1997, 289. On Lucian's Herakles Ogmios, see Elsner 2007, 58–66, and Bader 1996.

20 Loraux 1990 discusses Herakles' relationships with women, arguing that a feminine element is an essential part of his virile strength; cf. Llewellyn-Jones 2005 for some reservations concerning 'feminising' clothing. Pike 1977 provides an overview of Herakles' marriages and main love-affairs. On Herakles, Iolaos and initiation, see Jourdain-Annequin 1986 and 1992c, Sergent 1987, 137–78, Dowden 1992, 115–16 and Davidson 2007, 285–99.

21 The wool-working and clothes-swapping motifs are taken up e.g. in the Senecan *Hercules Oetaeus* 371–7, and Statius' *Thebaid* 10.646–9 and *Achilleid* 1.260–1. The idea of Herakles' emasculation is also reflected in two first-century AD epigrams (*Greek Anthology* 16.103) which purport to describe a statue of Herakles stripped of his arms by Eros. General discussion of the Omphale story is provided by Alonso 1996, while Bonnet 1996 reviews the debate about the cross-dressing motif. On the story's treatment in particular sources see: Easterling 2007 (on Ion's satyr play); above chapter 2 n. 3 (on Propertius 4.9); Parker 1997, 78–83 and 101–24 (on the *Fasti*); Brommer 1985, 210–13 fig. 34 (on the archaic amphora); Schauenburg 1960 (on the fourth-century BC as well as Roman images); Ritter 1996 (on Omphale's popularity as a subject for small-scale media of the first centuries BC/AD); Kampen 1996 (on first- and second-century AD art).

22 On the Kian ritual see Sourvinou-Inwood 2005. On Apollonios' Herakles, see Levin 1971. On Theokritos, *Idyll* 13, see Campbell 1991 and Mastronarde 1968.

5 POLITICAL HERAKLES

1 Huttner 1997 provides an in-depth study of Herakles' use in Greek ruler-propaganda. Palagia 1986 surveys imitation of Herakles in hellenistic and Roman portraiture.

2 Euripides' *Kresphontes* dealt with the murder of the original king of Messenia and the revenge taken by his son of the same name; too little survives of the *Temenos* and *Sons of Temenos* to be sure of their plots, but they clearly covered early events in the establishment of the Herakleids' rule at Argos; see further below n.6. Tomlinson (1972, 58–66) discusses the relationship between the mythological 'lot of Temenos' and early Argive history. On Corinth, see Salmon 1984, 38–54 (the relationship of the city with the Herakleidai) and 55–74 (on the Bakchiads). Kennell (2010, 20–30) provides an accessible discussion of Sparta's early myth-history; see also Malkin 1994, 15–45, and Tigerstedt 1965, 28–36.

3 On the Spartan royal genealogies, and the vexed question of their status as 'king-lists', see Cartledge 2002, 293–8; West 1985, 8–11; Henige 1974, 207–13.

4 On the hellenistic imagery, see Palagia 2006. Coins: Kraay and Hirmer 1966, nos 521–22.

5 On the Makedonian foundation myths, see Borza 1995, and see Borza 1990, 98–131, on Alexander I. On Alexander I's coinage, see Raymond 1953, 82–3 pl. 5 nos 23–33, and 127–8 pl. 11 nos 118–21. Iliadou 1998 includes coins in a survey of evidence for Herakles' cult in Makedonia.

6 For detailed discussion of the play, see Harder 1985, 125–44 (and 3–26 on the *Kresphontes*); on performance context see Sourvinou-Inwood 2003, 41–5. The historical reality of Euripides' sojourn in Makedonia has been challenged e.g. by Scullion 2003, who also (2006) argues that the *Archelaos* was the third play in a trilogy, after the *Temenos* and *Sons of Temenos*. On Archelaos' reign, see Borza 1990, 161–79; on his claim to the throne, see Ogden 1999, 7–8.

7 Coins: Kraay and Hirmer 1966, nos 560–1 (Amyntas and Perdikkas); Iliadou 1998, no. 119 pl. 37.98 (Amyntas). Philip at Kynosarges: see e.g. Parker 1996, 257 (compliment) v. Ogden 1996, 202 (insult); the issue is discussed at length by Versnel 1973, and cf. Bremmer 1977.

8 On Alexander as divine bastard, see Ogden 1999, 27–9. Bonnet 1992 surveys Alexander's encounters with eastern deities identified with Herakles, and on 'the creation of belief', see Bosworth 1996, 98–132.

9 On Arrian's presentation of Alexander, see Bosworth's commentary (1995) on the passages concerned.

10 On the use of imagery by Alexander and his Successors, see Stewart 1993, especially figures 30–1, 71, 104, 110 and 120–1. Coins: Kraay and Hirmer 1966, nos 569–72. Dahmen 2007 provides a convenient overview of Alexander's coin-types and their use by later imitators: see especially pls 1, 9, 11, 19,

26 and 28. Nicgorski (2005) argues that the knot also lent itself to Alexander's propagandistic programme because of its coincidence of shape with the Egyptian symbol of unity.

11 On naming, see above p. 9 with Introduction n. 3; Iliadou (1998, 146–8) catalogues Herakles-related names attested in Makedonia. Brunt 1975 reviews the contested evidence for Barsine and Herakles; on the question of Herakles' legitimacy, see Ogden 1999, 41–51.

12 On Maussolos' use of myth, see Ruzicka 1992, 46–55. Coins: Kraay 1976, no. 940; see also Sherwin-White 1978, 70–1.

13 Makedonian coins: Iliadou 1998, nos 117–18 pl. 36.96–7, nos 165–8 pl. 37.98–9. The Vergina inscription: Andronikos 1987, 38–42; Iliadou 1998, no. 91 pl. 20.48.

14 Mithradates' coins: Price 1968, 6–9 pls 2–3 nos 14–23.

15 Coins: Kraay and Hirmer 1966, nos 797–8, and see Nicgorski 2005.

16 On Attalid myth-making, see Kosmetatou 1995 and 2000, 45–7. Robert 1984 discusses the epigram alongside epigraphic evidence from Pergamon for the local cult of Herakles.

17 See Rawlings 2005 on Hannibal and Hercules.

18 On Sulla's games, see Wiseman 2000, and on Pompey see Rawson 1970.

19 Galinsky 1966 discusses political readings of *Aeneid* 8; Schilling 1942 considers the fortunes of Hercules' cult under Augustus. See Zanker (1988, 44–65 figs 34–50) on Antony and Augustus' competing use of divine imagery.

20 Nero's association with Hercules is discussed by Champlin 2003, 135–8; on the Corinth relief, see Salowey 1994, 94 pl. 29b.

21 On emperors from Trajan to Commodus, see Hekster 2005. Coins: e.g. Carson 1990, nos 128 and 142 (Trajan), 170 (Hadrian); Carson 1980, nos 538 (Trajan).

22 For in-depth study of Commodus–Hercules, see Hekster 2001; Gagé 1981 focuses on the Hercules-themed spectacles. Coins: e.g. Carson 1990, nos 213–14; Carson 1980, nos 663–5 and 667. See Hannah 1986 on the Capitoline bust; Vermeule (C.C. 1975, 329–31 pl.55) discusses the post-mortem portraits, and more generally see 1977.

23 Coins: e.g. Carson 1980, no. 679 (Septimius Severus), 910–11 and 918 (Postumus), 1081, 1090, 1099–1100, 1109–10, 1112, 1117, 1122, 1159, 1223 (Maximian), 1152 (Constantius), 1244 (Maxentius); Carson 1990, nos 413 (Postumus), 585 and 593 (Constantius), 560 and 575 (Maximian), 599 (Maxentius). Rees 2005 discusses the 'Herculius' title.

24 Coins: Kraay and Hirmer 1966, no. 726.

25 On Herakles in the west and his links with the Phoenician Melqart, see especially Jourdain-Annequin 1989; see also Malkin 2005, Jourdain-Annequin 1992b, and the articles collected in Mastrocinque 1993 (in particular Plácido 1993, on the roads). Coins: Kraay and Hirmer 1966, nos 270–1 (Kroton), 255–8 (Herakleia); Rutter 2001, nos 2139–40 (Kroton), 1358–410, 1421–35 and 1443–8 (Herakleia Lucania), 909–14 and 955 (Tarentum). Détienne 1960 connects Herakles and the development of Pythagoreanism in southern Italy.

26 Giangiulio 1983 discusses the Herakles' mediating role in Sicily; see Erskine (2001, 131–56) on the broader issue of mythological justifications for Greek colonization, and cf. Leigh 2000 on the baths at Himera and Segesta as a parallel for Aponus (modern Bagni d'Abano, near Padova). Coins: Kraay and Hirmer 1966, nos 125, 127 and 129 (Syracuse), cf. nos 147–9 (Kamarina). On Dorieus' expedition, see Malkin 1994, 203–18.

27 Proceedings of the conference and an exhibition catalogue: Bernardini and Zucca (eds 2005). On the *nuraghe* see Boardman 2002, 26–7 fig. 4; Ridgway 2006 reviews the evidence for early trade with Greece; see also Létoublon 1996, and Dowden 1992, 116–17.

28 On Herakleia Trahcinia, see especially Malkin 1994, 219–35; see also Hornblower 1992, 186–90, and Bowden 2005. Vickers (1995) argues controversially for a link between the foundation and Sophokles' *Women of Trachis*.

29 Accessible accounts of the ancient Olympic Games are provided by Young 2004 and Spivey 2004 (see 225–30 on the foundation myths). Golden (1998) discusses the Olympic foundation myths (12–14) and the ideology which equated cash prizes with wage labour (146–57). See Cairns 2010, 93–100 on Bakchylides 9, and Doffey 1992 on the Nemean myths. Valavanis 2004 provides sumptuously illustrated coverage of all the panhellenic sanctuaries.

30 Harrison (forthcoming) argues that much of Herodotus' account of Peisistratos' tyranny is historically unreliable. Criticisms and defences of political interpretations of the images include: Osborne 1983–4; Cook 1987; Cavalier 1995; Hannah 1995; Parker 1996, 84–5. Williams 1983 extends the Boardman approach to scenes of the sleeping Alkyoneus (p. 118), which he links to Peisistratos' victory at Attic Pallene (Herodotus 1.62–3). Discussions of the apotheosis scenes' religious significance include: Verbanck-Piérard 1987; Laurens 1988 and 1996: Shapiro 1989, 135–9. On Herakles' relationship with Athena, see Deacy 2005 and 2008, 62–7.

31 Miquel 1989 discusses the kithara-playing scenes. In extant literature, the story of Herakles' initiation is first certainly attested in Euripides (*Herakles* 610–13), but see Lloyd-Jones 1967 for the motif in a fragmentary poem possibly by Pindar.

32 On the tripod scenes, see e.g. Parke and Boardman 1957; Defradas 1972, 126–59; von Bothmer 1977; Boardman 1978; Watrous 1982, 167–8; Williams 1983; Neer 2003, 134–7. On the treasury's spatial context, see Scott 2010, 63–6.

33 On Theseus and Athens, see especially Walker 1995; more recently, see Hall 2007, 338–46, and Neer 2002, 154–68.

34 On the vases, see Steiner 2007, 221–3 figs 10.7–8. Neer 2004 examines the politics of the Athenian Treasury; see also Scott 2010, 77–81. Barringer (2008, 109–43) discusses the Hephaisteion in the spatial and political context of the fifth-century Agora.

35 On Herakles in the battle of Marathon, see Bowden 2005. The Stoa Poikile paintings: Pollitt 1993, 143–5. Boardman (2001, 202–9) reviews the debate concerning Herakles and Theseus as conveyors of 'civic messages'.

36 Cohen 1998 defends the Heraklean identity of Parthenon figure D. On the Athena Nike frieze, see Schultz 2009.

6 WORSHIP OF THE HERO-GOD

1 I discuss Asklepios' status in Stafford 2008, and see Stafford 2010 on the uniqueness of Herakles' apotheosis story; Brelich (1958, 362–5) comments on the paradox of Herakles' hero-god status, given his prototypically heroic character. See Currie 2005, 60–70 on Pindar's use of *heros*, and Pirenne-Delforge 2010 on Pausanias' definitions of the divine v. the heroic.

2 On the Hesiodic passages, see West 1966 and 1985. Holt 1992 surveys lost works which may have treated the apotheosis story.

3 The Samian krater is unpublished, but that the island continued to have a strong tradition of the apotheosis is suggested by a colossal statue-group of Herakles, Hera and Zeus said to have been made by the early classical sculptor Myron (Strabo 14.1.4).

4 Recent discussion of Olympian versus chthonic ritual, including contentious aspects of Herakles' cult: Verbanck-Piérard 1998; Ekroth 1999 and 2002; Scullion 1994 and 2000; Pirenne-Delforge 2008, 187–92. Against the duality of Herakles' cult: Verbanck-Piérard 1989, Georgoudi 1998. I consider the issue further in Stafford 2005b. On the treatment of Herakles in Herodotus Book 2, see Harrison 2000, 182–207.

5 There is no comprehensive, easily accessible account of Herakles' cult. The most detailed survey of the evidence is Gruppe 1918, while Farnell 1921 remains the lengthiest general discussion of his cult in English; both works have naturally been superseded on points of detail. There is much relevant material in *ThesCRA*, though the work's structure means that it is scattered between chapters on various elements of ritual (see e.g. under 'sacrifices', 'dedications'). The evidence for Herakles-derived names is collected in *LGPN*, and Parker (2000) discusses the practice of naming children after gods. On ships' names, see Casson 1995, 348–60. Tagalidou 1993 studies reliefs dedicated to Herakles, and many relevant images feature in van Straten 1995.

6 Woodford 1974 gives a detailed account of Herakles' cult in Athens and Attika; Shapiro (1989, 157–63) considers the archaic period; important aspects are discussed further in Jourdain-Annequin 1998a, 355–9, and Verbanck-Piérard 1992 and 1995; Lambert 1999 examines an example of the epigraphic evidence for *thiasoi*; see Jameson 2005 specifically on Attika. Some works on Athenian religion in general have useful material on Herakles (easily located via the index), especially Mikalson 1975, Parke 1977, Parker 1996 and 2005.

7 Statue at Melite: Woodford 1976. Lalonde (2006, 86–93) argues that the Melite Herakleion was a modest affair located within a sanctuary of Zeus on the Hill of the Nymphs, southwest of the Agora; Harrison (2002) locates it at a road-intersection a little way north of this, and associates with it a set of

three-figure reliefs representing the overcoming of death. Representations of the four-column structure have been much discussed: see e.g. van Straten 1995, 88–9 for a summary of the debate; Carabatea 1997 adds a previously unrecognized example. Riethmüller (1999) suggests that Herakles' shrine is a *bothros* for heroic ritual, but Verbanck-Piérard's objections (2000) seem to be insuperable. Ephebic Oath: *SEG* 21.519; Rhodes-Osborne 2003, 440–8 no.88. Herakles Menytes: van Straten 1981, 106 and 1995, 87.

8 On bull-raising, see van Straten 1995, 109–13. Scenes of Herakles sacrificing: e.g. van Straten 1995, figs 38–40, 124, 134–5. Scenes of Herakles banqueting: Wolf 1993, 12–21 pls 5–37.

9 On the political significance of the *nothoi* of Kynosarges, see Patterson 1990, 63–5 and Humphreys 1974. Billot reviews the evidence for the sanctuary's location (1992) and for activities there (1993).

10 Holocaust interpretation: Van Straten 1995, 158 fig. 168; *contra* Ekroth 2002, 289–90.

11 Inscriptions from Marathon: *SEG* 28.25 and *IG* I³ 3; see Vanderpool 1984 and Matthaiou 2003. Rhamnous relief: Petrakos 2000, fig. 189. The calendars are discussed in detail in Ekroth 2002: Marathonian Tetrapolis = *LSCG* 20; Erchia = *LSCG* 18; Thorikos = *IG* I³ 256 bis (translated in Price 1999, 172–3). Decree of the Salaminioi: *LSS* 19; Rhodes-Osborne 2003, 182–92 no. 37; Parker 1996, 308–16.

12 Aspects of the Peloponnesian cult are discussed by Jourdain-Annequin 1998a, 348–51 (Sparta), Piérart 1992 and Jost 1992.

13 Schachter (1979 and 1986, 1–37) surveys the evidence for Herakles' cult in Boiotia. On Thebes, see also Demand 1982, 49–52, and for the coins Kraay and Hirmer 1966, nos 450–5; on the shield, see Boardman 2002, 83 and 165 fig. 146. Connelly (2007, 40–1) considers the limited evidence for virgin priestesses.

14 Cole 1992, 106–7 and 2004, 100–4. See also Létoublon 1996 for discussion of the Thespiads story and its initiatory flavour.

15 On the excavations, see Béquignon 1937, 204–26 and Malkin 1994, 228. Interpretations: see Shapiro 1983, 15–17, and Finkelberg 1996 on possible reference to the festival in Sophokles' *Women of Trachis*.

16 Links between Herakles' cult on Oita and the springs at Thermopylai are discussed in Croon 1956, 210–17; cf. Croon 1952.

17 Inscriptions: Segre 1993, ED 149 pl. 44 (*LSCG* 177; Cole 1992, 107) and ED 140, pl. 37 (*LSCG* 151C). Coins: Kraay 1976, no. 940. Herakles' place in Koan cult is discussed by Sherwin-White 1978, 317–20. On transvestite elements in the wedding, see most recently Goff 2004, 119–20.

18 The story of Herakles' sacrifice at Lindos is told by Apollodoros (2.5.11), Konon (fr. 1), Lactantius (*Div. Inst.* 1.21.31–7), Philostratos (*Imagines* 2.24), and see below for Origen (p. 202): see Durand 1986, 145–73. Burkert (1970, 364–7) draws parallels with Athenian ritual. Dougherty (1993, 120–9) examines the Rhodian foundation story of Pindar, *Olympian* 7. Guilt may again lie

behind the strange offering made to Herakles at Melite in Athens and in Boiotia of an apple made into the rudimentary shape of an ox by the insertion of four twigs for legs and two for horns (Zenobios 5.22, Pollux 1.30). Higbie 2003 provides a useful commentary on the Lindian Chronicle (see especially on ll.23–36).

19 Thasos' archaeology is conveniently summarized in Grandjean and Salviat 2000: city gate (129–32 figs 85–7), sanctuary (142–5 figs 94–6), amphora stamp (fig. 132), coins (306–13 figs 271–83), Saliari relief (fig. 107). Coins: see also Kraay and Hirmer 1966, pl. 141 no. 439. Inscriptions: festival calendar = Salviat 1958; decree = Pouilloux 1954, no. 141 (translated in Zaidman and Pantel 1992, 76); sacred law = *IG* XII Suppl. 414, *LSS* 63; garden lease = *IG* XII Suppl. 353. Discussions of the archaeology and epigraphy: Launey 1944, Pouilloux 1954, 352–79 and 1974; Bergquist 1973, 1998 and 2005; Bonnet 1988, 346–71; des Courtils and Pariente 1988 and 1996; Ekroth 2000, 220–1. Iliadou (1998) includes Thasos in her study of Herakles in Makedonia.

20 The cult at Erythrai is discussed in detail by Graf 1985, 296–316. See Dowden (1992, 84–5) on the inexact use of the term 'Thracian' in a number of myths.

21 Sycretism of Herakles and Melqart has been the subject of extensive study by Bonnet (1988 and 2005) and Jourdain-Annequin (1989, 1992a and b); papers in Bernadini and Zucca 2005 focus on Herakles-Melqart in Sardinia. On Herakles and Sandan, see Goldman 1949.

22 Discussions of the cult on Sicily: Martin 1979, Giangiulio 1983, Bonnet 1988, 269–74. Jourdain-Annequin 1992c argues that the Agyrion ritual conserved traces of an ancient initiation rite; on ritual hair-cutting and hair-growing, see Leitao 2003. On Cicero's description of the Agrigento cult statue, see Stewart 2008, 127–31.

23 Fundamental works on the question of origins: Bayet 1926a (Greek); van Berchem 1959–60 (Phoenician); Toutain 1928 (Italic). Bayet was also responsible for the first major work on the Etruscan Hercle (1926b).

24 The most detailed account of Hercules' cult is still Wissowa 1912, 271–84; Dumézil (1970, 432–9) covers the Ara Maxima cult; Ritter 1995 surveys art connected with the cult; cult sites in Rome itself are discussed in the entries in Steinby ed. 1996, 11–26; Bradley 2005 surveys the evidence available for the cult in central Italy; Moitrieux 2003 is an exhaustive treatment of the cult in Gaul; see also Bonnet 1988, 294–312. The Hercules myths dealt with in Wiseman 2004 are all connected with cult: see 26–32 on myths surrounding the Ara Maxima, and 184 fig. 7 on Hercules Musarum. See above (chapter 2 n. 3) on the treatment of aetiologies for the Ara Maxima cult in Propertius 4.9. On the inscription from Artena, see Kajava 1997. Roymans 2009 explores the role of Hercules' cult in the construction of ethnic identity under Roman rule in a particular province.

7 POST-CLASSICAL VARIATIONS

1 Herakles' post-antique survival is placed in a broader context in Seznec's classic work of 1953.

2 Simon 1955 examines Hercules' place in Christian discourse from the Church Fathers to the twentieth century. Toynbee (1939, 465–76) lists twenty-four correspondances between Hercules and Christ; Pfister 1937 surveys analogies between Hercules' life and the Gospel stories. Tronzo (1986) discusses the Via Latina catacombs (Hesperides scene = fig. 52); all three scenes are illustrated in Grabar 1967, figs 35, 87, 229 and 251.

3 Whitman (1987, 104–21) discusses the place of Fulgentius and Boethius in the development of allegory; for detailed discussion of Boethius' use of mythical *exempla*, see O'Daly 1991, 178–235.

4 See Miller 1984 on Dante's use of Hercules.

5 Dulac 2002 examines Christine de Pizan's treatments of Hercules; Jung (1966, 105–25) surveys 'L'Hercule chrétien' in Renaissance French literature.

6 See Smarr 1977 on Boccaccio.

7 On Salutati, see Witt 1983, especially 213–19 on the *Labours*.

8 Thompson 1971 provides some facsimiles illustrations from the Houghton manuscript in his selective translation of de Bassi. Full details of Ercole I's wedding are provided by Licht 1996.

9 Nees 1991 provides a thorough analysis of the throne and its place in the development of Hercules' image.

10 See Friedländer and Rosenberg 1978 on Lucas Cranach. Utz 1971 examines the evidence for Rossi's Herculean fountain project.

11 Simons 2008 explores the homoerotic potential of the Renaissance Hercules.

12 Mommsen (1953) traces the re-emergence of the Choice story. On Prudentius, see Whitman 1987, 83–91.

13 In addition to Panofsky 1930, see Warner (1985, 88–126) on the influence of Athena's image on representation of the virtues.

14 On Dürer's parody, see Wind 1939.

15 Rosenthal 1993 argues that Rubens' pairing of the *Drunken Hercules* and *The Hero Crowned by Victory* is a variation on the Vice or Virtue theme.

16 Evidence for the snowman is cited by Brown 1991, 95 and n.11; for detailed discussion of the Florentine Hercules, see Ettlinger 1972.

17 The Saint Mark's reliefs are discussed in Brown 1991, 516–17 figs 5–6.

18 Jung (1966, 30–7) reconstructs the performance at the Burgundian court. See Rosenthal 1973 on the origins and meaning of Charles V's Herculean device.

19 Polleross 1998 discusses the phenomenon of identification with Hercules in ruler-portraiture of the Renaissance and later.

20 King 2005 provides a lively account of Rudbeck's search for Atlantis (see 149–51 on Hercules).

21 The triumphal entries of François I and Henri II are discussed in Huon 1955 and Saulnier 1955. Trousseau 1962 provides an overview of Ronsard's use of Hercules; Hallowell 1962 looks specifically at his engagement with the Gallic Hercules. Jung 1966 situates sixteenth-century French literary treatments of Hercules in the context of earlier literature and the hero's contemporary political significance.

22 Vivanti 1967 reviews Henri IV's Herculean imagery; Bardon 1974 looks more broadly at political use of classical mythology under Henri IV and Louis XIII.

23 On the French revolutionary Hercules, see Hunt 1983; Aghulon 1981 outlines the development of the Marianne figure; see also de Baecque 1997, 310–14.

24 Details of performances of the relevant plays are gathered by the *Archive of Performances of Greek and Roman Drama* (http://www.apgrd.ox.ac.uk/). Poduska (1999, 199 and 225–6) lists musical treatments of Herculean themes.

25 E. R. OKell's discussion, 'Sophocles' Trachiniae, Martin Crimp's Cruel and Tender and Handel's Hercules' is available at http://www.classicalassociation.org/Audio/226-end.html.

26 Riley 2004 is an early version of the discussion of the Macleish and Armstrong plays included in her thought-provoking 2008 monograph.

27 See Waith 1962 on the 'Herculean hero' in seventeenth-century English drama.

28 See Rutter 1997 for a detailed account of Harrison's play at Delphi.

29 Schultz 1999 discusses the novel's exploration of the relationship between masculinity and Christian virtue.

30 I owe the title of this section to Blanshard and Shahabudin 2003, a brief account of the Hercules phenomenon. Solomon 2001 provides a useful overview of Hercules on film from 1909 to 1998; see especially 103–31 and 307–23.

31 Wyke 1997 discusses *Hercules'* place in the development of the cinematic strongman figure, with useful observations especially on the classicizing rhetoric of early body-building and of 1950s homoerotic photography.

32 Clauss 2008 notes parallels between the mythological figures of Hercules, Ulysses and Oedipus (who makes a brief appearance in the film) and offers a reading of *Hercules Unchained* as an articulation of the universal themes of death, rebirth and homecoming.

33 Shahabudin 2009 discusses the relationship of *Hercules Conquers Atlantis* to the *peplum* genre, ably demonstrating the potential of such films as social-historical documents. Both *Atlantis* and another Reg Park film of the same year, *Hercules at the Centre of the Earth* (directed by Mario Bava), are singled out for discussion by Winkler (2007, 466–9 and 472–3) in his short survey of 'Greek myth on the screen', and by Pomeroy (2008, 49–58) in a chapter on the *peplum*. A good deal of information on the Hercules films can be found at 'The Many Face of Hercules' site (http://www.briansdriveintheater.com/hercules.html).

34 The Lou Ferrigno films have an informative fan-site (http://bugaev.tripod.com/index.html).

35 Full details of the *Legendary Journeys* series can be found on the Xena fan site *Whoosh!* (http://www.whoosh.org/epguide/herk/herk.html), including a synopsis and transcript for each episode of the six TV seasons.

36 For the statistics, see http://boxofficemojo.com/. Lindner 2008 provides an overview of Greek myth in children's animation films, noting at least five in the 1990s apart from Disney on the subject of Hercules.

37 Maguire 2008 is the exhibition catalogue, with useful essays by Elizabeth Rankin and Patrick O'Sullivan; see also http://www.papergraphica.co.nz/ for information on the artist and the tour.

38 See the interview at http://pitchfork.com/features/interviews/7133-hercules-love-affair/.

GLOSSARY

aetiology Properly 'the study of causes'. In the context of classical religion, an 'aetiological myth' is one which offers an explanation from the past for a historical ritual practice.

agora 'Market-place'. Used today especially of the Athenian Agora, but every Greek city had one.

akropolis The 'upper city' or 'citadel', usually fortified. Today especially associated with the Athenian Akropolis, but again common to all Greek cities.

amphora Narrow-necked vessel for storing and transporting wine or oil; some types have a pair of handles on the neck or belly. 'Tyrrhenian' amphoras were made specifically for export to Etruria.

Apulian Used of Greek vases made in the region of Apulia in south-east Italy, in the red-figure technique, c.420–300 BC.

archaic Applied to the period c.750–500 BC, sometimes thought of as beginning in 776 BC, the traditional foundation date of the Olympic Games, and often extended to include the Persian Wars of 490–479 BC. A certain formality and stylization is associated with art of the period.

aretê 'Virtue' or 'excellence', encompassing moral, physical and intellectual qualities. The Latin equivalent is *virtus*.

aryballos Small vessel for precious oils, used especially by men at the gymnasium.

Attic Used of vases made at Athens. 'Protoattic' is used of the pottery produced in the seventh century BC, Attic black-figure mostly dates from c.600–500 BC, and Attic red-figure from c.520–400 BC.

Caeretan Used of vases made at Caere in Etruria using the black-figure technique, probably by Greek craftsmen, c.600–500 BC.

Chalkidian Used of vases made at the Greek (Euboian) colony of Chalkis in southern Italy, using the black-figure technique, c.600–500 BC.

classical Though often used more loosely of antiquity in general, properly speaking the classical period consists of the fifth and fourth centuries BC, and is often defined as running from the end of the Persian Wars (479 BC) to the death of Alexander the Great (323 BC).

Corinthian Used of vases made at Corinth c.620–550 BC. 'Protocorinthian' is used of the pottery produced in the region c.720–620 BC.

deme Small community, village – basic unit of e.g. the Athenian political system.

dinos A type of wine-mixing bowl with a round base, requiring a stand.

enagizein To 'devote' or 'consecrate' an animal to a god or hero, usually by burning it whole.

ephebe Young man of around 18–20, an age-group regarded as on the brink of adulthood. Many cities had mandatory military service and specific religious rituals for ephebes.

frieze On a temple or treasury, the frieze usually runs along the top of the columns around the building's exterior. In the Doric architectural order the frieze consists of **metopes** (see below) interspersed with triglyphs (blocks carved with a | | | pattern), while the Ionic frieze is a continuous strip often decorated with relief sculpture. The term is also used to indicate a strip of decoration on a painted vase.

genos (pl. *gene*) 'Clan', or small kinship group, often involving aristocratic families and acting together in political and ritual matters.

Geometric Term applied to pottery of the ninth and eighth centuries BC because of the geometric patterning of its decoration; also used of the period c.900–700 BC. 'Protogeometric' is used of the pottery of the preceding two centuries.

hellenistic The period from the death of Alexander the Great (323 BC) to the Battle of Actium (31 BC). Earlier end-dates sometimes used are 86 BC (fall of Athens to the Romans under Sulla) or 146 BC (sack of Corinth by the Romans under Mummius).

hoplite Greek *hoplites*, from *hoplon*, a type of large shield: heavily armed infantry-man.

hydria Narrow-necked vessel for fetching and serving water, with a pair of horizontal handles either side of the belly (for lifting) and a third vertical handle on the neck (for pouring).

krater Bowl for mixing wine and water (Greeks generally drank a mixture of about 2 parts wine to 5 parts water). A wide variety of types are further qualified according to the shape of their body (bell krater) or handles (calyx and volute kraters).

Lakonian Used of vases made at Sparta, in the black-figure technique, c.600–500 BC.

lekythos Small vessel with long narrow neck for valuable liquids like perfumed oil. 'White-ground' lekythoi, decorated with a variety of colours on a white slip, were especially used as grave-goods.

Lucanian Used of Greek vases made in the region of Lucania in south-west Italy, in the red-figure technique, c.430–300 BC.

metope More or less square slab in a Doric **frieze** (above), often decorated with relief sculpture.

***nothos* (pl. *nothoi*)** 'Bastard', used at Athens of someone whose parents were not both of Athenian citizen status.

oinochoe A jug for pouring wine.

Paestan Used of vases made at the Greek colony of Paestum in south-west Italy, in the red-figure technique, c.360–300 BC.

pankration Literally 'all strength', an athletic contest combining boxing and wrestling, with no holds barred.

pediment The triangular space formed by the gable-ends of a temple or treasury, often decorated with figures sculpted in relief or in the round.

pelike Vessel for storing and serving wine with two vertical handles, similar to an amphora but with a wider neck and low-bulging belly.

phiale (pl. *phialai*) Shallow dish, used in the pouring of libations and often depicted in the hands of a god.

pithos A type of large storage jar, usually set into the ground, and used especially for wine.

pyxis Small clay container with a lid, used especially by women for jewellery and cosmetics.

skyphos Deep cup with two handles, for drinking wine.

stamnos Vessel for storing and serving wine with two horizontal handles, with a short wide neck and sometimes with a lid.

tetradrachm A silver coin equivalent to four drachmas.

thuein To 'fumigate', i.e. to sacrifice an animal to a god or hero, the slaughter usually being followed by a communal feast.

FURTHER READING

The works listed here have been selected as providing accessible avenues for further study. Although they have often informed my argument, I have not referred to them in the notes to each chapter, but acknowledge my debt to them here. Works which do appear in the notes may prove useful if you want to follow up a particular point, but they are often quite specialized, and may be in languages other than English.

GENERAL

Galinsky 1972, although showing its age a little, is the one book which covers the full spectrum of Herakles' incarnations in classical and post-classical literature, and is well worth reading for its attempt to follow Herakles through the ages, although questions of art and cult practice are beyond its scope. More recently, Blanshard 2005 provides a stimulating 'biography' of the hero, discussing a selection of ancient and post-classical representations of each episode of the myth. Recent scholarship on a variety of Heraklean topics is represented by the papers in Rawlings (ed.) 2005, which arises out of a conference held in Cardiff in 1997; topics include Herakles/Hercules in Greek and Roman historiography, tragedy, cult and political propaganda (individual papers are listed separately in our bibliography). Olalla 2002, 146–64 provides a more detailed geographical guide to Herakles' myth than has been possible in this volume.

INTRODUCING HERAKLES

Burkert 1979 usefully summarizes the evidence for Herakles' origins, discussing parallels in Indo-European mythology for various aspects of his character. On the influence of the Near East on Herakles' myth, West 1997, 458–72 is essential reading. Both Dowden 1992 and Graf 1993 provide useful introductions to the mythological theories and to the ways in which myth functioned within Greek society; Woodard (ed.) 2007 provides an up-to-date overview of myth in Greek literature and art, and modern reinterpretations. Buxton 1994 likewise considers the theories, but is primarily concerned with locating myth firmly within Greek culture – the contexts in which the stories were told, the relationship between myth and day-to-day reality, and the functions of storytelling. A more substantial introduction to the theories which have been, and continue to be, applied to Greek myths can be found in Csapo 2005, with chapters on comparative approaches, psychology, ritual theories, structuralism, and cultural ideology. For more extensive case-studies exemplifying various approaches, see Bremmer (ed.) 1987 and Edmunds (ed.) 1990.

Translations of ancient texts

The two surviving systematic accounts of Herakles' story are essential reading. There is a very convenient Oxford World's Classics translation of Apollodoros, with helpful introduction and notes: R. Hard (tr. 1997) *Apollodorus: The Library of Greek Mythology*, Oxford (see 69–92 on Herakles). Diodoros Book 4 is less well served in English (though there are recent French and German translations/commentaries), but can be found in the Loeb series: C.H. Oldfather (tr.) *Diodorus of Sicily* vol. 2 (Cambridge MA 1935).

CHAPTERS 1–5: HERAKLES IN ANCIENT LITERATURE AND ART

Since no other work organizes material in quite the same way as this volume, it is convenient to group the following references into paragraphs which cut across my chapter divisions.

The obvious place to start is Brommer 1986, a usefully straightforward account of the twelve labours in ancient art and literature, with the emphasis on the visual sources. There is discussion of the 'canon' of twelve labours (55–64), and some Etruscan material is included. There is a sequel covering the other exploits (Brommer 1984), but this is only available in German. Both the labours and other aspects of Herakles' career are covered in Carpenter 1991, a survey of mythology as depicted in Greek art which includes a whole chapter (117–59) on Herakles; the text is straightforward, and there are no fewer than sixty-eight illustrations of Herakles, all with helpful captions. Etruscan myth is similarly served by Grummond 2006, with a section on Hercle (180–8), and see the index, *s.v.* 'Hercle'. For further consideration of how different media present stories about Herakles, Shapiro 1994 is well worth reading, and includes some particularly relevant case studies: Stesichoros' *Geryoneis* and related images (71–7 figs 46–51), Pindar's *Nemean* 1 and images of the infant Herakles (105–9 figs 73–5), Sophokles' *Trachiniae* and images of Herakles' encounter with Nessos (155–60 figs 110–14). A lively and extensively illustrated introduction to the problems involved in representing Greek mythological narrative in visual form is provided by Woodford 2003; images of Herakles appear throughout, but see especially 23–7 on story cycles, 28–39 on 'choosing a moment', 143–7 on politics, 176–85 and 199–214 on problems of identification. Excellent introductions to the social-historical significance of Greek art are provided by Osborne 1998, for the archaic and classical periods, and Pollitt 1986, for the Hellenistic period; both include a good range of Herakles images (see the index, *s.v.* 'Herakles').

Herakles' appearance in the art specifically of the archaic period is discussed in two works by Karl Schefold, both with plentiful high quality illustrations. The 1966 volume is not arranged by mythological character, but includes the earliest known representations of Herakles' labours and other exploits (see the index, *s.v.* 'Heracles'). In the 1992 volume, on the later archaic period, material is conveniently gathered by theme: Herakles' arrival on Olympos (33–46 figs 31–47), the labours and other exploits (95–158 figs 105–94), and the Nessos encounter (158–61 figs 196–8). Schefold 1988 covers the classical and hellenistic periods (128–229 figs 155–281 on Herakles), although this is only available in German. In English quite thorough coverage of the period 450–300 BC, with over one hundred illustrations, is provided by Vollkommer 1988, although the catalogue format is a little off-putting. Another volume in the same series, Pipili 1987, catalogues appearances of gods and heroes in archaic Spartan art: see 1–13 nos 1–23 on Herakles.

The Duckworth Companions to Greek and Roman Tragedy series includes volumes on Sophokles' *Women of Trachis* (Levett 2004) and *Philoktetes* (Roisman 2005, see especially 106–11 on Herakles), and Euripides' *Herakles* (Griffiths 2006a). These provide a convenient introduction to each play's themes and original performance context, as well as considering its reception and offering guidance on further reading.

For detailed study of the myth's development over time, Gantz 1993 is invaluable. This carefully lays out exactly what the early literary sources say (including difficult and fragmentary texts, all paraphrased), and when individual elements of the story first appear in the visual arts. The chapter on Herakles is substantial (374–466), going into a great deal more detail than has been possible in this volume, systematically working through each element of the hero's story. The one drawback is the absence of illustrations (the focus is on the literature), but this is highly recommended for anyone seriously interested in the ancient sources. Fowler's forthcoming commentary on the fragments of early Greek mythography likewise devotes a substantial chapter to Herakles, helpfully placing the relevant fragments in the context of each episode's development.

On the visual material, the ultimate reference work is the *Lexicon Iconographicum Mythologiae Classicae*, in which the entry on 'Herakles' spans two volumes (Boardman et al. 1988 and 1990). *LIMC* is generally confined to university libraries, and is not for the faint-hearted, but it is the most comprehensive catalogue available of visual representations of Herakles in Greek and Roman art, with excellent b/w photographs in separate volumes. It is organized by iconographic subject, so, for example, you will find all images of Herakles' childhood grouped together. There is a useful introduction to the sources and an overview of the development of Herakles' iconography, while each catalogue entry has further bibliographic details on individual works.

Images

In addition to the works listed above, a convenient source of images is Thames and Hudson's extensively illustrated World of Art series – in each case images can be easily located via the indices. The volumes on Greek sculpture are all by John Boardman: 1991 includes the Siphnian and Athenian Treasuries at Delphi; 1985 includes the temple of Zeus at Olympia, the Hephaistion at Athens; 1995, despite the title, includes the Heraion at Foce del Sele and the archaic temples of Selinous. Also by Boardman, the 1998a volume includes Geometric, Corinthian and other non-Athenian pottery of the archaic period, and on Attic vases see 1991 (especially 221–5), 1975 (especially 226–8) and 1989. In addition see Trendall 1989 on South Italian vases and Smith 1991 on hellenistic sculpture.

Translations of ancient texts

Of the many versions of Homer's epics available, I particularly like the verse translations by R. Lattimore, which have the advantage of more or less maintaining the line-numbering of the originals: *The Iliad of Homer* (Chicago and London 1951), *The Odyssey of Homer* (New York 1967). Some find prose translations more accessible, however, and there are some relatively recent ones available which have useful introductions and notes: M. Hammond (tr.), *The Iliad: a new prose translation* (Penguin Classics, 1987); M. Hammond (tr.), *The Odyssey* (London 2000). A very accessible translation of Hesiod's *Theogony*, with helpful introduction and notes is:

A.N. Athanassakis (tr.) *Hesiod: Theogony, Works and Days, Shield* (2nd ed. Baltimore 2004). The fragmentary works traditionally attributed to Hesiod have recently been made accessible in a Loeb volume, with Greek text and facing translation: G.W. Most (tr.), *Hesiod vol. II: The Shield, Catalogue of Women, other fragments* (Cambridge MA 2008). A useful volume in the Oxford World's Classics series is M.L. West (tr.) *The Greek Lyric Poets* (Oxford 1993). This gathers together and translates all the more comprehensible fragments of archaic lyric poetry, with helpful notes on the poets and on the individual poems.

For Bakchylides and Pindar the best translations available are in the Loeb series: see D.A. Cambell (tr.) *Greek Lyric* vol. 4 (Cambridge MA 1991) for Bakchylides; for Pindar, see W.H. Race (tr.), *Olympian Odes, Pythian Odes*, and *Nemean Odes, Isthmian Odes, Fragments* (Cambridge MA 1997). Sophocles' *Women of Trachis* is included in the Penguin Classics, D. Raeburn (tr.) *Sophocles: Electra and Other Plays* (London 2008); Euripides' *Alkestis, Madness of Herakles* and *Children of Herakles* are conveniently grouped together in the Oxford World's Classics, R. Waterfield (tr.) *Euripides: Heracles and Other Plays* (Oxford 2003), with a useful introduction and notes. Euripides' fragmentary tragedies and satyr plays have recently been made accessible in two Loeb volumes, C. Collard and M. Cropp (tr.) *Euripides vol. VII: Fragments: Aegeus-Meleager* and *Euripides vol. VIII: Fragments: Oedipus-Chrysippus* (Cambridge MA 2008). Aristophanes' plays are covered by three Penguin Classics volumes: A. Sommerstein (tr., revised ed.) *Aristophanes: Lysistrata and Other Plays* (London 2003), A. Sommerstein and D. Barrett (tr., revised ed.) *Aristophanes: Birds and Other Plays* (London 2003), D. Barrett (tr., revised by S. Dutta) *Aristophanes: Wasps and Other Plays* (London 2007).

A good verse translation of Apollonios' epic, with useful supporting material, is provided by P. Green (tr., revised ed.) *The Argonautika: the story of Jason and the quest for the golden fleece* (Berkeley, 2008). A. Verity (tr.) *Theocritus: Idylls* (Oxford 2003) has the usual Oxford World's Classics introduction and notes.

Ovid is well served by Penguin Classics, including D. Raeburn's *Ovid: Metamorphoses* (London 2004). Seneca's tragedies are more difficult to find, but both *Hercules Furens* and *Hercules Oetaeus* are included in D.R. Slavitt, *Seneca: the tragedies* vol. 2 (Baltimore 1995).

CHAPTER 6: WORSHIP OF THE HERO-GOD

For the last twenty-five years or so the standard reference work on Greek religious practice has been Burkert 1985; see Chapter 4 (190–215) for a basic account of the distinction between Olympian and chthonic cult in general, and on figures like Herakles who cross the boundary, but be aware that there remains much debate in this area. More recent introductions to Greek religion are Mikalson 2004, in which Herakles makes several appearances, and the excellent Larson 2007, which includes an overview of Herakles' cult (183–7) and a section on other 'anomalous immortals' (187–95); Kearns 2010 discusses a number of relevant passages (see the index, s.v. 'Herakles'). A much more detailed account of the archaeological and literary evidence for the worship of Herakles specifically in Athens and Attika is provided by Woodford 1974.

Beard, North and Price 1998 is the standard modern work on Roman religious practice, with discussion in vol.1 and annotated, translated texts in vol. 2, including a number concerning Hercules (see the index to each volume, s.v. 'Hercules'). The fullest modern account of the Roman cult of Hercules in the imperial period, with details on the colleges and provincial cults, is Jaczynowska 1981 (in French).

Translated ancient text

Although information about ritual practices comes from a wide variety of sources, the single most important text is Pausanias' lengthy description of Greece, which runs to two 500-page volumes in the Penguin Classics series, translated by P. Levi (1972) as *Pausanias: Guide to Greece*, Harmondsworth. The sheer wealth of information can be a little overwhelming, but there is a detailed index to aid navigation.

CHAPTER 7: POST-CLASSICAL VARIATIONS

Galinksy 1972 (185–304) provides an extensive account of Herakles in post-classical literature, and Blanshard 2005 includes a good deal of post-classical material. More briefly, there are useful entries *s.v.* 'Hercules' in Grafton et al. (eds) 2010 (426–9), and on Renaissance and other art in Bull 2005 (86–140), Impelluso 2002 (106–22), Brumble 1998 (154–66) and Reid 1993 (515–61). Riley 2008 provides a thorough assessment of the changing fortunes of Euripides' tragedy *Herakles* from its reception in antiquity through to modern performances. A lively introduction to Hercules' place in the limited repertoire of ancient Greek-themed films can be found in Nisbet 2008 (especially 45–66).

WORKS CITED

Aghulon, M. (1981) *Marianne into Battle: Republican imagery and symbolism in France 1789–1880*, Cambridge.

Ahlberg-Cornell, G. (1984) *Herakles and the Sea-Monster in Attic Black-Figured Vase Painting*, Stockholm.

Allan, W. (2001) *Euripides: the Children of Heracles*, Warminster.

Alonso, F. Wulff (1996) 'L'histoire d'Omphalè et d'Héraklès', in Jourdain-Annequin and Bonnet (eds), 103–20.

Amyx, D. and Amandry, P. (1982) 'Héraclès et l'Hydre de Lerne dans la céramique corinthienne', *Antike Kunst* 25: 102–16.

Anderson, W.S. (1964) 'Hercules exclusus: Propertius 4.9', *American Journal of Philology* 85: 1–12.

Andreae, B. (1962) 'Herakles und Alkyoneus', *Jahrbuch des Deutschen Archäologischen Instituts* 77: 130–210.

Andronikos, M. (1987) *Vergina: The Royal Tombs and the Ancient City*, Athens.

Armitage, S. (2000) *Mister Heracles*, London.

Ashmole, B. and Yalouris, N. (1967) *Olympia: the sculptures of the Temple of Zeus*, London.

Bader, F. (1985) 'De la préhistoire à l'idéologie tripartie: les Travaux d'Héraklès', in Bloch, R. (ed.) *D'Héraklès à Poseidon: mythologie et protohistoire*, Geneva, 9–124.

Bader, F. (1992) 'Les travaux d'Héraklès et l'idéologie tripartie', in Bonnet and Jourdain-Annequin (eds), 7–42.

Bader, F. (1996) 'Héraklès, Ogmios et les Sirènes', in Jourdain-Annequin and Bonnet (eds), 145–85.

Baecque, A. de (1997) *The Body Politic: corporeal metaphor in revolutionary France*, Stanford, CA.

Bardon, F. (1974) *Le portrait mythologique à la cour de France sous Henri IV et Louis XIII: mythologie et politique*, Paris.

Barrett, W.S. (2007) 'Stesichoros and the story of Geryon' and 'Stesichoros, *Geryoneis*, *SLG* 11', in Barrett, W.S. (ed. West, M.L.) *Greek Lyric, Tragedy and Textual Criticism: collected papers*, Oxford, 1–24 and 25–37.

Barringer, J.M. (2005) 'The temple of Zeus at Olympia, heroes, and athletes', *Hesperia* 74: 211–41.

Barringer, J.M. (2008) *Art, Myth and Ritual in Classical Greece*, Cambridge.

Bartman, E. (1986) 'Lysippos' huge god in small shape', *Bulletin of the Cleveland Museum of Art* 73: 298–311.

Bauchhenss-Thüriedl, C. (1971) *Der Mythos von Telephos in der antiken Bildkunst*, Würzburg.

Baurain, C. (1992) 'Héraclès dans l'épopée homérique, in Bonnet and Jourdain-Annequin (eds), 67–09.

Bayet, J. (1926a) *Les Origines de l'Hercule Romain*, Paris.

Bayet, J. (1926b) *Herclé: etude critique des principaux monuments relatives à l'Hercule étrusque*, Paris.

Beard, M., North, J. and Price, S. (1998) *Religions of Rome*, 2 vols, Cambridge.

Béquignon, Y. (1937) *La vallée du Spercheios*, Paris.

Berchem, D. van (1959–60) 'Hercule Melqart à l'Ara Maxima', *Rendiconti della Pontificia Accademia romana di archeologia* 32: 61–8.

Berchem, D. van (1967) 'Sanctuaires d'Hercule-Melqart: contribution à létude de lexpansion phénicienne en méditerranée', *Syria* 44: 73–109, 307–38.

Bergquist, B. (1973) *Herakles on Thasos*, Stockholm.

Bergquist, B. (1998) 'Feasting of worshippers or temple and sacrifice? The case of Herakleion on Thasos', in Hägg, R. (ed.) *Ancient Greek Cult-Practice from the Archaeological Evidence*, Stockholm, 57–72.

Bergquist, B. (2005) 'A restudy of two Thasian instances of *enateuein*', in Hägg and Alroth (eds), 61–70.

Bernardini, P. and Zucca, R. (eds) (2005) *Il Mediterrane di Herakles: studi e ricerche*, Rome.

Billot, M.F. (1992) 'Le Cynosarges, Antiochos et les tanneurs. Questions de topographie', *Bulletin de Correspondance Héllenique* 116: 119–56.

Billot, M.F. (1993) 'Antisthène et le Cynosarges dans l'Athènes des Vᵉ et IVᵉ siècles', in Goulet-Cazé, M.-O., and Goulet, R. (eds) *Le Cynisme ancien et ses prolongements*, Paris, 69–116.

Binder, G. (1974) 'Hercules und Claudius', *Rheinisches Museum* 117: 288–317.

Blanshard, A. (2005) *Hercules: a heroic life*, London.

Blanshard, A. and Shahabudin, K. (2003) 'Hercules – the movie star', *Omnibus* 45: 4–6.

Boardman, J. (1972) 'Herakles, Peisistratos and sons', *Revue archéologique*, 57–72.

Boardman, J. (1975a) *Athenian Red Figure Vases: the archaic period*, London.

Boardman, J. (1975b) 'Herakles, Peisistratos and Eleusis', *Journal of Hellenic Studies* 95: 1–12.

Boardman, J. (1978) 'Herakles, Delphi, and Kleisthenes of Sikyon', *Révue archeologique*, 227–34.

Boardman, J. (1982) 'Herakles, Theseus and Amazons', in Kurtz, D.C. and Sparkes, B. (eds) *The Eye of Greece: studies in the art of Athens*, Cambridge, 1–28.

Boardman, J. (1985) *Greek Sculpture: the classical period*, London.

Boardman, J. (1989a) *Athenian Red Figure Vases: the classical period*, London.

Boardman, J. (1989b) 'Herakles, Peisistratos and the unconvinced', *Journal of Hellenic Studies* 109: 158–9.

Boardman, J. (1991a) *Greek Sculpture: the archaic period*, 2nd ed. London.

Boardman, J. (1991b) *Athenian Black Figure Vases*, 2nd ed. London.

Boardman, J. (1992) '"For you are the progeny of unconquered Herakles"', in Sanders, J.M. (ed.) *Philolakôn: Lakonian studies in honour of Hector Catling*, London, 25–9.

Boardman, J. (1995) *Greek Sculpture: the late classical period*, London.

Boardman, J. (1998a) *Early Greek Vase Painting*, London.

Boardman, J. (1998b) 'Herakles' monsters: indigenous or oriental?', in Bonnet, Jourdain-Annequin and Pirenne-Delforge (eds), 27–35.

Boardman, J. (2001) *The History of Greek Vases*, London.

Boardman, J. (2002) *The Archaeology of Nostalgia: how the Greeks re-created their mythical past*, London.

Boardman, J. et al. (1988) *s.v.* 'Herakles' in *LIMC* IV, 728–838 and (1990) *s.v.* 'Herakles' in *LIMC* V, 1–192.

Bolonyai, G. 'Das Gedicht des Aristoteles auf Areta an Hermias von Atarneus (*PMG* 842)', Acta *Antiqua Academiae Scientiarum Hungaricae* 44, (2004), 5–20.

Bonnet, C. (1988) *Melqart. Cultes et mythes de lHéraclès tyrien en Méditerranée*, Leuven-Namur.

Bonnet, C. (1992) 'Héraclès en orient: interprétations et syncrétismes', in Bonnet and Jourdain-Annequin (eds), 165–98.

Bonnet, C. (1996) 'Héraclès travesti', in Jourdain-Annequin and Bonnet (eds), 121–31.

Bonnet, C. (2005) 'Melqart in Occidente. Percorsi di approprizione e di acculturazione', in Bernadini and Zucca (eds), 17–28.

Bonnet, C. and Jourdain-Annequin, C. (eds) (1992) *Héraclès: d'une rive à lautre de la Méditerranée: bilan et perspectives*, Brussels and Rome.

Bonnet, C., Jourdain-Annequin, C. and Pirenne-Delforge, V. (eds) (1998) *Le Bestiaire d'Héraclès: IIIe Rencontre Héracléenne*, Liège.

Borg, B.E. (2002) *Der Logos des Mythos: Allegorien und Personifikationen in der frühen griechischen Kunst*, Munich.

Borza, E.N. (1990) *In the Shadow of Olympus: the emergence of Macedon*, Princeton, NJ.

Borza, E.N. (1995) 'Athenians, Macedonians, and the origins of the Macedonian royal house', in Thomas, C.G. (ed.) *Makedonika: essays by Eugene M. Borza*, Claremont, CA.

Bosworth, A.B. (1995) *A Historical Commentary on Arrian's History of Alexander*, Oxford.

Bosworth, A.B. (1996) *Alexander and the East: the tragedy of triumph*, Oxford.

Bothmer, D. von (1957) *Amazons in Greek Art*, Oxford.

Bothmer, D. von (1977) 'The struggle for the tripod', in Hockmann, Krug and Brommer (eds), 51–63.

Bowden, H. (2005) 'Herakles, Herodotus and the Persian Wars', in Rawlings (ed.), 1–14.

Bowie, A.M. (1993) *Aristophanes: myth, ritual and comedy*, Cambridge.

Bowie, A. (2000) 'Myth and ritual in the rivals of Aristophanes', in Harvey, D. and Wilkins, J. (eds) *The Rivals of Aristophanes: studies in Athenian Old Comedy*, London and Swansea, 317–39.

Bowra, C.M. 'Aristotle's hymn to virtue', *Classical Quarterly* 32 (1938), 182–9 [reprinted in Bowra, C.M. (1953) *Problems in Greek Poetry,* Oxford, 138–50].

Bradley, G. (2005) 'Aspects of the cult of Hercules in central Italy', in Rawlings (ed.),129–52.

Brelich, A. (1958) *Gli eroi greci: un problema storico-religioso,* Roma.

Bremmer, J. (1977) 'ΕΣ ΚΥΝΟΣΑΡΓΕΣ', *Mnemosyne* 30: 369–74.

Bremmer, J.N. (ed.) (1987) *Interpretations of Greek Mythology,* London and New York.

Bremmer, J.N. (2002) *The Rise and Fall of the Afterlife,* London and New York.

Bremmer, J.N. and Erskine, A. (eds) (2010) *The Gods of Ancient Greece: identities and transformations,* Edinburgh.

Brize, P. (1980) *Die Geroyneis des Stesichoros und die frühe griechische Kunst,* Würzburg.

Brize, P. (1985) 'Samos und Stesichoros zu einem Früarchaischen Bronzeblech', *Mitteilungen des Deutschen Archäologischen Instituts, Athenische Abteilung* 100: 53–90.

Brommer, F. (1944/5) 'Herakles und Syleus', *Jahrbuch des Deutschen Archäologischen Instituts* 59/60: 69–78.

Brommer, F. (1983) 'Herakles und Nereus', in Lissarrague and Thelamon (eds), Rouen, 103–10.

Brommer, F. (1984) *Herakles II: die unkanonischen Taten des Helden,* Darmstadt.

Brommer, F. (1985) 'Herakles und Theseus auf Vasen in Malibu', in *Greek Vases in the J. Paul Getty Museum* 2: 183–28.

Brommer, F. (1986) *Heracles: the twelve labours of the hero in ancient art and literature,* New York.

Brown, A. (1991) 'City and citizen: changing perceptions in the fifteenth and sixteenth centuries', in Molho, A., Raaflaub, K. and Emlen, J. (eds) *City States in Classical Antiquity and Medieval Italy: Athens and Rome, Florence and Venice,* Stuttgart, 93–111.

Brulé, P. (1996) 'Héraclès et Augé. À propos d'origines rituelles du mythe', in Jourdain-Annequin and Bonnet (eds), 35–50.

Brumble, H. D. (1988) *Classical Myths and Legends in the Middle Ages and Renaissance: a dictionary of allegorical meanings,* London.

Brundage, B.C. (1958) 'Herakles the Levantine: a comprehensive view', *Journal of Near Eastern Studies* 17: 225–36.

Brunt, P.A. (1975) 'Alexander, Barsine and Heracles', *Rivista di filologia e di istruzione classica* 103: 22–34.

Bull, M. (2005) *The Mirror of the Gods: classical mythology in Renaissance art,* London.

Burkert, W. (1970) 'Buzyge und Palladion: Gewalt und Gericht in altgriechischem Ritual', *Zeitschrift für Religions und Geistesgeschichte* 22: 356.

Burkert, W. (1972) 'Die Leistung eines Kreophylos: Kreophyleer, Homeriden und die archaische Heraklesepik', *Museum Helveticum* 29: 74–85.

Burkert, W. (1977) 'Le mythe de Géryon: perspectives préhistoriques et tradition rituelle', in Gentili and Paioni (eds), 273–84.

Burkert, W. (1979) 'Heracles and the Master of Animals', in *Structure and History in Greek Mythology and Ritual,* Berkeley, etc., 78–98.

Burkert, W. (1985) *Greek Religion: archaic and classical*, tr. Raffan, J., Oxford.

Burkert, W. (1987) 'Oriental and Greek mythology: the meeting of parallels', in Bremmer (ed.), 10–40.

Burkert, W. (1992a) *The Orientalizing Revolution: Near Eastern influence on Greek culture in the early archaic age*, Cambridge, MA.

Burkert, W. (1992b) 'Eracle e gli altri eroi culturali del Vicino Oriente', in Bonnet and Jourdain-Annequin (eds), 111–27.

Burkert, W. (1998) 'Héraclès et les animaux. Perspectives préhistoriques et pressions historiques', in Bonnet, Jourdain-Annequin and Pirenne-Delforge (eds), 11–26.

Burnett, A.P. (2005) *Pindar's Songs for Young Athletes of Aegina*, Oxford.

Burstein, S.M. (1976) *Outpost of Hellenism: the emergence of Heraclea on the Black Sea*, Berkeley, CA.

Burton, D.H. (1997) *The Search for Immortality in Archaic Greek Myth*, diss. London.

Buxton, R.G.A. (1985) 'Euripides' *Alcestis*: five aspects of an interpretation', *Dodone (Philologia)* 14: 75–89.

Buxton, R.G.A. (1988) 'Bafflement in Greek tragedy', *Metis* 3: 41–51.

Buxton, R.G.A. (1994) *Imaginary Greece: the contexts of Greek mythology*, Cambridge.

Cairns, D.L. (2010) *Bacchylides: Five Epinician Odes (3, 5, 9, 11, 13)*, Cambridge.

Cairns, F. (1992) 'Propertius 4.9: "Hercules exclusus" and the dimensions of the genre', in Galinsky, G.K. (ed.) *The Interpretation of Roman Poetry: empiricism or hermeneutics?*, Frankfurt, 65–95.

Calame, C. (2005) 'Heracles, animal and sacrificial victim in Sophocles' *Trachiniae*', in Hägg and Alroth (eds), 181–95 [= (1998) 'Héraclès, animal et victime sacrificielle dans les *Trachiniennes* de sophocle?', in Bonnet, Jourdain-Annequin and Pirenne-Delforge (eds), 197–216]

Caldwell, R. (1989) *The Origin of the Gods: a psychoanalytic study of Greek theogonic myth*, New York and Oxford.

Cameron, A. (2004) *Greek Mythography in the Roman World*, Oxford.

Campbell, M. (1990) 'Theocritus 13', in Craik, E.M. (ed.) *'Owls to Athens': essays on classical subjects presented to Sir Kenneth Dover*, Oxford, 113–19.

Carabatea, M. (1997) 'Herakles and a "man in need?"', in Palagia, O. (ed.) *Greek Offerings: essays on Greek art in honour of John Boardman*, Oxford.

Carandini, A., Ricci, A. and de Vos, M. (1982) *Filosofiana: the Villa of Piazza Armerina*, Palermo.

Carawan, E. (2000) 'Deianeira's guilt', *Transactions of the American Philological Association* 130: 189–237.

Carpenter, T.H. (1991) *Art and Myth in Ancient Greece*, London.

Carson, R.A.G. (1980) *Principal Coins of the Romans*, London.

Carson, R.A.G. (1990) *Coins of the Roman Empire*, London.

Carter, J. B. (1989) 'The Chests of Periander', *American Journal of Archaeology* 93: 355–78.

Cartledge, P. (2002) *Sparta and Lakonia: a regional history 1300 to 362 BC*, 2nd ed. London and New York.

Casson, L. (1995) *Ships and Seamanship in the Ancient World*, Baltimore and London.

Cavalier, K. (1995) 'Did not potters portray Peisistratos posthumously as Herakles?',

Electronic Antiquity 2.5 (http://scholar.lib.vt.edu/ejournals/ElAnt/V2N5/cavalier. html).

Champlin, E. (2003) *Nero*, Cambridge, MA.

Clauss, J.J. (2008) '*Hercules Unchained: contaminatio, nostos, katabasis*, and the surreal', *Arethusa* 41: 51–66.

Cohen, B. (1994) 'From bowman to clubman: Herakles and Olympia', *Art Bulletin* 76: 696–715.

Cohen, B. (1998) 'The Nemean Lion's skin in Athenian art', in Bonnet, Jourdain-Annequin and Pirenne-Delforge (eds), 127–40.

Cole, S.G. (1992) '*Gynaiki ou themis*: gender difference in the Greek *leges sacrae*', *Helios* 19: 104–22.

Cole, S.G. (2004) *Landscapes, Gender, and Ritual Space*, Berkeley, CA.

Coleman, K.M. (1990) 'Fatal charades: Roman executions staged as mythological enactments', *Journal of Roman Studies* 80: 44–73.

Conacher, D.J. (1988) *Euripides, Alcestis*, Warminster.

Connelly, J.B. (2007) *Portrait of a Priestess: women and ritual in ancient Greece*, Princeton, NJ.

Cook, R.M. (1987) 'Pots and Pisistratan propaganda', *Journal of Hellenic Studies* 107: 167–9.

Coralini, A. (2001) *Hercules domesticus: immagini di Ercole nelle case della regione vesuviana (I secolo a.C.-79. d.C)*, Naples.

Courtils, J. des, and Pariente, A. (1988) 'Excavations in the Heracles sanctuary at Thasos', in Hägg, R., Marinatos, N. and Nordquist, G.C. (eds) *Early Greek Cult Practice*, Stockholm, 121–3.

Courtils, J. des, Gardeisen, A., and Pariente, A. (1996) 'Sacrifices d'animaux à l'Hérakleion de Thasos', *Bulletin de Correspondance Héllenique* 120: 799–820.

Croon, J.H. (1952) *The Herdsman of the Dead: studies on some cults, myths and legends of the ancient Greek colonization area*, Utrecht.

Croon, J.H. (1953) 'Heracles at Lindos', *Mnemosyne* 6: 253–99.

Croon, J.H. (1956) 'Artemis Thermia and Apollo Thermios (with an excursus on the Oetaean Heracles-cult)', *Mnemosyne* 9: 193–220.

Crossett, J., 'Aristotle as a poet. The Hymn to Hermeias', *Philological Quarterly* 46 (1967), 145–55.

Csapo, E. (2005) *Theories of Mythology*, Oxford.

Currie, B. (2005) *Pindar and the Cult of Heroes*, Oxford.

Dahmen, K. (2007) *The Legend of Alexander the Great on Greek and Roman Coins*, London and New York.

Davidson, J. (2007) *The Greeks and Greek Love: a radical reappraisal of homosexuality in ancient Greece*, London.

Davidson, O.M. (1980) 'The Indo-European dimension of Herakles in *Iliad* 19.95–133', *Arethusa* 13: 197–202.

Davies, G. (1978) 'The door motif in Roman funerary sculpture', in Mc K. Blake, H., Potter, T.W. and Whitehouse, D.B. (eds) *Papers in Italian Archaeology I* (*BAR Supplementary Series* 41), Oxford, 203–20.

Davies, M. (1988) 'Stesichorus' *Geryoneis* and its folktale origins', *Classical Quarterly* 38: 277–90.

Davies, M. (1989) *The Epic Cycle*, Bristol.

Davies, M. (1984) 'Lichas' lying tale: Sophocles, *Trachiniae* 260 ff', *Classical Quarterly* 34: 480–3.

Davies, M. (1991) *Sophocles: Trachiniae*, Oxford.

Deacy, S. (2005) 'Herakles and his "girl": Athena, heroism and beyond', in Rawlings (ed.), 37–50.

Deacy, S. (2008) *Athena*, London and New York.

Defradas, J. (1972) *Les thèmes de la propagande delphique*, 2nd ed. Paris.

Demand, N.H. (1982) *Thebes in the Fifth Century: Heracles resurgent*, London.

Détienne, M. (1960) 'Héraclès, héros pythagoricien', *Revue de l'histoire des religions* 158: 19–53.

Dillon, M. (1995) 'By gods, tongues, and dogs: the use of oaths in Aristophanic comedy', *Greece and Rome* 42: 135–51.

Dodd, D.B. and Faraone, C.A. (eds 2003) *Initiation in Ancient Greek rituals and narratives*, Oxford.

Doffey, M. C. (1992) 'Les mythes de fondation de concours néméens', in Piérart, M. (ed.) *Polydipsion Argos: Argos de la fin des palais mycéniens à la constitution de l'état classique* (*Bulletin de Correspondance Héllenique* Supplement 22), Paris, 185–93.

Dougherty, C. (1993) *The Poetics of Colonization*, Oxford.

Dowden, K. (1992) *Uses of Greek Mythology*, London and New York.

Dowden, K. (2005) *Zeus*, London and New York.

Dulac, L. (2002) 'Le chevalier Hercule de l'*Ovide moralisé* au *Livre de la mutacion de fortune* de Christine de Pizan', *Cahiers de recherches médiévales et humanistes* 9 (http://crm.revues.org//index68.html).

Dumézil, G. (1970a) *The Destiny of the Warrior*, tr. Hiltebeitel, A., Chicago, IL.

Dumézil, G. (1970b) *Archaic Roman Religion*, Chicago and London.

Dunn, F.M. (1997) 'Ends and means in Euripides' *Heracles*', in Roberts, D.H., Dunn, F.M. and Fowler, D. (eds) *Classical Closure: reading the end in Greek and Latin literature*, Princeton, NJ, 83–111.

Dupont, F. (1989) 'Apothéose et héroïsation dans Hercule sur l'Oeta de Sénèque' in Laurens (ed.), 99–106.

Durand, J.-L. (1986) *Sacrifice et labour en Grèce ancienne*, Paris and Rome.

Durand, J.L. and Lissarrague, F. (1983) 'Héros cru ou hôte cuit: histoire quasi cannibale d'Héraclès chez Busiris', in Lissarrague and Thelamon (eds), Rouen, 153–67.

Easterling, P.E. (1982) *Sophocles Trachiniae*, Cambridge.

Easterling, P.E. (2007) 'Looking for Omphale', in Jennings, V. and Katsaros, A. (eds) *The World of Ion of Chios*, Leiden, 282–92.

Eden, P.T. (ed.) (1984) *Seneca: Apocolocyntosis*, Cambridge.

Edmonds, R.G. (2003) 'Who in Hell is Heracles? Dionysus' disastrous disguise in the *Frogs*', in Dodd and Faraone (eds), 181–200.

Edmonds, R.G. (2004) *Myths of the Underworld Journey: Plato, Aristophanes, and the 'Orphic' gold tablets*, Cambridge.

Edmunds, L. (ed. 1990) *Approaches to Greek Mythology*, Baltimore and London.

Edwards, C.M. (1969) 'Lysippos', in Palagia, O. and Pollitt, J.J. (eds) *Personal Styles in Greek Sculpture* (Yale Classical Studies 30), Cambridge, 130–53.

Ekroth, G. (1999) 'Pausanias and the sacrificial rituals of Greek cult', in Hägg, R. (ed.) *Ancient Greek Hero Cult*, Stockholm, 145–58.

Ekroth, G. (2002) *The Sacrificial Rituals of Greek Hero-Cults* (= *Kernos* Suppl. 12), Liège.

Elsner, J. (2007) *Roman Eyes: visuality and subjectivity in art and text*, Princeton, NJ.

Erskine, A. (2001) *Troy Between Greece and Rome: local tradition and imperial power*, Oxford.

Essarts, E. des (1871) *Du type d'Hercule dans la literature grecque depuis les origins jusqu'au siècle des Antonins*, Paris.

Ettlinger, L.D. (1972) 'Hercules Florentinus', *Mitteilungen des Kunsthistorischen Instituts in Florenz* 16: 119–42.

Farnell, L.R. (1921) *Greek Hero Cults and Ideas of Immortality*, Oxford.

Faraone, C.A. (1994) 'Deianeira's mistake and the demise of Heracles: erotic magic in Sophocles' *Women of Trachis*', *Helios* 21: 115–35.

Finster-Hotz, U. (1984) *Der Bauschmuck des Athenatempels von Assos*, Rome.

Finkelberg, M. (1996), 'The second stasimon of the *Trachiniae* and Heracles' festival on Mount Oeta', *Mnemosyne* 49: 129–43.

Fisher, N.R.E. (1992) *Hybris: a study in the values of honour and shame in ancient Greece*, Warminster.

Fitch, J.G. (1987) *Seneca's Hercules Furens*, Ithaca.

Fittschen, K. (1969) *Untersuchungen zum Beginn der Sagendarstellungen bei den Griechen*, Berlin.

Fitzgerald, G.T. (1991) 'The Euripidean Heracles. An intellectual and a coward', *Mnemosyne* 44: 85–95.

Flacelière, R. and Devambez, P. (1966) *Héraclès: images et récits*, Paris.

Fontenrose, J. (1959) *Python: a study of Delphic myth and its origins*, Berkeley and Los Angeles, CA.

Fowler, R.L. (forthcoming) *Early Greek Mythography*, vol. 2, Oxford.

Frazer, J.G. (1898) *Pausanias's Description of Greece* (6 vols.), London.

Friedländer, M.J. and Rosenberg, J. (1978) *The Paintings of Lucas Cranach*, London.

Friedländer, P. (1907) *Herakles: Sagengeschichtliche Untersuchungen*, Berlin.

Friedländer, P. (1914) 'Kritische Untersuchungen zur Geschichte der Heldensage', *Rheinisches Museum* 69: 299–341.

Gagé, J. (1981) 'La mystique impériale et l'épreuve des "jeux". Commode-Hercule et l' "anthropologie" héracléene', *Aufstieg und Niedergang der römischen Welt* II 17.2, 662–83.

Galinsky, G.K. (1966) 'The Hercules-Cacus episode in *Aeneid* VIII', *American Journal of Philology* 87: 18–51.

Galinsky, G.K. (1972) *The Herakles Theme: the adaptations of the hero in literature from Homer to the twentieth century*, Oxford.

Gantz, T. (1993) *Early Greek Myth: a guide to literary and artistic sources*, Baltimore, MD.

Gentili, B. and Paioni, G. (eds) *Il mito Greco: atti del convegno internazionale (Urbino 7–12 maggio 1973)*, Roma.

George, D.B. (1994) 'Euripides' *Heracles* 140–235: staging and the stage iconography of Heracles' bow', *Greek, Roman and Byzantine Studies* 35: 145–57.

Georgoudi, S. (1998) 'Héraclès dans les pratiques sacrificielles des cités', in Bonnet, etc. (eds), 301–17.

Giangiulio, M. (1983) 'Greci e non Greci in Sicilia alla luce dei culti e delle leggende di Eracle', in *Modes de contacts et processus de transformation dans les sociétés anciennes*, Pisa and Rome, 785–846.

Glynn, R. (1981) 'Herakles, Nereus and Triton: a study of iconography in sixth-century Athens', *American Journal of Archaeology* 85: 121–32.

Goff, B. (2004) *Citizen Bacchae: women's ritual practice in ancient Greece*, Berkeley, CA.

Golden, M. (1990), *Children and Childhood in Classical Athens*, Baltimore, MD.

Golden, M. (1998) *Sport and Society in Ancient Greece*, Cambridge.

Goldfarb, B.E. (1992) 'The conflict of obligations in Euripides' *Alcestis*', *Greek, Roman and Byzantine Studies* 33: 109–26.

Goldman, H. (1949) 'Sandon and Herakles', *Hesperia Supplement* 8: 164–74.

Grabar, A. (1967) *The Beginnings of Christian Art, 200–395*, London.

Graf, F. (1985) *Nordionische Kulte: religionsgeschichtliche und epigraphische Untersuchen zu den Kulten von Chios, Erythrai, Klazomenai und Phokaia*, Rome.

Graf, F. (1993) *Greek Mythology: an introduction*, tr. Marier, T., Baltimore, MD.

Graf, F. (2008), *Apollo*, London and New York.

Grafton, A., Most, G.W. and Settis, S. (eds) (2010) *The Classical Tradition*, Cambridge, MA.

Grandjean, Y. and Salviat, F. (2000) *Guide de Thasos*, 2nd ed. Paris.

Green, S.J. (2004) *Ovid Fasti I: a commentary*, Leiden.

Greengard, C. (1987) *Theatre in Crisis: Sophocles' reconstruction of genre and politics in Philoctetes*, Amsterdam.

Griffiths, E. (2002) 'Euripides' *Herakles* and the pursuit of immortality', *Mnemosyne* 55: 641–56.

Griffiths, E. (2006a) *Euripides: Herakles*, London.

Griffiths, E. (2006b) *Medea*, London.

Grummond, N.T. de (2006) *Etruscan Myth, Sacred History, and Legend*, Philadelphia, PA.

Gruppe, O. (1918) s.v. 'Herakles', in Paulys *Realencylopädie der Classischen Altertumswissenschaft*, Suppl. III, cols 910–1121.

Hägg, R. and Alroth, B. (eds) (2005) *Greek Sacrificial Ritual, Olympian and Chthonian*, Stockholm.

Hall, J.M. (2007) 'Politics and Greek myth', in Woodard, R.D. (ed.) *The Cambridge Companion to Greek Mythology*, Cambridge, 331–54.

Hallowell, R.E. (1962) 'Ronsard and the Gallic Hercules myth', *Studies in the Renaissance* 9: 242–55.

Hampe, R. (1936) *Frühe griechische Sagenbilder in Böotien*, Athens.

Hannah, R. (1986) 'The emperor's stars: the Conservatori portrait of Commodus', *American Journal of Archaeology* 90: 337–42.

Hannah, R. (1995) 'Peisistratos, the Peisistratids and the Introduction of Herakles to Olympos: an alternative scenario', *Electronic Antiquity* 3.2 (http://scholar.lib.vt.edu/ejournals/ElAnt/V3N2/hannah.html).

Hansen, H.M. and Nielsen, T.H. (eds) (2004) *An Inventory of Archaic and Classical Poleis*, Oxford.

Hard, R. (2004) *The Routledge Handbook of Greek Mythology*, London and New York.

Harder, A. (1985) *Euripides* Kresphontes *and* Archelaos (= *Mnemosyne* Suppl. 87), Leiden.

Harris, E.M. (1990) 'Did the Athenians regard seduction as a worse crime than rape?', *Classical Quarterly* 40: 370–7.

Harrison, E.B. (2002) 'The aged Pelias in the Erechtheion frieze and the meaning of the three-figure reliefs', in A.J. Clark and J. Gaunt (eds) *Essays in Honour of Dietrich von Bothmer*, Amsterdam, 137–46.

Harrison, J.E. (1912) *Themis: a study of the social origins of Greek religion*, Cambridge.

Harrison, T. (2000) *Divinity and History: the religion of Herodotus*, Oxford.

Harrison, T. (forthcoming) 'Herodotus, Heracles and Peisistratus: the invention of tyranny in Athens (Hdt 1.59–64), unpublished paper.

Hartigan, K. (1987) 'Euripidean madness: Herakles and Orestes', *Greece and Rome* 34: 26–35.

Haubold, J. (2005) 'Heracles in the Hesiodic *Catalogue of Women*', in Hunter (ed.), 85–98.

Hekster, O. (2001) 'Commodus-Hercules: the people's *princeps*', *Scripta Classica Israelica* 20: 51–83.

Hekster, O. (2005) 'Propagating power: Hercules as an example for second-century emperors', in Rawlings (ed.), 205–22.

Henige, D.P. (1974) *The Chronology of Oral Tradition: quest for a chimera*, Oxford.

Hermary, A. (1992) 'Quelques remarques sur les origines proche-orientales de l'iconographie d'Héraclès', in Bonnet and Jourdain-Annequin (eds), 129–43.

Higbie, C. (2003) *The Lindian Chronicle and the Greek Creation of Their Past*, Oxford.

Hockmann, U., Krug, A. and Brommer, F. (eds) (1977) *Festschrift für Frank Brommer*, Mainz.

Hoïstad, R. (1948) *Cynic Hero and Cynic King*, Uppsala.

Holt, P. (1989) 'The end of the *Trachiniae* and the fate of Herakles', *Journal of Hellenic Studies* 109: 69–80.

Holt, P. (1992) 'Herakles' apotheosis in lost Greek literature and art', *L'Antiquité classique* 61: 38–59.

Hornblower, S. (1992) 'The religious dimension to the Peloponnesian War, or, what Thucydides does not tell us', *Harvard Studies in Classical Philology* 94: 169–97.

Hornblower, S. and Morgan, C. (eds) (2007) *Pindar's Poetry, Patrons, and Festivals*, Oxford.

Howard, S. (1978) *The Lansdowne Herakles*, Malibu, CA.

Hughes, D.D. (1991) *Human Sacrifice in Ancient Greece*, London and New York.

Humphreys, S.C. (1974) 'The *nothoi* of Kynosarges', *Journal of Hellenic Studies* 94: 88–95.

Hunt, L. (1983) 'Hercules and the radical image of the French Revolution', *Representations* 2: 95–117.

Hunter, R. (ed.) (2005) *The Hesiodic Catalogue of Women*, Cambridge.

Huttner, U. (1997) *Die politische Rolle der Heraklesgestalt im griechischen Herrschertum* (*Historia Einzelschriften* 112), Stuttgart.

Huon, A. (1955) 'Le theme du prince dans les entrées parisiennes au XVIe siècle', in Jacquot (ed.), 21–30.

Huxley, G.L. (1969) *Greek Epic Poetry from Eumelos to Panyassis*, London.

Iliadou, P. (1998) *Herakles in Makedonien*, Hamburg.

Impelluso, L. (2003) *Gods and Heroes in Art*, Malibu, CA.

Jacobson, H. (1974) *Ovid's Heroides*, Princeton, NJ.

Jacquot, J. (ed.) (1955) *Les fêtes de la Renaissance*, vol. 1, Paris.

Jaczynowska, M. (1981) 'Le culte de l'Hercule romain au temps du Haut-Empire', *Aufstieg und Niedergang der römischen Welt* II 17.2, 631–61.

Jameson, M. (2005) 'The family of Herakles in Attica', in Rawlings (ed.), 15–36.

Janko, R. (1986) 'The *Shield of Heracles* and the Legend of Cycnus', *Classical Quarterly* 36: 38–59.

Jongste, P.F.B. (1992) *The Twelve Labours of Hercules on Roman Sarcophagi*, Rome.

Jost, M. (1992) 'Héraklès en Arcadie', in Bonnet and Jourdain-Annequin (eds), 245–61.

Jourdain-Annequin, C. (1986) 'Héraclès Parastatès', in *Les grandes figures religieuses*, Besançon and Paris, 283–31.

Jourdain-Annequin, C. (1989) *Héraclès aux portes du soir: mythe et histoire*, Paris.

Jourdain-Annequin, C. (1992a) *Héraclès-Melqart à Amrith: recherches iconographiques: contribution à l'étude d'un syncrétisme*, Paris.

Jourdain-Annequin, C. (1992b) 'Héraclès en Occident', in Bonnet and Jourdain-Annequin (eds), 263–91.

Jourdain-Annequin, C. (1992c) 'A propos d'un rituel pour Iolaos à Agyrion. Héraclès et l'initiation des jeunes gens', in Moreau, A. (ed.) *L'initiation. Actes du colloque international de Montpellier 11–14 avril 1991*, Montpellier, vol. 1 121–41.

Jourdain-Annequin, C. (1998a) 'Public ou privé? À propos de quelques cultes d'Héraclès dans la cité grecque', *Ktema* 23: 345–64.

Jourdain-Annequin, C. (1998b) 'Héraklès et le bœuf?', in Bonnet, Jourdain-Annequin and Pirenne-Delforge (eds), 285–300.

Jourdain-Annequin, C. and Bonnet, C. (eds) (1996) *IIe Rencontre Héracléene: Héraclès: les femmes et le féminin*, Brussels and Rome.

Jucker, H. (1977) 'Herakles und Atlas auf einer Schale des Nearchos in Bern', in Hockmann, Krug and Brommer (eds), Mainz, 191–9.

Jung, M.-R. (1966) *Hercule dans la literature française du XVIe siècle: de l'Hercule courtois à l'Hercules baroque*, Geneva.

Kajava, M. (1997) 'Heracles saving the shipwrecked', *Arctos* 31: 55–86.

Kampen, N.B. (1996) 'Omphale and the instability of gender', in Kampen (ed.), 233–46.

Kampen, N.B. (ed.) (1996) *Sexuality in Ancient Art*, Cambridge.

Karwiese, S. (1980) 'Lysander as Herakliskos Draknopnigon', *Numismatic Chronicle* 140: 1–27.

Kearns, E. (1989) *The Heroes of Attica*, London.

Kearns, E. (2010) *Ancient Greek Religion: a sourcebook*, Oxford.

Kellum, B. (1985) 'Sculptural programs and propaganda in Augustan Rome: the temple of Apollo on the Palatine', in R. Winkes (ed.) *The Age of Augustus*, Louvain-la-Neuve, 169–76.

Kennell, N.M. (2010) *Sparta: a new history*, London.

Kerenyi, K. (1959) *The Heroes of the Greeks*, tr. Rose, H.J., London.

Keuren, F. van (1989), *The Frieze from the Hera I Temple at Foce del Sele*, Rome.

King, D. (2005) *Finding Atlantis: the true story of genius, madness, and an extraordinary quest for a lost world*, New York.

Kirk, G.S. (1974) *The Nature of Greek Myths*, London.

Kirk, G.S. (1977) 'Methodological reflexions on the myths of Heracles', in Gentili and Paioni (eds), 285–97.

Kirkpatrick, J. and Dunn, F. (2002) 'Heracles, Cercopes, and Paracomedy', *Transactions and Proceedings of the American Philological Association* 132: 29–61.

Knauss, J. (1990) 'Der Graben des Herakles im Becken von Pheneos und die Vertreibung der stymphalischen Vogel', *Mitteilungen des Deutschen Archäologischen Instituts, Athenische Abteilung* 105: 1–33.

Kosmetatou, E. (1995) 'The legend of the hero Pergamus', *Ancient Society* 26: 133–44.

Kosmetatou, E. (2000) 'Lycophron's *Alexandra* reconsidered: the Attalid connection', *Hermes* 128: 32–53.

Kraay, C.M. (1976) *Archaic and Classical Greek Coins*, London.

Kraay, C.M. and Hirmer, M. (1966) *Greek Coins*, London.

Kunze, E. (1950) *Archaische Schildbänder (Olympische Forschugen* II), Berlin.

Kuntz, M. (1994) 'The Prodikean "Choice of Herakles": a reshaping of myth', *Classical Journal* 89: 163–81.

Lada-Richards, I. (1999) *Initiating Dionysus: ritual and theatre in Aristophanes' Frogs*, Oxford.

Lalonde, G.V. (2006) *Horos Dios: an Athenian shrine and cult of Zeus*, Leiden.

Lambert, S.D. (1999) '*IG* II² 2345, thiasoi of Herakles and the Salaminioi again', *Zeitschrift für Papyrologie und Epigraphik* 125: 93–130.

Larson, J. (2007) *Ancient Greek Cults: a guide*, London.

Launey, M. (1944) *Le sanctuaire et le culte dHérakès à Thasos (Etudes Thasiennes* I), Paris.

Laurens, A.-F. (1988) *s.v.* 'Hebe I', *LIMC* IV, 458–64.

Laurens, A.-F. (1996) 'Héraclès et Hébé dans la céramique grecque ou les noces entre terre et ciel', in Jordain-Annequin and Bonnet (eds), 235–58.

Laurens, A.-F. (ed.) (1989) *Entre hommes et dieux. Le convive, le héros, le prophète*, Besançon and Paris.

Laurens, A.-F. and Lissarrague, F. (1989) 'Le bûcher d'Héraclès: l'empreinte du dieu', in Laurens (ed.), 81–98.

Leigh, M. (2000) 'Founts of identity: the thirst of Hercules and the Greater Greek world', *Journal of Mediterranean Studies* 10, 125–38.

Leitao, D. (2003) 'Adolescent hair-growing and hair-cutting rituals in ancient Greece: a sociological approach', in Dodd and Faraone (eds), 109–29.

Létoublon, F. (1996) 'Héraclès et les Thespiades', in Jordain-Annequin and Bonnet (eds), 77–87.

Lévêque, P. and Verbanck-Piérard, A. (1992) 'Héraclès héros ou dieu?', in Bonnet and Jourdain-Annequin (eds), 43–65.

Levett, B. (2004) *Sophocles: Women of Trachis*, London.

Levin, D.M. (1971) 'Apollonius' Heracles', *Classical Journal* 67: 22–8.

Levy, G.R. (1934) 'The oriental origin of Herakles', *Journal of Hellenic Studies* 54: 40–53.

Liapis, V. (2006) 'Intertextuality as irony: Heracles in epic and in Sophocles', *Greece and Rome* 53: 48–59.

Licht, M. (1996) 'Elysium: a prelude to Renaissance theater', *Renaissance Quarterly* 49: 1–29.

Lincoln, B. (1976) The Indo-European cattle-raiding myth', *History of Religions* 16: 42–65.

Lissarrague, F. and Thelamon, F. (eds) (1983) *Image et céramique grecque*, Rouen.

Littlewood, A.R. (1968) 'The symbolism of the apple in Greek and Roman literature', *Harvard Studies in Classical Philology* 72: 147–81.

Livingstone, N. (2001) *A Commentary on Isocrates'* Busiris, Leiden.

Llewellyn-Jones, L. (2005) 'Herakles re-dressed: gender, clothing and the construction of a Greek hero', in Rawlings (ed.), 51–70.

Lloyd-Jones, H. (1967) 'Heracles at Eleusis', *Maia* 19: 206–29.

Long, T. (1986) *Barbarians in Greek Comedy*, Corbendale and Edwardsville, Ill.

Loraux, N. (1990) 'Herakles: the super-male and the feminine', in Halperin, D.M, Winkler, J.J. and Zeitlin, F.I. (eds) *Before Sexuality: the construction of erotic experience in the ancient Greek world*, Princeton, NJ, 21–52.

Maas, P. (1958) 'The GRYLLOS Papyrus', *Greece and Rome* 27: 171–3.

Maguire, M. (2008) *The Labours of Herakles as a New Zealand Pioneer*, Christchurch.

Mackay, E.A. (2002) 'The hairstyle of Herakles', in Clark, A.J. and Gaunt, J. (eds) *Essays in Honor of Dietrich von Bothmer*, Amsterdam, 203–10.

Malkin, I. (1994) *Myth and Territory in the Spartan Mediterranean*, Cambridge.

Malkin, I. (2005) 'Herakles and Melqart: Greeks and Phoenicians in the middle ground', in Malkin, I. and Gruen, E. (eds) *Cultural Borrowings and Ethnic Appropriations in Antiquity*, Stuttgart, 238–58.

March, J. (1987) *The Creative Poet (Bulletin of the Institute of Classical Studies* Suppl. 49), London.

March, J. (1998) *Cassell Dictionary of Greek Mythology*, London.

Marconi, C. (2007) *Temple Decoration and Cultural Identity in the Archaic Greek World: the metopes of Selinus*, Cambridge.

Marshall, C.W. (2000) '*Alcestis* and the problem of prosatyric drama', *Classical Journal* 95: 229–38.

Martin, P.M. (1972) 'Héraclès en Italie d'après Denys d'Halicarnasse *AR* I.34–44', *Athenaeum* 56: 252–75.

Martin, R. (1976) 'Bathykles de Magnésie et le trône d'Apollon à Amyklae', *Revue archéologique*, 205–18.

Martin, R. (1979) 'Introduction à l'étude du culte d'Héraclès en Sicile', in *Recherches sur les cultes grecs et l'Occident* I (*Cahiers du Centre Jean Bérard* V), Naples, 11–17.

Martin, R.P. (2005) 'Pulp epic: the *Catalogue* and the *Shield*', in Hunter (ed.), 153–75.

Mastrocinque, A. (1993) 'Ercole "iperboreo" in Etruria', in Mastrocinque (ed.), 49–61.

Mastrocinque, A. (ed. 1993) *Ercole in Occidente*, Trento.

Mastronarde, D.J. (1968) 'Theocritus' *Idyll* 13: love and the hero', *Transactions and Proceedings of the American Philological Association* 99: 273–90.

Matthaiou, A. (2003) "Ἀθηναίοισι τεταγμένοισι ἐν τεμένει Ἡρακλέος (Hdt 6.108.1)', in P. Derow and R. Parker (eds) *Herodotus and His World: essays from a conference in memory of George Forrest*, Oxford, 190–202.

Matthews, V.-J. (1974) *Panyassis of Halikarnassos* (*Mnemosyne* Suppl. 33), Leiden.

McDonough, C. (2002) 'Hercle and the Ciminian Lake legend: source study for an Etruscan mirror', *Classical Journal* 98.1: 10–17.

McPhee, I. (1979) 'An Apulian oinochoe and the robbery of Herakles', *Antike Kunst* 22: 38–42.

Merkelbach, R. and West, M.L. (1965) 'The wedding of Ceyx', *Rheinisches Museum für Philologie* 108: 300–17.

Mikalson, J.D. (1975) *The Sacred and Civil Calendar of the Athenian Year*, Princeton, NJ.

Mikalson, J.D. (1986) 'Zeus the father and Heracles the son in tragedy', *Transactions of the American Philological Association* 166: 89–98.

Mikalson, J.D. (2004) *Ancient Greek Religion*, Oxford.

Miller, C.H. (1984) 'Hercules and his labours as allegories of Christ and his victory over sin in Dante's *Inferno*', *Quaderni d'Italianistica* 5.1: 1–17.

Mills, S. (1997) *Theseus, Tragedy and the Athenian Empire*, Oxford.

Miquel, C. (1989) 'Héraclès sonore', in Laurens (ed.), 69–79.

Moitrieux, G. (2002) *Hercules in Gallia: recherches sur la personnalité et le culte d'un dieu romain en Gaule*, Paris.

Mommsen, T.E. (1953), 'Petrarch and the story of the Coice of Hercules', *Journal of the Warburg and Courtauld Institutes* 16: 178–92.

Moore, M.B. (1977) 'The Gigantomachy of the Siphnian Treasury: reconstruction of three lacunae', *Bulletin de Correspondance Héllenique* Suppl. 4: 305–35.

Moore, M.B. (1979) 'Lydos and the Gigantomachy', in *American Journal of Archaeology* 83: 79–99.

Moore, M.B. (1995) 'The central group in the Gigantomachy of the old Athena temple on the Acropolis', *American Journal of Archaeology* 99: 633–40.

Morford, M.P.O. and Lenardon, R.J. (2003) *Classical Mythology*, 7th ed., Oxford and New York.

Müller, K.O. (1830) *The History and Antiquities of the Doric Race*, tr. Tufnell, H. and Cornewall, G., London.

Murgatroyd, P. (2007) *Mythical Monsters in Classical Literature*, London.

Murray, G. (1946) 'Heracles: best of men', in *Greek Studies*, Oxford, 106–26.

Neer, R.T. (2002) *Style and Politics in Athenian Vase-Painting: The Craft of Democracy, ca. 530–460 BCE*, Cambridge.

Neer, R.T. (2003) 'Framing the gift: the Siphnian Treasury at Delphi and the politics of public art', in Dougherty, C. and Kurke, L. (eds) *The Cultures Within Ancient Greek Culture*, Cambridge, 129–49.

Neer, R.T. (2004) 'The Athenian Treasury at Delphi and the material of politics', *Classical Antiquity* 23: 63–94.

Nees, L. (1991) *A Tainted Mantle: Hercules and the classical tradition at the Carolingian court*, Philadelphia, PA.

Neils, J. and Oakley, J.H. (2003) *Coming of Age in Ancient Greece: images of childhood from the classical past*, Hanover, NH.

Nicgorski, A. (2005) 'The magic knot of Herakles, the propaganda of Alexander the Great and Tomb II at Vergina', in Rawlings (ed.), 97–128.

Nieto Hernández, M.P. (1993) 'Herakles and Pindar', *Metis* 8: 75–102.

Nilsson, M.P. (1932), *The Mycenaean Origins of Greek Religion*, Berkeley, CA.

Nimmo Smith, J. (2001) *A Christian's Guide to Greek Culture: the pseudo-Nonnus Commentaries on Sermons 4, 5, 39 and 43 by Gregory of Nazianzus*, Liverpool.

Nisbet, G. (2002) 'Barbarous verses: a mixed-media narrative from Greco-Roman Egypt', *Apollo* 15–19.

Nisbet, G. (2008) *Ancient Greece in Film and Popular Culture*, 2nd ed. Bristol and Exeter.

Noel, D. (1983) 'Du vin pour Héraklès!', in Lissarrague and Thelamon (eds), Rouen, 141–50.

O'Daly, G. (1991) *The Poetry of Boethius*, London.

Ogden, D. (1996) *Greek Bastardy in the Classical and Hellenistic Periods*, Oxford.

Ogden, D. (1999) *Polygamy, Prostitutes and Death: the Hellenistic dynasties*, Swansea.

O Kell, E.R. (2005) '*Hercules Furens* and Nero: the didactic purpose of Senecan Tragedy', in Rawlings (ed.), 185–204.

Olalla, P. (2002) *Mythological Atlas of Greece*, Athens.

Osborne, R. (1983–4) 'The myth of propaganda and the propaganda of myth', *Hephaistos* 5–6: 61–70.

Osborne, R. (1998) *Archaic and Classical Greek Art*, Oxford.

Pache, C.O. (2004) *Baby and Child Heroes in Ancient Greece*, Chicago: IL.

Padilla, M. (1992) 'The Heraclean Dionysus: theatrical and social renewal in Aristophanes' *Frogs*', *Arethusa* 25: 359–84.

Padilla, M. (1994) 'Heroic paternity in Euripides' *Heracles*', *Arethusa* 27: 279–302.

Padilla, M.W. (1998a) *The Myths of Herakles in Ancient Greece: survey and profile*, Lanham, MD and New York.

Padilla, M. (1998b) 'Herakles and animals in the origins of comedy and satyr-drama', in Bonnet, Jourdain-Annequin and Pirenne-Delforge (eds), 217–30.

Page, D.L. (1973) 'Stesichoros: the *Geryoneis*', *Journal of Hellenic Studies* 93: 138–54.

Palagia, O. (1986) 'Imitation of Herakles in ruler portraiture: a survey from Alexander to Maximus Daza', *Boreas* 9: 137–51.

Palagia, O. (2006) 'Art and royalty in Sparta of the third century BC', *Hesperia* 75: 205–17.

Panofsky, E. (1930) *Hercules am Scheidewege und andere antike Bildstoffe in der neueren Kunst* (*Studien der Bibliothek Warburg* 18), Leipzig.

Papadopoulou, T. (2004) 'Herakles and Hercules: the hero's ambivalence in Euripides and Seneca', *Mnemosyne* 57: 257–83.

Papadopoulou, T. (2005) *Heracles and Euripidean Tragedy*, Cambridge.

Parisi Presicce, C. (1998) 'Eracle e il leone: *paradeigma andreias*', in Bonnet et al. (eds), 141–50.

Parke, H.W. (1977) *Festivals of the Athenians*, London.

Parke, H.W. and Boardman, J. (1957) 'The struggle for the tripod and the first sacred war', *Journal of Hellenic Studies* 77: 276–82.

Parker, H.C. (1997) *Greek Gods in Italy in Ovid's* Fasti, Lewiston, etc.

Parker, R. (1996) *Athenian Religion: a history*, Oxford.

Parker, R. (2000) 'Theophoric names and the history of Greek religion', in Hornblower, S. and Matthews, E. (eds) *Greek Personal Names: their value as evidence* (= *Proceedings of the British Academy* 104), Oxford, 53–79.

Parker R. (2005) *Polytheism and Society at Athens*, Oxford.

Patterson, C.B. (1990) 'Those Athenian bastards', *Classical Antiquity* 9: 40–73.

Pavese, C. (1968) 'The new Heracles poem of Pindar', *Harvard Studies in Classical Philology* 72: 47–88.

Pfister, F. (1937) 'Herakles und Christus', *Archiv für Religionswissenschaft* 34: 42–60.

Piérart, M. (1992) 'Les honneurs de Persée et d'Héraclès', in Bonnet and Jourdain-Annequin (eds), 223–44.

Pike, D.L. (1977) 'Heracles: the superman and personal relationships', *Acta Classica* 20: 73–83.

Pike, D.L. (1978) 'Hercules Furens. Some thoughts on the madness of Heracles in Greek literature', *Proceedings of the African Classical Associations* 14: 1–6.

Pike, D.L. (1984) 'Pindar's treatment of the Heracles myths', *Acta Classica* 27: 15–22.

Pipili, M. (1987) *Laconian Iconography of the Sixth Century BC*, Oxford.

Pirenne-Delforge, V. (2008) *Retour à la Source: Pausanias et la religion grecque* (*Kernos* suppl. 20), Liège.

Pirenne-Delforge, V. (2010) 'Reading Pausanias: cults of the gods and representation of the divine', in Bremmer and Erskine (eds), 375–87.

Plácido, D. (1993) 'Le vie di Ercole nell'estremo Occidente', in Mastrocinque (ed.), 63–80.

Poduska, D.M. (1999) 'Classical myth in music: a selective list', *Classical World* 92.3: 195–276.

Pötscher, W. (1971) 'Der Name des Herakles', *Emerita* 39: 169–84.

Polleross, F. (1998) 'From the *exemplum virtutis* to the apotheosis: Hercules as an identification figure in portraiture: an example of the adoption of classical forms of representation', in Ellenius, A. (ed.) *Iconography, Propaganda, and Legitimation*, Oxford, 37–62.

Pollitt, J.J. (1986) *Art in the Hellenistic Age*, Cambridge.

Pollitt, J.J. (1990) *The Art of Ancient Greece: sources and documents*, Cambridge.

Pomeroy, A.J. (2008) *Then It Was Destroyed by the Volcano: the ancient world in film and on television*, London.

Pouilloux, J. (1954) *Recherches sur l'histoire et les cultes de Thasos* I: *de la fondation de la cité à 196 avant J.-C.* (*Etudes Thasiennes* III), Paris.

Pouilloux, J. (1974) 'L'Héraclès thasien', *Revue des études anciennes* 76: 305–16.

Powell, A. (1998) 'Sixth-century Lakonian vase-painting', in Fisher, N. and van Wees, H. (eds) *Archaic Greece: new approaches and new evidence*, Swansea and London, 119–46.

Pralon, D. (1996) 'Héraclès-Iole', in Jourdain-Annequin and Bonnet (eds), 51–76.

Price, M.J. (1968) 'Mithradates VI Eupator, Dionysus, and the coinages of the Black Sea', *Numismatic Chronicle* 8: 1–12.

Price, S. (1999) *Religions of the Ancient Greeks*, Cambridge.

Propp, V. (1968 [1928]) *Morphology of the Folktale*, tr. L. Scott, 2nd ed. Austin and London.

Puhvel, J. (1987) *Comparative Mythology*, Baltimore, MD.

Rankin, H.D. (1986) *Antisthenes Sokratikos*, Amsterdam.

Rawlings, L. (2005) 'Hannibal and Hercules', in Rawlings (ed.), 153–84.

Rawlings, L. (ed.) (2005), *Herakles and Hercules: exploring a Greco-Roman divinity*, Swansea.

Rawson, B. (1970) 'Pompey and Hercules', *Antichthon* 4: 30–7.

Raymond, D. (1953) *Macedonian Regal Coinage to 413 BC* (= *Numismatic Notes and Monographs* 126), New York.

Rees, R. (2005) 'The emperors' new names: Diocletian Jovius and Maximian Herculius', in Rawlings (ed.), 223–40.

Reid, J.D. (1993) *The Oxford Guide to Classical Mythology in the Arts, 1300–1990s*, Oxford.

Renehan, R. (1982) 'Aristotle as lyric poet. The Hermias poem', *Greek, Roman and Byzantine Studies* 23: 251–74.

Rhodes, P.J. and Osborne, R. (2003) *Greek Historical Inscriptions 404–323 BC*, Oxford.

Ricci, G. (1946–8) 'Una hydria ionica da Caere', *Annuario della Regia Scuola Archeologica di Atene e delle Missioni Italiane in Oriente* 24–6 (n.s. 8–10): 47–57.

Ridgway, B.S. (1997) *Fourth-Century Styles in Greek Sculpture*, London.

Ridgway, D. (2006) 'Early Greek imports in Sardinia', in Tsetskhladze, G.R. (ed.) *Greek Colonisation: an account of Greek colonies and other settlements overseas* (*Mnemosyne* Suppl. 293), Leiden, 239–52.

Riethmüller, J.W. (1999), '*Bothros* and tetrastyle: the *heroon* of Asclepius in Athens', in Hägg, R. (ed.) *Ancient Greek Hero Cult*, Stockholm, 123–43.

Riley, K. (2004) 'Heracles as Dr Strangelove and GI Joe: male heroism deconstructed', in Hall, E., Macintosh, F. and Wrigley, A. (eds) *Dionysus since 69: Greek tragedy at the dawn of the third millennium*, Oxford, 113–42.

Riley, K. (2008) *The Reception and Performance of Euripides' Herakles: reasoning madness*, Oxford.

Ritter, S. (1995) *Hercules in der römischen Kunst von den Anfängen bis Augustus*, Heidelberg.

Ritter, S. (1996) 'Ercole e Onfale nell'arte romana dell'età tardo-repubblicana e augustea', in Jourdain-Annequin and Bonnet (eds), 89–102.

Robert, L. (1984) 'Héraclès à Pergame et une épigramme de l'Anthologie 16.91', *Revue de philologie, de littérature et d'histoire anciennes* 58: 7–18.

Roberts, C.H. (1954) 'Verses on the Labours of Heracles', *Oxyrhyncus Papyri* 22: 84–8.

Robertson, M. (1969) '*Geryoneis*: Stesichoros and the vase-painters', *Classical Quarterly* 19: 207–21.

Rochette, B. (1998) 'Héraclès à la croissé des chemins: un *topos* dans la literature gréco-latine', *Études Classiques* 66: 105–13.

Roisman, H.M. (2001), 'The ever-present Odysseus: eavesdropping and disguise in Sophocles' *Philoctetes*', *Eranos* 99: 38–53.

Roisman, H.M. (2005) *Sophocles: Philoctetes*, London.

Rosen, R.M. (2007) *Making Mockery: the poetics of ancient satire*, New York.

Rosenmeyer, T.G. (1989) *Senecan Drama and Stoic Cosmology*, Berkeley etc.

Rosenthal, E.E. (1973) 'The invention of the columnar device of Emperor Charles V at the court of Burgundy in Flanders in 1516', *Journal of the Warburg and Courtauld Institutes* 36: 198–230.

Rosenthal, L. (1993) 'Manhood and statehood: Ruben's construction of heroic virtue', *Oxford Art Journal* 16.1: 92–111.

Roymans, N. (2009) 'Hercules and the construction of a Batavian identity in the context of the Roman empire', in Derks, T. and Roymans, N. (eds), *Ethnic Constructs in Antiquity: The role of power and tradition* (*Amsterdam Archaeological Studies* 13), Amsterdam, 219–38.

Rutter, C. Chillington (1997) 'Harrison, Herakles, and wailing women: "Labourers" at Delphi', *New Theatre Quarterly* 13.50: 133–43.

Rutter, N.K. (2001) *Historia Numorum Italy*, 3rd ed. London.

Ruzicka, S. (1992) *Politics of a Persian Dynasty: the Hecatomnids in the fourth century BC*, Oaklahoma (= *The Oklahoma series in classical culture* 14).

Sadurska, A. (1964) *Les tables Iliaques*, Warsaw.

Salmon, J.B. (1984) *Wealthy Corinth: a history of the city to 338 BC*, Oxford.

Saloway, C.A. (1994) 'Herakles and the waterworks: Mycenaean dams, classical fountains, Roman acqueducts', in Sheedy, K.A., *Archaeology in the Peloponnese* (*Oxbow Monograph* 48), Oxford, 77–94.

Salviat, F. (1958) 'Une nouvelle loi thasienne: institutions judiciaires et fêtes religieuses à la fin du IVᵉ s. av. J.-C.', *Bulletin de Correspojndance Héllenique* 82: 193–267.

Sansone, D. (2004) 'Heracles at the Y', *Journal of Hellenic Studies* 124: 125–42.

Saulnier, V.L. (1955) 'L'entrée de Henri II à Paris et la revolution poétique de 1550', in Jacquot (ed.), 31–59.

Scarpi, P. (1998) 'Héraclès entre animaux et monstres chez Apollodore', in Bonnet et al. (eds), 231–40.

Schachter, A. (1979) 'The Boiotian Heracles', in Fossey, J.M. and Schachter, A. (eds) *Proceedings of the Second International Conference on Boiotian Antiquities*, Montreal (= *Teiresias* Suppl. 2), 37–43.

Schachter, A. (1986) *Cults of Boiotia* II, London.

Schauenburg, K. (1960) 'Herakles und Omphale', *Rheinisches Museum* 103: 57–76.

Schefold, K. (1966) *Myth and Legend in Early Greek Art*, tr. Hicks, A., London.

Schefold, K. (1988) *Die Urkönige, Perseus, Bellerophon, Herakles und Theseus in der klassischen und hellenistischen Kunst*, Munich.

Schefold, K. (1992) *Gods and Heroes in Late Archaic Greek Art*, tr. Griffiths, A.H., Cambridge.

Schlesier, R. (1991–2) 'Olympian versus Chthonian religion', *Scripta Classica Israelica* 11: 38–51.

Schilling, R. (1942) 'L'Hercule romain en face de la reforme religieuse d'Auguste', *Revue de philologie, de littérature, et d'histoire anciennes* 68: 31–57.

Schnapp-Gourbeillon, S. (1998) 'Les lions d'Héraclès', in Bonnet et al. (eds), 109–26.

Schoo, J.H. (1969) *Hercules' Labors: fact or fiction?*, Chicago, IL.

Schroeder, L. Von (1914) *Herakles und Indra: eine mythenvergleichende Untersuchung*, Vienna.

Schultze, C. E. (1999) 'Manliness and the myth of Hercules in Charlotte M. Yonge's *My Young Alcides*', *International Journal of the Classical Tradition* 5.3: 383–414.

Schultz, P. (2009) 'The north frieze of the temple of Athena Nike', in Palagia, O. (ed.) *Art in Athens during the Peloponnesian War*, Cambridge, 128–67.

Schwab, K.A. (1996) 'Parthenon east metope XI: Herakles and the Gigantomachy', *American Journal of Archaeology* 100: 81–90.

Schwarz, S.J. (1990) *s.v.* 'Hercle' in *LIMC* V, 196–253.

Schweitzer, B. (1922) *Herakles: Aufsätze zur griechischen Religions- und Sagengeschichte*, Tübingen.

Scott, M.C. (2010) *Delphi and Olympia: the spatial politics of panhellenism in the archaic and classical periods*, Cambridge.

Scullion, S. (1994) 'Olympian and chthonian', *Classical Antiquity* 13: 75–119.

Scullion, S. (2000) 'Heroic and chthonian sacrifice: new evidence from Selinous', *Zeitschrift für Papyrologie und Epigraphik* 132: 163–71.

Scullion, S. (2003) 'Euripides and Macedon, or the silence of the *Frogs*', *Classical Quarterly* 53: 389–400.

Scullion, S. (2006) 'The opening of Euripides' *Archelaus*', in Cairns, D.L. and Liapis, V. (eds) *Dionysalexadros: Essays on Aeschylus and his fellow tragedians in honour of A.F. Garvie*, Swansea, 185–200.

Seaford, R. (2006) *Dionysos*, London and New York.

Secci, D.A. (2009) 'Ovid *Met.* 9.1–97: through the eyes of Achelous', *Greece and Rome* 56: 34–54.

Segre, M. (1993) *Iscrizioni di Cos*, Rome.

Segura, M.O. (1996) *Hércules en Hispania: una aproximacíon*, Barcelona.

Sergent, B. (1987) *Homosexuality in Greek Myth*, London.

Seznec, J. (1953) *The survival of the pagan gods: the mythological tradition and its place in Renaissance humanism and art*, Princeton NJ.

Shahabudin, K. (2009) 'Ancient Mythology and modern myths: *Hercules Conquers Atlantis* (1961)', in Lowe, D. and Shahabudin, K. (eds) *Classics For All*, Cambridge, 196–216.

Shapiro, H.A. (1983) '*HEROS THEOS*: the death and apotheosis of Herakles', *Classical World* 77: 7–18.

Shapiro, H.A. (1984) 'Herakles and Kyknos', *American Journal of Archaeology* 88: 523–9.

Shapiro, H.A. (1986) 'The origins of allegory in Greek art', *Boreas* 9: 4–23.

Shapiro, H.A. (1988) *s.v.* 'Geras' in *LIMC* IV, 180–2.

Shapiro, H.A. (1989) *Art and Cult under the Tyrants in Athens*, Mainz.

Shapiro, H.A. (1993) *Personifications in Greek Art: the representation of abstract concepts 600–400 B.C.*, Zurich.

Shapiro, H.A. (1994) *Myth Into Art: poet and painter in Classical Greece*, London and New York.

Shefton, B.B. (1989) 'The Auge bowl', in Cook, B.F. (ed.) *The Rogozen Treasure*, London, 82–90.

Sherwin-White, S.M. (1978) *Ancient Cos (Hypomnemata* 51), Göttingen.

Silk, M.S. (1985) 'Herakles and Greek tragedy', *Greece and Rome* 32: 1–22.

Simon, E. (1982) 'Satyr plays on vases in the time of Aeschylus', in Kurtz, D.C. and Sparkes, B. (eds) *The Eye of Greece: studies in the art of Athens*, Cambridge, 123–48.

Simon, E. (1983) *Festivals of Attica: an archaeological commentary*, Madison, WI.

Simon, M. (1955) *Hercule et le Christianisme*, Paris.

Simons, P. (2008) 'Hercules in Italian Renaissance art: masculine labour and homoerotic libido', *Art History* 31.5: 632–64.

Slater, P.E. (1968) *The Glory of Hera: Greek mythology and the Greek family*, Boston, MA.

Small, J.P. (1982) *Cacus and Marsyas in Etrusco-Roman Legend*, Princeton, NJ.

Small, J.P. (2003) *The Parallel Worlds of Classical Art and Text*, Cambridge.

Smarr, J.L. (1977) 'Boccaccio and the Choice of Hercules', *Modern Language Notes* 92.1: 146–52.

Smith, R.R.R. (1991) *Hellenistic Sculpture*, London.

Snodgrass, A. (1998) *Homer and the Artists*, Cambridge.

Solomon, J. (2001) *The Ancient World in the Cinema*, 2nd ed. New Haven, CT.

Sommerstein, A.H. (1987) *Aristophanes: Birds*, Oxford.

Sommerstein, A.H. (1996) *Aristophanes: Frogs*, Oxford.

Sourvinou-Inwood, C. (2005) *Hylas, the Nymphs, Dionysos and Others: myth, ritual, ethnicity*. Stockholm.

Spencer, D. (2001) 'Propertius, Hercules, and the dynamics of Roman mythic space in *Elegy* 4.9', *Arethusa* 34: 259–84.

Spivey, N. (2004) *The Ancient Olympics*, Oxford.

Stafford, E.J. (2000) *Worshipping Virtues: personification and the divine in ancient Greece*, Swansea.

Stafford, E.J. (2003) 'Brother, son, friend and healer: Sleep the god', in Dowden, K. and Wiedemann, T. (eds) *Sleep*, Nottingham, 71–106.

Stafford, E.J. (2005a) 'Herakles and the art of allegory', in Rawlings (ed.), 71–96.

Stafford, E.J. (2005b) 'Héraklès: encore et toujours le problème de l'héros theos', *Kernos* 18: 391–406.

Stafford, E.J. (2007) 'Personification in Greek religious thought and practice', in Ogden, D. (ed.) *Blackwell Companion to Greek Religion*, Oxford, 71–85.

Stafford, E.J. (2008) 'Cocks to Asklepios: sacrificial practice and healing cult', in Brulé, P. and Mehl, V. (eds), *Le sacrifice, nouvelles perspectives* (Actes du colloque de Lampeter, 29 août – 3 septembre 2006), Rennes, 205–21.

Stafford, E.J. (2009) 'Visualising creation in ancient Greece', in Merolla, D. (ed.) *Creation Myths and the Visual Arts: an ongoing dialogue between word and image* (Religion and the Arts vol. 13), Leiden, 419–47.

Stafford, E.J. (2010) 'Herakles: between gods and heroes', in Bremmer and Erskine (eds), 228–44.

Steinby, E.M. (ed. 1996) *Lexicon Topographicum Urbis Romae*, Rome.

Steiner (2007) *Reading Greek Vases*, Cambridge.

Stern, J. (1974) 'Theocritus *Idyll* 24', *American Journal of Philology* 95: 348–61.

Stern, J. (1996) *Palaephatus: On Unbelievable Tales* (Peri apiston),Wauconda, IL.

Stern, J. (1999) 'Rationalizing myth in Palaephatus', in Buxton, R.G.A. (ed.) *From Myth to Reason? Studies in the development of Greek thought*, Oxford, 215–22.

Stewart, A.F. (1993) *Faces of power: Alexander's image and Hellenistic politics*, Berkeley, etc.

Stewart, A.F. (1996) 'Reflections', in Kampen (ed.), 136–54.

Stewart, A.F. (1997) *Art, Desire and the Body in Ancient Greece*, Cambridge.

Stewart, P. (2008) *The Social History of Roman Art*, Cambridge.

Stössl, F. (1945) *Der Tod des Herakles: Arbeitsweise und Formen der antiken Sagendichtung*, Zurich.

Straten, F.T. van (1981) 'Gifts for the gods', in Versnel, H.S. (ed.) *Faith, Hope and Worship*, Leiden, 65–151.

Straten, F.T. van (1995) *Hierà kalà: images of animal sacrifice in archaic and classical Greece*, Leiden, etc.

Sutton, D.F. (1984) *The Lost Sophocles*, Lanham, MD.

Stupperich, R. (1996) 'Neue Reliefs vom Athena-Tempel von Assos', in Serdaroglu, U. and Stupperich, R. (eds) *Ausgrabungen in Assos 1992*, Bonn.

Tagalidou, E. (1993) *Weihreliefs an Herakles aus klassicher Zeit*, Jonsered.

Taplin, O. (1993) *Comic Angels and Other Approaches to Greek Drama Through Vase-Painting*, Oxford.

Taplin, O. (2007) *Pots and Plays: interactions between tragedy and Greek vase-painting of the fourth century BC*, Malibu, CA.

Thompson, W.K. (1971) *The Labors of Hercules by Pietro Andrea di Bassi*, Barre, MA.

Tigerstedt, E.N. (1965) *The Legend of Sparta in Classical Antiquity*, Stockholm.

Tomlinson, R.A. (1972) *Argos and the Argolid: from the end of the Bronze Age to the Roman occupation*, London.

Too, Y.L. (1995) *The Rhetoric of Identity in Isocrates: text, power, pedagogy*, Cambridge.

Toynbee, A. (1939) *A Study of History* VI, Oxford and London.

Toutain, J. (1928) 'Observations sur le culte d'Hercule à Rome', *Revue des études latines* 6: 200–12.

Trendall, A.D. (1989) *Red Figure Vases of South Italy and Sicily: a handbook*, London.

Tronzo, W. (1986) *The Via Latina Catacomb: imitation and discontinuity in fourth-century Roman painting*, London.

Trousson, R. (1962) 'Ronsard et la legend d'Hercule', *Bibliothèque d'humanisme et de Renaissance* 24: 77–87.

Tyrrell, W.B. (1984) *Amazons: a study in Athenian mythmaking*, Baltimore, MD.

Uhlenbrock, J.P. (ed. 1986) *Heracles: passage of the hero through 1,000 years of Classical art*, New Rochelle, NY.

Utz, H. (1971) 'The Labors of Hercules and Other Works by Vincenzo de' Rossi', *The Art Bulletin* 53: 344–66.

Valavanis, P. (2004) *The Games and Sanctuaries in Ancient Greece*, Los Angeles, CA.

Vanderpool, E. (1984) 'Regulations for the Herakleian Games at Marathon', *Greek, Roman and Byzantine Monographs* 10: 295–6.

Verbanck-Piérard, A. (1982) 'La rencontre d'Héraklès et de Pholos: variantes iconographiques du peintre d'Antiménès', in Hadermann-Misguich, L. and Raepsaet, G. (eds) *Rayonnement grec: hommages à Charles Delvoye*, Brussels, 143–54.

Verbanck-Piérard, A. (1987) 'Images et croyances en Grèce ancienne: représentations de l'apothéose d'Héraclès au V^{ie} siècle', in Bérard, C. (ed.) *Images et société en Grèce ancienne*, Lausanne, 187–99.

Verbanck-Piérard, A. (1989) 'Le double culte d'Héraklès: légende ou réalité?', in Laurens (ed.), 43–65.

Verbanck-Piérard, A. (1992) 'Herakles at feast in Attic art: a mythical or cultic iconography?', in Hägg, R. (ed.) *The Iconography of Greek Cult* (*Kernos* Suppl. 1), Athens and Liége, 85–106.

Verbanck-Piérard, A. (1995) 'Héraclès l'Athénien', in Verbanck-Piérard, A. and Viviers, D. (eds) *Culture et Cité: lavènement dAthènes à l'époque archaïque*, Brussels, 103–25.

Verbanck-Piérard, A. (1998) 'Héros attiques au jour le jour: les calendriers des dèmes', in Pirenne-Delforge, V. (ed.) *Les panthéons des cités, des origines à la* Périégèse *de Pausanias* (*Kernos* Suppl. 8), Athens and Liége, 109–27.

Verbanck-Piérard, A. and Gilis, E. (1998) 'Héraclès, pourfendeur de dragmos', in Bonnet et al. (eds), 37–60.

Vermeule, C.C. (1975) 'The weary Herakles of Lysippos', *American Journal of Archaeology* 79: 323–32.

Vermeule, C.C. (1977) 'Commodus, Caracalla and the Tetrarchs: Roman Emperors as Hercules', in Hockmann, Krug and Brommer (eds), 289–94.

Vermeule, E.T. (1977) 'Herakles brings a tribute', in Hockmann, Krug and Brommer (eds), 295–301.

Versnel, H.L. (1973) 'Philip II and Kynosarges', *Mnemosyne* 26: 273–9.

Vickers, M. (1995) 'Heracles Lacedaemonius: the political dimension of Sophocles *Trachiniae* and Euripides' *Heracles*', *Dialogues d'histoire ancienne* 21.2: 41–69.

Vivante, P. (1985) 'Héraclès chez Pindare', in *Actes du 3e Congrès Internationale sur la Béotie antique (Montréal 1979)*, Amsterdam, 159–63.

Vivanti, C. (1967) 'Henry IV, the Gallic Hercules', *Journal of the Warburg and Courtauld Institutes* 30: 176–97.

Vollkommer, R. (1988) *Herakles in the Art of Classical Greece* (= *Oxford University Committee for Archaeology Monograph* 25), Oxford.

Waith, E.M. (1962) *The Herculean Hero in Marlowe, Chapman, Shakespeare and Dryden*, London.

Walker, H. (1995) *Theseus and Athens*, Oxford.

Warner, M. (1985) *Monuments and Maidens*, London.

Watrous, L.V. (1982) 'The sculptural program of the Siphnian Treasury at Delphi', *American Journal of Archaeology* 86, 159–72.

West, M.L. (1966) *Hesiod's Theogony*, Oxford.

West, M.L. (1983) *The Orphic Poems*, Oxford.

West, M.L. (1985) *The Hesiodic Catalogue of Women*, Oxford.

West, M.L. (1997) *The East Face of Helicon: West Asiatic elements in Greek poetry and myth*, Oxford.

West, M.L. (2003) *Greek Epic Fragments*, Cambridge, MA and London.

Whitman, J. (1987) *Allegory: the dynamics of an ancient and medieval technique*, Oxford.

Wilamowitz-Moellendorf, U. von (1895) *Euripides: Herakles*, vol. I, Berlin.

Wilamowitz-Moellendorf, U. von (1932) *Der Glaube der Hellenen*, vol. II, Berlin.

Wilkins, J. (1990) 'The young of Athens: religion and society in the *Herakleidae* of Euripides', *Classical Quarterly* 40: 329–39.

Wilkins, J. (1993) *Euripides: Children of Herakles*, Oxford.

Williams, D.J.R. (1983) 'Herakles, Peisistratos and the Alcmeonids', in Lissarrague and Thelamon (eds), Rouen, 131–40.

Wind, E. (1939), '"Hercules" and "Orpheus": two mock-heroic designs by Dürer', *Journal of the Warburg Institute* 2: 206–18.

Winkler, M.M. (2007) 'Greek myth on the screen', in Woodard (ed.), 453–79.

Winterson, J. (2006) *Weight*, Edinburgh.

Wiseman, T.P. (2000) 'The games of Hercules', in Bispham, E. and Smith, C. (eds) *Religion in Archaic and Republican Rome and Italy: evidence and experience*, Edinburgh, 108–114.

Wiseman, T.P. (2004) *The Myths of Rome*, Exeter.

Wissowa, G. (1912) *Religion und Kultus der Römer*, Munich.

Witt, R. (1983) *Hercules at the Crossroads: the life, work, and thoughts of Coluccio Salutati*, Durham, NC.

Wolf, S.R. (1993) *Herakles beim Gelage: eine motiv- und bedeutungsgeschichtliche Untersuchung des Bildes in der archaisch-frühklassischen Vasenmalerei*, Köln.

Wonterghem, F. van (1998) 'Hercule et les troupeaux en Italie centrale: une nouvelle mise en point', in Bonnet, Jourdain-Annequin and Pirenne-Delforge (eds), 241–55.

Woodard, R.D. (ed.) (2007) *The Cambridge Companion to Greek Mythology*, Cambridge.

Woodford, S. (1974) 'Cults of Heracles in Attica', in *Studies presented to George M.A. Hanfmann*, Cambridge, MA, 211–25.

Woodford, S. (1976) 'Herakles Alexikakos reviewed', *American Journal of Archaeology* 80: 291–4.

Woodford, S. (1983) 'The iconography of the infant Herakles strangling snakes', in Lissarrague and Thelamon (eds), Rouen, 121–29.

Woodford, S. (1989) 'Herakles' attributes and their appropriation by Eros', *Journal of Hellenic Studies* 109: 200–4.

Woodford, S. (2003) *Images of Myths in Classical Antiquity*, Cambridge.

Woodford, S. and Spier, J. (1992) *s.v.* 'Kerberos' in *LIMC* VI, 24–32.

Worman, N. (1999) 'The ties that bind. Transformations of costume and connection in Euripides' *Heracles*', *Ramus* 28.2: 89–107.

Wyke, M. (1997) 'Herculean muscle! The classicizing rhetoric of body-building', *Arion* 4.3: 51–79.

Young, D. (2004) *A Brief History of the Olympic Games*, Oxford.

Zaidman, L. Bruit, and Pantel, P. Schmitt (1992) *Religion in the Ancient Greek City*, Cambridge.

Zancani Montuoro, P. and Zanotti-Bianco, U. (1954) *Heraion alla Foce del Sele II: il primo thesauro*, Rome.

Zanker, G. (1996) 'Pictorial description as a supplement for narrative: the labour of Augeas' Stables in Heracles Leontophonos', *American Journal of Philology* 117: 411–23.

Zanker, P. (1988) *The Power of Images in the Age of Augustus*, Ann Arbor, MI.

Zanobi, A. (2008) 'The influence of pantomime on Seneca's tragedies', in Hall, E. and Wyles, R. (eds) *New Directions in Ancient Pantomime*, Oxford, 227–57.

Zardini, F. (2009) *The Myth of Herakles and Kyknos: a study in Greek vase-painting and literature*, Verona.

INDEX

Mythological characters are generally listed under their Greek name, after which the Latin name is given in brackets if it has been used in this book. A separate entry for the Latin name is only given in cases where it differs radically from the Greek (see pp. xx–xxi on spelling conventions).